Business Environment and Concepts

Allen H. Bizzell, Ph.D, CPA
Douglas Clinton, Ph.D., CPA, CMA
Janet Gillespie, Ph.D
Robert Prentice, J.D.
Dan Stone, Ph.D. MPA

PO Box 4223 Sedona, AZ 86340-4223
888.884.5669 N.America   928.204.1066 International

www.cpaexcel.com

Edward Foley, President & CEO
Gun Granath, Editor

ISBN 978-0-9746541-0-2

Printed in the United States of America

ABOUT THE CPAexcel™ CPA EXAM REVIEW COURSES

The Surest Way to Pass the CPA Exam

Since 1998, a growing number of CPA exam candidates have used CPAexcel to pass the CPA exam. The performance of our students on the exam, as well as their feedback to us, confirms that CPAexcel is the easiest way to pass the CPA exam.

Key reasons why our students chose CPAexcel:

- They consistently pass the exam at a rate almost twice that of all other candidates
- They learn from leading professors who are CPA exam experts at top accounting schools
- They master more knowledge in less time than other students, by using CPAexcel's unique bite-sized lessons℠ and software-driven, highly-interactive Efficient Learning System™
- They benefit from using the most powerful learning tools of any CPA exam review course
- They select from among CPAexcel's basic learning modules to create customized courses that fit their individual learning needs, lifestyle, schedule, and budget.
- They have unlimited use of Simulated CPA Exams with exam-identical formats, functions and time limits – plus representative scores and identification of weak spots.
- They receive free electronic updates and their CPAexcel course has no expiration date
- They pay about half the price of other leading review courses

CPAexcel's Basic Learning Modules Are:

- ***Core Study Materials***. All CPAexcel courses include: Bite-sized lessons, Efficient Learning System, Diagnostic Exams, Study Text, Proficiency Questions, Past Exam Questions, Simulations, Electronic Flashcards, Performance Metrics, Exam Tutor, Simulated CPA Exams, Final Review, Personalized Exam Planning, Course Manager and Student Discussion Groups.
- ***Professor Mentoring.*** Provide prompt answers to each student's questions from subject-expert professors, guidance and progress monitoring.
- ***Video Lectures with Printable Slides.*** Leading professors from top accounting schools present information essential to passing the exam. These lectures are integrated into bite-sized lesson and typically run between five and fifteen minutes.
- ***Textbooks.*** Include copies of CPAexcel's Study Text typically organized into 3 to 10 page lessons that follow the same sequence as our courseware.
- ***Printed Flashcards.*** 1000 printed flashcards help you learn and test yourself on the go.

How CPAexcel's Basic Learning Modules Fulfill the Needs of Different Types of Learners:

Learners' Needs	Appropriate CPAexcel Course
You learn best in a classroom-type setting watching and listening to an instructor and then using textbooks to study the details.	**Video Gold Medal Course.** (Core Study Materials, Professor Mentoring and then using textbooks to study Video Lectures, Textbooks)
You learn best in a structured learning program, with assignments and grades. You learn well by simply reading.	**Gold Medal Course** (Core Study Materials, Professor Mentoring, Textbooks)
You learn best studying at your own pace in your own way using recorded lectures, with reading materials and self-scoring tests.	**Video Self-Study Course** (Core Study Materials, Video Lectures, your own way using recorded lectures, with Textbooks)
You learn best studying at your own pace in your own way using reading materials and self-scoring tests.	**Classic Self-Study Course** (Core Study Materials, Textbooks)

ABOUT THE CPAexcel™ CPA EXAM REVIEW COURSES

OUR AUTHORS & MENTORS

CPAexcel™ content is authored by a team of accounting professors and CPA exam experts from top accounting colleges such as the University of Texas at Austin (frequently ranked the #1 accounting school in the country), California State University at Sacramento, Northern Illinois University, and University of North Alabama. Via the Internet, students using CPAexcel's Professor Mentoring receive unlimited mentoring and personalized answers to their questions from subject-expert professors. Team members are:

Professor Craig Bain
CPAexcel Guided Seminar Professor
Ph.D., CPA
Northern Arizona University - Flagstaff

Professor Allen H. Bizzell
CPAexcel Author, Guided Seminar Professor and Video Lecturer
Ph.D., CPA
Former Associate Dean and Accounting Faculty, University of Texas (Retired)
Associate Professor, Department of Accounting, Texas State University (Retired)

Professor Gregory Carnes
CPAexcel Author and Video Lecturer
Ph.D., CPA
Raburn Eminent Scholar of Accounting, University of North Alabama
Former Dean, College of Business, Lipscomb University
Former Chair, Department of Accountancy, Northern Illinois University

Professor B. Douglas Clinton
CPAexcel Video Lecturer
Ph.D., CPA, CMA
Alta Via Consulting Professor of Management Accountancy, Department of Accountancy, Northern Illinois University

Professor Charles J. Davis
CPAexcel Author, Guided Seminar Professor and Video Lecturer
Ph.D., CPA
Professor of Accounting, Department of Accounting, College of Business Administration, California State University - Sacramento

Professor Donald R. Deis Jr.
CPAexcel Video Lecturer
Ph.D., CPA, MBA
Ennis & Virginia Joslin Endowed Chair in Accounting, College of Business, Texas A&M University - Corpus Christi
Former Director of the School of Accountancy, University of Missouri - Columbia
Former Professor and Director of the Accounting Ph.D. Program, Louisiana State University - Baton Rouge

Professor Janet D. Gillespie
CPAexcel Author and Guided Seminar Professor
Ph.D.
Lecturer, Department of Accounting, McCombs School of Business, University of Texas - Austin

Professor Marianne M. Jennings
CPAexcel Video Lecturer
J.D.
Professor of Legal and Ethical Studies, W.P. Carey School of Business, Arizona State University

Professor Gaylord A. Jentz
CPAexcel Author
J.D., MBA
Herbert D. Kelleher Centennial Professor Emeritus in Business Law, Department of Management Science and Information Systems, McCombs School of Business, University of Texas - Austin

Professor John E. Karayan
CPAexcel Guided Seminar Professor
J.D., Ph.D
Chair, Department of Accounting and IT, Woodbury University - Burbank, California

Professor Claire Latham
CPAexcel Guided Seminar Professor
Ph.D, CPA
Washington State University

Professor Christopher Meakin
CPAexcel Guided Seminar Professor
MA, J.D., BBA
University of Texas - Austin

Professor Pam Smith
CPAexcel Video Lecturer
Ph.D., MBA, CPA
KPMG Professor of Accountancy, Department of Accountancy, Northern Illinois University

Professor Dan Stone
CPAexcel Video Lecturer
Ph.D., MPA
Gatton Endowed Chair, Von Allmen School of Accountancy and the Department of Management, University of Kentucky

Professor Donald Tidrick
CPAexcel Author and Video Lecturer
Ph.D., CPA, CMA, CIA
Deloitte Professor of Accountancy, Northern Illinois University
Former Associate Chairman of the Department of Accounting, Director of the Professional Program in Accounting and Director of the CPA Review Course, University of Texas at Austin, 1991 - 2000

Professor Jeanne Yamamura
CPAexcel Guided Seminar Professor
Ph.D., CPA, MIM
University of Nevada - Reno (Retired)

CPAexcel's BITE-SIZED LESSONS^{SM} AND EFFICIENT LEARNING SYSTEM^{TM}

A key reason why CPAexcel students pass the CPA exam at rates almost twice that for all other students is that they study using CPAexcel's bite-sized lessons^{SM} and Efficient Learning System.

Bite-Sized Lessons:

CPAexcel's course materials are broken down into many lessons each one of which covers a single topic that can often be learned in about 30 minutes. The course materials available in each bite-sized lesson are shown below in an image of a typical "Lesson Overview" panel displayed alongside a part of the Table of Contents for that section of the course materials. Each of the learning resources listed in the Lesson Overview are linked to that particular learning resource for that lesson.

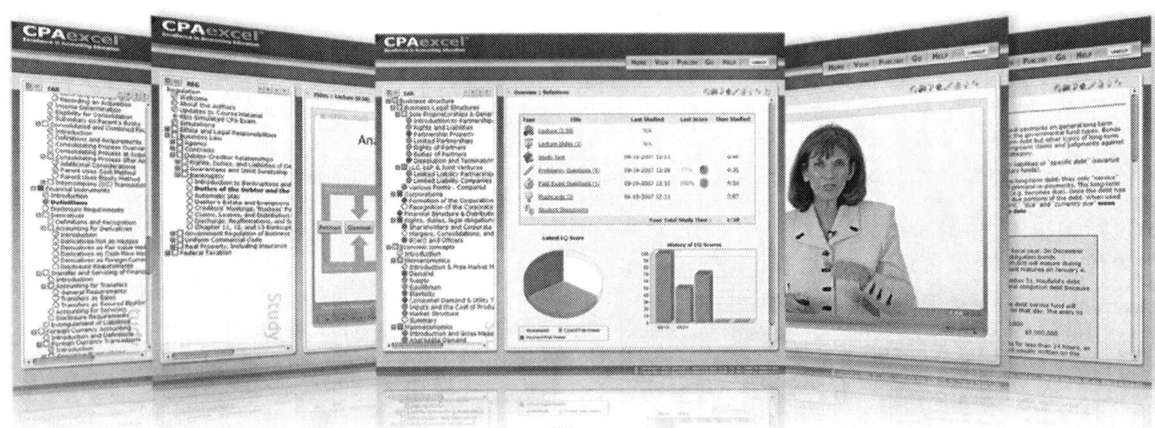

Students may use each lesson's learning resources in any desired sequence. Typically, a student will first watch and listen to the Video Lecture and then either review the Study Text or go directly to the Proficiency Questions to test and reinforce his or her knowledge of the lesson content. Then he or she might test his or her knowledge on Past Exam Questions. Note that each of the learning resources are just one click away from each other, enabling the student to easily access all the resources needed to quickly master that bite-sized topic before moving to the next topic.

Compared to other review courses, CPAexcel's bite-sized lessons are a much more efficient way to master the large body of knowledge required to pass the CPA exam. They are a key contributor to the exam success of CPAexcel's students.

Efficient Learning System:

CPAexcel's software-driven Efficient Learning System tightly-integrates the use of all CPAexcel's learning functions including bite-sized lessons. Key benefits to students are:

- Significant increases in knowledge gained and retained per hour of study
- Increased student focus and motivation
- Automatic progress measurement, tracking, and reporting
- Two-click access to fellow students and professors worldwide
- Exact replication of the formats and software functions used in the CPA exam itself
- 24/7/365 courseware access from any computer anywhere, with synchronization of scores
- Online and offline personalized updates with automatic alerts

Free Demonstration:

Free demonstrations of CPAexcel are available at http://www.cpaexcel.com/student_center/tutorial/

Table of Contents

Business Environment and Concepts

Welcome

Overview
According to the Board of Examiners (BOE) of the AICPA, the Business Environment and Concepts (BEC) section of the exam tests:

A. Knowledge of the general business environment and business concepts that candidates need to know in order to understand the underlying business reasons for and accounting implications of business transactions; and

B. The skills needed to apply that knowledge in performing financial statement audit and attestation engagements and other functions normally performed by CPAs that affect the public interest.

Content covered in this section includes knowledge of business structure; economic concepts essential to obtaining an understanding of an entity's operations, business and industry; financial management; information technology; and planning and measurement.

According to the BOE, approximately 70% of the content of this section was not tested before the exam became computerized in 2004. Therefore, there is little "historical information" from prior to 2004 as to the nature and focus of exam questions for most of this section of the exam. Consequently:

C. The outline for this section is patterned after the "Examination Content Specifications" provided by the BOE for the BEC section of the exam; and

D. Many of the multiple choice questions used in this section have been created by CPAExcel authors based on the content of the material presented.

The content specifications for this section are present in the following area headings, together with the point range for each area:

AREA	Point Range
Business Structures	17% - 23%
Economic Concepts	8% - 12%
Financial Management	17% - 23%
Information Technology	22% - 28%
Planning & Measurement	22% - 28%
Total Points	100%

The material in this section covers all topics in the content specifications, but they are not necessarily covered in the same order as listed in the specifications. Those specifications are intended to identify all of the topics that might be on the exam, but they are not listed in the most logical order or groupings for learning purposes. In this material the topics listed in the specifications have been arranged and grouped to facilitate learning.

Each of the five areas covered in this material is described briefly below.

Business Structure
This area covers material concerned with:

E. The characteristics, advantages and disadvantages of various legal forms of business organization;

F. How the various legal forms are formed, operate and terminate;

G. The rights, duties/obligations and authority of owners and managers;

H. Issues related to the capitalization and to profit/loss allocation and distribution in the various forms of legal entity

For presentation purposes, the material begins by considering sole proprietorships and partnerships, then discusses limited liability forms of organization, and concludes with matters related to the corporate form of business. A section that compares the characteristics of each form of structure is included to facilitate an understanding of the basic differences of each form and the circumstances under which each form may be the appropriate form of organization.

Economic Concepts
This area covers material concerned with:

I. The effects of economic events, including business cycles, on an entity's financial position and operation;

J. National economic measures and reasons for changes in the economy;

K. How the economy and markets influence business and customer management strategies;

L. Implications of dealing in foreign currencies, including exchange rate fluctuations and hedging.

Some of the topics covered will be familiar to you from basic economics courses, especially microeconomics and macroeconomics. Other topics may be new to you, especially if you have not taken an international economics course.

While the content specifications provided by the BOE covers a broad range of economic topics, that coverage is not particularly deep. An understanding of the material covered in this section should provide more than adequate preparation for the exam.

Financial Management
This area covers material concerned with:

M. Concepts and tools used in financial management, as well as in other areas of management and accounting;

N. The capital budgeting process and analytical techniques used in capital budgeting;

O. Short-term and long-term strategies for financing and appropriate financing strategies;

P. Techniques for managing working capital;

Q. The use of ratios and other quantitative techniques for financial management;

R. The various categories of risk faced by a business and ways to mitigate those risks.

Some of these topics were covered on the exam prior to it becoming computerized in 2004; however, on the current exam more financial management topics are covered than previously, and in more depth.

In covering this section, it is important to understand the concepts and tools covered in the first set of lessons before considering the other subsections in this area. Those concepts and tools - including cost concepts, and time value of money and interest rate concepts and calculations - are used in the subsequent subsection of this area, as well as in various other topics covered on the exam.

Information Technology
This area covers material concerned with:

S. The purposes and types of information technology (IT) systems, including E-business and E-commerce systems, and the development and implementation of IT systems;

T. The fundamental elements of information systems, including hardware, software, operating systems, data and data structures, and networks;

U. The types of risks inherent in different types of information systems and the controls appropriate to mitigate those risks.

In covering these topics, this section provides an overview of the types of systems now available, the manner in which they can be used to support both low-level and high-level activities within the organization, and the processing methodologies employed.

Basic to understanding these information technology topics is to understand the myriad technical terms and concepts used. These terms and concepts may be the basis for exam questions, or may be needed to answer broader exam questions. Therefore, an "Information Technology Glossary" is presented as the final lesson in the section.

Planning and Measurement
This area covers material concerned with:

V. The various methods of measuring and assigning costs, especially as they related to a production process;

W. Financial planning and control functions, including budgeting, forecasting and post-performance analysis;

X. Issues involving the determination of costs that are relevant in making certain financial decisions;

Y. Forms of both financial and non-financial performance measurement.

Most of the topics in this area are covered in college "Management Accounting" courses and were covered on the exam prior to 2004, though in a different part of the exam. Therefore, there is a longer "historical record" of the occurrence of these topics on the exam, and more Exam Questions for this topic come from actual old exams than for the other areas in BEC.

~ *Prof. Allen Bizzell*

About the Authors

Dr. Allen Bizzell has been involved with the CPA Exam for almost 30 years as a researcher, developer of exam-related materials and review course instructor. He has conducted numerous CPA Exam-related studies, including several analyses of CPA Exam Candidates' Characteristics and Performance for the Texas State Board of Public Accountancy. He has developed CPA review materials and taught review courses at both the national and local levels. Included in his innovative review materials is the use of simple network diagrams to depict the relationships between related accounting concepts/topics and the appropriate treatment for each. These diagrams are powerful tools for not only understanding accounting materials, but also for retaining the knowledge needed to pass the CPA Exam.

Several publishers have approached Dr. Bizzell to develop financial accounting textbooks incorporating his instructional methodology. According to Dr. Bizzell, he has not done so because the traditional textbook does not lend itself to using all the elements of the methodology. He believes, "The CPAexcel approach is the first to provide the capabilities to capture and deliver to the user the benefits of the methodology."

Professor B. Douglas Clinton is the Alta Via Consulting Professor of Management Accountancy at Northern Illinois University. Doug serves as an Editorial Board Member of *Strategic Finance and Management Accounting Quarterly*, is the IMA's Contributing Editor for Strategic Cost Management, and is Senior Content Advisor to the IMA Research Centre of Excellence. Doug is Associate Editor for *Advances in Accounting Behavioral Research*, and a member of the Editorial Board of the *Journal of Accounting Education* and *Issues in Accounting Education*. His research emphasizes strategic costing and he publishes regularly in *Strategic Finance and Management Accounting Quarterly*. Doug has made numerous presentations at national and international conferences and was recently awarded the 2006 IMA Faculty Leadership Award.

Professor Jan Gillespie has over twelve years experience teaching CPA Review courses. Her major areas of interest, fund accounting and managerial accounting, are supported by work experience in private industry and governmental organizations. In addition, Jan has been on the faculty of the University of Texas since 1988, teaching Accounting Information Systems and Fund Accounting, and a variety of other courses. Having passed the CPA exam after being out of school for seven years, and while working full-time and raising a family, she is a great believer in the ability of anyone to achieve this goal if they are willing to dedicate themselves to the task.

Professor Robert A. Prentice is the Ed and Molly Smith Centennial Professor of Business Law at the University of Texas at Austin and has taught both UT's and other CPA courses for fifteen years. He created a new course in accounting ethics and regulation that he has taught for the last decade. Professor Prentice has written several textbooks, many major law review articles on securities regulation and accountants' liability, and has won more than thirty teaching awards.

Professor Dan N. Stone is a Gatton Endowed Chair at the University of Kentucky, where he holds a joint appointment in the Von Allmen School of Accountancy and the School of Management (Decision Science Information Systems.) He is Director of Graduate studies and Director of the PhD program for the Von Allmen School of Accountancy. His joint PhD degree is in accounting and management information systems from the University of Texas at Austin. He has published over 40 academic works, including articles, essays, short stories, and poetry in a variety of journals, including the *Journal of Accounting Research, Accounting, Organizations, Organizations, and Society, Organizational Behavior and Human Decision Processes, and Auditing: A Journal of Theory and Practice*. His recent research investigates online deception, information technologies, dysfunctional effects of financial rewards, and knowledge management and motivation quality among professionals.

Business Structure

Sole Proprietorships & General and Limited Partnerships

Introduction to Partnerships

As in other areas of the law, a good place to begin study is to acquire a familiarity with the key terminology in a given subject matter area. The terminology in partnership law is fairly simple to grasp.

I. Definitions and Governing Law

Definitions:

General Partnership: An association of two or more persons to carry on as co-owners a business for profit."

Joint Venture: An association of two or more persons in a single business enterprise; the term can be used to distinguish a general partnership which can connote an ongoing business relationship rather than a one-shot deal.

Limited Partnership: A partnership with at least one general partner and at least one limited partner; it is distinguishable from a general partnership in that its limited partners will enjoy limited legal liability.

Limited Liability Partnership: A relatively new form of business organization carrying much greater protection from liability than exists in either general or limited partnerships.

II. Governing Law

A. General partnership law is governed by model acts that the states adopt. The original Uniform Partnership Act (UPA) was promulgated in 1916, but most states have now adopted some variant of the Revised Uniform Partnership Act (RUPA). The most recent version of the RUPA was promulgated in 1994, and amended in 1997. Because the AICPA must take a nationwide view of the law, this course concentrates on the areas of similarity between the two regimes, although some differences will be noted. RUPA will be our focus.

B. Joint ventures are essentially identical to general partnerships and are governed by either the UPA or RUPA, depending on the jurisdiction.

C. The Revised Uniform Limited Partnership Act (RULPA) governs limited partnership law in most jurisdictions.

D. The RUPA was amended in 1996 to provide limited liability for partners in a Limited Liability Partnership (LLP). LLPs are examined later in this portion of the partnership discussion.

III. Introduction to General Partnerships

A. RUPA is functionally a *form contract*, which provides default rules.

B. By agreement, partners may vary (most) RUPA provisions to meet their business needs, but may not prejudice rights of third parties.

C. A written partnership agreement is a good idea, but not required unless it is to last for a specified period longer than one year.

D. No official filing is required to form a general partnership, although RUPA provides for a voluntary **Statement of Partnership Authority** in the Secretary of State's Office.

IV. Characteristics of a General Partnership

A. Unlimited Liability for Partners.

Example:
A, B, and C form the ABC partnership. On its second day of existence one of its employees drives the firm truck into the back of a busload of nuns. The firm's insurance policy is not yet effective, and the nuns sue A, B, and C as well as the partnership and recover a judgment of $10,000,000. After the partnership's assets are depleted, the nuns may proceed against A, B, and C personally. They are generally liable for the firm's debts, contractual and tort-based.

B. Pass-through Taxation

1. Partnership files an informational return, but pays no taxes.
2. Individual partners pay tax on allocated income, whether or not it is actually distributed.

C. A **partnership** is an association of two or more persons to carry on as co-owners a business for profit.

Note:
It is surprising in how many contexts the issue will arise as to whether a particular business relationship was a partnership. The issue is usually resolved by detailed application of the definition of a partnership contained in the UPA or RUPA.

V. Elaboration of Determining the Existence of a Partnership:

A. Association

1. **Voluntariness --** Delectus Personae: Partners are allowed to choose with whom they will become partners; that is, all existing partners must consent to the addition of another partner.
2. **Intent --** The key is not an intent to be "partners", but simply an intent to enter into the type of business relationship that the law deems a partnership; that is, content controls form.
3. **Two or More Persons Having Legal Capacity --** Minors can become partners, but can disaffirm a partnership contract like any other.

B. Business for Profit

1. Includes: Every trade, occupation, or profession.
2. Excludes: Charitable, religious, and fraternal groups, which are deemed simply other unincorporated associations.

C. Co-ownership

1. *Community of interest* involves sharing:
   a. Capital;
   b. Control;
   c. Profits and Losses.
2. Sharing of profits and losses is prima facie evidence of a partnership, unless the profits were received in payment:
   a. Of a debt;
   b. As wages of an employee or rent to a landlord;
   c. As an annuity to a widow or representative of a deceased person.

d. As interest on a loan; or

e. As consideration for the sale of goodwill.

D. Partnership by Estoppel/Purported Partners

1. Generally, persons who are not partners as to each other are not partners as to others. There is an important exception to this general rule. Partnership by estoppel is based on traditional agency law and is important to grasp.

2. Persons who are not partners may be treated as partners on an estoppel theory.

3. RUPA calls them purported partners.

4. This is not a true partnership, but a method of fixing liability on one who has held herself out as a partner (or allowed herself to be so held out by others).

5. Elements of:

   a. Words or conduct by or attributable to the party to be charged amounting to a representation of partnership;

   b. Detrimental action taken by plaintiff in reliance on the representation; and

   c. The representation was reasonably believed by plaintiff.

Example:
Attempting to induce D to make a loan to their business, partners A and B tell D that C, a wealthy person, is their partner. C is present and does not deny this. If D makes the loan and is not repaid by A and B, he may sue C as their partner even though he was not truly their partner.

VI. Aggregate Theory vs. Entity Theory -- Under the original UPA, a partnership is usually viewed as simply an aggregation of its partners with no separate existence of its own like that enjoyed by a corporation.

A. Example -- Pass-through taxation.

VII. RUPA -- Treats a partnership as a separate entity for most purposes, although partners continue to have pass-through taxation.

A. RUPA makes this change primarily so that the partnership entity can continue to exist even though individual partners come and go.

Rights and Liabilities

The rights and liabilities of partners regarding third parties is also based on traditional agency law. If you have mastered agency law, then you already know everything you need to know to handle this part of partnership law, although some attention to the rules of joint and several liability would probably be helpful.

I. Partnership Contractual Liability to Third Parties

A. Overview -- The law in this area is largely an application of agency principles discussed in the Agency Unit to the specific partnership situation.

B. General Principles

1. An act of a partner for apparently carrying on in the ordinary course the partnership business binds the partnership, unless the partner had no authority to act for the partnership in the particular matter and the person with whom the partner was dealing knew or had received notification that the partner lacked authority.
2. An act of a partner which is not apparently for carrying on in the ordinary course the partnership business binds the partnership only if the act was authorized by the other partners.

C. A partner binds both the partnership and the other partners if she acts with

1. Actual Authority, or
    - a. Expressed, or
    - b. Implied,
        - i. Customary,
        - ii. Incidental, or
        - iii. Emergency.
2. Apparent Authority. Apparent authority cannot exist where:
    - a. Third party knows of a partner's lack of authority, or
    - b. The partner's action is one that requires unanimity, such as an "extraordinary" contract.

D. Scope of Authority is determined by

1. Past practices of the partnership, and
2. Practices of similar businesses in the area.

Example:

1. Implied and apparent authority typically encompass the power to hire and fire employees, open bank accounts, buy supplies, sell inventory, rent office space, etc.

2. After a falling out with Partners B and C, Partner A of the ABC Furniture Co. is forbidden by majority vote to sell any partnership property without the consent of the other partners. Nonetheless, acting on his own A sells to a customer a couch and the company's fleet of seven delivery trucks. The sale of the couch is probably within the scope of apparent authority, but the sale of the trucks probably is not.

E. **Ratification --** Even if a partner acted without actual or apparent authority, the partnership may still be liable if it ratifies the action.

II. **Tort Liability**

A. **Overview --** Partnership tort liability is largely an application of agency tort law principles to the partnership setting. Generally speaking, a partnership is liable for the torts of its partners.

B. **Key question --** Was the partner acting within the scope of partnership business?

C. **Negligence Cases --** The common "car wreck" scenario:

1. Personal car/Personal errand: partnership not liable;
2. Partnership car/Personal errand: partnership not liable;
3. Partnership car/Partnership business: partnership liable;
4. Personal car/Partnership business: partnership liable if delivery is a regular part of partnership's business.

D. **Intentional Torts --** The partnership is liable if the partner was attempting to advance partnership interests, even if he did so in a wrongful way.

Example:

In attempting to acquire more prominent shelf space for the partnership's products in a grocery store carrying those products, partner A gets into a fist fight with an employee of a competitor also seeking the shelf space. The partnership is probably liable.

E. **Misapplication of Funds --** RUPA imposes virtually strict liability on a partnership for the misapplication of money received by the partnership "in the course of its business."

III. **Joint and Several Liability --** Under RUPA, contract and tort liability are typically joint and several, meaning that a creditor may sue any one partner and hold that partner completely liable without suing the others.

A. RUPA, and even most UPA states require, in cases of both contract and tort liabilities, that assets of the partnership be exhausted before the partnership creditor proceeds against individual assets of partners and many states provide for joint and several liability for contract as well as tort liabilities.

Example:
A is owed $50,000 by the XYZ Partnership and is fairly certain that the partnership does not have sufficient assets to pay the debt. A should sue the partnership as well as individual partners X, Y, and Z. Achieving a judgment against the individual partners will enable A to proceed against their individual assets if, after exhausting partnership assets, some of the debt remains unpaid.

B. If a partner joins an existing partnership, she is generally liable for all subsequently-incurred debts, but is liable for preexisting debts only out of her firm contribution.

Example:
D joins the ABC partnership by contributing $20,000. At the time D joined the partnership, it owed X Bank $50,000. Soon after D joined, ABC borrowed $50,000 more from Y Bank. Both obligations went unpaid. X Bank can seize what is available of D's $20,000 contribution (after following proper procedures), but cannot reach D's personal assets if there is a shortfall. Y Bank, however, can pursue D's personal assets if it goes unpaid out of partnership assets.

Partnership Property

One of the more intricate areas of partnership law is that of partnership property. This section will emphasize the process of determining whether a particular piece of property belongs to the partnership or to one of the partners, the nature and extent of a partner's interest in partnership property, and the rights of individual creditors regarding partnership property.

I. **Partnership Versus Individual Property**

   A. **RUPA Provision --** RUPA provides that "Property transferred to or otherwise acquired by a partnership is property of the partnership and not of the partners individually."

   B. **Additional Factors --** Consistent with earlier UPA rules, RUPA goes on to provide that property is "partnership property" if acquired in the name of:

      1. The partnership; or

      2. One or more of the partners with an indication in the instrument that transferred title of the person's capacity as a partner or of the existence of the partnership.

   C. **Partnership Assets --** Property is presumed to be partnership property if purchased with partnership assets.

   D. **Separate Property --** Property acquired in the name of one or more of the partners without any indication of partnership capacity or of the existence of the partnership and without the use of partnership assets is presumed to be separate property, even if it is used for partnership purposes.

   E. **Entity Ownership --** Partnership property is owned by the partnership entity, not by the partners in common.

II. **Partnership Interest:** A partner's *partnership interest* is personal property and consists of the right to:

   A. Share in the partnership's profits, and

   B. Share in the partnership's net assets upon dissolution.

III. **Creditor Restriction --** No creditor of an individual partner may attach partnership property to satisfy an individual debt.

   A. **Charging Order --** The proper approach for creditors of individual partners is the charging order, in which the judge orders the other partners to pay any distribution due to the debtor partner to that partner's creditor instead.

   B. **Assignment --** Debtor partners may assign (and creditors of debtor partners may seize) only the individual partner's interest in the partnership (i.e. profits and net assets).

      1. **Satisfying Debts of Partners --** Individual partners may not assign and creditors of individual partners may not seize partnership property to satisfy the debts of individual partners.

      2. **Assignment to Creditor --** If an individual partner does assign to an individual creditor his or her partnership interest, the creditor does not become a partner for any purpose.

Example:

Partner A goes to Las Vegas and runs up large gambling debts. His creditors seek to collect on the debt. All A owns is his interest in the ABC Partnership. The creditors cannot reach any partnership property. All A can assign to the creditors is his right to receive his share of partnership profits upon distribution and his share of partnership net assets in the event of dissolution.

C. **Partnership Creditor** -- A partnership creditor is required in most states to proceed against the partnership's assets first and, if they prove to be inadequate, then may proceed against the assets of individual partners.

Limited Partnerships

Limited partnership law is governed by the ULPA or the RULPA. Any questions that cannot be answered by either the limited partnership agreement or ULPA and RULPA are answered by resort to general partnership law. Traditionally the AICPA has not asked too many questions about limited partnerships specifically.

I. Introduction

> **Definition:**
>
> *Limited Partnership*: A partnership consisting of at least one general partner (GP) and at least one limited partner (LP).

1. Limited Liability for LPs.
2. Partnership (Pass-Through) Taxation.
3. Transferability of LP interests.
4. Centralized management by GPs.

B. **Forfeit of Control --** Limited partners forfeit right to *control* their investment and, in exchange, are accorded limited liability.

C. **Limited Partners --** General partners can simultaneously become limited partners by purchasing limited partnership interests.

D. **Governing Law --** The Revised Uniform Limited Partnership Act (RULPA) governs in most states.

II. Partnership Formation

A. **Limited partnerships** can be formed only by filing the appropriate documents at the Secretary of State's Office.

B. One of those documents must be a written limited partnership agreement.

C. The **limited partnership name** should indicate its status by use of the term "limited partnership" or "L.P.," or "Ltd.," etc.

III. Loss of Limited Liability Status

A. **Creditors: Personal Liability --** Creditors of a limited partnership who go unpaid will seek to impose personal liability upon limited partners.

B. **Forfeit of Limited Liability --** Limited partners can, in some circumstances, forfeit their limited liability:

C. **Defective Formation**

1. If a limited partnership is defectively formed, an LP may be held liable if he knew or should have known that no certificate had been filed or that one erroneously referred to him as a general partner.
2. However, this liability (a) extends only to third parties who, reasonably believed based on the LP's conduct that he was a GP, extended credit to the partnership, and (b) may be terminated by the filing of an appropriate certificate with the Secretary of State's office and the withdrawing from participation in profits.

D. **False Statements --** If an LP (a) signs an LP certificate knowing that it contains false statements or omissions, or (b) learns of such misrepresentations and fails to amend or cancel it, the LP may forfeit limited liability.

E. **Exercising Control**

1. If an LP takes part in the control of the partnership business, he may forfeit limited liability.
2. However, liability to the LP extends only to persons who transact business with the limited partnership believing, based on the LP's conduct, that the LP is a GP.
3. A limited partner does not take part in control by virtue of the following:
   a. Being a contractor for or an agent or employee of the limited partnership;
   b. Consulting with and advising a general partner;
   c. Acting as surety for the limited partnership or guaranteeing its loans;
   d. Taking any action required or permitted by law to sue on behalf of the limited partnership;
   e. Requesting or attending a meeting of the partners;
   f. Winding up the partnership;
   g. Exercising any right permitted to limited partners; or
   h. voting on any important partnership matter.

F. **Use of Name**

1. An LP who knowingly permits his name to be used in the name of the limited partnership forfeits limited liability.
2. This liability extends only to persons who extend credit to the limited partnership without knowledge that the LP is not a GP.

IV. **Rights and Responsibilities of Limited Partners**

A. **Control and Approval**

1. LP powers should be set out in LP agreement.
2. LPs often have veto power over certain "extraordinary" acts by GPs.
3. LPs usually have power to replace GPs.

B. **Information and Inspection Rights**

1. A limited partnership must maintain and permit the inspection by limited partners of all important partnership records.
2. Access to Courts.
3. LPs have the right to file derivative suits, just like corporate shareholders.

C. **Assignability**

1. A limited partner's interest (in share of profits and assets on dissolution) is considered personal property and is freely assignable.
2. A limited partner's rights to inspect, to bring derivatives suits, etc. are not assignable unless they are assigned to a substitute limited partner.

V. **General Partners' Rights and Responsibilities --** The general partners' right to control leads to:

A. Unlimited personal liability, and

B. Enhanced fiduciary duty owed to limited partners.

VI. Allocation of Profits and Losses

A. Profits and losses shall be allocated in the manner provided in the written partnership agreement.

B. If not otherwise provided, profits and losses shall be allocated in accordance with the current percentage or other interest in the partnership stated in its records.

C. Partners who lend money to the partnership share in distributions along with outside creditors.

D. The partnership agreement may provide for LPs and GPs to be treated equally.

Rights of Partners

This section introduces you to the rights of partners, including the right to choose associates, the right to manage partnership business, the right to return of capital, the very limited right to interest, the right to profits, the limited right to compensation for services, the right to reimbursement for expenses incurred on behalf of the partnership, the right to use partnership property for partnership purposes, the right to inspect partnership records, and the right to an accounting.

I. Right to Choose Associates (Delectus Personae)

Example:
A, B, C. and D were partners. A, B, and C wish to add E as a partner. D does not. D will prevail unless he has waived his delectus personae right.

II. Right to Manage -- All partners have equal rights in the management and conduct of business affairs, absent agreement to the contrary.

A. Majority vote governs, absent agreement to the contrary.

Example:
A, B, and C are partners. A and B vote to borrow money from the bank. C votes against. A and B prevail. The loan is valid and C is liable to repay it.

B. However, unanimity is needed for "extraordinary matters"

1. Any act in contravention of the partnership agreement;
2. Any decision to vary from the default rules, such as to provide a right of compensation for work performed; and
3. Any matter outside ordinary business affairs. Examples from the UPA include:
   a. Assign partnership property;

Example:
Creditor A is owed money by ABC partnership. It wishes to have the partnership assign its trucks to A so that A can sell them to pay the debt. Partners A, B, and C must all agree.

b. Dispose of goodwill;

Example:
A, B, and C own an ice cream store with the name "ABC Creamery." X wishes to buy the store and to operate it under the name "ABC Creamery." All partners must agree to the sale.

c. Do any other act which would make it impossible to carry on the ordinary business of the partnership;

Example:
A, B, and C own a furniture store in a small town. There is only one building in town suitable for housing the business. D wishes to buy the building. A, B, and C must unanimously agree.

d. Confess judgment; and

Example:
A, B, and C run a partnership and wish to borrow money from D bank. The bank wishes the partners to sign a note containing a "confession of judgment" clause that essentially promises that the partners will not defend on the merits if sued on the note. All three partners must sign the note.

e. Submit a partnership claim or liability to arbitration.

Example:
Partners A, B, and C sued customer D for nonpayment of debt. D suggests that the claim be arbitrated rather than litigated. A, B, and C must all agree.

III. Capital Accounts

A. Under RUPA, each partner is deemed to have an account that is

1. Credited with an amount equal to the money plus the value of any other property, net of the amount of any liabilities, the partner contributes to the partnership and the partner's share of the partnership profits;
2. At the same time, this account is charged with an amount equal to the money plus the value of any other property, net of the amount of any liabilities, distributed by the partnership to the partner and the partner's share of partnership losses.

B. Partners are to be reimbursed for payments made and indemnified for liabilities incurred in the ordinary course of the partnership business.

C. Partners are to be reimbursed for advances to the partnership made beyond agreed capital contributions.

IV. **Interest** -- Under RUPA, partners should receive interest on a payment or advance made by a partner which gives rise to a partnership obligation.

V. **Right to Profits**

A. Absent agreement, profits and losses are to be shared equally.

Example:
A contributes $100,000 to a partnership with B, who contributes $10,000. The partnership makes $20,000 the first year. Absent contrary agreement, the $20,000 is distributed equally to A and B.

B. If the partners agree to share profits in some proportion other than equally, but make no agreement regarding losses, losses will be shared in the same proportion as profits.

Example:
A, B, and C are partners. Because A contributed more to the partnership than B and C, it is agreed that A will receive 50% of the profits and B and C will each receive 25%. The partners never even considered losses, but things do not go well and the partnership loses $200,000. A is responsible for 50% of the losses and B and C 25% each.

VI. **Right to Compensation for Services**

A. Generally, absent agreement, a partner is not entitled to be compensated for services performed for the partnership, for his compensation is to come exclusively in his share of profits.

Example:
A and B are partners. A works 40 hours a week on the partnership business. B works 5 hours a week. The partnership profits $20,000 in the first year. Each is entitled to $10,000. Absent agreement, A receives no compensation for his extra work.

B. **Exception - A partner will be entitled to compensation for services rendered in**

1. Winding up partnership affairs;
2. Performing tasks expected to be done by hired help; or
3. Performing "extraordinary services."

VII. Right to Use Property

Example:

1. Partner A has the right to use the partnership truck to deliver furniture to a customer.

2. Partner A does not have the right to use the partnership truck to move his sister's furniture on a weekend, absent consent of the other partners.

VIII. Right to Inspect Partnership Records

IX. Right to an Accounting

Duties of Partners

As in a democratic society, rights of partners carry reciprocal duties. This section introduces you to the duties of loyalty and care emphasized by the RUPA.

I. Fiduciary Duties

A. The RUPA provides that a partner owes only two fiduciary duties to the other partners:

1. The Duty of Loyalty; and

2. The Duty of Care.

II. Duty of Loyalty

A. The Duty of Loyalty entails the same basic precepts discussed in the Agency Unit:

1. No competition;

2. No conflicts of interest;

a. Nonetheless, transactions between a partner and the partnership are fully permissible if certain criteria (including notice and fairness) are met.

3. No appropriation of a partnership business opportunity; and

4. No disclosure of confidential information.

III. Duty of Care -- The Duty of Care is limited to "refraining from engaging in grossly negligent or reckless conduct, intentional misconduct, or a knowing violation of law."

IV. Discharge of Duties -- RUPA also provides that partners must discharge their duties to the partnership and other partners "consistently with the obligation of good faith and fair dealing."

V. UPA -- The partners' fiduciary obligations in UPA jurisdictions are roughly analogous to those just spelled out for RUPA.

Dissolution and Termination

Dissolution and termination are key stages in the life (and death) of a partnership.

I. The UPA approach provides three distinct phases

A. Dissolution

1. Causes of Dissolution Include:
   a. Death of a partner;
   b. Bankruptcy of a partner;
   c. Partner's declaration of an intent to leave the partnership.
2. **Effect of Dissolution --** The partnership ends, and the remaining partners must settle up with the departing partner or his estate or guardian, absent agreement to the contrary.

B. Winding Up

1. During the winding up phase, the partners gather together partnership assets and pay off firm debts.
2. Liquidation right: generally, departing partners (or their estates) have the right to have the partnership property applied to discharge its liabilities, and the surplus applied to pay in cash the net amount owing to the respective partners.

C. Termination -- Occurs when the winding up process is completed.

D. If the partnership continues during the wind up phase, continuing partners generally must hold harmless departing partners.

II. The RUPA makes several changes from the UPA in this area, including

A. The fact that partners are added or subtracted does not automatically lead to dissolution of the partnership, as in the UPA.

1. Rather, what are causes of dissolution *of the partnership* under UPA are merely causes of "dissociation" of a partner under RUPA.
2. Among the grounds for dissociation listed in RUPA are:
   a. Notice of a partner's express will to dissolve;
   b. Death;
   c. Bankruptcy;
   d. Expulsion;
   e. Etc.

B. Rule 801 lists situations in which a partnership *must* be wound up; in all other situations, a buyout of a partner must occur under Rule 701. Thus, a partner's dissociation must always lead to either a buyout or dissolution.

C. If dissolution does *not* occur, the partnership shall purchase the interest of the dissociating partner at the amount that would have been distributable to the dissociating partner from his or her partnership account if, on the date of dissociation, the assets of the partnership were sold at the *greater* of liquidation or going-concern value (offset by damages caused if the dissociation was harmful).

D. While dissociation normally does not cause dissolution, and thus partners may leave or be added without any technical dissolution, events that will cause dissolution include partner choice in an at-will partnership, death of a partner, incapacity of a partner, etc.

E. RUPA provides a 90-day "cooling off" period between dissolution and liquidation in order to give the parties a chance to negotiate an amicable buyout.

III. UPA Rules for Distribution

A. Partnership Assets include

1. All partnership property; and
2. Any additional contributions of partners necessary to pay obligations.

B. Order of Payment

1. Outside creditors;
2. Partners as creditors;
3. Unpaid capital contributions;
4. Surplus, if any, to partners.

Question:
Upon dissolution of the ABC partnership, the partnership assets are $80,000. Debts owed outsiders are $40,000; C has loaned the partnership $10,000. Original capital contributions were A's $5,000, B's $4,000, and C's $3,000. They have not been repaid. In what order are the assets applied?

Answer:
1. $40,000 to outsiders, leaving $40,000.
2. $10,000 to C as creditor, leaving $30,000
3. $5,000 to A, $4,000 to B, and $3,000 to C to repay capital contributions, leaving $18,000.

$6,000 to A, B, and C representing their shares of the $18,000 profit.

Question:
Upon dissolution of the ABC partnership, the partnership assets are $50,000. Debts owed outsiders are $40,000. C has loaned the partnership $10,000. Original capital contributions were A's $5,000, B's $4,000, and C's $3,000. They have not been repaid. In what order are the assets applied?

Answer:
1. $40,000 to outside creditors, leaving $10,000.
2. $10,000 to C as creditor, leaving $0

Capital contributions of $12,000 remain unpaid. Because, absent agreement to the contrary, all partners are to share losses equally, each partner should lose $4,000. So, C should contribute $1,000 to be paid to A. If this is done, all three partners share the $12,000 loss equally.

IV. RUPA provides two basic categories for distribution

- **A.** Creditors, *including partners.*
- **B.** Partners "in accordance with their right to distributions..."
  - **1.** RUPA sensibly consolidates capital contributions and profits and losses to determine distribution rights.
  - **2.** In most cases, UPA and RUPA distribution rules lead to the same result.

LLC, LLP & Joint Ventures

Limited Liability Partnerships

The AICPA has long concentrated its questions on traditional forms of business organization -- partnerships, limited partnerships, and corporations. With the advent and sweeping popularity of LLCs (studied in the corporate law section) and LLPs (studied here and in the corporate law section), it makes sense that these areas will now receive their share of attention.

I. **LLP Statutes --** In recent years most states have passed LLP statutes in order to shelter professionals, such as accountants, from liability for the torts of other members of their firm.

II. **Characteristics of LLPs --** Like limited partnerships (and unlike general partnerships), LLPs must be formed by filing appropriate documents with the Secretary of State.

   A. LLPs feature partnership pass-through taxation with limited liability for the torts of other members of the firm.

   B. Typically, LLP members are liable for their own torts and for the torts of those they supervise.

Example:
Ann, an accountant supervised by Chuck, is a member of the ABC LLP. Ted is another member of the firm who does not supervise Ann. Ann commits malpractice. Ann is liable. Chuck is liable. Ted is not liable, as he would be if this were a general partnership rather than an LLP. Firm assets are reachable by injured plaintiffs in either event.

   C. Most LLP statutes protect members from liability for LLP contract-based obligations, but some do not.

   D. Many states require that LLPs carry certain levels of malpractice insurance to ensure that injured plaintiffs are protected.

   E. LLP liability protection has been called "death insurance," because it kicks in only when liabilities exceed firm assets.

Limited Liability Companies

As noted earlier, LLCs and LLPs have become a very important part of the legal landscape in the last few years . They are now so important that they will likely garner significant attention.

I. Two new forms of business organization

A. In order to encourage business activity and cater to accountants concerned about their liability, states have invented two new forms of business organization

1. Limited Liability Companies (LLCs), and

2. Limited Liability Partnerships (LLPs), which are discussed in more detail in the Unit on Partnerships.

II. Characteristics -- Both feature the limited liability and pass-through taxation of limited partnerships (LPs) and Subchapter S corporations, but:

A. Unlike LPs, do not require that there be at least one party who is generally liable; and

B. Unlike Subchapter S corporations, do not involve a lot of prickly federal requirements (100 or fewer shareholders, no foreign shareholders, no partnerships, limited passive income, etc.);

C. LLPs and LLCs join currently existing professional corporations and Subchapter S corporations as major ways for business people to enjoy both limited liability and pass-through taxation.

III. LLCs

A. Are currently authorized in all states.

B. Many national accounting firms have restructured themselves as LLCs.

C. Most, but not all, jurisdictions authorize "single-member" LLCs.

D. Owners are called "members," rather than shareholders or partners.

IV. Comparison of Various Forms of Organization -- Both LLCs and LLPs were invented as part of this quest.

A. Check the Box Rules -- However, in 1997 the IRS promulgated the **check the box** rules for taxing business organizations in an attempt to minimize the influence that tax factors have upon choice of forms.

> **Note:**
> Importantly, the new rules largely eliminate the old test focusing on the various supposed features of **corporate**, including limited liability, perpetual duration, centralized control, and transferability of interests.

B. Under the new rules

1. Taxed as Corporations -- Certain entities are always taxed as corporations:

a. State law corporations; and

b. Publicly traded entities.

2. Taxed as Partnerships -- Other incorporated associations with two or more members are taxed as partnerships, *unless* they affirmatively elect to be taxed as corporations:

a. General Partnerships;

b. Limited Partnerships;

c. LLCs;

d. LLPs.

3. **Taxed as Sole Proprietorships --** Single-member LLCs (not allowed in some jurisdictions) are treated as sole proprietorships (and, therefore, taxed as "nothings"), unless they affirmatively elect corporate treatment.

V. **Other Unincorporated Forms of Business Organizations --** In addition to joint ventures, partnerships, limited partnerships, LLCs, and LLPs, other unincorporated forms of business organization include:

A. **Business Trusts --** Business trusts are formed by contracts in the form of written declarations. Management is centralized in the hands of trustees who operate the business on behalf of the owners. The goal is to attain the limited liability and free transferability of corporations, yet evade state corporate regulation and corporate taxation. They are used primarily as an organizational form for money market funds and real estate investments, and are taxed as corporations if they reflect too many corporate characteristics.

B. **Joint Stock Companies --** Joint stock companies are organized under a contract normally called the articles of association. Their affairs are typically handled by a group of directors or managers. Like a partnership, the owners have unlimited liability. However, unlike a partnership, the owners are not agents of the organization and cannot bind it. Only the directors or managers can.

C. **Business Cooperatives --** Credit unions, farming cooperatives, and rural power and telephone cooperatives operate as business cooperatives. These organizations may operate commercially for a profit, but they are formed primarily to benefit members. They are characterized by features such as equal ownership and control by members, ownership limited to those who avail themselves of services furnished by the cooperative, limited return on capital investments, and services provided primarily to members. They are usually taxed as partnerships, yet provide limited liability to owners.

Corporations

Formation of the Corporation

Unlike partnerships, corporations are separate legal entities. They carry the advantage of protecting their owners from legal liability; they have the concomitant disadvantage of subjecting those same owners to double taxation (unless they are Subchapter S corporations). Corporations can be formed only by compliance with statutory formalities. The AICPA wants you to know the basics of these formalities. It may seem silly, but it pays to memorize the provisions that must be included in corporate articles of incorporation.

I. Characteristics, Types & Governing Law of Corporations

A. Characteristics of Corporations

1. Limited liability for shareholders

Example:
ABC Computer Corporation has several bad quarters in a row, racks up millions of dollars in losses, and takes bankruptcy. It owes millions in non-dischargeable debts. Creditors of ABC generally cannot sue its shareholders for those sums. Unlike partners, they are not generally liable. Their losses are limited to the amount of their investment, for the company's stock is now probably worth zero.

2. Centralized management by officers and directors

a. Shareholders exert control indirectly by voting on directors who, in turn, choose officers to run the day-to-day affairs of the company.

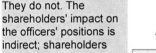

Note:
Misconception: Many people believe that shareholders vote on the officers of the company. They do not. The shareholders' impact on the officers' positions is indirect; shareholders vote on the directors who, in turn, select the officers.

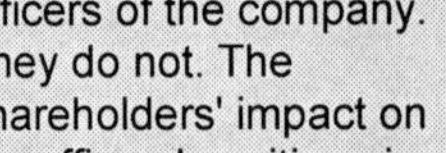

3. Ownership Interests -- Free transferability of ownership interests.

a. Shareholders own easily-sold (usually) shares, rather than the underlying assets which are in the corporation's name.

4. Perpetual duration

Example:
All fifty shareholders of ABC Corp. die in a plane crash as they travel to ABC's planned annual shareholders meeting in Hawaii. The death of all shareholders does not affect ABC's legal existence. It still exists; its new owners are the heirs of the fifty deceased shareholders.

5. Double taxation (except for Subchapter S corporations)

a. Corporation pays corporate income tax on profits.

b. Shareholders pay individual income tax on dividends. The desire to couple limited liability with pass-through taxation has led to creation not only of Subchapter S Corporations, but also Limited Liability Companies (LLCs) (discussed later in this Unit) and Limited Liability Partnerships (LLPs).

B. Types of Corporations

1. **Publicly Held --** shares freely traded, large numbers of shareholders, division of ownership and control;

2. **Closely Held --** relatively few shareholders, shares not freely traded, shareholders may be actively involved in the business;

3. **Subchapter S**

    a. **Pass-through Status --** Partnership pass-through status can be achieved for the corporate form, if the corporation complies with the requirements of Subchapter S of the IRS Code:

        i. It has only one class of stock (judged by economic criteria; the same class can include both voting and nonvoting stock);

        ii. There are no more than 100 shareholders, each being an individual, individual estate, qualified trust, or certain tax exempt entities such as qualified charities, pension funds, or ESOPs (partnerships, corporations, and nonresident aliens are not allowed to be shareholders);

        iii. No more than 25% of the corporation's gross profits over a 3-year period come from "passive" sources (e.g., rents, dividends, or interest payments);

        iv. All shareholders consent to the Subchapter S election.

    b. Sub. S corporations may own subsidiaries, including foreign corporations.

C. Governing Law -- There is substantial state-to-state variation in corporate codes, but most largely follow either:

1. The Revised Model Business Corporation Act (RMBCA); or

2. The Delaware Corporate Code.

II. The Incorporation Process -- Like limited partnerships, LLCs, and LLPs (and unlike general partnerships), corporations can only be formed by filing the appropriate documents with the jurisdiction's Secretary of State.

A. Draft Articles of Incorporation

1. **Mandatory Contents**

    a. The corporate name;

    b. The number of shares the corporation is authorized to issue;

    c. The street address of the corporation's registered office and the name of its registered agent;

    d. The name and address of each incorporator.

2. **Contains More Information --** Usually contains much more information, including:

    a. Duration (typically perpetual);

    b. Purposes (any legal purpose is allowable;)

    c. Capital Structure;

    d. Minimum Capitalization ($1,000 in many states);

    e. Directors;

    f. Management Provisions, such as quorum requirements, dates of annual meetings, cumulative voting provisions, preemptive rights, etc.

B. Execute and File Articles

C. Hold Organizational Meeting

1. Elect board-of-directors;
2. Adopt contracts entered into by promoters.

D. Draft and adopt By-Laws -- which are the corporation's internal procedural rules.

E. Obtain Certificate of Authority to Do Business in Foreign Jurisdictions. A corporation that is incorporated in one jurisdiction (e.g., Delaware) may do business in foreign jurisdictions (e.g., Nebraska) only after obtaining the foreign jurisdiction's permission to do so.

III. Promoters and Their Contracts -- Before a corporation is officially formed, promoters typically lay the groundwork for the business by hiring employees, renting office space, buying supplies, etc. Many legal issues can arise out of this activity, including the enforceability of the contracts the promoter negotiates.

Definition:

Promoter: A promoter is a person who takes the initiative in founding and organizing a business.

A. Fiduciary Duties of a Promoter

1. The promoter owes a fiduciary duty to:
   - **a.** The proposed corporation;
   - **b.** Other promoters;
   - **c.** Contemplated investors.

Example:
A promotes a corporation, forming it and issuing 10,000 shares to himself at $5/share. A then immediately sells 100,000 more shares to other investors who pay $20/share, assuming that this is the amount that A paid for his shares. A has breached his fiduciary duty to the later investors by issuing shares to himself at a discount without revealing that fact.

B. Safe ways for a promoter to profit:

1. Make full disclosure to an independent board of directors; or
2. Make full disclosure to all original shareholders.

C. Promoter Liability on Pre-Incorporation Contracts

1. Promoters are liable on the contracts they negotiate on the prospective corporation's behalf unless the contract clearly and explicitly indicates that the third party is looking only to the corporation for performance.
2. **Continued Liability --** Even if the corporation is formed and adopts the contract, the promoter remains liable, absent a novation (an express release from the third party).

D. Corporation Liability on Contracts -- A corporation is liable on contracts negotiated by its promoters if it comes into existence and adopts the contract:

1. Expressly (e.g., via board of directors resolution); or
2. Impliedly (e.g., via voluntary acceptance of the benefits of the contract).

Example:
While promoting ABC Corporation, Al signs a contract renting an office from Joe at $2,000/month. ABC comes into existence, but its board of directors does not expressly adopt the contract. Nonetheless, ABC occupies the office and uses it for several months. ABC has impliedly adopted the contract and must pay the specified rent. Absent a novation, Al is also liable on the contract.

E. Right to Enforce -- The corporation, once it adopts the promoter's contracts, has the right to enforce them against the third parties.

Recognition of the Corporate Entity

Corporate creditors who are unsuccessful in being paid by the corporation will always want to look to individual shareholders for payment notwithstanding the concept of the corporate entity and the supposed limited liability of shareholders. It is important to know when those creditors may succeed.

I. Background

A. One of the greatest inventions of Western law is the corporate entity, which encourages the formation of business enterprises by allowing investors to limit the amount they can lose if a venture fails; limited liability is an expected attribute of a properly formed corporation.

B. Existence Recognized -- Existence of a corporate **entity** is well-recognized.

Example:
England once had a law that persons from France could not charter ships in England. Three French persons formed a British corporation and chartered a ship in England in the name of the corporation. This was perfectly permissible because the corporate entity was recognized and in the eyes of the law the ship was chartered by a British corporation not its three French owners.

II. Piercing the Corporate Veil --

Notwithstanding strong recognition of the corporate entity, occasionally courts will **pierce the corporate veil**, disregarding the corporate entity and imposing personal liability upon shareholders.

A. Background -- Courts will never pierce the corporate veil of a public held corporation like an IBM or General Motors; this is strictly a closely held corporation phenomenon.

B. Rationale -- The corporate form should not be used to defeat public convenience, to justify wrong, protect fraud, or defend crime.

C. Factors for Piercing -- The following factors (usually in combination) may induce a court to pierce the corporate veil:

1. Commingling of funds and other assets of the corporation with those of the individual shareholders:
   - a. Diversion of the corporation's funds or assets to the personal use of shareholders;
   - b. Failure to maintain the necessary corporate formalities;
   - c. Failure to adequately capitalize the corporation for the reasonably foreseeable risks of the enterprise;
   - d. Use of the corporation as a mere shell or conduit to operate a single venture or some particular aspect of the business of an individual shareholder;
   - e. Absence of separately held corporate assets;
   - f. Formation and use of the corporation to assume the existing liabilities of another person or entity.

Financial Structure & Distributions

People invest in corporations because they want financial return. Therefore, this section of financial matters is one of the most important parts of corporate law. Make sure you are familiar with the terminology, especially the different types of securities. Beyond that, it is most important to concentrate on the conditions under which dividends and other corporate distributions may properly be paid.

I. Introduction and Definitions

A. Types of Corporate Securities -- There are several types of corporate securities.

1. Equity Securities

a. **Common stock --** Owners of common stock are the true owners of the corporation. They bear the most risk and have the most to gain. They have the right to vote for directors, to share pro rata in the profits of the corporation when paid out as dividends and to share in the surplus of assets over liabilities, if any, when the corporation dissolves.

b. **Preferred stock --** Preferred shareholders may have economic rights that are superior to those of common shareholders in terms of either dividend rights or assets upon dissolution. Preferred shareholders are entitled to have their preferences respected. Preferred shares are usually cumulative, meaning that if the board chooses not to declare any preferred dividends in a given year, the right to receive them accumulates and in a subsequent year the board must pay both that year's preferred dividends and those that have cumulated unpaid from previous years before paying any dividends to common shareholders. If the preferred shares are noncumulative, however, no arrearages arise from one year's non-declaration and nonpayment. Once dividends are declared, the receiving shareholders are unsecured creditors of the corporation for that amount until they are actually paid.

c. **Treasury stock --** Common stock that, once issued to shareholders, has now been repurchased by the corporation is called treasury stock. Such stock is often distributed to shareholders pro rata as a **share dividend**.

2. Debt Securities -- are issued to creditors who, functionally, loan money to the corporation. They are not shareholders and do not have the rights to vote, to inspect, etc. that belong to shareholders. However, like other lenders and unlike common shareholders, they do have the right to be repaid and to be paid specified interest whether the corporation is prospering or not

a. **Notes --** short-term unsecured debt instruments.

b. **Debentures --** long-term unsecured debt instruments.

c. **Bonds --** debt instruments secured by corporate property.

B. Other terms

1. **Redeemable --** redeemable shares must be repurchased by the corporation under specified conditions and at specified prices if the shareholder so desires.
2. **Callable --** shares that are redeemable at the corporation's option.
3. **Convertible --** debt securities that are convertible to equity securities at specified ratios at the request of the holder.

4. **Warrants, rights, and options** -- legal entitlements to purchase equity (not debt) securities at a specified price and time at the request of the holder. Until exercised, these entitlements carry no dividend, inspection, or other rights.

II. **Consideration** -- It is important for corporate fiscal soundness and to prevent fraud that shares not be simply given away. Therefore, shares must be issued only in exchange for consideration that meets both quality and quantity tests.

A. **Quality Tests**

1. Traditionally, proper consideration included only money paid, services performed, and property received.
2. Traditionally, improper consideration included unsecured promissory notes, promises to perform future services, and promises to transfer property.
3. However, the modern trend is to recognize as valid consideration: "Any tangible or intangible benefit to the corporation, including cash, promissory notes, services performed, contracts for services to be performed, or other securities of the corporation....."
    a. The board of directors can adequately protect the corporation by issuing the shares only where there is a good chance it will benefit because the promissory notes will probably be paid, the services will probably be performed, etc.

B. **Quantity Tests**

1. Par Value: This means **face value**.
    a. The RMBCA has abolished the concept, but its use persists in many states.
    b. Issuance of **no par** is also permitted.
    c. Par value is not always a gauge of a corporation's solvency, because watered stock (stock issued in exchange for consideration that is less than the par value of the shares) is sometimes issued.
    d. In states which still require that consideration be at least equal to par value, corporations use **nominal** par value
2. Today, if stock is issued for less than par (in states where that concept is still recognized) or less than the authorized (by the board of directors) purchase price, then liability to creditors and other stockholders may be placed upon:
    a. The board who allowed the sale;
    b. The buyer who paid too little; and
    c. Transferees of the original buyer who both know that he paid too little and who pay too little themselves.

Note:
Treasury stock may be purchased at less than par value; if the company's share prices have dropped since the shares were originally issued, that may be the only way the company can resell them.

Example:
The board of directors authorizes the issuance of 10,000 shares of $1 par value stock for $20/share. The board allows 1,000 shares to be sold to Sue for $10/share. Sue sells 500 of the shares to Sam for $10/share. She sells the other 500 shares to Ace for $10/share. Sam knows that Sue did not pay the authorized sale price; Ace does not know it. If creditors of the corporation go unpaid, they may sue the board and Sue for $10,000 and Sam for $5,000 (total recovery cannot exceed $10,000). Ace, however, is not liable because he did not know that Sue had not paid the authorized price.

3. Valuation of Consideration Received

4. General Rule: absent a showing of bad faith, the board's valuation of consideration received in exchange for stock is presumptively valid.

Example:
The board of directors of ABC Corporation wishes to purchase a tract of land from X so that it can build a factory thereon. X likes ABC's prospects and wishes to receive 10,000 ABC shares as the sale price for the land rather than cash. The board authorizes the transaction. Disgruntled shareholder Z challenges the transaction on grounds that the shares issued to X were worth more than the land received from X. To prevail, Z must prove not only that land was worth less than the shares but also that the directors acted in bad faith.

III. **A primary purpose of most corporations --** To provide income for owners through a stream of dividend payments

A. **Types of dividends**

1. **Cash**

2. **Stock**

   a. A **stock dividend** might be issued by a corporation that has no readily available funds for cash dividends. Such a dividend does not reduce the assets in the corporate till nor transfer anything but paper to shareholders. Typically, shareholders are issued 1 new share for each 50 or so that they already hold.

   b. Related is the **stock split**, which involves a greater increase in outstanding shares than does a stock dividend. Typically, shareholders are issued 2 or 3 shares for each one that they already hold. Again, the transaction has no effect on the net worth of the corporation, which has no more or fewer assets. Only paper has been transferred to the shareholders.

   c. **Difference: Dividend and Split**. The primary difference between a stock dividend and a stock split is an accounting difference. In a stock split, a division of the shares of stock, not of the earnings or profits of the corporation, takes place without any change in or impingement upon the existing status on the corporate books of the earned surplus and capital accounts. However, in a stock dividend, an addition of shares of stock and a division of, at least, some of the earnings or profits of the corporation take place, such division being reflected on the corporate books by an irreversible allocation of corporate funds from the earned surplus to the capital account.

3. **Property**

Example:
One company in England which operates a crematorium occasionally delivers as a dividend to its shareholders a certificate for a free cremation. More typically, property dividends are in the form of shares of stock of other corporations that the distributing corporation has acquired.

B. **To be proper, dividends must be paid**

1. Only out of legally available funds; and
2. Only in accordance with applicable preferences.

C. Repurchase of shares has the same effect as a dividend payment (taking money out of the corporate treasury and putting into shareholders' pockets) and must meet the same standards.

D. **A distribution may not be made by a corporation if**

1. After giving effect to the distribution, the corporation would be insolvent; or
   a. Key is bankruptcy solvency: Can the corporation meet its debt obligations as they come due?
2. The distribution exceeds the **surplus** (defined as the "excess of the net assets of a corporation over its stated capital") of the corporation.
   a. Key is **equity solvency**: Do the corporation's assets exceed its liabilities?

E. **Board Discretion**

1. **General Rule --** The board of directors' decision to pay or not pay dividends and choice of amounts is presumed legitimate.
2. **Exception --** To overcome this presumption and force a board to pay more dividends, shareholders must prove:
   a. The board acted in bad faith; and
   b. Funds to pay dividends existed in a legally available source.

Shareholders and Corporate Management

The management structure of corporations is often visualized as a triangle. At the base are the shareholders; the owners of the corporation. Next up the line is the board of directors. Elected by the shareholders, the directors make the long-term corporate policy and select the officers who will run the day-to-day operations of the corporation. At the top of the corporation are the officers who make the day-to-day decisions.

I. Shareholder Voting

A. A basic shareholder right is the right to vote

1. For directors at annual meetings; and
2. Upon matters of important shareholder concern at special meetings, including:
    a. Mergers or consolidations;
    b. Sales of major corporate assets;
    c. Dissolution;
    d. Amendments to the articles of incorporation

Note:
The shareholders' influence on corporate management is indirect. Remember (the AICPA likes to test this point), shareholders vote for directors. They do not play any direct role in selection of officers.

B. Proxies

1. Shareholders are generally entitled to sign proxy cards granting others the right to cast their votes at shareholder meetings.
2. This is a necessity for acquiring a quorum at meetings of publicly held corporations.

C. Preemptive Voting Rights -- Especially in a small corporation, it may be important for a shareholder to maintain a particular proportion of ownership. For example, Indy and Kira may form a small corporation as 50-50 owners, each owning 100 shares of the 200 outstanding. Both like having a check on the other. Neither can accomplish major changes without the other's consent. But what if the corporation issues additional shares? If they are all purchased by Indy or half by Indy and the others by third parties, Kira's ownership position and control will be diluted. Therefore, the common law of corporations began granting existing shareholders "preemptive rights." That means that if the corporation issues another 100 shares, for example, both Indy and Kira would have the right to maintain their current control position by purchasing 50 shares each before any nonshareholders would have the opportunity to purchase. If both exercise those rights, they will remain 50-50 owners. However, if Kira, for example, waives her preemptive rights, perhaps because she is not interested in investing more money in the corporation, then Indy or third parties may purchase the shares. Today, some states presume that preemptive rights exist unless they are eliminated in the articles of incorporation. Other states presume that preemptive rights do not exist unless they are provided for in the articles of incorporation. Preemptive rights are not particularly significant in larger corporations and are usually eliminated in the articles of incorporation, if necessary.

D. Cumulative Voting Rights -- In most director elections, "straight voting" occurs. Assume that shareholder A owns 51 outstanding shares of X Corporation and that B owns the other 49. Assume that there are seven directors. If A and B have a disagreement and each nominates seven director candidates, though A has only two more shares than B. his candidates will be the top seven vote getters - each with 51. B's nominees will each get only 49 votes. Thus, A will be represented by all seven directors and B by none.

1. Because of the arguable unfairness of this result, many jurisdictions provide for "cumulative voting," which is a method of achieving proportional representation in director elections. In cumulative voting, each share is entitled to the number of votes corresponding to the number of directors to be elected. Furthermore, those votes may be cumulated - grouped for one or just a few candidates. Thus, if B owns 49 shares and if seven directorships are up for election, B will have a total of 343 votes (7 x 49). If B were to nominate only three candidates and cast 114 votes for B1, 114 for B2 and 114 for B3, there would be no way that A could spread his 357 votes (51 x 7) around so that he could prevent B from having B's three candidates be among the top seven vote getters. If both A and B vote wisely, A will be able to elect four candidates and B will elect three. In that way, B's interests are proportionately represented on the board. In most states cumulative voting may be prohibited in the articles of incorporation, and usually is in the case of large corporations.

II. **Corporate shareholders --** enjoy both common law and statutory inspection rights to aid them in keeping track of their investment.

   A. **Common Law Rights**

      1. **General Rule --** shareholders may inspect at proper times in proper places for proper purposes.

      2. **Proper purposes include**

         a. To ascertain financial status;

         b. To detect mismanagement;

         c. To ascertain value of shares;

         d. To aid legitimate personal or derivative litigation against management;

         e. To communicate with other shareholders regarding director elections or other matters of legitimate shareholder concern.

      3. **Improper purposes include**

         a. Merely to harass the corporation;

         b. To obtain shareholder list in order to use for personal business or to sell at profit;

         c. To learn trade secrets from a competitor;

         d. To find technical defects in transactions in order to bring frivolous litigation;

         e. To further the shareholder's political, moral, or religious views.

      4. **The burden of proof is on the shareholder to convince the court that s/he has a proper purpose for the inspection.**

   B. **Statutory Inspection Rights**

      1. **Any shareholder can inspect for a proper purpose, if he or she**

         a. Owns 5% or more of the company's shares; or

         b. Has owned company shares for more than six months.

      2. **Wrongful denial penalty --** P's costs and attorney's fees.

      3. **The burden of proof is on the company to show an improper purpose (as opposed to the common law right, where the burden is on the plaintiff shareholder to show a proper purpose).**

Mergers, Consolidations, and Dissolution

Organic changes in corporate structure must be accomplished pursuant to statutory formalities. This section summarizes those formalities. In the early days of corporate law, any single shareholder could veto a significant change in corporate structure. That proved impractical so now a majority vote of shareholders is usually sufficient to accomplish a major change. The trade-off is that the minority, deprived of its veto over change, is protected by its appraisal rights that are explained in this part.

I. These internal organic changes include

A. Amendments to the Articles of Incorporation

1. Dissolution

a. Corporations may be voluntarily dissolved upon approval of their directors and shareholders.

b. Corporations may be involuntarily dissolved administratively by the Secretary of State for such reasons as:

i. Failure to pay franchise taxes;

ii. Failure to file annual reports; or

iii. Failure to properly establish a registered agent or office.

c. Corporations may be involuntarily dissolved judicially in

i. An action by the attorney general, where:

1. The corporation obtained approval for its articles of incorporation through fraud; or

2. The corporation has abused its legal authority.

ii. An action by shareholders:

1. If management is deadlocked;

2. If those controlling the corporation are acting in an illegal or oppressive way, such as by looting the corporation or wasting its assets; or

3. If the shareholders are deadlocked and cannot elect directors.

iii. An action by creditors

iv. If a judgment creditor's claim is unsatisfied and the corporation is insolvent or if the corporation admits in writing that the creditor's claim is due and owing and that it is insolvent.

II. Such significant external organic changes include

A. Sale of All or Substantially All of a Corporation's Assets (Not in the Normal Course of Business).

B. Mergers -- when two corporations combine their assets.

C. Consolidations -- another form of corporate combination.

D. Typically, Corporation A merges with Corporation B, creating new Corporation C.

Note:
Typically, Corporation A merges with Corporation B, and only Corporation A survives.

III. Procedures and Protections

Note:
The modern trend is to not distinguish between mergers and consolidations.

A. Procedures -- for all of the internal and external changes noted above.

B. The board of directors will propose the change.

C. A majority of the shareholders must approve the change at a special election.

1. This election, like a directors' election, requires due notice and full disclosure of reasonable details.

D. Short Form Mergers

1. If Company A already owns 90% of Company B and wishes to **squeeze out** the minority shareholders, it may well form a wholly-owned subsidiary and propose a merger between Company B and the subsidiary for the purpose of buying out the 10% minority shareholders. Because most states require only 51% approval for a merger and Company A controls 90% of the shares, it is clear that this merger between Company B and Company A's wholly-owned subsidiary will be approved no matter how the 10% minority shareholders vote their shares.

2. Therefore, most states allow a "short-form" merger in such a case where no vote need be taken. Minority shareholders are simply informed of the merger. They have no right to vote, but may still exercise appraisal rights if they believe they are not receiving a fair price.

IV. Protections -- For all these changes noted above:

A. Dissenting shareholders may request that their shares be purchased at a court-valued rate pursuant to their **dissenters' rights** or **appraisal rights** if their interests are fundamentally altered by the transaction.

Board and Officers

*In the middle of the **pyramid** management structure of corporations sits the board of directors. Directors are elected by shareholders and select the officers who will run the day-to-day operations of the corporation under the guidance of the directors. Both officers and directors are agents of the corporation and as such owe it a fiduciary duty of loyalty. Again, a grasp of basic agency law should make much of this part a breeze to master.*

I. **Directors**

A. **Typical state statute --** "The business and affairs of a corporation shall be managed under the supervision of a board of directors."

1. **Directors' Broad Power --** Because the board sets broad company policy (to be implemented by the officers), directors have broad power to:

   a. Borrow money;

   b. Sell corporate property;

   c. Hire and fire officers and other employees;

   d. Declare or refuse to declare dividends;

   e. Make or refuse to make other distributions of funds to shareholders;

   f. Set the salaries of employees, officers, and even themselves;

   g. Propose for shareholder approval:

      i. Sale of major corporate assets;

      ii. Mergers or consolidations with other firms;

      iii. Dissolution; and

      iv. Amendments to the articles of incorporation.

B. **Board of Directors Meetings --** The board of directors usually discharges its duties at meetings with a quorum.

1. **Acting Without a Meeting --** However, directors can act without a meeting, if they unanimously agree to do so.

2. They can act by serially signing the same document, by conference telephone call, etc.

3. **Acting Through Committees --** The board can act through committees of directors (such as audit committees) for all but the most important actions, such as:

   a. Selecting officers; and

   b. Paying dividends

C. **Sarbanes-Oxley --** Although corporation law has traditionally been primarily state law, Congress passed Sarbanes-Oxley with a major purpose of reforming internal corporate governance, at least in public corporations. First, Congress provided that public companies should have audit committees composed entirely of independent directors. Second, those audit committees are directly responsible for the appointment, compensation, and oversight of the work by outside auditors. Also, the audit committee should establish procedures for the receipt, retention, and treatment of complaints regarding accounting matters and regarding confidential submissions by whistleblowers.

II. Officers

A. Usually consist of:

Note:
In many states, one person can hold all four positions.

1. President;
2. Vice-President(s);
3. Secretary;
4. Treasurer.

B. Officers Chosen by Board -- Officers are chosen by the board and can be removed by the board at any time with or without cause.

C. Types of Officer Authority

1. **Express, derived from**
   - **a.** By-laws;
   - **b.** Board of directors' resolutions;
   - **c.** Articles of incorporation;
   - **d.** Statutes.
2. **Implied**
   - **a.** Also called "inherent" or "by virtue of office"
   - **b.** President (not others) has implied authority to bind corporation.
   - **c.** But not in "extraordinary transactions," such as:
     - **i.** Merger;
     - **ii.** Sale of major corporate assets;
     - **iii.** Borrowing an unusually large amount of money;
     - **iv.** Signing managers to long-term contracts.
3. **Apparent**
   - **a.** Trend is to hold that officers have substantial power to act on the corporation's behalf, and to allow outsiders to rely more on officers' statements of authority.
   - **b.** Still, to be perfectly safe, if a third party has any questions, she should require the officer with whom she is dealing to produce a board of directors' resolution authorizing the transaction.
4. **Ratification**
   - **a.** As in all other areas of agency law, an unauthorized contract may be ratified by the principal, in this case the corporation.

III. Duties of Management

A. Duty of Attention

1. Directors should, at a minimum:
    - a. Attend most board meetings;
    - b. Gain a basic familiarity with the company's business;
    - c. Study the company's financial statements.

Example:
After her husband died, a woman became a director of a corporation founded by her husband. Before his death, her husband told her to keep an eye on their sons who would run the corporation after he died. Indeed, the sons stole around $9 million from the company. Their mother was not a sophisticated businessperson and became depressed and alcoholic following her husband's death. This was not viewed as an excuse and she was held liable for breaching her duty of attention in letting her sons rob the company blind. Directors must direct.

B. Duty of Care

1. Most state laws impose on the director a duty to act:
    - a. In good faith;
    - b. With the care an ordinarily prudent person in a like position would under similar circumstances; and
    - c. In a manner he reasonably believes to be in the best interests of the corporation.
2. **Imposed higher duties --** Courts tend to impose higher duties on **inside** directors.
3. **Right to Rely --** Directors do have the right to rely in good faith upon the reports of officers and other directors unless they have some reason to be suspicious.

Example:
Company A's officers committed an antitrust violation. Thirty years before, other officers had committed such a violation. The board of directors was sued, but showed that the directors knew nothing of the earlier violations nor of the newer violations. Therefore, in the absence of "red flags" that should have alerted them to the violations, the directors were justified in assuming that the officers were acting honestly.

- a. **Court review of board of director decisions.**
- b. Because courts are not experts in business, they do not normally second-guess the business judgments of directors. When challenged, such decisions are reviewed under the relatively generous **Business Judgment Rule:**

"In the absence of a showing of bad faith on the part of the directors or of a gross abuse of discretion, the business judgment of the directors will not be interfered with by the courts. ... The acts of directors are presumptively acts taken in good faith and inspired for the best interests of the corporation, and a minority stockholder who challenges their bona fides of purpose has the burden of proof." (Warshaw v. Calhoun, Del. 1966)

Example:
The board of directors of ABC Computer Corporation, after carefully studying the situation, decides to borrow a large sum of money in order to expand production capacity. Demand for the product flattens and ABC clearly has too much capacity. The new production lines are shut down, but the debt must still be paid off. Angry shareholders sue the board for its error in judgment. The court will probably hold the board not liable.

c. **Protection for the Board --** Additional protection of the BOD from liability for their decisions comes in statutory form; many states allow shareholders to amend articles to eliminate BOD (and officer) liability for errors of judgment or even carelessness.

d. Most such statutes do not allow shareholders to exonerate the board or officers in advance for errors involving fraud and dishonesty.

4. **Duty of Loyalty**

   a. Conflicts of interest should be avoided.

   b. **Void Transactions --** Many state laws provide that no transaction between a director and the corporation is void solely because of the financial interest or solely because the interested directors participate in the meeting authorizing the action, if:

      i. The transaction is approved by an affirmative majority of disinterested directors who are fully knowledgeable of the conflict; or

      ii. The transaction is approved by a majority of shareholders who are fully knowledgeable; or

      iii. The transaction was "fair" to the corporation.

Example:
Pursuant to a board of directors decision, ABC Corporation signs a long-term lease with Landlord Corp. Later, it is discovered that Mr. X, a director of ABC Corporation, is also a major owner of Landlord Corp. This should have been disclosed to the board at the time it made its decision, but the transaction is not a breach of fiduciary duty if it is fair to ABC (for example, if the rent specified in the lease is a fair one and the building is in good shape).

c. **Corporate Opportunity Doctrine**

   i. Corporate directors (and officers) should not appropriate for themselves business opportunities that rightfully belong to the corporation.

   ii. Again, Sarbanes-Oxley raised the bar for officers of public companies by imposing specific duties in what had traditionally been strictly a state law realm. For example, to pin responsibility for accurate financial reporting directly on CEOs and CFOs, Congress required in Section 302 that they certify annual and quarterly reports filed with the SEC.

   iii. The certification indicates that they have reviewed the report and it does not contain any material inaccuracies of half-truths, that based on their knowledge it fairly presents the issuer's financial condition and results, and that they (a) are responsible for establishing and maintaining internal controls, (b) have designed internal controls to ensure that material information is known to the officers, (c) have recently evaluated the effectiveness of the internal controls, and (d) have presented in their report their conclusions about that effectiveness.

   iv. Furthermore, the officers must certify that they have disclosed to the auditors and to the audit committee all significant deficiencies in the internal controls and any frauds, whether or not material, that involve management or other employees with a significant role in the issuer's internal controls.

Various Forms - Compared

This section shows a table comparing various forms of business organization with respect to limited liability, continuity, transferability, cost, and taxation.

I. Background

A. Business organizations date back to ancient times. Many early forms resembled today's general partnership. This form works well for small businesses, but is not optimal for accumulating large amounts of capital. Because general partners are personally liable for all the business' debts, they generally wish to do business only with close friends and relatives whom they know and trust. Eventually, limited liability was invented for the corporate form and that encouraged investors to take more risks with their money, because the most they could lose was their investment in the enterprise. They were not personally liable for the corporation's debts.

B. While corporations have the advantage of limited liability, they suffer the comparative detriment of double taxation in that the company pays income tax on its earnings and then its shareholders pay income tax on the dividends they are paid from corporate profits. Partnerships, on the other hand, enjoy single, pass-through taxation. The partnership entity pays no taxes, but its profits are "passed through" to the partners who pay individual income tax on their allocable share.

C. For most of the 1900s, the major forms of business organization in the United States were the corporation (limited liability for owners, but double taxation), general partnerships (single taxation, but general liability for owners), and limited partnerships (single taxation and limited liability for limited partners, but general liability for the general partner(ships)).

D. In the late 1900s, to encourage economic development, states started creating new forms of business organizations that would allow entrepreneurs and investors to enjoy both limited liability and single taxation, without leaving at least one person exposed to general liability, as in the limited partnership.

E. Thus, limited liability companies (LLCs), limited liability partnerships (LLPs), and limited liability limited partnerships (LLLPs) were created.

F. These were made popular by IRS decisions to allow these new entities to elect partnership taxation, even though they embodied so many corporate characteristics that under previous law they likely would have been subject to double taxation. Most accounting firms are either LLPs or LLCs.

II. Feature of Various Forms of Business Organization

A. Promoters seeking to organize a business venture decide, by comparing features, which organizational form will work best for them.

1. Limited liability.
2. Single taxation.
3. Legal personality.
4. Perpetuity.
5. Ease of Formation.

III. Comparing Features among the Various Forms

A. Sole Proprietorships

1. **Limited Liability --** No. A sole proprietorship is an informal, single-owner business. Because the owner is the business and the business is the owner, the owner has unlimited liability for the business's obligations.

2. **Single Taxation --** Yes. The sole owner of the business pays taxes on all of the business's taxable income. There is no entity apart from the owner that could pay taxes.

3. **Legal Personality --** No. In a sole proprietorship, there is no artificial business entity.

4. **Perpetuity --** No. If the owner of the sole proprietorship dies, the proprietorship ends, although with planning a sole proprietorship's business can be sold or conveyed by will.

5. **Ease of Formation --** Yes. No forms need be filed to create a sole proprietorship, although often licenses to do business and the like must be obtained.

B. General Partnerships

1. **Limited liability --** No. General partners face general liability for all partnership debts. If the partnership entity cannot pay its obligations, the partners may have to reach into their own pockets to pay their share (and may have to pay the other partners' share as well if they are unable to do so). However, if the partnership purchases liability insurance, it can minimize the risk that partners will face liability for partnership torts.

2. **Single taxation --** Yes. The partnership files an informational return, but does not pay taxes; only the partners do on the amount of income that is deemed to have "passed through" to them.

3. **Legal personality --** Yes. The general partnership today is viewed, at least to a significant extent, as a separate legal entity. It is no longer viewed, as it once was, as simply an aggregation of its individual partners. It can sue, be sued, and own property in its own name.

4. **Perpetuity --** Yes. Earlier versions of partnership law, such as the UPA, provided that general partnerships dissolved whenever a partner died or left the partnership for some other reason. Thus, partnerships did not enjoy perpetuity. However, the current majority approach of the RUPA makes it so easy for partners to plan in such a way as to maintain the entity in most cases when a partner departs that it no longer makes sense to say that general partnerships lack perpetuity.

5. **Ease of Formation --** Yes. No formalities are required to form a general partnership. Although partners may file papers with the Secretary of State under the RUPA, they need not do so. All that is needed is an intent by the parties to enter into a relationship that the law deems a partnership.

C. Limited Partnerships

1. **Limited Liability --** Partial. Under the RULPA, a limited partnership can have an unlimited number of limited partners who enjoy limited liability, but must have at least one general partner exposed to general liability. The fact that the general partner can be a corporation, however, allows a limited partnership to get much closer to total limited liability than a general partnership. On the other hand, if a limited partner becomes actively involved in the day to day affairs of a limited partnership, he or she can forfeit limited liability.

2. **Single Taxation --** Yes. Limited partnerships have the same single, pass-through taxation as general partnerships.

3. **Legal Personality --** Yes. A limited partnership is more than just an aggregation of its partners; it can own property, sue, and be sued in its own name.

4. **Perpetuity --** Yes. As with general partnerships, it is so easy for the partners of a limited partnership to contract around dissolution even if partners depart that it no longer makes sense to say that limited partnerships lack continuity.

5. **Ease of Formation --** No. Unlike general partnerships, a limited partnership cannot be formed without filing proper documents with the Secretary of State in the state of formation.

D. Corporation - Subchapter C

1. **Limited Liability --** Yes. Shareholders of corporations taxed under Subchapter C of the Internal Revenue Code enjoy limited liability for the corporation's obligations. Absent very unusual circumstances, when the corporate veil is pierced, shareholders can lose no more than the amount of their investment.

2. **Single Taxation --** No. Shareholders of Subchapter C corporations pay income tax on dividend revenue after the corporate entity pays tax on its income. That is double taxation. It can be minimized, especially in closely-held corporations, by minimizing the amount of dividends paid and funneling corporate income to shareholders in other ways, such as through salaries.

3. **Legal Personality --** Yes. The invention of the legal fiction of the corporate entity is viewed as one of the great inventions of western law.

4. **Perpetuity --** Yes. Because the corporate entity is clearly recognized as separate and apart from its owners, even if all shareholders of a corporation happened to die in a single accident, the corporate entity would continue without skipping a beat. Its new owners would be the heirs of the previous shareholders.

5. **Ease of Formation --** No. To form a corporation, like a limited partnership, proper documents must be filed with the Secretary of State's office.

E. Corporation - Subchapter S

1. **Limited Liability --** Yes. Shareholders of both Subchapter C and Subchapter S corporations enjoy limited liability.

2. **Single Taxation --** Yes. Subchapter S corporations were created to allow small corporations to provide limited liability to shareholders, yet also receive single taxation. The complication is that Subchapter S corporations must meet many requirements, such as no more than 100 shareholders, mostly active income, only certain types of shareholders, etc. It is these limitations that led states to create the LLCs, LLPs, and LLLPs soon to be discussed.

3. **Legal Personality --** Yes. Subchapter S corporations are legally separate entities that can own property, sue and be sued, etc. in their own names.

4. **Perpetuity --** Yes. Like Subchapter C corporations, the Subchapter S corporate entity survives the deaths of even all of its shareholders.

5. **Ease of Formation --** No. To form Subchapter S corporations, promoters must not only meet the federal requirements for single taxation but must file incorporation papers with the Secretary of State in the state of formation just like other corporations.

F. Professional Corporations

1. **Limited Liability --** Yes. Shareholders in PCs enjoy limited liability for the obligations of the corporation with one exception - they are naturally personally liable for torts such as malpractice that they commit. They are not, however, personally liable for the malpractice of other shareholders as they would be in a general partnership.

2. **Single Taxation** -- No (unless). Shareholders in PCs are subject to double taxation unless they qualify as Subchapter S corporations. Many can and do.

3. **Legal Personality** -- Yes. Like other corporations, PCs are legal entities separate and apart from their shareholders.

4. **Perpetuity** -- Yes. Professional corporations survive the leaving of individual shareholders.

5. **Ease of Formation** -- No. Like other corporations, promoters of PCs must file proper documents with state government.

G. **Limited Liability Companies**

1. **Limited Liability** -- Yes. Members of LLCs enjoy limited liability. In most states they are not liable for the contractual or tort obligations of the LLC nor of other members. However, they are liable for the torts they personally commit. In a few states, LLC members do not receive limited liability for contractual debts of the LLC, only for tort liabilities.

2. **Single Taxation** -- Yes. LLCs typically choose single taxation, although they have the option to choose corporate taxation. If they happen to be publicly traded, then they cannot choose single taxation, but must be taxed as corporations.

3. **Legal Personality** -- Yes. LLCs are legal entities separate and apart from their members that can own property and sue and be sued in their own names.

4. **Perpetuity** -- Yes. It is relatively easy for members of LLCs to provide for continuity of the entity notwithstanding the departure of members.

5. **Ease of Formation** -- No. Like corporations and limited partnerships, LLCs can be formed only by filing proper documents with the Secretary of State.

H. **Limited Liability Partnerships**

1. **Limited Liability** -- Yes. In most jurisdictions, but not all, partners in LLPs are not generally liable for the firm's contractual obligations. Regarding tort liability, the main point of an LLP is to provide limited liability for the torts of the firm or other partners. However, partners remain liable for their own torts, of course. Second, they are liable for the torts of those they supervise. Many states require the LLP to carry a minimum level of liability insurance in exchange for according partners limited liability.

2. **Single Taxation** -- Yes. LLPs typically choose single taxation, although they have the option to choose corporate taxation. If they happen to be publicly traded, they must have corporate taxation.

3. **Legal Personality** -- Yes. LLPs are legal entities separate and apart from their partners that can own property and sue and be sued in their own names.

4. **Perpetuity** -- No. However, it is relatively easy for partners of LLPs to contract around this default setting and provide contractually for continuity of the entity notwithstanding the departure of partners.

5. **Ease of Formation** -- No. Like corporations and limited partnerships, LLPs can be formed only by filing proper documents with the Secretary of State.

I. **Limited Liability Limited Partnerships**

1. **Limited Liability** -- Yes. The purpose of LLLPs is to provide full corporation-like limited liability for all partners. Therefore, general partners in LLLPs enjoy limited liability, as do limited partners. Indeed, unlike under the traditional limited partnership rule, limited partners in an LLLP retain limited liability *even if they take part in control of the partnership.*

Note:
LLLPs are the newest form of business organization and are not yet authorized in a majority of states.

   a. Both general partners and limited partners would remain liable for the torts they personally commit, of course.

2. **Single Taxation --** Yes. LLLPs typically choose single taxation, although they have the option to choose corporate taxation.
3. **Legal Personality --** Yes. LLLPs are legal entities separate and apart from their partners that can own property and sue and be sued in their own names.
4. **Perpetuity --** Yes. It is relatively easy for partners of LLLPs to provide for continuity of the entity notwithstanding the departure of partners.
5. **Ease of Formation --** No. Like corporations and limited partnerships, LLLPs can be formed only by filing proper documents with the Secretary of State.

Form	Limited Liability	Continuity	Transferability	Cost	Taxation
Sole Proprietor	No	No	No	Low	Single
General Partnership	No	No*	No	Low	Single
Limited Partnerships	GP: No LP: Yes	Yes**	GP: No LP: Yes	High	Single
Corporation (Ch.C)	Yes	Yes	Yes	High	Double
Subchapter S Corporation	Yes	Yes	Yes	High	Single
Professional Corporation	Yes***	Yes	Yes	High	Double
LLC	Yes***	Yes	Yes	High	Single****
LLP	Yes***	No	No	High	Single****

*The UPA provides for nearly automatic dissolution upon the departure of any partner, but in RUPA jurisdictions continuity is much more likely.

**Limited partnerships usually continue despite changes in limited partners, but changes in general partners often lead to dissolution.

***Naturally, those who commit malpractice remain liable for their own negligence (but not that of their colleagues) in professional corporations and LLCs. In LLPs, such malpractice liability often extends to those who supervised the wrongdoer as well.

**** Unless publicly traded (in which case, the LLC is taxed as a corporation) or a single-member LLC (permissible in some states, in which case the LLC is not a taxable entity). Before advent of the check-the-box rules in 1997, in order to qualify for non-corporate taxation, LLCs had to be formed in such a way as to eliminate at least two of the following three signs of "corporateness"--perpetual duration, free transferability, and centralized management.

Economic Concepts

Introduction

Economics is a social science concerned with the study of the allocation of scarce economic resources among alternative uses, usually to achieve desired objectives. This introductory lesson: (1) Provides an overview of the material covered in the Economic Concepts subsection. (2) Defines economics and identifies the areas of economic study. (3) Summarizes the use of graphs in economics. (4) Distinguishes between free market and command economic systems.

I. Content Coverage -- Economics is the study of the allocation of scarce economic resources among alternative uses. From a business perspective, economics is concerned with studying the production, distribution and consumption of goods and services, generally so as to maximize desired outcomes. The field can be divided into three general areas for study purposes: microeconomics, macroeconomics and international economics.

A. Economic Concepts covers material concerned with:

1. The effects of economic events, including business cycles, on an entity's financial position and operation;
2. National economic measures and reasons for changes in economy;
3. How the economy and markets influence business and customer management strategies;
4. Implications of dealings in foreign currency, including exchange rate fluctuations and hedging.

B. This unit begins by reviewing basic economic terms and concepts, including demand, supply and pricing, at both the individual unit and the aggregate market levels.

II. Economics Defined

> **Definition:**
>
> *Economics*: The study of the allocation of scarce economic resources among alternative uses.

A. From a business perspective, economics is concerned with studying the production, distribution and consumption of goods and services, generally so as to maximize desired outcomes. The field can be divided into three general areas for study purposes: microeconomics, macroeconomics and international economics.

1. **Microeconomics --** studies the economic activities of distinct decision-making entities, including individuals, households and business firms. Major areas of interest include demand and supply, prices and outputs, and the effects of external forces on the economic activities of these individual decision makers.
2. **Macroeconomics --** studies the economic activities and outcomes of a group of entities taken together, typically of an entire nation or major sectors of a national economy. Major areas of interest include aggregate output, aggregate demand and supply, price and employment levels, national income, governmental policies and regulation, and international implications.

3. **International economics --** studies economic activities that occur between nations and outcomes that result from these activities. Major areas of concern include socio-economic issues, balance of payments, exchange rates and transfer pricing.

4. Each of these three general areas of economic study are covered in sections below.

III. Use of Graphs

A. Many economic concepts and relationships are depicted using graphs. These graphs often show the relationship between two variables, an independent variable (usually shown on the horizontal "X" axis) and a dependent variable (usually shown on the vertical "Y" axis).

B. Thus, the variable plotted using values on the "Y" (vertical) axis (the dependent variable) depends on the value shown on the "X" (horizontal) axis (the independent variable). The point at which the plotted relationship (i.e., the "graphed line") intersects the "Y" axis (which is the left end of the "X" axis) is called the "intercept."

C. In economics, any influence that other variables (other than the one shown on the graph) may have on the dependent variable is assumed to be held constant, a concept referred to in economics as *ceteris paribus.*

D. The relationship between variables may be positive, negative or neutral, as shown in the following graphs:

1. **Positive --** The dependent variable moves in the same direction as the independent variable.

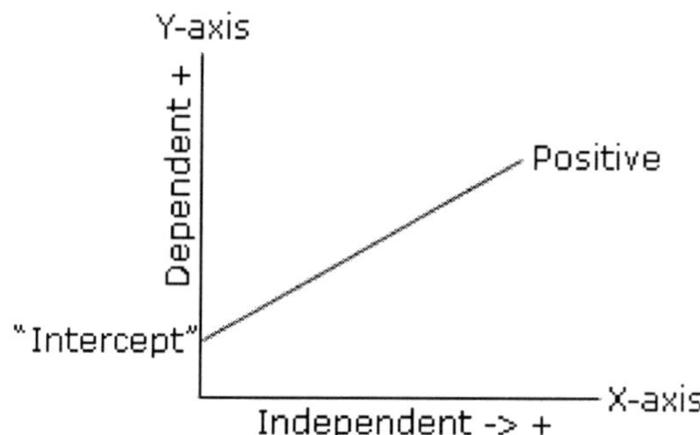

2. **Negative --** The dependent variable moves in the opposite direction as the independent variable.

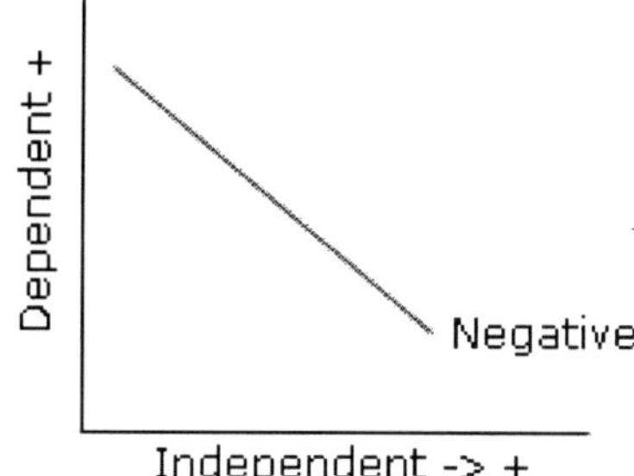

3. **Neutral --** One variable does not change as the other variable changes: (This indicates that the variables are not interdependent.)

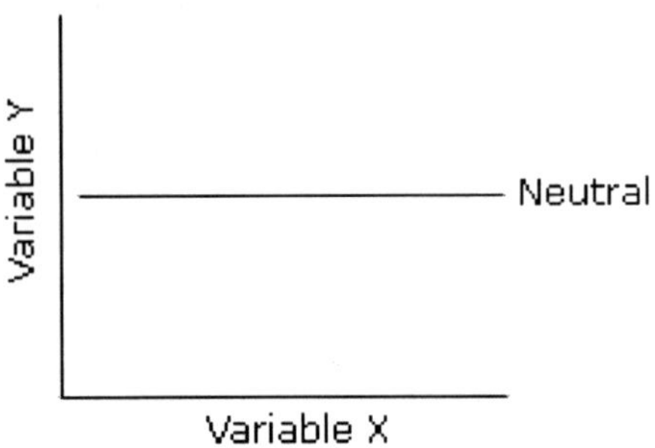

E. When the independent variable is time, the vertical axis shows the behavior of the dependent variable over time and is called a "time series graph." Such a graph might take the following form:

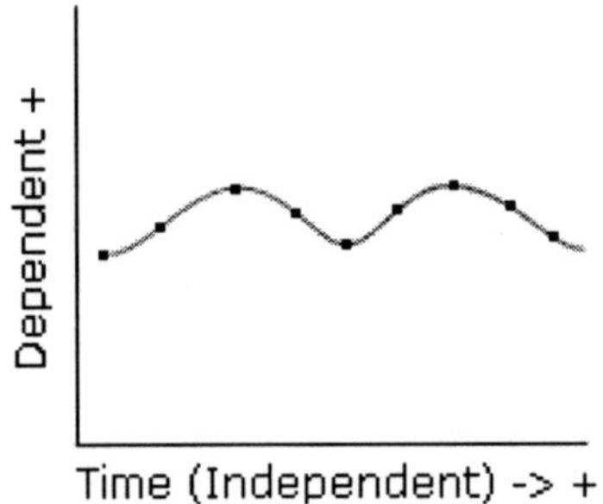

F. Relationships shown in graphic form often can be expressed as mathematical formulas. Such formulas provide a quantitative expression of the relationships between variables and are basic to making economic projections.

IV. **Economic Systems - Command and Market Economies --** The nature of economic activity, at the microeconomic, macroeconomic and international levels, depends on the political environment (or economic system) within which the economic activity takes place.

A. **Command Economic System --** A system in which the government largely determines the production, distribution and consumption of goods and services. Communism and socialism are prime examples of command economic systems.

Note:
The material in this unit assumes a free market economic system as it operates in the U.S.

B. **Market (Free-enterprise) Economic System --** A system in which individuals, businesses and other distinct entities determine production, distribution and consumption in an open (free) market. Capitalism is the prime example of a market economic system.

Microeconomics

Introduction & Free-Market Model

In a free-market or capitalist economy, resources are privately owned and economic decisions are made by individual decision-making entities, including individuals and business firms. This lesson describes the flow of resources between individuals and businesses in a free-market economy.

I. Flow Model

A. In a free market economy, economic decisions are made by individual decision-making entities, including individuals and business firms.

B. The roles and relationships of these decision-making entities (individuals and business firms) are depicted in the following model:

Free-Market Flow Model

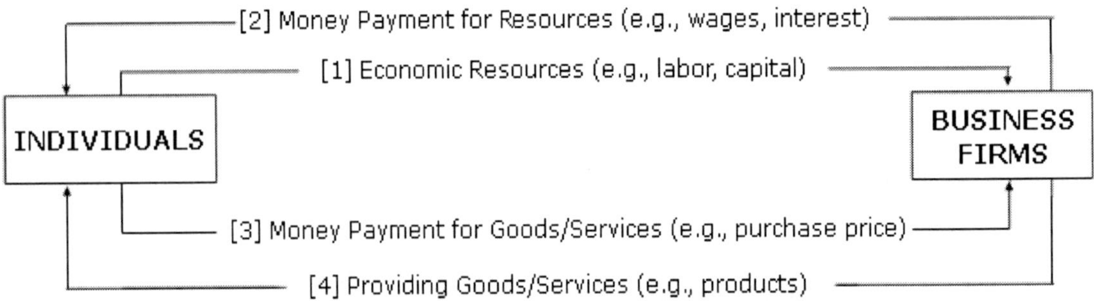

C. In the top half of the model (flow lines [1] and [2]):

1. [1] -- Business firms acquire economic resources from individuals, including:
   - **a.** **Labor --** human work, skills, and similar human effort;
   - **b.** **Capital --** financial resources (e.g. savings) and man-made resources (e.g. equipment, buildings, etc.);
   - **c.** **Natural Resources: --** land, minerals, timber, water, etc.
   - **d.** These resources are essential to the production of (other) goods and services, and they are scarce.
2. [2] -- Individuals receive compensation from business firms for the use of individuals' resources, including:
   - **a.** Wages, salaries and profit sharing for labor;
   - **b.** Interest, dividends, rental and lease payments for capital;
   - **c.** Rental, lease and royalty payments for natural resources.

D. As a consequence of the reciprocal relationship (in the top half of the model) between the economic resources provided by individuals and the compensation received for those resources, the cost of production (price of economic recourses) to business firms is equal to the money compensation (income) of individuals.

E. In the bottom half of the model (flow lines [3] and [4]):

1. [3] -- Individuals use the compensation received for their economic resources to pay for goods and services acquired from business firms.

2. [4] -- Business firms produce goods and services which are purchased by individuals.

F. As a consequence of the reciprocal relationship (in the bottom half of the model) between goods and services produced by business firms and the payment for those goods and services by individuals, the cost of purchasing (price of goods and services) to individuals is equal to the money income of business firms.

II. Characteristics of Free-Market Economy

A. The relationships in the model show, among other things, that in a true free market economy:

1. The interdependent relationship between individuals and business firms. Individuals depend on business firms for money (income) to use in the purchase of goods and services provided by the business firms. Business firms depend on individuals for economic resources to carry out production and for the money (purchase price) individuals pay for goods and services provided by the firms.
2. What gets produced by business firms and how those goods and services are distributed depends on the preferences (needs and wants) of individuals who have the ability (money resources) to pay for those goods and services.
3. How goods and services get produced by business firms depends on the availability of economic resources (labor, capital and natural resources), the level of technology available, and how business firms choose to use available resources and technology.
4. Business firms will produce goods and services only if the price at which those goods and services can be sold to individuals is equal to or greater than the cost (price) of the economic resources acquired from individuals.

B. Central to the relationships in the free market model is the role of price. The prices of economic resources and of goods and services produced are determined by demand and supply in the market.

Demand

Demand is the desire, willingness, and ability to acquire a commodity. It can be measured and analyzed for an individual decision-maker, for a market (e.g., a particular good or service), or for a multi-market economy. This lesson considers demand at the individual and market levels; aggregate (or economy) demand is considered in the macroeconomics subsection.

I. Existence of Demand -- Demand is the desire, willingness and ability to acquire a commodity. Thus, the existence of demand depends not only on having needs and wants, but also on having the financial ability to act on those needs and wants in the market. Because demand depends on having the financial ability to acquire a commodity (good or service), the quantity of a commodity for which there will be demand (quantity demanded) will be negatively associated with the price of the commodity. If other influences are held constant, the higher the price, the lower quantity demanded and, the lower the price, the higher the quantity demanded.

II. Individual Demand -- A demand schedule for an individual shows the quantity of a commodity that will be demanded at various prices during a specified time, ceteris paribus (holding variables other than price constant). The graphic representation of a demand schedule presents a demand curve which has a negative slope.

Individual Demand Curve

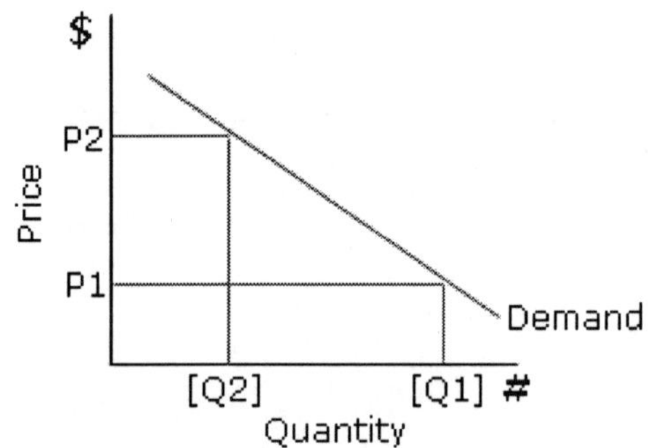

A. At P1, the lower price, quantity demanded (Q1) is greater than the quantity demanded (Q2) at P2, the higher price. Two factors account for an increase in individual demand at lower prices:

1. **Income Effect --** a given amount of income can buy more units at a lower price;
2. **Substitution Effect --** lower priced items will be purchased as substitutions for higher priced items.

III. Market Demand -- A market demand schedule shows the quantity of a commodity that will be demanded by all individuals (and other entities) in the market at various prices during a specified time, *ceteris paribus.* A market demand curve, like an individual demand curve, is negatively sloped.

A. As the market demand curve D1 shows, holding other variables constant, as price falls aggregate demand for a commodity increases. However, if certain other variables in the market change, aggregate demand will change and a new market demand curve will result. Changes in other market variables that may change aggregate demand include:

1. **Size of Market --** As the size of the market for a commodity changes, the demand for a commodity may change. For example, if the population of individuals in a market increases, the market demand for a commodity (e.g., bread) may increase, and vice versa. This increase in market demand will result in a new demand curve, shown as D2 in the graph.
2. **Income or Wealth of Market Participants --** As the spendable income or level of wealth of market participants change, the demand for a commodity may change:
    - **a.** An increase in the income of individuals in the market may increase demand for normal (or preferred) goods (e.g., fresh meat), and decrease the demand for inferior (or less than preferred) goods (e.g., canned meat);
    - **b.** A decrease in the income of individuals in the market may increase demand for inferior goods, and decrease the demand for normal goods.
3. **Preferences of Market Participants --** As the tastes of individuals in the market change, the demand for a commodity may change. The change in preference from standard 2 and 4-door automobiles to the SUV-type vehicle decreased market demand for automobiles, but increased demand for SUVs. A market "fad" represents an extreme shift in market preference for a commodity.
4. **Change in Prices of Other Goods and Services --** A change in the prices of other goods and services may change the demand for a particular commodity. The effect of a change in other prices depends on whether the other goods/services are substitutable for or complementary to a particular commodity.
    - **a.** Substitute commodities are those which satisfy the same basic purpose for the consumer as another commodity. The demand for a commodity may increase when the prices of substitute commodities increase, and vise versa. For example, the demand for rice may increase as the price of potatoes (a substitute for rice) increases.
    - **b.** Complementary commodities are those which are used together. Therefore, the demand for a commodity may increase when the price of a complementary commodity decreases, and vice versa. For example, the demand for shoe laces may increase when the price of shoes decreases because consumers buy more shoes and, thus, more shoe laces.

IV. It is important to distinguish a change -- In quantity of a commodity demanded from a change in the demand for a commodity:

A. Change in quantity demanded is movement along a given demand curve (for an individual or for the market) as a result of a change in price of the commodity. Variables other than price are assumed to remain unchanged.

B. Change in demand results in a shift of the entire demand curve that is caused by changes in variables other than price. The demand curve will shift to the left and down when aggregate demand decreased (D1 to D0), and to the right and up when aggregate demand increases (D1 to D2).

Supply

Supply is the quantity of a commodity that will be provided at alternative prices during a specified time. Like demand, supply can be measured and analyzed for an individual producer, for all producers of a good or service (market supply), or in the aggregate for all providers of all goods and services in an economy. This lesson considers supply at the individual producer and at the market levels; aggregate (or economy) supply is considered in the macroeconomics subsection.

Definition:

Supply: The quantity of a commodity that will be provided by an individual producer or by all producers of a good or service (market supply) at alternative prices during a specified time.

I. Individual Supply

A. A supply schedule for an individual producer shows the quantity of goods or services that the producer is willing to provide (supply) at alternate prices during a specified time, *ceteris paribus*. The graphic representation of a supply schedule presents a supply curve, which normally has a positive slope.

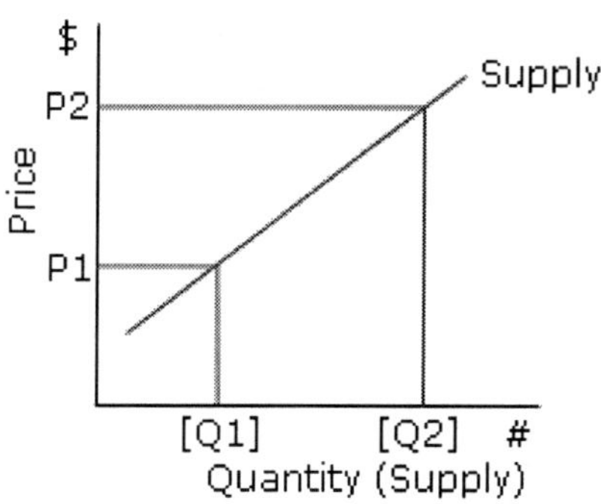

B. At P2, the higher price, the quantity supplied (Q2) is greater than the quantity supplied (Q1) at P1, the lower price. Producers normally are willing to provide higher quantities of goods and services only at higher prices because higher production costs are normally incurred in increasing production in the short run. The higher production costs (known as the principle of increasing cost) occurs because the additional resources used to increase production typically are not as efficient in producing the commodity as the resources previously used.

II. Market Supply

A. A market supply schedule shows the quantity of a commodity that will be supplied by all providers in the market at various prices during a specified time, *ceteris paribus*. A market supply curve, like and individual supply curve, is positively sloped.

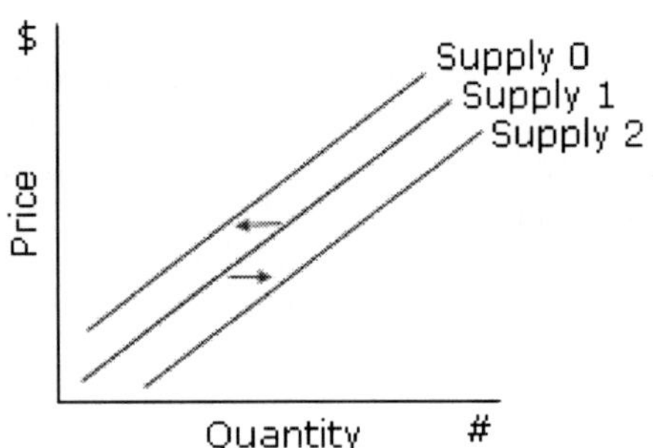

B. As the market supply curve S1 shows, holding other variables constant, as price increases aggregate supply for a commodity (quantity) increases. However, if certain other variables in the market change, aggregate supply will change and a new market supply curve will result (S2 or S0). Changes in other market variables that may change aggregate supply include:

1. **Number of Providers --** As the number of providers of a commodity increase, the market supply of the commodity increases, and vice versa. An increase in market supply will result in a new supply curve, shown as S2 in the graph. The new supply curve shows more of the commodity being provided at a give price. If the number of suppliers of the product decrease, the supply curve would move (up and left) to S0, showing less of the commodity provided at a given price.

2. **Cost of Inputs (Economic Resources) Change --** As the cost of inputs to the production process change (e.g., labor, rent, raw materials, etc.), so also will the supply curve. An increase in input prices would cause per unit cost to increase and the supply curve would shift up and to the left (S1 to S0), indicating less output at a given price. A decrease in input prices would reduce per unit cost and would shift the curve from S1 to S2, with more output at a given price.

   a. **Related Commodities --** Changes in the prices of other commodities that use the same inputs as a given commodity will result in more or less demand for the inputs and change the cost of inputs for the given commodity and, thus, change supply of that commodity.

   b. **Government Influences --** If government taxes or subsidizes the production of a commodity, it effectively increases cost (taxes) or decreases cost (subsidizes) of the product. Thus, government can influence aggregate supply through its taxation and subsidization programs.

3. **Technological Advances --** Improvements in technology for the production of a commodity reduces the per unit cost and would shift the supply curve down and to the right (S1 to S2), showing more of a commodity provided at a given price.

III. **It is important to distinguish a change --** In the quantity of a commodity supplied from a change in supply of a commodity.

A. Change in the quantity supplied is movement along a given supply curve (for an individual provider or for the market) as a result of a change in price of the commodity. Variables other than price are assumed to remain unchanged.

B. Change in supply results in a shift of the entire supply curve that is caused by changes in variables other than price. The supply curve will shift right and down when aggregate supply increases (S1 to S2), and to the left and up when aggregate supply decreases (S1 to S0).

Market Equilibrium

Economic equilibrium occurs when, in the absence of external influences, there is no tendency for change in economic values. Market equilibrium occurs at the intersection of the market demand and market supply curves; quantity demanded equals quantity supplied. This lesson considers the determination of market equilibrium, the consequences of a price that is higher or lower than the equilibrium price, the effects of changes in market demand and/or market supply on market equilibrium, and how government influences market equilibrium.

I. **Market Equilibrium --** The equilibrium price for a commodity is the price at which the quantity of the commodity supplied in the market is equal to the quantity of the commodity demanded in the market. Graphically, the market equilibrium price for a commodity occurs where the market demand curve and the market supply curve intersect.

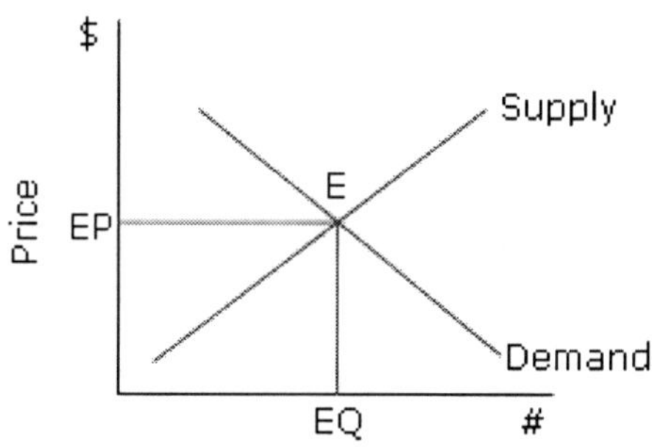

A. Equilibrium for the commodity occurs at the intersection (E) of the demand and supply curves. The equilibrium price is EP and the equilibrium quantity is EQ. For the given supply and demand curves, at the equilibrium price (EP), the quantity of the commodity demanded (i.e., that can be sold) is exactly equal to the quantity of the commodity that will be supplied at that price. There will be no shortage or surplus of the commodity in the market.

B. Shortages and surpluses in quantity occur when the actual price (AP) of the commodity is less (shortage) or more (surplus) than the equilibrium price (EP).

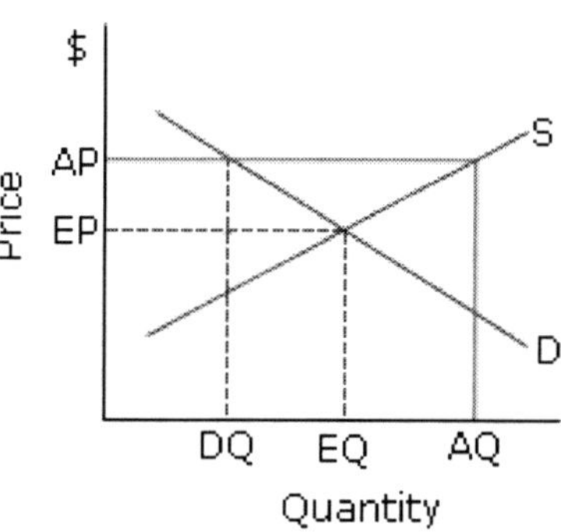

C. When market equilibrium is attained it will continue until there is a change in demand and/or supply of the commodity. The shifts in the demand and/or supply curves that result will change market equilibrium.

II. Change in Equilibrium -- The effect of change(s) in demand and/or supply on market equilibrium depends on whether demand changes, supply changes or both change.

A. Change in Market Demand (only) -- An increase in market demand D1 to D2 due to an increase in the size of the market (or increased income, changes in consumer preferences, etc.) causes the demand curve to shift up and to the right. If there is no change in market supply, the results will be an increase in both the equilibrium price (EP1 to EP2) and equilibrium quantity (EQ1 to EQ2). A decrease in market demand would cause both equilibrium price and equilibrium quantity to decrease.

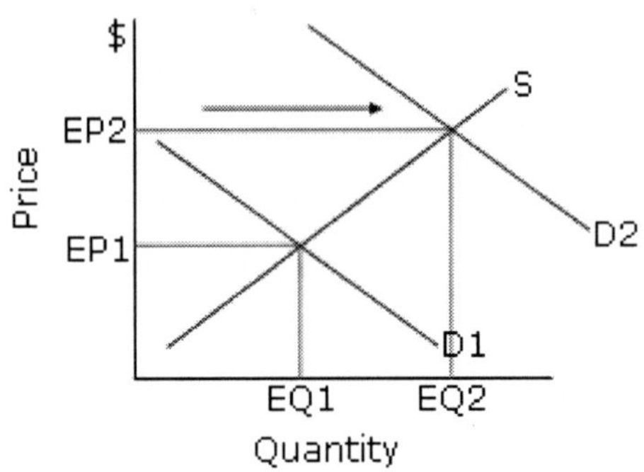

B. Change in Market Supply (only) -- An increase in market supply (S1 to S2) due to an increase in the number of providers in the market (or lower cost of inputs, technological advances, etc.) causes the supply curve to shift down and to the right. If there is no change in market demand, the results will be a decrease in equilibrium price (EP1 to EP0) and an increase in equilibrium quantity (EQ1 to EQ2). A decrease in market supply would cause a higher equilibrium price and a lower equilibrium quantity.

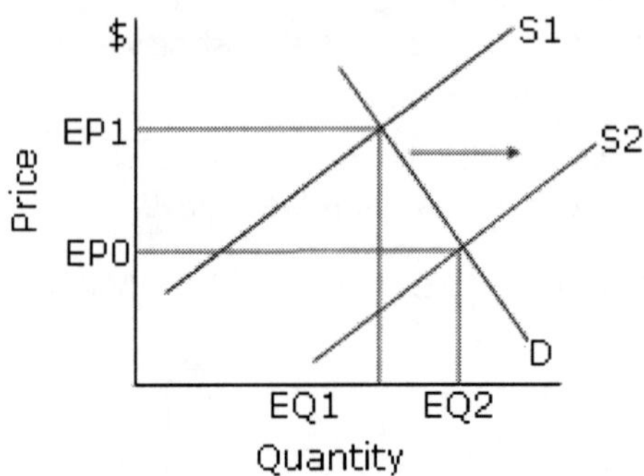

C. Changes in Both Market Demand and Market Supply -- The effect of simultaneous changes in both market demand and market supply depends on the direction of the changes (increase or decrease) and the relative magnitude of each change.

1. Increases in both market demand and market supply will shift both curves to the right resulting in a higher equilibrium quantity, but the resulting equilibrium price will depend on the magnitude of each change. The equilibrium price could remain unchanged, increase or decrease.

2. Decreases in both market demand and market supply will shift both curves to the left resulting in a lower equilibrium quantity, but the resulting equilibrium price will depend on the magnitude of each change.

3. The effects of a simultaneous increase in one market curve (demand or supply) and a decrease in the other market curve (supply or demand) on market price and market equilibrium can be determined only when the specific magnitude of each change is known.

III. Governmental Influences on Equilibrium

A. As noted earlier, government taxation and subsidization have the effect of increasing and decreasing the effective cost of production (supply). For example, a tax on a commodity at the production level increases the cost and shifts the market supply curve up and to the left. If demand remains constant, equilibrium price increases and equilibrium quantity decreases. Government subsidies have the opposite effects.

B. By imposing a rationing system, government can change market demand and, thereby, the equilibrium. Rationing would be intended to shift the demand curve down and to the left, thus lowering equilibrium price and equilibrium quantity.

C. Government also can affect the price of a commodity through price fiat by establishing an (artificial) price ceiling or price floor. These artificial prices result in disequilibrium in the market. An imposed market ceiling (less than free market equilibrium price) results in market supply being less than market demand at the imposed price. Market demand and market supply are not in equilibrium. An imposed market floor (greater than free market equilibrium price) results in market supply being more than market demand at the imposed price.

Elasticity

Elasticity measures the percentage change in a market factor (e.g., demand) as a result of a given percentage change in another market factor (e.g., price). This lesson considers four major measures of elasticity and the usefulness of one of these measures (elasticity of demand) in estimating the effects on total revenue likely to result from a change in price.

I. Elasticity Measures -- Elasticity measures the percentage change in a market factor (e.g., demand) as a result of a given percentage change in another market factor. Elasticity measures often have specific practical applications. For example, elasticity is used in estimating the change in demand (and total revenue) likely to result from a change in price.

Definition:

Elasticity: Measures the percentage change in a market factor (e.g., demand) as a result of a given percentage change in another market factor

II. Elasticity of Demand -- Elasticity of demand (ED) measures the percentage change in quantity of a commodity demanded as a result of a given percentage change in the price of the commodity. Therefore, it is computed as:

ED = % change in quantity demanded / % change in price

This formula expresses the slope of the demand curve when demand is shown graphically

A. Expanded the formula is:

ED = (change in quantity demanded / pre-change quantity demanded) / (change in price / pre-change price)

B. The calculation also can use the following as the denominator:

1. New quantity and new price

2. Average of old and new quantity and price

Example:
Assume that as a result of a change in price from $1.50 to $2.00 demand decreased from 1,500 units to 1,200 units. Using the old quantity and price the calculation would be:

% change in quantity: 1,500 - 1,200 = 300/1,500 = .20

% change in price: $2.00 - $1.50 = $ .50/$1.50 = .333

ED = .20/.333 = .60

Alternate Calculation: ED = 300/1,500 x 1.50/.50 = 450/750 = .60

C. In the above example, a 33.3% increase in price (from $1.50 to $2.00) will result in only a 20% decrease in demand; the elasticity of demand (.20/.333) of .60 is less than 1. When elasticity of demand is less than 1, demand is inelastic - demand does not change proportionally as much as a change in price. The calculation of elasticity of demand results in the following possible outcomes:

Calculated Elasticity Coefficient	Elasticity of Demand	Meaning
greater than 1	Elastic	% change in demand greater than % change in price
= 1	Unitary	% change in demand = % change in price
less than 1	Inelastic	% change in demand less than % change in price

D. The effect of a change in price on total revenue can be directly estimated from the elasticity of demand coefficient. Using the data from the example above:

	Quantity	**x**	**Price**	**=**	**Total Revenue**
Before price change	1,500	x	$1.50	=	$2,250
After price change	1,200	x	$2.00	=	2,400
Change in Revenue (increase)					$ 150

E. The relationship between elasticity of demand and total revenue (TR) generated can be summarized as:

Elasticity Coefficient	Price Increase	Price Decrease
greater than 1	TR Decrease	TR Increase
= 1	TR No change	TR No change
less than 1	TR Increase	TR Decrease

III. Elasticity of Supply -- Elasticity of supply (ES) measures the percentage change in the quantity of a commodity supplied as a result of a given percentage change in the price of the commodity. Therefore, it is computed as:

ES = % change in quantity supplied / % change in price

This formula expresses the slope of the supply curve when supply is shown graphically.

A. Expanded the formula is:

ES = (change in quantity supplied / pre-change quantity supplied) / (change in price / pre-change price)

B. As with the calculation of elasticity of demand, the above calculation also can use the following as the denominator:

1. New quantity and new price
2. Average of old and new quantity and price

C. The calculation of elasticity of supply would be done in the same manner as the calculation of elasticity of demand, and the resulting outcomes could be:

Calculated Elasticity Coefficient	Elasticity of Supply	Meaning
greater than 1	Elastic	% change in supply greater than % change in price
= 1	Unitary	% change in supply = % change in price
less than 1	Inelastic	% change in supply less than % change in price

IV. **Elasticity of Other Market Factors --** In addition to measurement of elasticity of demand (and related total revenue) and elasticity of supply, other measures of elasticity include:

A. *Cross Elasticity of Demand* - measures the percentage change in quantity of a commodity demanded as a result of a given percentage change in the price of another commodity.

B. *Income Elasticity of Demand* - measures the percentage change in quantity of a commodity demanded as a result of a given percentage change in income.

Consumer Demand & Utility Theory

Consumer demand derives from the need or desire for goods and services; those goods and services provide utility to the consumer. This lesson covers the concept of utility theory and, related thereto, indifference curves.

I. Utility -- Consumers (individually and in the aggregate) demand a commodity because it satisfies a need or a want. In economics, the satisfaction derived from the acquisition or use of a commodity is referred to as "utility." Thus, demand for a good or service occurs because of the utility derived from that good or service. A hypothetical unit of measure called "utils" is often used to assign value (or measure) an individual's utility (or satisfaction) derived from each commodity.

II. Marginal Utility -- The more of each commodity an individual acquires during a given time, the greater total utility (or utils) the individual derives. However, while total utility increases as acquisition increases, the utility (or utils) derived from each additional unit of a commodity decreases. The last unit acquired is referred to as the "marginal unit," and the decreasing utility derived from each (additional) marginal unit is referred to as the law of diminishing marginal utility. Graphically, diminishing marginal utility (MU) would be depicted as:

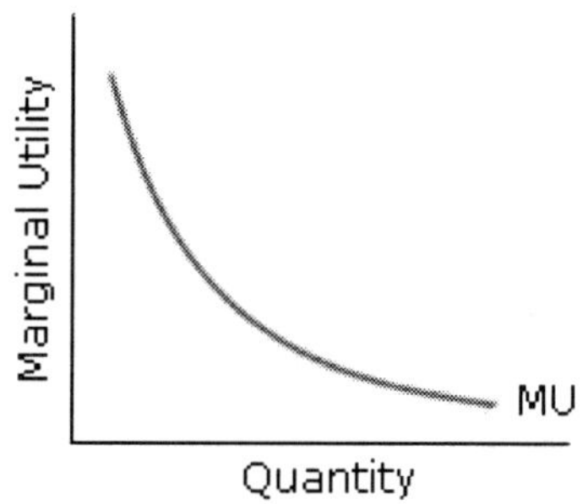

A. An individual will maximize total utility (satisfaction) for a given amount of income when the marginal utility of the last dollar spent on each and every commodity acquired is the same. Thus, total utility is maximized when:

(MU of A) / (A Price) = (MU of B) / (B Price) = (...MU of Z) / (Z Price)

B. When this condition exists, the individual is said to be in equilibrium.

III. Indifference Curves -- When the various quantities of two commodities that give an individual the same total utility are plotted on a graph, the result is an indifference curve. Assume, for example, that with a fixed income and given prices, an individual would be equally satisfied (have the same total utility) with the following combination soft drinks and beer:

Soft Drinks	Beers
10	1
7	2
5	3
2	4

According to this schedule, an individual would be equally happy with 10 soft drinks and 1 beer as with 2 soft drinks and 4 beers; there is no preference for any of the shown combinations of soft drinks and beers.

A. The resulting indifference curve (I) would take the form:

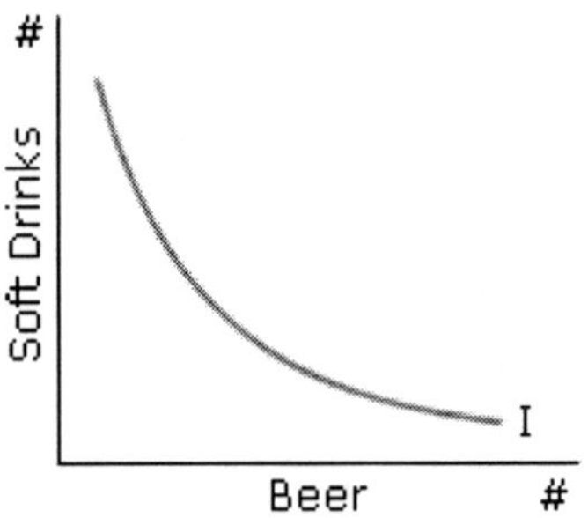

B. Along this curve the individual would receive equal utility, and therefore be indifferent as to which combination of soft drinks and beer is acquired.

Inputs and the Cost of Production

The costs of a firm's input factors - labor, capital and natural resources - are the primary determinants of a firm's supply curve. For analytical purposes, the costs of these factors can be classified in a number of ways. This lesson considers several cost concepts and how the different cost concepts apply in the economic analysis of the cost of production.

I. **Inputs --** In the free-market model it was shown that business firms acquire economic resources in order to produce (other) goods and services. These inputs to the production process are the major determinants of a firm's supply curve. As noted in the discussion of supply, changes in the cost of inputs to the production process cause a shift in an entity's supply curve (i.e., change the quantity of goods supplied at a given price).

II. **Periods of Analysis**

A. The analysis of cost of production (and other areas of economics) distinguishes between analysis in the short-run and analysis in the long-run.

1. **Short-run --** the time period during which the quantity of at least one input to the production process can not be varied; the quantity of at least one input is fixed.

2. **Long-run --** the time period during which the quantity of all inputs to the production process can be varied.

B. Since business firms can vary all inputs in the long-run and since they must nevertheless operate in the short-run, analysis of production costs tends to focus on the short-run.

III. **Short-run Cost Analysis**

A. **Total Cost --** Because some costs cannot be changed in the short-run, total production costs are separated into fixed costs and variable costs:

1. **Total Fixed Cost (FC) --** costs incurred which cannot be changed with changes in the level of output (including no output). Examples include property taxes, contracted rent, insurance, etc.

2. **Total Variable Cost (VC) --** costs incurred for variable inputs and which will vary directly with changes in the level of output. Examples include raw materials, most labor, electricity, etc.

3. **Total Costs (TC) --** the sum of total fixed and total variable costs.

4. These costs can be presented as curves in graph form as:

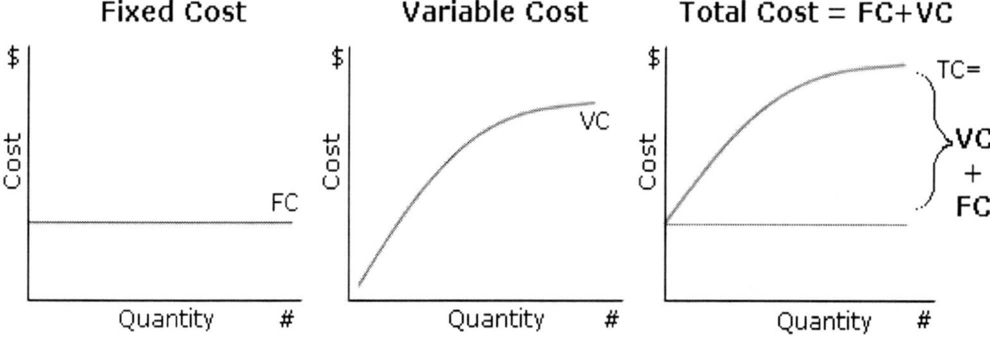

B. Average Cost -- Average cost is the cost per-unit of commodity produced. Average fixed cost (AFC), average variable cost (AVC) and average total cost (ATC) are computed by dividing the cost (FC, VC or TC) by the quantity of units produced. The resulting curves take the form:

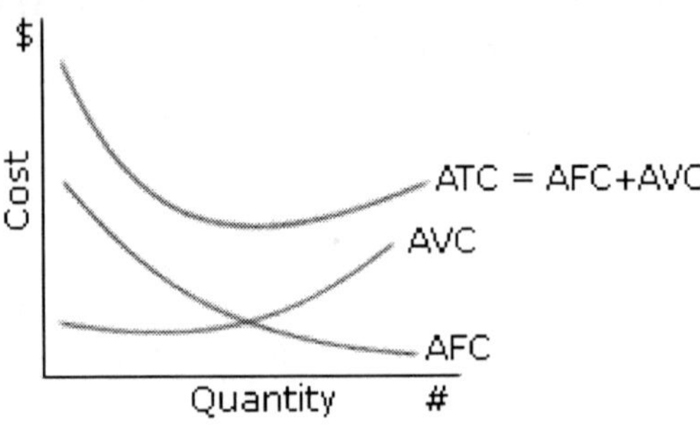

C. Marginal Cost -- Marginal cost (MC) is the cost of the last acquired unit of an input. It is computed as the difference between successive total costs, or because only variable costs change, successive total variable costs. When plotted, a marginal cost curve takes the form:

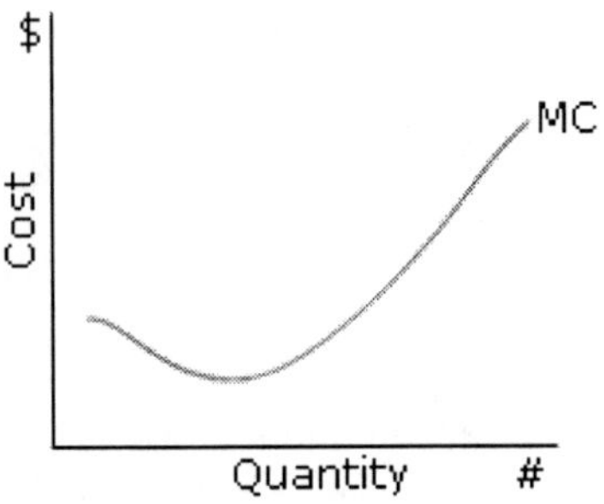

Note:
The lowest MC occurs at lower output than the lowest point on the AVC or ATC. The MC curve crosses the AVC and ATC at their respective lowest point.

D. Average Cost and Marginal Cost -- When the marginal cost curve is combined with the average cost curves, the following results:

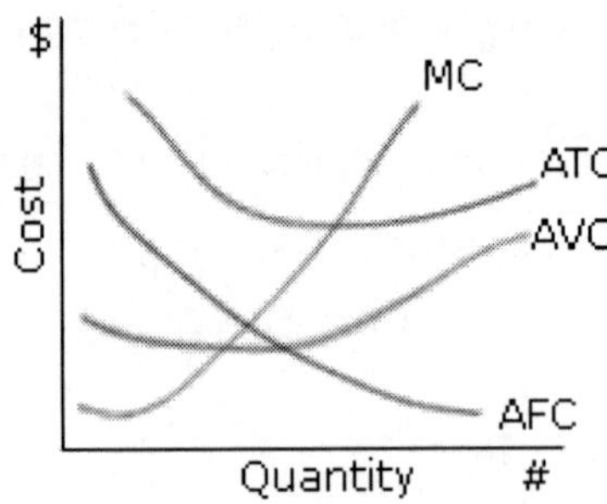

IV. Law of Diminishing Returns

A. In the foregoing graphs the ATC, AVC and MC curves all have a general "U" shape. That shape is basic to each curve and occurs because of eventual diminishing returns from adding more variable inputs. In the short-run, as the quantity of variable inputs increases, output initially increases, causing AC, AVC and MC to decrease.

B. However, at some quantity of variable inputs the addition of more units, in combination with the fixed inputs, results in decreasing output per unit of variable input. Simply put, at some point the quantity of variable inputs begins to overwhelm the fixed factors resulting in inefficiencies and diminishing return on marginal units of variable inputs. As a consequence of diminishing returns as inputs increase, ATC, AVC and MC all begin to increase. Thus, their curves are "U" shaped. (Note, however, that AFC continues to decline.)

V. Long-run Cost Analysis -- In the long-run all costs are considered variable, including plant size. Thus plants of various sizes can be assumed in the long-run, but in the short-run a plant of a particular size will operate. By plotting the short-run average cost (SAC) curve of plants of various sizes (1 - 4), the long-run average cost (LAC) curve can be constructed.

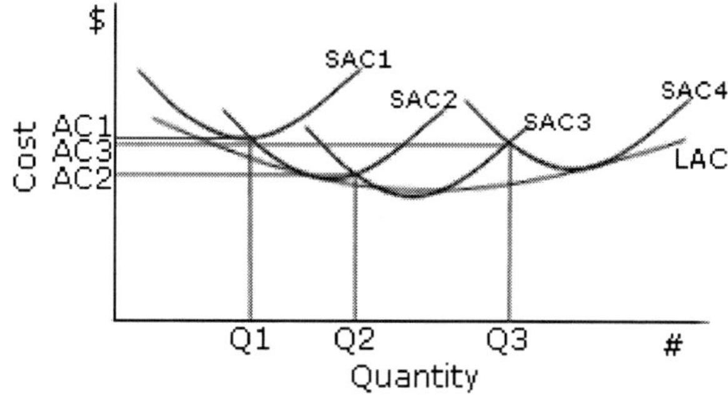

VI.

A. As shown, the LAC is determined by the relevant segments of SAC for plants 1, 2, 3 and 4. This curve (LAC) shows the minimum average cost of production with various size plants. Note that:

1. Up to the quantity at Q1, plant 1 is the most efficient size plant;
2. From the quantity at Q1 to Q2, plant 2 is the appropriate size plant, and from Q2 to Q3, plant 3 is the appropriate size;
3. Above the quantity at Q3, plant 4 is the appropriate size plant.

B. The long-run average cost curve (LAC) is also "U" shaped, reflecting that as plant size (scale) increases there are various returns to (or economics of) scale. Three possible cost outcomes exist:

1. Economies of (or increasing return to) scale - as shown where the LAC curve is decreasing, quantity of output increases in greater proportion than the increase in all inputs, primarily due to specialization of labor and equipment;
2. Neither economy nor diseconomy of (constant return to) scale - as shown at the bottom of the LAC curve, output increases in the same proportion as inputs;
3. Diseconomies of (or decreasing return to) scale - as shown where the LAC curve is increasing, quantity of output increases in lesser proportion than the increase in all inputs, primarily due to problems or managing very large scale operations.

Market Structure

Introduction

Market structure describes the nature of the economic environment in which firms operate and economic activity occurs. Conceptually, a number of different environments or market structures can exist along a hypothetical continuum with perfect competition at one extreme and perfect monopoly at the other. This lesson introduces four of the most common market structures, each of which is considered in detail in subsequent lessons.

I. Market Structures

A. The extent to which competition exists, or does not exist, in an industry or market determines how prices are established, operating results at various levels of production, and other performance characteristics. Four assumptions as to market structure are considered in the following lessons:

1. **Perfect Competition**;
2. **Perfect Monopoly**;
3. **Monopolistic Competition**; and
4. **Oligopoly**.

B. Analysis of factors in each of these assumed structures provides insights into real-world economic activity and outcomes which are useful in explaining and predicting business activity. For each assumed structure, both short-term and long-term analysis are presented.

Perfect Competition

This lesson considers the conditions that would constitute a perfectly competitive market, one end of a hypothetical market structures continuum. The nature of demand, revenue, costs, and profit in both the short-run and long-run in such a market are described and illustrated.

I. Characteristics

A. Perfect Competition exists in industries or markets characterized by:

1. A large number of independent buyers and sellers, each of which is too small to separately affect the price of a commodity;
2. All firms sell homogeneous products or services;
3. Firms can enter or leave the market easily;
4. Resources are completely mobile;
5. Buyers and sellers have perfect information;
6. Government does not set prices.

B. A market (or industry) meeting all of these criteria is virtually impossible to identify. Nevertheless, analysis under assumed conditions of perfect competition is useful in understanding pricing, production, profit and related elements.

C. In a perfectly competitive market, a firm is a "price taker" that must (and can) sell any quantity of its commodity at market price. Therefore, for firms in a perfectly competitive market, the demand curve is a straight line for any price.

II. Short-run Analysis

A. In the short-run a firm in a perfect competition environment will maximize profit when total revenue exceeds total costs by the greatest amount, or where its marginal revenue is equal to (rising) marginal cost. Said another way, it maximizes profit when the amount received (revenue) from the last unit sold equals the incremental (marginal) cost of producing that unit. Since, in perfect competition, each unit will be sold at the market price, marginal revenue is (the same as) market price. The relevant graph would show:

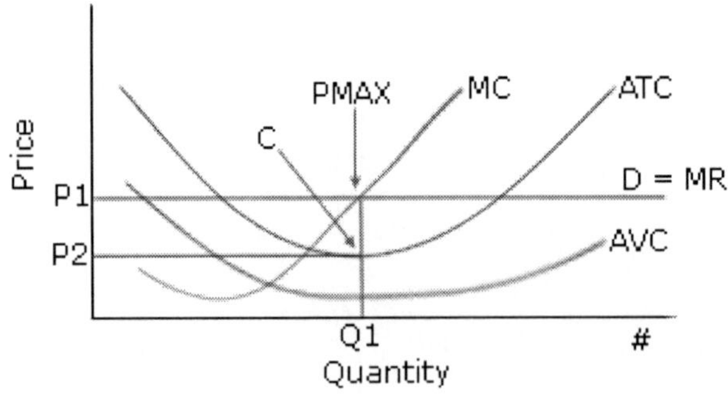

B. Short-run profit would be maximized where MC intersects MR (also D), labeled PMAX at Q1 in the graph. Each unit of output up to that quantity would add more to total revenue than to total cost, therefore total profit would increase. Units after that quantity (Q1) would cost more to produce than the price at which the additional units could be sold; therefore, the amount of profit would decline with each additional unit greater than Q1.

C. In the above graph, total revenue would be P1 x Q1 and total cost would be P2 x Q1, which is less that P1 x Q1. Total profit would be (P1 - P2) x Q1, or on a per unit basis PMAX - C. If, however, demand (which is also marginal revenue) shifts downward, with the same cost structure, the results may be different.

1. MR = ATC: At this level the firm would break even.
2. MR less than ATC but greater than AVC: At this level the firm would cover variable cost, but not total cost. The excess of sales price (also D) over AVC would contribute to paying fixed cost (in the short-run).
3. MR less than AVC: At this level the firm would shut down because each unit it produces fails to cover the direct cost of producing the unit.

III. Long-run Analysis

A. When firms in a perfectly competitive market are making profit in the short-run, in the long-run more firms will enter the market. As more firms enter the market, supply (output) increases and the market price will fall until all firms just break even. When firms in a perfectly competitive market are suffering losses in the short-run, some of the firms will exit the market, causing the market price to increase until all firms just break even. Therefore, in a perfectly competitive market there are no long-run economic profits.

B. Because demand price and marginal revenue are the same, long-run equilibrium occurs where marginal revenue, marginal cost and the lowest long-run average cost intersect.

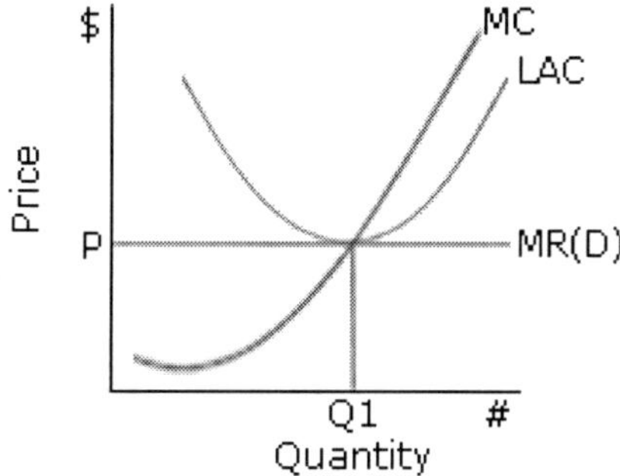

C. Thus, in the long-run, at Q1 inputs are used most efficiently and price is the lowest possible.

Perfect Monopoly

This lesson considers the conditions that would constitute a perfectly monopolistic market, one end of a hypothetical market structures continuum. The nature of demand, revenue, costs, and profit in both the short-run and long-run in such a market are described.

I. Characteristics

A. Perfect monopoly exists in industries or markets characterized by:

1. A single seller;
2. A commodity for which there are no close substitutes;
3. Restricted entry into the market.

B. A monopoly may exist as a result of:

1. Control of raw material inputs or processes (e.g., a patent);
2. Government action (e.g., a government granted franchise);
3. Increasing return to scale (or natural monopolies) (e.g., public utilities).

C. In a perfect monopoly market, a single firm is the industry. Therefore, for that firm the demand curve takes the traditional negative slope (down and to the right).

II. Short-run Analysis

A. In the short-run a monopolistic firm will maximize profit where marginal revenue is equal to (rising) marginal cost. Because the demand curve is downward sloping, in order to sell additional units, the firm must (continuously) lower its price. Therefore, the marginal revenue curve will be below the demand curve. The price charged at the point of profit maximization (MR = MC) is determined by the level of the demand curve for that quantity. These relationships are graphed as:

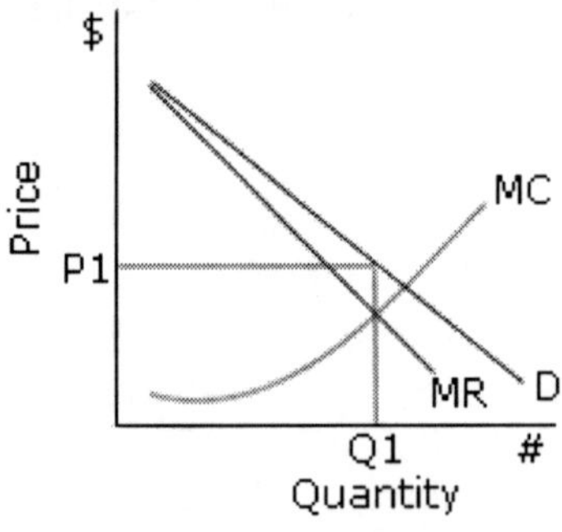

B. In the graph, the firm maximizes profit at Q1 (MR = MC) and can sell that quantity at the price level called for by demand, or P1 in the graph. Whether the monopolistic firm makes a profit or not depends on the average cost (AC) of producing at Q1. The following results are possible:

1. Profit: If AC less than P1;
2. Break even: If AC = P1;
3. Loss: If AC greater than P1.

C. Since demand is fixed in the short-run, the monopolistic firm can increase revenue only by selling at different prices to different customers. For example, the firm could sell at different prices to different classes of customers or in different markets. Since some of Q1 will be sold at more than P1, total revenue and total profits will increase.

III. Long-run Analysis

A. If a firm maintains its monopolistic position in the long-run, it has two basic ways to improve its total profits:

1. Reduce its cost by changing the size of its plant so as to produce the best level of long-run production;
2. Increase demand for it commodity through advertising, promotion, etc.

B. Like the firm in a perfectly competitive environment, the monopolistic firm will produce where MR = MC. In either environment, to produce at a lesser quantity (MR greater than MC) or at a greater quantity (MC greater than MR) would result in less total revenue than MR = MC. For the monopolistic firm, however, production at MR = MC results in an inefficient use of resources and a higher price than would result from a firm with the same costs under perfect competition. These less than optimum outcomes occur because for the monopolistic firm facing a downward sloping demand curve MR less than P, whereas for an individual firm in perfect competition MR = P (=D). (Recall that in a perfectly competitive environment the market demand is downward sloping, but for a single firm in that environment the demand curve is horizontal and the firm can sell any quantity at the market price.)

Monopolistic Competition

This lesson considers the conditions that would constitute a market structure that is a blend of competition and monopoly, known as monopolistic competition. The nature of demand, revenue, costs, and profit in both the short-run and long-run in such a market are described.

I. Characteristics

A. Monopolistic competition exists in industries or markets characterized by:

1. A large number of sellers;
2. Firms sell a differentiated product or service (similar but not identical), for which there are close substitutes;
3. Firms can enter or leave the market easily.

B. Thus, this market environment has elements of both perfect competition and perfect monopoly.

II. Short-run Analysis

A. A monopolistic competitive environment has a downward sloping demand curve that is highly elastic. It is downward sloping because of product differentiation and highly elastic because there are close substitutes for the good or service. Again, optimum profit (and output) occur where MR = MC (provided P greater than AVC). The following graph is representative:

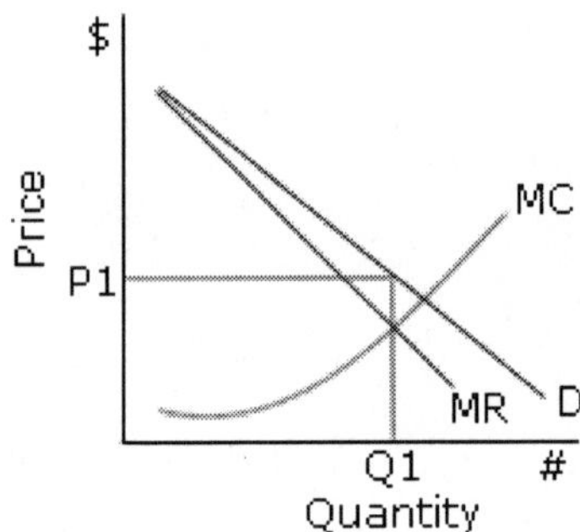

B. MR = MC at Q1 with a price of P1. Whether the firm makes a profit, breaks even or has a loss depends on its average cost curve (AC) at Q1. The following short-run results are possible:

1. Profit: If AC < P1;
2. Break even: If AC = P1;
3. Loss: If AC > P1.

III. Long-run Analysis

A. If firms in a monopolistic competitive environment experience short-run profits, in the long-run more firms will enter the industry. More firms in the industry result in a lower demand curve for each firm. Equilibrium will result where the demand curve becomes tangential to the average cost curve and each firm just breaks even. Conversely, if firms are experiencing losses in the long run, firms will leave the industry and the demand curve will shift up so that remaining firms just break even.

B. A firm in a monopolistic environment incorrectly allocates economic resources in the long-run because the price at which it sells is greater than marginal cost of production. Further, such firms operate with smaller scale plants than the optimum and, as a consequence, more firms than would exist in perfect competition.

Oligopoly

This lesson considers the final market structure, oligopoly. It describes the nature of an oligopoly market, and production and profit characteristics in both the short-run and long-run in such a market.

I. Characteristics

A. Oligopoly exists in industries or markets characterized by:

1. A few sellers;
2. Firms sell either a homogeneous product (standardized oligopoly) or a differentiated product (differentiated oligopoly);
3. Restricted entry into the market.

B. Because there are few firms in an oligopolist market, the action of each firm is known by and affects other firms in the market. Therefore, if one firm lowers its price to increase its share of the market (demand), other firms in the market are likely to reduce their prices. In the extreme a "price war" will result. Consequently, oligopolist firms tend to compete on factors other than price (e.g., quality, service, distinctions, etc.).

C. In order to change price without triggering a price war, oligopolist firms may engage in collusion, either overt or tacit. Overt collusion, in which firms (a cartel) conspire to set output, price or profit, is illegal in the U.S. The Organization of Petroleum Exporting Countries (OPEC) is an example of a cartel. Tacit collusion occurs when the firms tend to follow price changes initiated by the price leader in the market. Tacit collusion (firms do not conspire in setting output, price or profits) is not illegal in the U.S.

II. Short-run/Long-run Analysis

A. In the short-run the oligopolist firm will produce where MC = MR and may make a profit, break even or have a loss, depending on the relationship between price and average cost for the quantity produced. In the long-run, however, firms incurring losses (because average cost exceeds market price) will cease to operate in the industry. Further, firms operating at a profit (because average cost is less than market price) can continue to make profits in the long-run because new firms are restricted from entering the market.

B. As with monopolies and monopolistically competitive firms, oligopolist firms produce at the quantity of output where MR = MC and, therefore, where P > MC. As a consequence, the oligopolist firm under allocates resources to production and produces less, but charges more than would occur in a perfectly competitive market.

Summary

This lesson summarizes four market structures as they exist and operate in the U.S. economy.

I. A Mix of Structures

A. The U.S. economy is a mix of market economic structures. Different commodities (goods and services) and industries tend to operate in different market structures. While a perfectly competitive segment of the U.S. economy may not exist in today's socio-political environment, the framework of a perfectly competitive market provides a useful model for understanding fundamental economic concepts and for evaluating other market structures.

1. **A monopoly --** Exists where there is a single provider of a good or service for which there are no close substitutes. Monopolistic firms do exist in the U.S. economy. Historically, public utilities have been permitted to operate as monopolies with the justification that market demand can be fully satisfied at a lower cost by one firm than by two or more firms. To limit the economic benefits of such monopolies, governments generally impose regulations which affect pricing, output and/or profits. Monopolies also can exist as a result of exclusive ownership of raw materials or patent rights. In most cases, however, exclusive ownership monopolies are of short duration as a result of the development of close substitutes, the expiration of rights, or government regulation.
2. **Monopolistic competition --** Is common in the U.S. economy, especially in general retailing where there are many firms selling similar (but not identical) goods and services. Because their products are similar, monopolistic competitive firms engage in extensive non-price competition, including advertising, promotion, and customer service initiatives, all of which are common in the contemporary U.S. economy.
3. **Oligopoly --** Exists in markets where there are few providers of a good or service. Such markets exist for a number of industries in the U.S. The markets for many metals (steel, aluminum, copper, etc.) are oligopolistic. So also are the markets for such diverse products a automobiles, cigarettes and oil. Firms in oligopolistic markets tend to avoid price competition for fear of creating a price war, but do rely heavily on non-price competition.

Macroeconomics

Introduction and Gross Measures

Macroeconomics is concerned with the economic activities and outcomes of an entire economy, typically an entire nation or sectors of a national economy. This lesson identifies and describes gross measures of macroeconomic activity, especially as they relate to the U.S. economy.

I. **Introduction --** Macroeconomics is concerned with the economic activities and outcomes of an entire economy, typically an entire nation or sectors of a national economy. This macroeconomics section will consider gross measures of economic activity, aggregate demand and supply, business cycles, price levels, and inflation/deflation. The material presented is based on the concepts, measures, policies, and regulations found in the U.S. economy.

II. **Gross Measures --** Common measures of the total activity or output of the U.S. economy are:

   A. **Nominal Gross Domestic Product (Nominal GDP) --** Measures the total output of final goods and services produced for exchange in the domestic market during a period (usually a year).

      1. GDP does not include:

         a. Goods or services which require additional processing before sold for final use (i.e., raw materials or intermediate goods);

         b. Activities for which there is no market exchange (i.e., do-it-yourself productive activities);

         c. Goods or services produced in foreign countries by U.S.-owned entities;

         d. Adjustment for changing prices of goods and services over time.

      2. This output may be quantified (measured) in two ways:

         a. Expenditure approach: derived by summing the spending of individuals, businesses, governmental entities, and net exports (imports) of U.S. goods and services;

         b. Cost approach: derived by summing the value added at each step in producing a final good or service.

   B. **Real Gross Domestic Product (Real GDP) --** Measures the total output of final goods and services produced for exchange in the domestic market during a period (usually a year) at constant prices. Real GDP measures production in terms of prices that existed at a specific prior period; that is, it adjusts for changing prices.

   C. **Potential Gross Domestic Product (Potential GDP) --** Measures the maximum final output that can occur in the domestic economy at a point in time without creating upward pressure on the general level of prices in the economy. The point of maximum final output at a point in time will be a point on the production-possibility frontier for the economy.

      1. The production-possibility frontier is the (conceptual) maximum amount of various goods and services an economy can produce at a given time with available technology and full utilization of current economic resources.

2. A production-possibility frontier represented by a curve in a simple two-dimensional graph (assuming available inputs are totally committed to only two outputs) would be shown as:

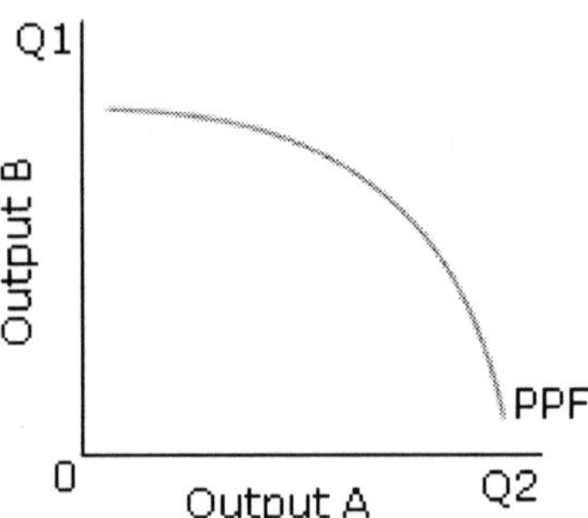

3. The curve Q1 to Q2 shows conceptually the various maximum combinations (potential production) of products A and B that could be produced with available inputs and technology.

4. If the curve Q1 to Q2 is assumed to represent all possible goods and services then:

   a. Points on the curve represent all input resources (labor, plant capacity, etc.) are being used to generate maximum output. There is no inefficiency in the economy;

   b. At points within the curve actual output (i.e., real GDP) is less than potential output (potential GDP). The difference (potential GDP - real GDP) is the (positive) GDP gap, a measure of inefficiency in the economy;

   c. At points outside the curve actual output (i.e., real GAP exceeds potential output) there is a negative GDP gap which will result in price level increases.

D. **Gross National Product (GNP) --** Measures the total output of all goods and services produced worldwide using economic resources of U.S. activities. In 1992 GNP was replaced by GDP as the primary measure of the U.S. economy. GNP includes both the cost of replacing capital (the depreciation factor) and the cost of investment in new capital.

E. **Net National Product (NNP) --** Measures the total output of all goods and services produced worldwide using economic resources of U.S. entities, but unlike GNP, NNP only includes the cost of investment in new capital (i.e., there is no amount included for depreciation).

F. **National Income --** Measures the total payments for economic resources included in the production of all goods and services, including payments for wages, rent, interest, and profits, but not taxes included in the cost of final output.

G. **Personal Disposable Income --** Measures the amount of income individuals have available for spending, after taxes are deducted from total personal income.

H. **Employment/Unemployment Measures --** Measures of the level of employment and unemployment in the U.S. economy, and associated characteristics.

1. In the U.S., official employment/unemployment measures are determined by the Bureau of Labor Statistics (BLS), a unit of the U.S. Department of Labor. The data the BLS provides comes primarily from two different surveys, the Current Employment Survey and the Current Population Survey:

   a. Current Employment Survey (CES): A monthly sample survey of 160,000 businesses and government entities designed to measure employment (only), with industry and geographical details.

b. Current Population Survey (CPS): A monthly sample survey of approximately 60,000 households designed to measure both employment and unemployment, with demographic details.

2. In developing measures of employment/unemployment, the population is considered to be comprised of two major subsets, those in the labor (or work) force and those not in the labor force. The (civilian) labor force consists of those at least 16 years old who are working (excluding those on active military duty) or who are seeking work; all others are not considered part of the labor force (including those who previously were seeking employment but have become discouraged and are no longer looking for work). Microeconomic employment/unemployment statistics are based almost exclusively on the size of the labor force.

3. The labor force, in turn, is comprised of two subgroups, the employed (employment) and the unemployed (unemployment):

   a. Employment Measures: While the primary focus of employment-related measures is concerned with the unemployed, measures of the employed provide information not only about the level of employment, but also details about the characteristics of the labor force. Those details include employment statistics by race, sex, age, marital status, educational attainment, class of worker (e.g., agricultural, government, private industry, self-employed, etc.) and full-time/ part-time status.

   b. Unemployment Measures: The primary focus of employment-related measures is concerned with the unemployed (i.e., measures of unemployment). In addition to statistics which provide details similar to those provided for the employed, unemployment statistics provide information by duration of unemployment and unemployment by occupation and industry. In order to better understand unemployment, economists and policy-makers have established categories which seek to describe the causes of and reasons for unemployment. These categories include:

      i. Frictional Unemployment: Members of the labor force who are not employed because they are in transition or have imperfect information. For example, members of the labor force who are in search of a job that is in line with their talents (education, skills, experience, etc.) or who are moving to a different part of the country.

      ii. Structural Unemployment: Members of the labor force who are not employed because their prior types of jobs have been greatly reduced or eliminated and/or because they lack the skills needed for available jobs. For example, the advent of computers and accounting software has greatly reduced the demand for bookkeepers in the economy.

      iii. Seasonal Unemployment: Members of the labor force who are not employed because their work opportunity regularly and predictably varies by the season of the year. For example, school teachers are regularly unemployed during summer months when school is not in session. (This category sometimes is viewed as a kind of temporary structural unemployment.)

      iv. Cyclical Unemployment: Members of the labor force who are not employed because a downturn in the business cycle (i.e., an economic contraction) has reduced the current need for workers.

   c. Special Employment/Unemployment Concepts: In considering measure of employment/unemployment, the following should be understood:

i. The official unemployment rate is the percentage of the labor force that is not employed, not the percentage of the population that is not employed. The calculation would be:

Unemployment Rate = Unemployed (including all categories)/Size of Labor Force

ii. The natural rate of unemployment is the percentage of the labor force that is not employed as a result of frictional, structural and seasonal unemployment. The calculation would be:

Natural Rate of Unemployment = Frictional + Structural + Seasonal Unemployed/Size of Labor Force

iii. Officially, full employment is when there is no cyclical unemployment. Even with frictional and structural unemployment, officially, full employment can exist. Said another way, if unemployment is due solely to frictional, structural and seasonal causes (i.e., the natural rate of unemployment), the economy is in a state of full employment.

d. Model of Employment/Unemployment Elements: The elements and categories of employment/unemployment may be summarized as follows:

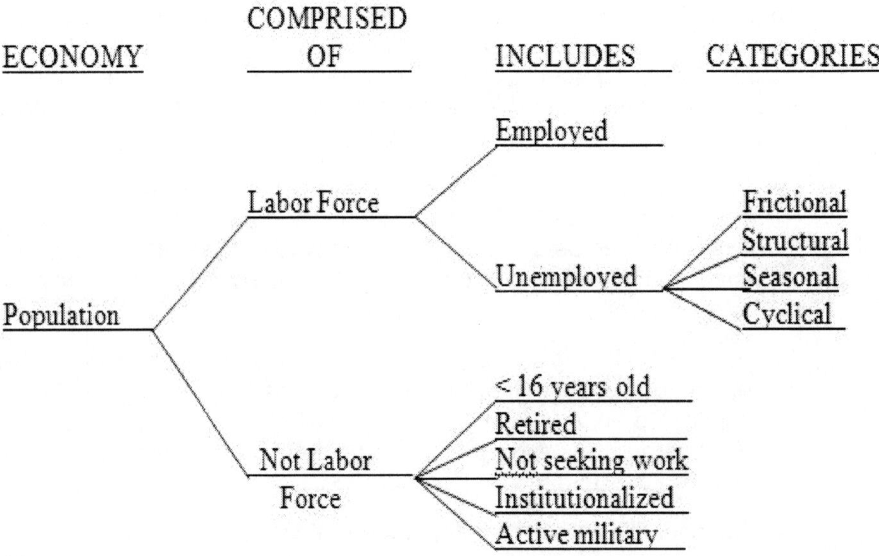

Aggregate Demand

At the macroeconomic (economy) level, demand measures the total spending of all entities on goods and services in an economy at different price levels. This lesson describes aggregate demand and analyzes the role of individual consumers, businesses, governmental entities, and net foreign spending in determining aggregate demand.

I. Introduction

A. **Aggregate Demand Curve --** At the macroeconomic (economy) level, demand measures the total spending of individuals, businesses, governmental entities, and net foreign spending on goods and services at different price levels. The demand curve that results from plotting the aggregate spending (AD) is negatively sloped and can be represented as:

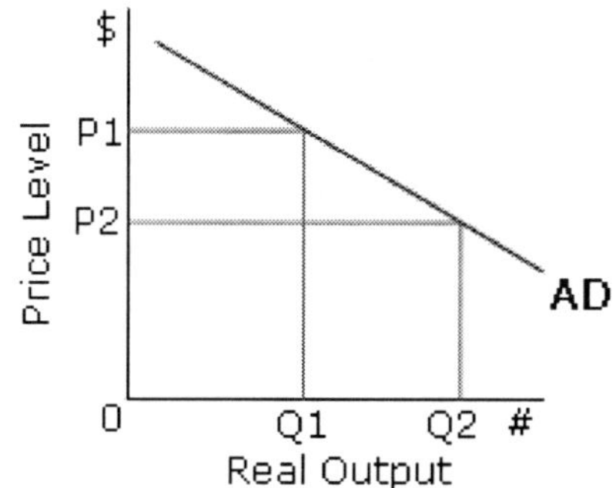

B. Like its microeconomic counterpart, the aggregate demand curve shows quantity demanded at various prices (aggregate prices = price level), assuming all other variables that affect spending are held constant (*ceteris paribus*). Thus, aggregate demand at price level P2 will be greater (Q2) than at price level P1 with demand (Q1).

C. **Components of Aggregate Demand --** Aggregate demand is the total spending by individual consumers (consumption spending) and businesses on investment goods, by governmental entities and by foreign entities on net exports. Each is considered in the following subsections.

II. Consumer Spending --

Spending on consumable goods accounts for about 70% of total spending (aggregate demand) in the U.S. Personal income and the level of taxes on personal income are the most important determinants of consumption spending. Personal income less related income taxes determines individual income available for spending, called disposable income. The relationship between consumption spending (CS) and disposable income (DI) is the consumption function. Graphically, the consumption function can be plotted as a positively sloped curve.

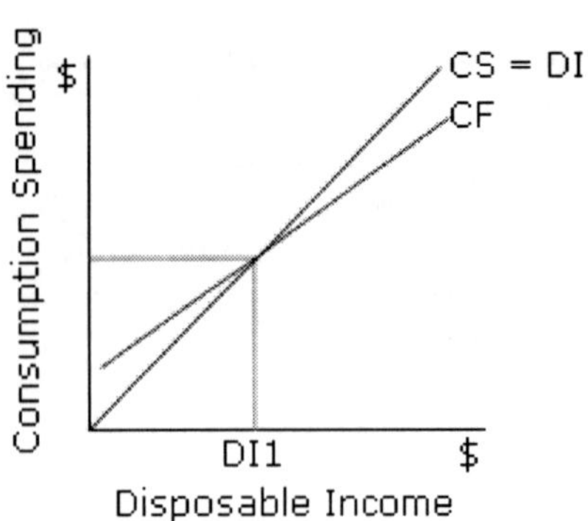

A. At the intersection of the CS = DI and CF (Consumer Function) curves on the graph, consumers are spending all of their disposable income. At other points on the CF curve, spending is either more or less than disposable income.

1. Where the CF curve is greater than the CS = DI curve (below DI1), consumer spending exceeds disposable income. This excess spending over disposable income can occur as a result of consumers spending accumulated savings or borrowing for current consumption spending.
2. Where the CF curve is less than the CS = DI curve (above DI1), consumers are not spending all available disposable income. The excess of disposable income over consumption spending is a measure of consumer savings.

B. Several ratios -- are used to measure the relationship between consumption spending and disposable income:

1. Average propensity to consume (APC): Measures the percent of disposable income spent on consumption goods.
2. Average propensity to save (APS): Measures the percent of disposable income not spent, but rather saved.

> APC + APS = 1 (because each measure is the reciprocal of the other)

3. Marginal propensity to consume (MPC): Measures the change in consumption as a percent of a change in disposable income.
4. Marginal propensity to save (MPS): Measures the change in savings as a percent of a change in disposable income.

> MPC + MPS = 1 (because each measure is the reciprocal of the other)

III. Investment

A. In the macroeconomic context, investment includes spending on

1. Residential construction;
2. Nonresidential construction;
3. Business durable equipment;
4. Business inventory.

B. The level of spending on these investment goods is influenced by a number of factors, including

1. Interest rate;
2. Demographics;
3. Consumer confidence;
4. Consumer income and wealth;
5. Current vacancy rates;
6. Level of capacity utilization;
7. Technological advances;
8. Current and expected sales levels.

C. The **most significant of these factors** over time is the interest rate. Higher interest rates are associated with lower levels of investment, and lower interest rates are associated with higher levels of investment. The graphic representation (an investment demand [ID] curve) shows the negative relationship.

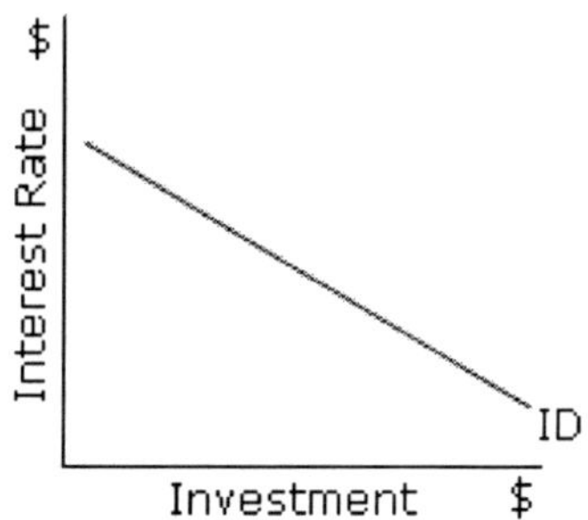

D. Investment spending is the most volatile component of aggregate spending (demand) and considered to be a major impetus for the business cycle. Monetary policy targets the investment component in order to moderate fluctuations of the business cycle. (See section on Business Cycles, below.)

IV. Government Spending and Fiscal Policy

A. Government spending increases aggregate spending (and demand) in the economy. However, much of that spending comes as a result of the reduced disposable income available to consumers due to taxes imposed to finance government spending. While taxes on income reduce aggregate demand and government spending and transfer payments (e.g., unemployment payments, social security, etc.) increase that demand, there will not be equal "offsetting" for a period because the two events - government taxing and government spending - are not absolutely interdependent, especially in the short run.

B. As a consequence, government can directly affect aggregate demand by changing tax receipts, government expenditures, or both. Intentional changes by the government in its tax receipts and/or its spending so as to increase or decrease aggregate demand in the economy is called discretionary fiscal policy.

C. The following chart summarizes possible fiscal policy initiatives to increase or decrease demand in the economy (*ceteris paribus*):

	To Increase Aggregate Demand	To Decrease Aggregate Demand
Government Spending	Increase	Decrease
Taxation	Decrease	Increase
Transfer Payments	Increase	Decrease

D. **Discretionary fiscal policy --** initiatives are used to close recessionary gaps (increase demand to the full employment level) or to close inflationary gaps (reduce demand to the full employment level).

V. **Net Exports/Imports**

A. Exports measure foreign spending for domestic (U.S.) goods and services, while imports measure U.S. spending on foreign goods and services. Exports increase demand for domestic products; imports lower spending for domestic products. Net exports measures the excess of gross exports over gross imports.

1. When net exports is positive (exports greater than imports) aggregate demand is increased.

2. When net exports is negative (exports less than imports) aggregate demand is decreased.

B. A number of factors enter into determining a country's level of imports and exports with other countries, including:

1. Relative levels of income and wealth;

2. Relative values of currencies;

3. Relative price levels;

4. Import and export restrictions and tariffs;

5. Relative inflationary rates.

C. During the past 20 years, the U.S. has been a **net import** country (negative net exports), causing a decrease in aggregate demand for U.S. goods.

D. **The aggregate demand curve**, as shown above, is negatively sloped because of three significant factors:

1. **Interest Rate Factor --** Generally, the higher the price level, the higher the interest rate. As the interest rate increases, interest-sensitive spending (e.g. new home purchases, business investment, etc.) decrease.

2. **Wealth-level factor --** As price levels (and interest rates) increase, the value of financial assets may decrease. As wealth decreases, so also may spending decrease.

3. **Foreign Purchasing Power Factor --** As the domestic price level increases, domestic goods become relatively more expensive than foreign goods. As a consequence, spending on domestic goods decreases and spending on foreign goods increases.

E. If **variables other than price** affect total spending in the economy, aggregate demand will change and the aggregate demand curve will shift to create a new curve. The curve will shift outward (to the right) when demand increases and inward (to the left) when demand decreases. Aggregate demand typically increases as a result of the following kinds of occurrences (among others):

1. Personal taxes are reduced, which increases disposable income;
2. Consumer confidence in the economy improves markedly;
3. New technology engenders increased investment;
4. Corporate taxes are reduced, which increases funds for investment and distribution to shareholders;
5. Interest rates decline as a result of monetary policy;
6. Government spending increases;
7. Net exports increase.

F. **Two additional points** should be noted about these factors:

1. The opposite effect on these factors (e.g., increases in taxes, declines in consumer confidence, etc.) likely will cause a contraction in aggregate demand.
2. The government can act so as to effect increases or decreases to many of these factors (i.e., change tax rates, government spending, etc.).

Aggregate Supply

At the macroeconomic (economy) level, supply measures the total output of goods and services in an economy at different price levels. This lesson describes aggregate supply and the three alternative supply curves used in economics - classical, Keynesian, and conventional.

I. **Three Theoretical Curves --** At the macroeconomic (economy) level, supply measures the total output of goods and services at different price levels. The exact slope of the aggregate supply curve that results from plotting the output depends on which of three theoretical curves is accepted as representing aggregate supply. These possibilities are:

A. **Classical Aggregate Supply Curve --** This curve is completely vertical, reflecting no relationship between aggregate supply and price level.

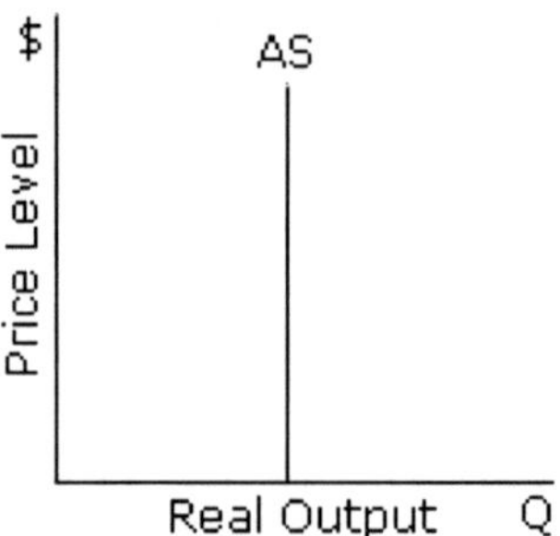

B. **Keynesian Aggregate Supply Curve --** This curve is horizontal up to the (assumed) level of output at full employment, and then slopes upward, reflecting that output is not associated with price level until full employment is reached, at which point increased output is associated with higher price levels.

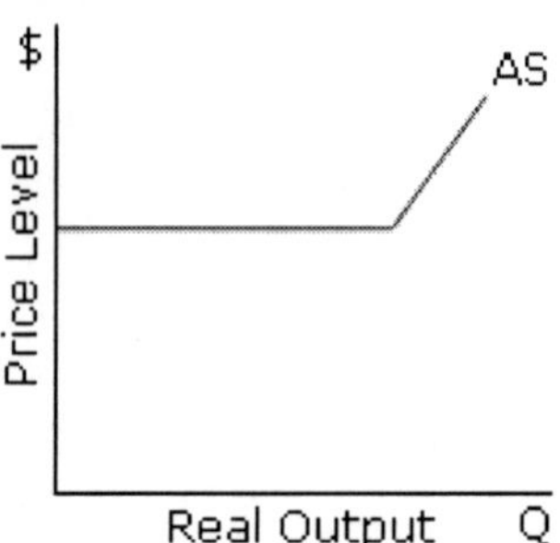

C. **Conventional Aggregate Supply Curve --** This curve has a continuously positive slope with a steeper slope beginning at the (assumed) level of output at full employment, reflecting that at full employment increased output is associated with proportionately higher increases in price levels.

Note:
In the remaining material, the supply curve being used will be identified.

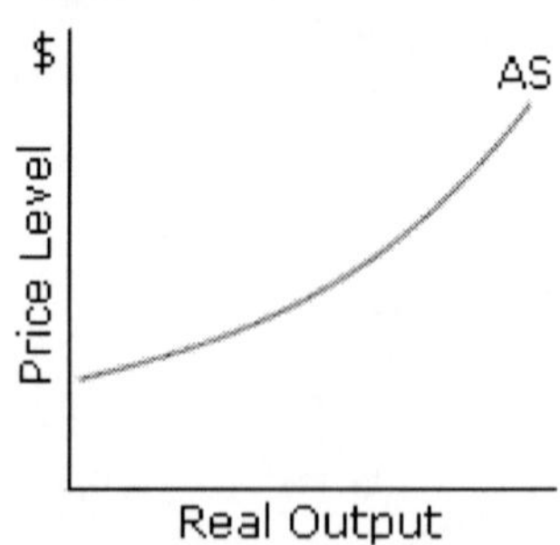

II. **Changes in variables --** other than price level will affect aggregate supply and shift the aggregate supply curve under any of the theoretical assumptions described above. Factors that may change the position of the supply curve include:

A. **Resource Availability --** An increase in economic resources (e.g., increase in working age population) will shift the curve outward (to the right); a decrease would have the opposite effect.

B. **Resource Cost --** A decrease in the cost of economic resources (e.g., lower oil prices) will shift the curve outward (to the right); an increase would have the opposite effect.

C. **Technological Advances --** (e.g., more efficient production processes) will shift the curve outward (to the right). Government prohibitions on the use of an existing technology, in the absence of a comparable alternative, would shift the curve inward (to the left).

Aggregate (Economy) Equilibrium

Aggregate equilibrium occurs when aggregate demand and aggregate supply of a multi-market economy are in balance and, in the absence of external influences, will not change. This lesson describes aggregate equilibrium and analyzes the effect on that equilibrium when externalities change aggregate demand or any of the three possible aggregate supply curve assumptions.

I. Introduction

A. The equilibrium real output and price level for an economy are determined by its aggregate demand and supply curves. Graphically, equilibrium occurs where the aggregate demand and supply curves intersect. Assuming a conventional supply curve, the graph would be:

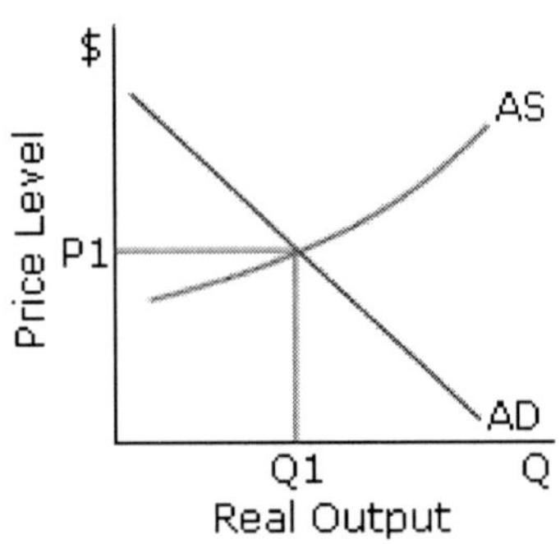

B. Equilibrium real output would be Q1 and the price level P1. The effect of a shift in the aggregate demand and/or aggregate supply curve(s) on equilibrium output and the price level would depend on:

1. Which of the three theoretical supply curves is assumed; and
2. The degree of shift in the curve(s) relative to prechange equilibrium.

II. Classical Supply Curve

Classical Supply Curve -- If the classical supply curve is assumed, an increase in aggregate demand alone results only in higher price levels. An increase in aggregate supply alone results in more output at a lower price.

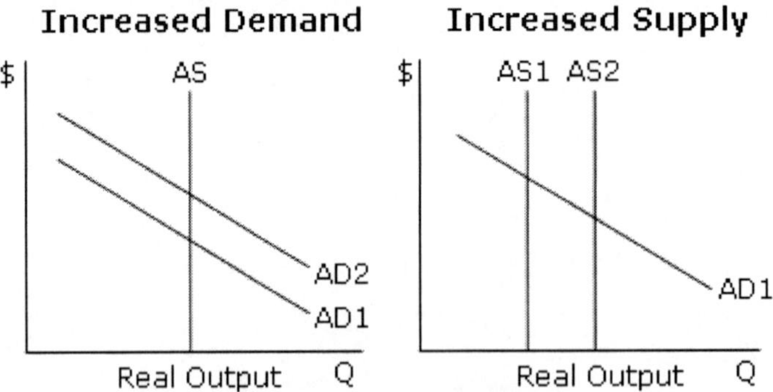

III. Keynesian Supply Curve -- If the Keynesian Supply Curve is assumed, an increase in aggregate demand alone results only in more output until output at full employment, at which point output and price level each increase. An increase in supply alone will not affect either output or price level unless aggregate demand intersects supply where it is positively sloped.

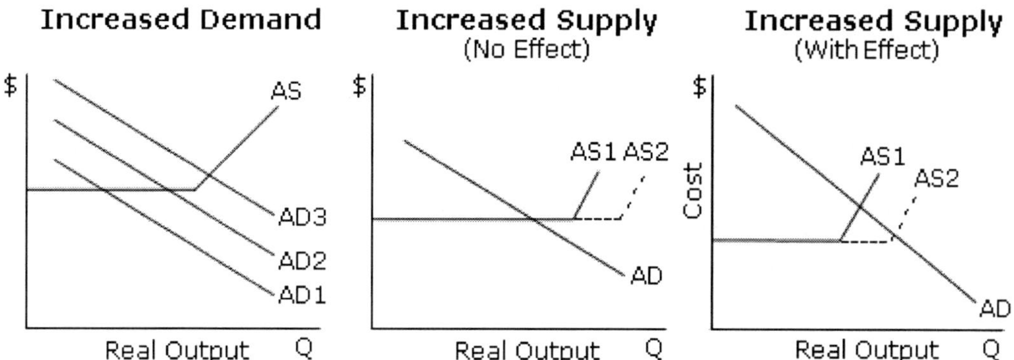

IV. Conventional Supply Curve -- If the conventional supply curve is assumed, an increase in aggregate demand alone will increase both the output and price level. An increase in supply alone will increase output, but reduce the price level.

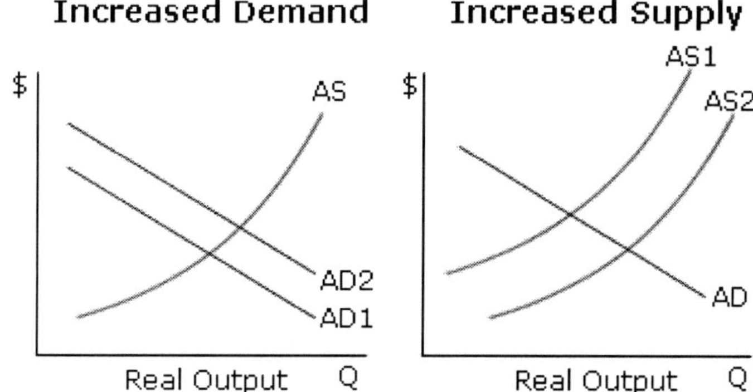

Business Cycles

Business cycles describes the cumulative fluctuations in aggregate real gross domestic product (GDP), generally that last for two or more years. This lesson defines business cycles, the components and causes of business cycles, and identifies leading and lagging indicators associated with business cycles.

I. Cyclical Economic Behavior

A. Business cycles is the term used to describe the cumulative fluctuations (up and down) in aggregate real GDP, generally that last for two or more years. These increases and decreases in real GDP tend to recur over time, though with no consistent pattern of length or magnitude. These increases and decreases also tend to impact individual industries at somewhat different times and with different intensities. A graphic representation of generic cyclical economic behavior can be shown as:

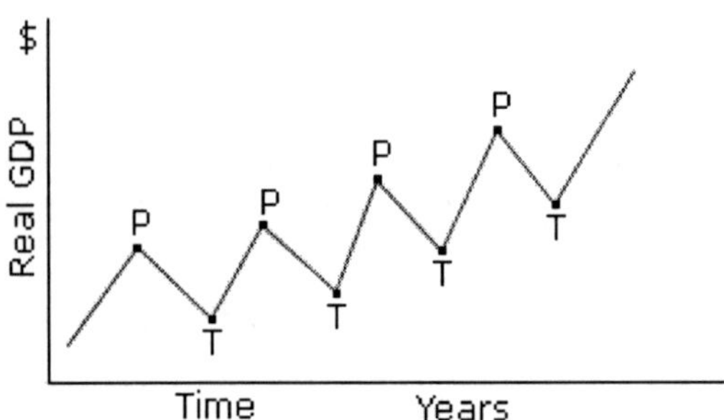

II. Components of Business Cycle

II. Components of Business Cycle -- The following terms are used to refer to components of the business cycle:

A. Peak -- A point in the economic cycle that marks the end of rising aggregate output and the beginning of a decline in output. (Ps in the graph).

B. Trough -- A point in the economic cycle that marks the end of a decline in aggregate output and the beginning of an increase in output. (Ts in the graph).

C. Economic Expansion or Expansionary Period -- Periods during which aggregate output is increasing. (Periods from T to P in the graph).

D. Economic Contraction or Recessionary Period -- Periods during which aggregate output is decreasing. (Periods from P to T in the graph).

III. Primary Cause of Business Cycles -- While no single theory fully explains the causes and characteristics of business cycles, a major cause is changes in business investment spending (i.e., on plant, equipment, etc.) and consumer spending on durable goods (i.e., on goods used over multiple periods, like major appliances, automobiles, etc.). The effects of such declines in spending are shown as follows (assuming the Keynesian supply curve):

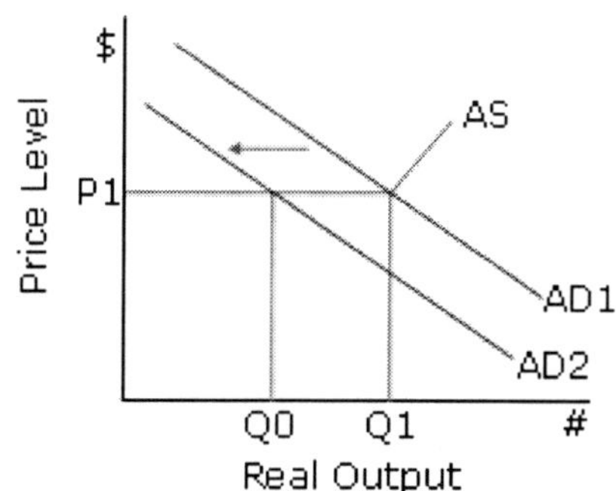

A. If the economy is in equilibrium at AD1 = AS, quantity Q1 will be produced and resources (labor, plant, and equipment, etc.) are being fully utilized. A decrease in investment and consumer spending causes demand to shift to AD2 and real output drops to Q0. The period during which output declines is recessionary and results in less than full utilization of economic resources. Unemployment will increase and plant and equipment will be underutilized.

B. As previously noted, declines in consumer and business spending may be caused by such factors as:

1. Taxes increase;
2. Confidence in the economy declines;
3. Interest rates rise and/or borrowing becomes more difficult.

IV. Leading and Lagging Indicators of Business Cycles

A. In an effort to anticipate changes in the business cycle, economists and business groups have attempted to establish relationships between changes in the business cycle and other measures of economic activity that occur before a change in the business cycle. These measures of economic activity (which change before the aggregate business cycle) are called "leading indicators" and include measures of:

1. Consumer expectations;
2. Initial claims for unemployment;
3. Weekly manufacturing hours;
4. Stock prices;
5. Building permits;
6. New orders for consumer goods;
7. Real money supply.

B. Measures of economic activity associated with changes in the business cycle, but which occur after changes in the business cycle, are called lagging or trailing indicators. These lagging indicators are used to confirm elements of business cycle timing and magnitude. Lagging indicators include measures of:

1. Changes in labor cost per unit of output;
2. Ratio of inventories to sales;
3. Duration of unemployment;
4. Commercial loans outstanding;
5. Ratio of consumer installment credit to personal income.

Price Levels & Inflation/Deflation

Price is the money amount used to measure the value of goods and services. The money amounts (or prices) change over time. This lesson describes how changing prices, or different price levels, can be adjusted to a common level, how changes in the price level results in inflation or deflation, and the consequences of inflation on economic activity.

I. **Changes --** Changes in prices and price levels over time will cause changes in various measures of economic activity and economic outcomes. For example, earlier we saw that changing price levels created the need for a measure of gross domestic product (GDP) adjusted for changing price levels, called real GDP. Adjustments to squeeze out the effects of changing price levels on economic measures are accomplished using price indexes (or indices).

II. **Price indexes --** convert prices of each period to what those prices would be in terms of prices of a specific prior (or sometimes subsequent) reference period. Mathematically, the price of the reference period is set equal to 100 (100%) and the price of other periods is measured as a percent of the reference (or base) period. Commonly used indexes prepared by the Bureau of Labor Statistics (BLS) are:

   A. **Consumer Price Index (CPI-U) --** The Consumer Price Index for All Urban Consumers (published monthly) relates the prices paid by all urban consumers for a "basket" of goods and services during a period to the price of the "basket" in a prior reference period. The current reference period for CPI-U is the 36-month average of prices for 1982-84. The average prices in that period are taken as 100. Prices in subsequent periods are measured as percentage changes related to that base period.

   B. For example, the CPI-Us for November 2004 and 2005 were:

	CPI- U
Annual, 2004	188.9
Annual, 2005	195.3

   C. The Annual 2004 index of 188.9 indicates that prices (in the CPI-U basket) were 88.9% higher in Annual 2004 than they were during the 1982-84 base period.

   D. For the period Annual 2004 through Annual 2005 the CPI-U went from 188.9 to 195.3. The change for the period is 6.4 (195.3 - 188.9), but the rate of change would be computed as (195.3 - 188.9)/188.9 = 3.38%, which is the rate of inflation (price increases) for the period Annual 2004 through Annual 2005.

   E. **Wholesale Price Index (WPI) --** The WPI relates the prices paid for a "basket" of raw materials, intermediate goods, and finished goods at the wholesale level to prices for comparable goods in a reference (base) period. The calculations are done in the same manner as for the CPI-U index.

   F. **Gross Domestic Product (GDP) Deflator --** The GDP Deflator relates nominal GDP to real GDP (both as previously defined), and is the most comprehensive measure of price level since GDP includes not only consumer and business spending, but also government spending and net exports.

   G. The calculation is:

(Nominal GDP/Real GDP) x 100 = GDP Deflator

III. Inflation and Deflation -- Inflation (or inflation rate) is the annual rate of increase in the price level; deflation (or deflation rate) is the annual rate of decrease in the price level. The most common yardstick used to measure inflation or deflation in the U.S. is the CPI-U. Although there have been month-to-month decreases in the CPI-U (i.e., deflation), most recently in November 2003, the U.S. has experienced annual inflation since the 1930s.

A. There are two fundamental causes of inflation, one related to demand, the other related to supply.

1. Demand-induced (demand-pull) inflation -- Results when levels of aggregate spending for goods and services exceeds the productive capacity of the economy at full employment. As a consequence, the excess demand pulls up prices.

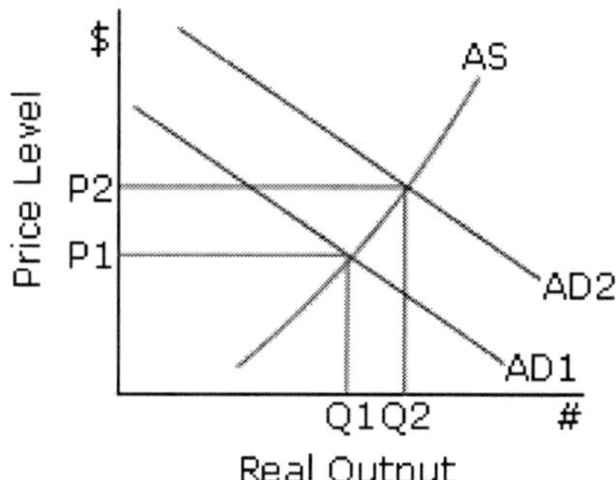

2. If demand exceeds Q1 at price level P1, the excess demand (AD1 to AD2) increases the price level and, generally, the quantity produced (to P2 and Q2).

B. Supply-induced (cost-push or supply-push) inflation -- Results from increases in the cost of inputs to the production process - raw materials, labor, taxes, etc. - which are passed on to the final buyer in the form of higher prices.

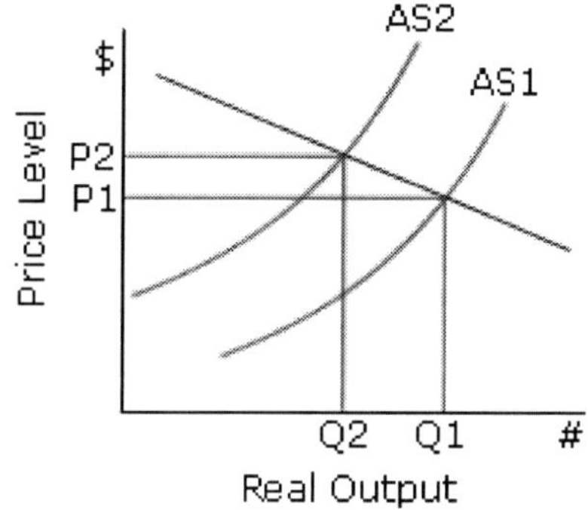

C. An increase in the cost of inputs (say, oil) shifts aggregate supply from AS1 to AS2. As a result, the price level increases and, generally, output decreases causing unemployment to increase.

D. Generally, deflation would result under conditions of greatly reduced demand and/or significantly lower cost of input resources.

IV. Consequences of Inflation

A. The occurrence of inflation, especially when unanticipated, usually has significant economic consequences. Major consequences include:

1. **Lower current wealth and lower future real income --** As a result of inflation, monetary items (those fixed in dollar amount) lose purchasing power. Consumers on fixed incomes, or those with incomes that don't keep pace with inflation, will reduce consumption. Similarly, creditors being repaid with fixed number of dollars will be able to purchase less with those dollars. The effect of less consumption is a reduction in aggregate demand leading to lower output and higher unemployment.
2. **Higher interest rates --** In order to offset declines in purchasing power derived from loans, creditors increase interest rates. Higher interest rates increase the cost of borrowing which reduces both consumer spending and business investment in capital goods. Further, lenders may tighten loan requirements and, thereby, squeeze marginal borrowers out of the market, which also would reduce spending.
3. **Uncertainty of economic measures --** The changing real value of the dollar makes it an uncertain measure for making economic decisions. Price increases create uncertainty about future costs, prices, profitability, and cash flows. As a consequence, individuals and businesses are likely to postpone investments, which in turn, reduce current demand and future productive capacity.

B. Because inflation has significant adverse consequence for the economy, control of inflation is a primary economic objective of government fiscal and monetary policy.

Money, Banking & Monetary Policy

The use of money is central to contemporary economic activity. The management of the money supply is essential to accomplishing desired aggregate economic outcomes. This lesson describes the role of money, measures of money, and management of the money supply in the U.S. economy.

I. **Overview --** As shown in the free market model, money flows from business firms to individuals for economic resources, and from individuals to business firms for goods and services. Thus, money is central to economic activity. In the U.S. the Federal Reserve System (the Fed) manages the money supply and regulates the banking system. Through its management of the money supply, and related activities, the Fed can exercise significant influence over elements of the economy.

II. **Money**

   A. Money serves multiple functions in the economy, including as:

      1. A medium of exchange-money is accepted as a means of payment by buyers and sellers in exchanges of goods and services.

      2. A measure of value-money is a common denominator for assigning value to diverse goods and services and, therefore, for measuring economic activity.

      3. A store of value-money retains value over time (although often with some loss of purchasing power), therefore it can be saved for use in the future.

   B. Conventionally, money is considered to consist of paper currency and coins. For economic purposes, however, money is comprised of a variety of financial items. The Federal Reserve System provides three definitions (and measures) of money for the U.S. economy:

      1. **M1 --** Includes paper and coin currency held outside banks and check-writing deposits. This is the narrowest definition of money and is based on including instruments used for transactions.

         a. The U.S. paper currency takes the form of Federal Reserve notes. These notes ("dollar" bills of various denomination) have no intrinsic value in that they do not represent a claim to any specific commodity (e.g. gold). Rather, their value derives from the good faith and credit of the U.S. government.

         b. Check-writing deposits are amounts held by banks, savings and loans, and credit unions for which ownership can be transferred by writing a check.

      2. **M2 --** Includes M1 items plus savings deposits, money-market deposit accounts, certificates of deposit (less than $100,000), individual-owned money-market mutual funds, and certain other deposits. This measure of money is the primary focus of Fed actions to influence the economy.

      3. **M3 --** Includes M2 items plus certificates of deposit (greater than $100,000), institutional-owned money-market mutual funds and certain other deposits.

III. **Banking System**

   A. The U.S. does not have a central bank, but rather a central banking system, the Federal Reserve System, consisting of:

      1. **Board of Governors --** The seven-member policy-making body of the Federal Reserve System.

2. **Federal Open Market Committee --** The 12-member body responsible for implementing monetary policy through open-market operations to affect the money supply (M1).

3. **Federal Reserve Banks --** The twelve district banks, each responsible for a specific geographical area of the U.S. Within their area, each federal bank supervises, regulates, and examines member institutions, provides currency to and clears checks for those institutions, and holds reserves and lends to those institutions. The Federal Reserve Banks are owned by its member institutions, but they operate under uniform policies of the Federal Reserve System. Member institutions, which function as financial intermediaries, include:

    a. Commercial banks;

    b. Savings and loan associations;

    c. Mutual savings banks;

    d. Credit Unions.

B. Individual, business firms, and other entities deal with these financial intermediaries, but not directly with the Federal Reserve Banks.

IV. Monetary Policy

A. Monetary policy is concerned with managing the money supply to achieve national economic objectives, including economic growth and price level stability. The Federal Reserve System can regulate the money supply (exercise monetary policy) in a number of ways:

1. **Reserve-requirement changes --** A bank's ability to issue check-writing deposits is limited by a reserve-requirement by the Fed on check-writing deposits. Simply put, loans made by banks are paid to borrowers by checks drawn on the lending bank. For every dollar of such checks issued as loans, the bank must have a required amount held as a reserve, either at the bank or on deposit at a Federal Reserve Bank.

Example:
Assume the reserve requirement established by the Fed is 10% (a real reserve-requirement in recent years). A bank would be required to have $1.00 in reserves for every $10.00 it loans. By changing the reserve requirement the Fed can influence greatly the check-writing deposits by banks.

    a. By decreasing (or increasing) the reserve requirement on check-writing deposits the Fed enables banks to increase (or requires them to decrease) the amount of loans the bank can make using check-writing deposits, and thus increase (or decrease) M1 money supply. Decreasing the requirement would affect monetary easing; increasing the requirement would affect monetary tightening.

2. **Open-Market Operations --** The Fed engages in open-market operations by purchasing and selling U.S. Treasury debt obligations (e.g., Treasury Bonds) from/to banks. The effect of purchasing Treasury obligations is to replace debt held by banks with additional reserves for the banks. The increase in reserves permits additional check-writing deposits (i.e., lending ability) by the banks. Sale of Treasury obligations has the opposite effect. Thus, open-market purchasing implements monetary easing; open-market sales implements monetary tightening.

a. Open-market operations is one of the preferred methods of changing the money supply because it permits changes of various degrees.

3. **Discount Rate --** The rate of interest banks pay when they borrow from a Federal Reserve Bank in order to maintain reserve requirements is called the "discount rate." Borrowing from a Fed bank increases a bank's reserves with the Fed because the borrowing is credited to the banks reserve with the Fed, not withdrawn from the Fed bank. As a result of increased reserves, banks are able to increase loans. By increasing or decreasing the discount rate, the Fed encourages or discourages borrowing from the Fed and, thereby, eases or tightens the money supply.

   a. The Fed intent in making changes in the discount rate is to keep it at an appropriate "spread" below other rates available to banks. Therefore, changes in the discount rate usually follow changes in the short-term rate of interest in the broad market. As a consequence, changes in the discount rate, which are widely publicized, signal Fed expectations about interest rates. For example, if the Fed increases the discount rate to maintain an appropriate spread with rising rates in the market, this tends to confirm that the Fed expects general interest rates to remain at the higher level.

B. **Changes in the money supply (M1)**, especially when accomplished through open-market operations, will affect short-term interest rates (*ceteris paribus*). For example, if other factors are held constant, an increase in M1 money supply will lower the short-term interest rate in the market. This can be shown as follows:

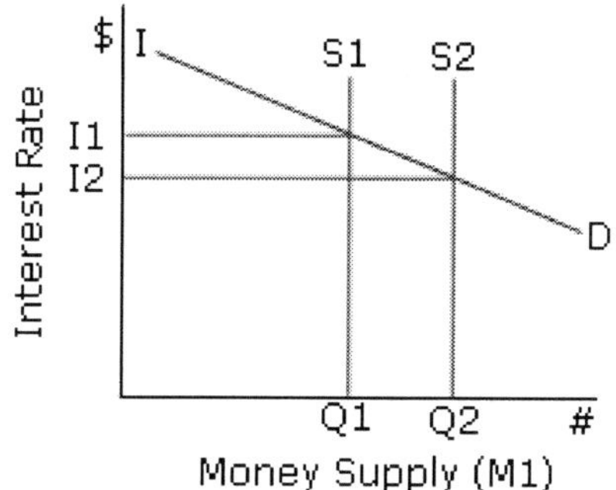

1. D represents the demand for money. If the supply of money increases from Q1 to Q2, the interest rate drops from I1 to I2. At a lower interest rate, individuals and businesses are more likely to borrow to finance purchase of high cost items (e.g. cars, houses, property, plant and equipment, etc.). The increase in demand (supported by more borrowing) will spur production, increase employment and raise GDP.

V. Fiscal and Monetary Policy Summary

A. Both fiscal and monetary policy provide means for the government to influence aggregate spending (demand). Fiscal policy is implemented through changes in government spending and/or taxes. Monetary policy is implemented primarily through control of the money supply. Thus, for example, governmental efforts to increase aggregate spending (and reduce unemployment, increase GDP, etc.) would include:

Action	Policy Type
Increase government spending	Fiscal
Reduce taxes	Fiscal
Increase money supply	Monetary

B. To reign-in aggregate spending the reverse types of action would be implemented. While the general effect of each type of policy action is known, the timing and net effects of the alternative forms of action are less certain.

1. **Lag-Time Element --** There are differences in how quickly the alternative forms of policy can be implemented and how quickly economic activity will be affected. Changes in fiscal policy of significant magnitude generally require congressional approval and may be delayed (or never approved) if there is not agreement by members of Congress. Once approved, however, changes in government spending can be implemented quickly and with almost immediate impact on demand. Changes in tax rates, once approved, have less immediate impact and a less certain magnitude of influence.
2. Generally, changes in monetary policy can be made more quickly than fiscal policy because monetary policy is changed by the Federal Reserve Board, not by Congress. Once approved, monetary policy has an almost immediate effect on the interest rate, but the full effect on spending may not occur immediately because of the time lags inherent in "ramping-up" (or "ramping-down") large-scale projects commonly sensitive to changes in the interest rate.
3. Of the two approaches, monetary policy has been the primary approach to achieving economic objectives. Changes can be approved more quickly to respond to changing economic circumstances and monetary policy changes have fewer artificial influences on the economy. Fiscal policy, on the other hand, causes a redistribution of output and income.

International Economics

International Economic Activity

Economic activity occurs not only at the individual, market, and national levels, but also at the international level. This lesson addresses the reasons for international economic activity.

I. **Overview --** The U.S. economy (and that of most other nations) is not a closed system, but rather is connected (open) to the economies of many other nations through trade, investment, and other financial activities. These international economic relationships provide important benefits to, and create challenges for, not only the national economy, but also for entities engaged in international economic activities.

II. **Important Reasons**

   A. There are a number of reasons entities seek to benefit from international economic activities. Among the most important are the following:

      1. To develop new markets for the sale of goods and services abroad. Exports increase demand, which raises output, revenues, and employment, thus benefiting both firms engaged in export activities and national economic measures.

      2. To obtain commodities not otherwise available in the U.S., or available only in limited supply. Certain raw materials, like tin, tungsten, and tea, are available only from foreign sources. Other important goods, like oil, are available domestically only in limited supply which must be supplemented with substantial imports. To obtain these economic resources, in the quantities needed, firms must import commodities from other countries (economies).

      3. To obtain goods and services at lower costs than are available in the U.S. Although certain goods and services may be available domestically, they cost more than if acquired in a foreign country. Thus, in a completely open system, entities will acquire economic resources from the lowest cost provider, wherever located.

III. **Comparative Advantage**

   A. From an international economics perspective, the ability of one country (A) to produce a good or service at a lower cost (or with lower opportunity cost) relative to what the good or service would cost in another country (B) is the "comparative advantage" of country A to provide the particular goods or service. Comparative advantage in the production of goods and services derives from differences in the availability of economic resources, including labor and technology, among nations.

Issues at National Level

While international economic activity benefits the national economy, it also creates issues for the national economy. This lesson considers matters that revolve around socio-political issues and balance of payment issues.

I. Socio-Political Issues

A. It is often argued that international trade causes or exacerbates certain domestic social and economic problems, including:

1. Unemployment resulting from the direct or indirect use of "cheap" foreign labor;
2. Loss of certain basic manufacturing capabilities;
3. Reduction of industries essential to national defense;
4. Lack of domestic protection for start-up industries.

B. Political responses to such concerns have taken the form of:

1. Import quotas, which restrict the quantity of goods that can be imported;
2. Import tariffs, which tax imported goods and thereby increase their cost.

C. Such forms of protectionism generally are inappropriate because they are based on economic misconceptions or because there are more appropriate fiscal and monetary policy responses.

II. Balance of Payments Issues

A. The U.S. balance of payments is a summary accounting of all U.S. transactions with all other nations for a calendar year. The U.S. reports international activity in three main accounts:

1. **Current Account --** Reports the dollar value of amounts earned from export of goods and services, amounts spent on import of goods and services, and government grants to foreign entities, and the resulting net (export or import) balance.
2. **Capital Account --** Reports the dollar amount of inflows from investments and loans by foreign entities, amount of outflows from investments and loans U.S. entities made abroad, and the resulting net balance.
3. **Official Reserve Account --** Reports the net dollar amount that results from the Current Account and the Capital Account taken together.
    - **a.** When the sum of earnings and inflows exceeds the sum of spending and outflows, a balance of payment surplus exists. This surplus would result in an increase in U.S. reserves of foreign currency or in a decrease in foreign government holdings of U.S. currency.
    - **b.** When the sum of spending and outflows exceeds the sum of earnings and inflows, a balance of payment deficit exits. This deficit would result in a decrease in U.S. holding of foreign currency reserves or in an increase in foreign government holdings of U.S. Currency.

B. A deficit in the U.S. balance of payments means that U.S. entities have a combined amount of imports and investments made abroad that exceeds the combined amount of exports and investments made in the U.S. by foreign entities. As a consequence, the U.S. demand for foreign currencies will exceed the amount of foreign currencies provided by U.S. exports and foreign investment in the U.S., and (other things remaining equal) the exchange rates between the dollar and other currencies will rise (i.e., the value of the dollar relative to other currencies will fall).

Issues at Entity Level

Exchange Rate Issue

At the entity level, a primary issue for firms involved in international economic activities is the uncertainty associated with foreign currency exchange rates. This lesson defines exchange rate, risks associated with exchange rates, and how hedging can be used to mitigate those risks.

I. **Exchange Rate --** While exchange rates create issues for the national economy, for individual entities engaged in international trade and investment activities, exchange rates are central in determining the success or failure of their international activities.

> **Definition:**
>
> *Currency Exchange Rate*: The exchange rate is the price of one unit of a country's currency expressed in units of another country's currency.

A. It may be expressed as:

1. **Direct exchange rate --** the domestic price of one unit of a foreign currency. For example: 1 Euro = $1.10;
2. **Indirect exchange rate --** the foreign price of one domestic unit of currency. For example: $1.00 = .909 Euro.

II. **Exchange Rate Determination**

A. In 1944, delegates from 45 nations meeting in Bretton Woods, New Hampshire reached agreement (Bretton Woods Agreement) to establish a post-war international monetary system, including fixed currency exchange rates. The fixed exchange rate system remained in operation until 1973, when it was abandoned and replaced by a system of floating exchange rates. The worldwide exchange system in operation today is not completely free-floating because monetary authorities in one country can and do intervene in the exchange markets of other countries so as to influence exchange rates. Nevertheless, the current exchange system is largely determined by aggregate demand and supply for a currency.

B. A number of factors play a role in determining the demand for a country's currency and, therefore, in determining a country's exchange rate with other countries. Five of the major factors are:

1. **Political and Economic Environment --** Currencies of countries that are politically stable and economically strong are more desirable than are the currencies of countries with political turmoil and a risky economic environment. For example, investors are more likely to make investments in a politically stable country with a history of strong economic performance than in a country with political unrest and a fragile economy.
2. **Relative Interest Rates --** The interest rates in a country relative to the rates in other countries will influence the exchange rates between the currency of that country and the currencies of other countries. If the interest rate in one country is higher than the rate in another country, foreign capital will flow into the country with the higher interest rate to earn the higher return. The exchange rate for the currency of the country with the higher interest rate will tend to be higher relative to the currency of the country with the lower interest rate.

3. **Relative Inflation --** The inflation rate in one country relative to the rates in other countries will influence the exchange rates between the currency of that country and the currencies of the other countries. If the inflation rate in one country is consistently lower than the rate in another country, the purchasing power in the country with the lower inflation rate will be higher relative to the purchasing power in the other country. The currency which better retains its purchasing power tends to increase in value relative to currencies of economies with higher inflation.

4. **Public Debt Level --** The level of deficit spending and the resulting level of public debt of a country influences the exchange rate between the currency of that country and the currencies of other countries. A country with a high level of public debt is likely to experience inflation, which will deter foreign investment and, thereby, weaken the country's currency relative to other currencies. Further, if government services its debt by increasing the money supply (called "monetizing debt"), even higher inflation will occur, causing a further decline in the country's currency exchange rate with other currencies.

5. **Current Account Balance --** The current account balance (in the Balance of Payments measure) of a country influences the exchange rate between the currency of that country and the currencies of other countries. A deficit in the current account of a country shows that it is spending more on foreign trade and related payments than it is receiving from foreign trading partners. This excess spending means that the country has a greater demand for foreign currencies than is demanded for the domestic currency by the foreign partners. This excess demand for foreign currencies will lower the country???s exchange rate with countries which have a favorable (net positive) current account balance with it.

C. These factors , and other generally less important factors, each play a role in determining the exchange rate of a country's currency with currencies of other countries. These factors are both interrelated and of varying relative importance over time. Therefore, the exact role of each often is difficult to measure at any particular time.

III. Exchange Rate Risk

A. Entities that engage in foreign trade and investments face the risk associated with changes in the exchange rate, a risk not encountered in domestic transactions. Foreign activity may be in the form of:

1. Importing (buying);
2. Exporting (selling);
3. Borrowing or Lending with a foreign entity;
4. Investing in a foreign investment.

B. When an entity engages in these activities and the transactions are settled (denominated) at a later date in a foreign currency, the number of dollars (the dollar amount) received or paid will change as the exchange rate between the currencies changes. A change in exchange rate may have a positive or negative effect on financial results.

1. **Import Illustration**

   a. Assume: On 10/15/05 a U.S. entity purchases goods (an import transaction) from a foreign supplier for 500,000 units of the foreign currency with terms of net 60. The relevant exchange rates between the dollar and the foreign currency (FC) are:

10/15/05 1 FC = $.75
12/14/05 1 FC = $.72

b. If the goods had been paid for at the date of purchase, 10/15, dollar cost would have been 500,000 FC x $.75 = $375,000. However, because the U.S. entity deferred payment (had a payable) and the exchange rate changed from $.75 to $.72 per FC unit, the dollar cost at date of payment (12/14) was 500,000 FC x $.72 = $360,000. In this case, the exchange rate change resulted in a benefit of $15,000, because the dollar strengthened relative to the foreign currency.

2. **Export Illustration**

a. Assume: On 9/18/05 a U.S. entity sells merchandise to a foreign buyer for 300,000 units of the foreign currency with terms net 90. The relevant exchange rates between the dollar and the foreign currency (FC) are:

9/8/05 1 FC = $1.18
12/17/05 1 FC = $1.10

b. If the U.S. entity had sold the goods for cash, it would have collected 300,000 FC x $1.18 = $354,000. However, because the U.S. entity extended payment terms (had a receivable) and the exchange rate changed from $1.18 to $1.10, the dollars received at date of collection (12/17) was 300,000 FC x $1.10 = $330,000. In this case, the exchange rate change resulted in a loss of $24,000 because the dollar strengthened relative to the foreign currency.

3. **Investment Illustration**

a. Assume: On 4/1/05 a U.S. entity purchases shares of a foreign company's securities as an investment for 1,500,000 units of the foreign currency. The U.S. entity sells the investment 11/14/03 for 1,600,000 units of the foreign currency. The relevant exchange rates between the dollar and the foreign currency (FC) are:

4/1/05 1 FC = $.95
11/14/05 1 FC = $.90

b. The collar cost of the investment on 4/1 was 1,500,000 FC x $.95 = $1,425,000 (excluding any transaction costs). The investment was sold on 11/14 for 1,600,000 FC, a gain of 100,000 FC units. However, because the exchange rate changed from $.95 to $.90, the dollar amount received from the sale is 1,600,000 FC x $.90 = $1,440,000, resulting in a dollar gain of only $15,000. In this case, the exchange rate change resulted in a reduction in the dollar amount received of $80,000 (1,600,000 FC x $.05).

IV. Hedging Exchange Rate Risks

A. An entity can avoid the risk associated with changing exchange rates by engaging only in dollar denominated transactions. The international nature of business, however, requires that firms of any significant size conduct business with foreign entities, often in terms of a foreign currency. Therefore, rather than avoid currency risk entirely, firms seek to minimize the degree of risk associated with such activity.

B. The risk associated with a change in exchange rates can be mitigated with hedging. Hedging is a risk management strategy which involves using offsetting (or contra) transactions so that a loss on one transaction would be offset (at least in part) by a gain on another transaction (and vice versa).

1. You would "hedge a bet" by offsetting a possible loss from betting on one team to win by also betting on the other team to win.
2. You would hedge against a possible loss in the dollar value of a foreign currency to be received in the future by selling that foreign currency now at a specified rate for delivery when you receive it in the future.

V. Illustration of a hedge (simplified)

A. Facts: Assume a U.S. entity provides services to a German entity and agrees to accept 100,000 Euros (E) in payment. The services are completed and the Germany company is billed on March 1, 20X1 with payment due in 90 days, on May 29. At 3/1 the spot and 90 day forward exchange rates are both 1 E = $1.10. Thus, at 3/1 the dollar value of revenue is $110,000 (100,000 E X $1.10 spot rate = $110,000). Since the US entity will receive 100,000 E in 90 days, it decides to hedge the risk that 100,000 E will not be worth (exchange for) $110,000 at that time (5/29/X1). To execute the hedge, on 3/1/X1 it enters into a forward exchange contract to sell 100,000 E to an International Bank for delivery on 5/29/X1. Between 3/1 and 5/29 the Euro weakens against the dollar so that the spot exchange rate on 5/29 is 1 E = $1.05.

B. Entries made by the US entity to record transactions related to the hedged item (receivable from sale of services) and the hedge (forward exchange contract) would be:

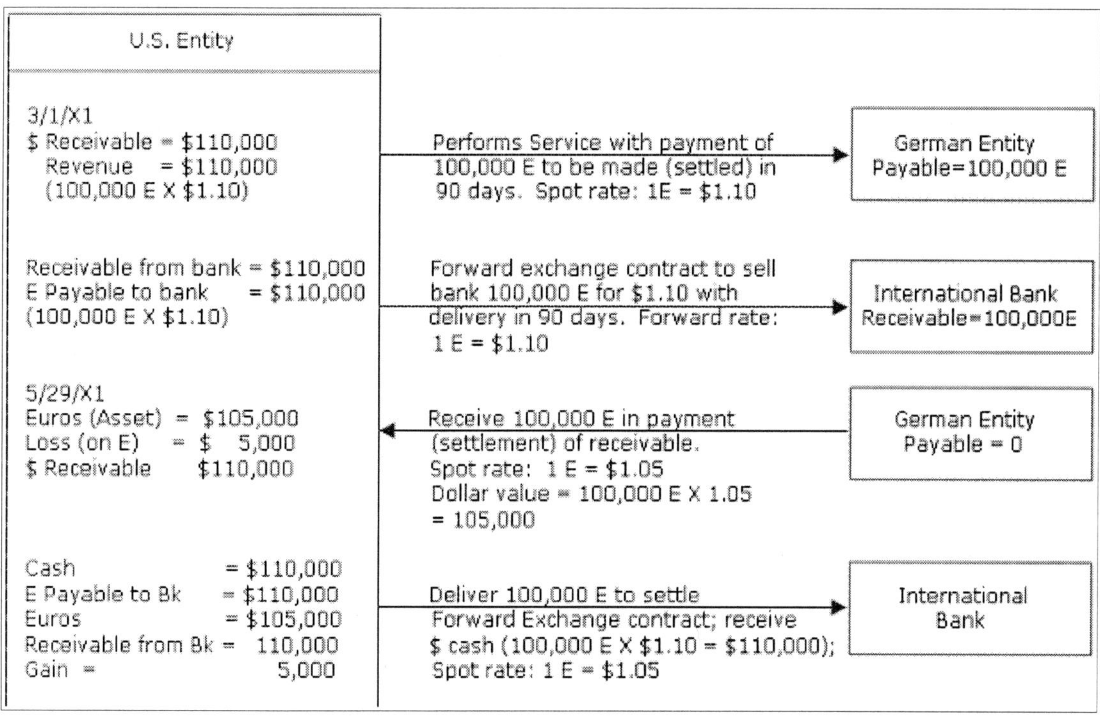

C. The net effect of the hedged item (receivable) and the hedge (forward contract) is:

Loss on Receivable	$5,000
Gain on Hedge Contract	5,000
Net Loss/Gain	-0-

D. Comments on the Illustration: The illustration above has been simplified to highlight the basic nature of a hedge. Simplifications include: (a) assuming spot rate and forward rate are the same on 3/1/X1, (2) initiation and settlement of the hedged item and the hedge within the same fiscal period, and (3) ignoring other costs which may be associated with the hedge.

E. Hedging minimizes or prevents losses from exchange rate changes (per se), but usually involve some costs of doing so, including:

1. fees or other changes imposed by the other party to the forward contract; and
2. differences between spot rates and forward rates at the date the forward contract is initiated.

VI. Foreign Currency Hedging

A. **A foreign currency hedge is the hedge of an exposure to changes in the dollar value of assets or liabilities (including certain investments) and planned transactions, which are denominated (to be settled) in a foreign currency.**

B. An entity may **hedge the foreign currency exposure** of the following kinds:

1. **Forecasted foreign-currency-denominated transactions --** (including inter-company transactions) The risk being hedged is the risk that exchange rate changes will have an effect on the cash flow from non-firm, but planned transactions to be settled in a foreign currency. For example, the dollar value of royalty revenue forecasted to be received in a foreign currency from a foreign entity.
2. **Unrecognized firm commitments --** The risk being hedged is the risk that exchange rate changes will have an effect on the fair value of firm commitments for a future sale or purchase to be settled in a foreign currency. For example, a commitment (contract) to purchase custom-built equipment from a foreign manufacturer with payment to be made in a foreign currency.
3. **Foreign-currency-denominated recognized assets --** (e.g., receivables) **or liabilities** (e.g., payables). The risk being hedged is the fair value or cash flow, measured in dollars, of an already booked asset or liability to be settled in a foreign currency. The dollar value of such assets and liabilities may change as a result of changes in the foreign exchange rate between recognition and settlement of the asset or liability.
4. **Investments in available-for-sale securities --** The risk being hedged is the risk that exchange rate changes will have an effect on the fair value of investments in available-for-sale securities denominated in a foreign currency.
5. **Net investments in foreign operations --** The risk being hedged is the risk that exchange rate changes will have an effect on the fair (economic) value of financial statements converted from a foreign currency to the functional currency.

Note:
The accounting treatments for these foreign currency hedging purposes are discussed in detail in the FARE unit on "Foreign Currency Accounting".

VII. Foreign Currency Hedging Instruments -- Foreign currency hedging is accomplished primarily through the use of forward contracts. Forward contracts are agreements (contracts) to buy or sell (or which give the right to buy or sell) a specified commodity in the future at a price (rate) determined at the time the forward contract is executed. The most important types of forward contracts are:

A. Foreign Currency Forward Exchange Contracts (FCFX): an agreement to buy or sell a specified amount of a foreign currency at a specified future date at a specified (forward) rate.

1. Under an FCFX contract the obligation to buy or sell is firm; the exchange must occur.
2. This contract is an "exchange" because the contract provides for trading (exchanging) one currency for another currency. Example: A U.S. entity enters into a FCFX to pay U.S. dollars for Euros.

B. Foreign Currency Option Contracts (FCO): an agreement which gives the right (option) to buy (call option) or sell (put option) a specified amount of a foreign currency at a specified (forward) rate during or at the end of a specified time period.

1. Under an FCO contract, the party holding the option has the right (option) to buy (call) or sell (put), but does not have to exercise that option; the exchange will occur at the option of the option holder. Example: A U.S. entity acquires an option (right) to buy Euros, but does not have to buy the Euros.
2. If the option is exercised, there is an exchange of currencies.
3. FCO contracts usually involve fees which make them significantly more costly to execute than FCFX contracts.

C. FCFXs and FCOs are financial instruments.

Transfer Price Issue

A second major issue for firms involved in international economic activity revolves around the use of transfer prices for activities which cross international borders. This lesson defines transfer price, the tax consequences of setting transfer prices, and methods of determining appropriate transfer prices.

I. For multinational entities transfer pricing often relates to the transfer of goods and services across international borders. Establishing transfer pricing policies is an important function for multinational entities because it determines, in part, the allocation of profits among affiliated units and, therefore, among different taxing jurisdictions with different tax rates. By manipulating transfer prices entities can avoid taxes in countries with higher rates and thereby increase profits. In addition, transfer prices are likely to have implications for performance evaluation and related motivational issues.

Definition:

Transfer Price: The amount (price) at which goods or services are transferred between affiliated entities

II. Effects of setting different transfer prices -- The following examples illustrate the effects of setting different transfer prices for the same goods.

A. Assume -- Company P, located in the U.S., owns controlling interest in Company S, located in a foreign country. The respective tax rates are:

Co.P (U.S.)	50%
Co. S (Foreign)	20%

B. Company S buys or produces goods for $100. These goods are sold (transferred) to Company P, which sells the goods to a third-party for $300. Before tax consolidated income is $200 ($300 - $100), but after tax income depends on the amount of income recognized in each of the two countries, which is determined by the price at which the goods are transferred from Company S to Company P.

1. Example 1 -- Transfer Price = $200

	Co. S Original Cost		Co.S to Co.P Transfer Price		Co. P Selling Price	Totals
	$100.00		$200		$300	
Pretax Profit		$100		$100		$200
Tax Rate		.20		.50		
Tax		$ 20		$ 50		$ 70
After Tax Profit		$ 80		$ 50		$130

2. **Example 2** -- Transfer Price = $250

	Co. S Original Cost		Co.S to Co.P Transfer Price		Co P. Selling Price	Totals
	$100		$250		$300	
Pretax Profit		$150		$50		$200
Tax Rate		.20		.50		
Tax		$ 30		$25		$ 55
After Tax Profit		$120		$25		$145

C. As shown in the two examples above, a transfer price of $200 results in a combined income of $130, whereas a transfer price of $250 results in a combined income of $145, an increase of $15, or more than 10%. That increase was achieved without any change in operations or other procedures. It resulted from simply changing the transfer price between affiliated entities. Insofar as international entities have discretion in setting transfer prices, they can manipulate the country in which revenue is recognized and, thereby, taxes incurred and profit reported.

III. Determining Transfer Price

A. In the U.S., guidance on the appropriate allocation of income between entities under common control, and therefore appropriate transfer pricing, is provided by the Internal Revenue Code (Sec. 482). That guidance provides that income should be allocated based on the functions performed and the risks assumed by each of the entities involved in such transactions. Transfer pricing guidelines also are provided by the Organization for Economic Co-operation and Development (OECD), an international body with representatives from 30-member nations. The OECD guidelines embody transfer pricing based on the principle of arm's length transactions.

B. In practice, transfer prices are determined using a variety of methods, including:

1. **Cost** -- Where the transfer price is a function of the cost to the selling unit.
    a. Commonly used when no external market exists for the good or service.
    b. Less costly implement than a negotiated price.
2. **Market Price** -- Where the transfer price is based on the price of the good or service in the market (if available).
    a. Commonly used when an external market for the good or services exists.
    b. Typically a valid "arms-length" basis for transfer price.
3. **Negotiated Price** -- Where the transfer price is based on a negotiated agreement between buying and selling affiliates.
    a. Commonly used when no external market exists for the good or service.
    b. May be more costly to implement than a predetermined cost-based transfer price.

C. In addition to its role in determining the total profit of firms with multinational operations, transfer pricing also affects the profit reported by the individual affiliated units. Because unit profit is usually used to evaluate the unit's management, individual unit managers may prefer a transfer price that is different than the price which maximizes total profit to the consolidated entities. Therefore, the transfer pricing methodology used by multinational firms is important not only to profit determination, but also to performance throughout the multinational entity.

Introduction to Financial Management

This lesson defines financial management and provides a summary of the material covered in the Financial Management subsection of CPAexcel.

I. Financial Management

A. This Financial Management area accounts for 17% - 23% of the Business Environment and Concepts section of the CPA Exam.

B. This unit begins by consideration of selected concepts and tools that are widely used in business, but which are particularly relevant in financial management applications. These concepts and tools can be used in various financial management applications.

C. This area covers materials concerned with:

1. Concepts and tools that are especially appropriate to financial management, including certain concepts of cost, time value of money concepts and calculations, and various interest rate concepts and calculations.
2. Financial modeling applications, especially as applied to capital budgeting decisions.
3. Alternatives for short-term and long-term financing and appropriate financing strategies, including consideration of related risk-reward trade-offs and the cost of capital.
4. Techniques for working capital management.
5. Use of ratios and other measures to assess effectiveness.
6. Summary of different kinds of risks faced in the business environment.

Cost Concepts

Cost is a measure of the money amount given up or the obligation incurred to acquire a resource. In this lesson different concepts of cost are identified, described and illustrated.

I. **Overview --** Cost is the monetary measure of a resource; it is the money amount paid or obligation incurred for a good or service. Many different types and classifications of cost are distinguished and used for business purposes. Certain of these distinctions are especially important for financial management.

II. **Cost vs. Expense**

A. Cost and expense are not the same concept. While cost is the amount paid for a resource (or asset), expense is the portion of cost that relates to the portion of the resource (or asset) that has been used up. As described in FASB Statement of Concepts No. 6, "...the value of cash or other resources given up (or the present value of an obligation incurred) in exchange for a resource measures the cost of the resource acquired." Expenses result from using up acquired resources and are measured as the portion of the cost of a resource that has been used up.

B. While cost and expense for a resource can occur simultaneously and be of the same amount, the two concepts are different and in the short-run, their amounts can be different for the same resource. The following diagrams illustrate the differences and relationship between the concepts using assumed amounts:

C. Cost and Expense Occurring at Different Times and at Different Amounts within Different Time Periods:

Cost	=> =>	Resource => =>	Period Expense
		(Asset)	(e.g., Depreciation)
$10,000		$10,000	$2,000

D. Cost and Expense Occurring Simultaneously and at the Same Amount:

COST
$10,000

↓

Expense
(e.g., Wages)
$10,000

E. In the long run (over the life of a resource) cost will equal expenses, but the concepts are different and the amounts may be different within a fiscal period. The concept of cost is more important for most financial management purposes than the concept of expense.

III. **Various Costs**

A. **Sunk Cost --** Sunk costs are costs of resources that have been incurred in the past and cannot be changed by current or future decisions. Therefore, sunk costs are irrelevant to current and future decision-making. The following examples illustrate sunk costs:

Example:

1. In making a decision concerning the replacement of equipment, the original cost (or the book carrying value) of the current equipment is a sunk cost and, therefore, not relevant in making the replacement decision. Only expected future costs (and/or future revenues and cost savings) resulting from the acquisition of the new equipment should enter into the decision whether or not to replace the equipment.

2. In making a new product decision, the costs incurred in conducting technical and market research prior to making the decision of whether or not to introduce the product are sunk costs and, therefore, not relevant to the decision. Only expected future revenues and costs are relevant in deciding whether the product is economically justifiable.

B. **Opportunity Costs --** Opportunity cost is the discounted dollar value of benefits lost from an opportunity as a result of choosing another opportunity. Economic resources normally can be used in two or more economically feasible, but mutually exclusive undertakings. The choice of one alternative precludes the choice of other alternatives. The revenue or other benefit, which would have been derived from an alternative not selected is the opportunity costs associated with the selected alternative. Although opportunity costs do not involve actual cash transactions, they are relevant in current decision-making. The following examples illustrate opportunity costs:

Example:

1. In making a decision between whether to go to school full-time or go to school part-time and work part-time, the pay foregone by choosing to go to school full-time would be an opportunity cost. Since going to school full-time and working part-time are mutually exclusive (an assumption in this illustration), by choosing to go to school full-time, the pay that would have been received by selecting the other alternative is an opportunity cost.

2. In considering the use of vacant space or unused equipment in new production undertakings, the net revenue that would be foregone by not leasing or selling the resource (if possible) would be an opportunity cost. By using the space or equipment for its own activities, an entity gives up the opportunity to receive a net lease or sales revenue. That foregone revenue (measured at present value) is an opportunity cost that should enter into the assessment of proposed uses of the resources.

Note:
It is important to note that the cost of financing a project-the interest and any other financing costs-are NOT incremental cost in assessing the project. The discounting of these costs to their present value will account for the costs associated with the source of financing.

C. **Differential (or Incremental) Costs --** Differential costs (also called incremental costs) are those costs that are different between two or more alternatives. Cost elements that do not differ between alternatives are not relevant in making economic comparisons, but cost elements that are different between alternatives are relevant in making such comparisons. The following examples illustrate differential costs:

Example:

1. In considering whether to accept a special order for a product, only the incremental revenues and costs should be included in assessing the net benefit (profit) inherent in the order. For example, while certain variable cost elements would be different between accepting and not accepting the special order and would be relevant, fixed cost elements may not change and, because these elements would not be different between accepting and not accepting the order, would be irrelevant in making the decision.

2. In comparing two or more alternative projects, some cost elements and amounts may be the same for each project. Those costs would not be relevant in making a decision between the alternatives. Any cost elements and/or amounts that are different between the alternatives would be relevant in making an economically based decision between the alternatives.

D. **Cost of Capital --** A firm's capital (or capital structure) is comprised of the long-term sources of funds used in financing the firm's assets. The major categories of capital elements typically include long-term debt, preferred stock, and common stock, though a variety of other instruments with various characteristics also are used. There is a cost associated with using each element of capital structure. The cost for each element identified above is defined in a similar way.

1. **Cost of Debt --** the rate of return that must be earned in order to attract and retain lenders' funds. The required rate would be determined by such factors as the level of interest in the general market, the perceived default risk of the firm, perceived interest-rate and inflationary risks, and similar factors. Historically, debt has been considered less risky than equity and the required rate of return has been less than the rate required on preferred and common stock. (These risk factors and the determination of the required rate of return on debt are discussed in detail in a later section.)

2. **Cost of Preferred Stock --** the rate of return that must be earned in order to attract and retain preferred shareholders' investment. Preferred stock has characteristics of both debt (a dividend rate paid before common stock dividends) and equity (possible claim to additional dividends and claim to assets on liquidation after debt). Therefore, the required rate of return is determined by factors which enter into determining the rates for each of those securities. Normally, preferred stock is considered more risky than debt, but less risky than common stock and, as a consequence, the rate of return required by investors has been higher than the cost of debt, but lower than the cost of common stock. (The required rate of return on common stock is discussed in detail in a later section.)

3. **Cost of Common Stock --** the rate of return that must be earned in order to attract and retain common shareholders' investment. The required rate would be determined by such factors as the various perceived risks associated with the firm's common stock, as well as expected dividends and price appreciation. Historically, common stock has been considered more risky than debt or preferred stock and, as a consequence, the required rate of return has been higher than the rate on debt or preferred stock.

4. **The Underlying Concept --** for the cost of each of these (and other) forms of financing is that the rate of return required by all sources of financing is based on each source's opportunity cost in the capital markets.

a. <u>The **opportunity cost** for each source of financing is the expected rate of return that investors could earn from the best available alternative investment with perceived comparable risk</u>. Thus, in order to attract and retain capital, an entity must earn, and be prepared to pay, a rate of return at least equal to the rate that investors could earn on investments with comparable risk elsewhere in the capital markets.

b. While the **cost of capital** can be calculated for each element of capital and these separate rates used for analytical purposes, more commonly the weighted average cost of all elements of capital is used. In most cases, this is appropriate since an entity's income stream or cash flow is not determined by or attached to the separate capital elements, but rather relates to the aggregate operations of the entity. Therefore, a weighted average cost of capital is usually appropriate and used for analytical purposes. (How the cost of capital is calculated for each element of capital is discussed in a later section.)

5. The **weighted average cost** of capital is calculated as the required rate of return on each source of capital weighted by the proportion of total capital provided by each source, and the resulting weighted costs summed to get the total weighted average. To illustrate the weighted average cost of capital, assume the following facts and calculations:

Capital Elements	Amount	Percent of Total	x Cost of Capital	= Weighted Cost
Bonds Payable	$400,000	.20	6%	1.2%
Preferred Stock	200,000	.10	10%	1.0%
Common Stock	1,400,000	.70	12%	8.4%
TOTALS	$2,000,000	1.00		
WEIGHTED AVERAGE COST OF CAPITAL =				10.6%

a. In the above illustration, the individual elements of capital have assumed costs of 6%, 10%, and 12%, but each is used to a different extent in the total financing. When each source is weighted by the extent to which it is used, the resulting weighted average cost of capital is 10.6%.

b. Since, as previously described, the cost of capital is the minimum rate of return that a firm must pay in order to attract and retain capital (that is, the rate of return required by investors based on their opportunity cost), the cost of capital is also the minimum rate of return that a firm must earn on its use of capital. In order for the value of common stock to increase, a firm must earn a return greater than its cost of capital. Because the weighted average cost of capital is the minimum average rate of return that a firm must earn to fund its capital elements, the weighted average cost of capital is used as the hurdle rate used in analyzing a firm's investment opportunities - if the rate of return on an investment can't clear the hurdle rate, it is not economically feasible for the firm. The weighted average cost of capital also establishes the discount rate used in various forms of economic analysis.

IV. **Conclusion --** The concepts of cost identified, defined, and illustrated in this section will be used in carrying out application analysis in later sections of this unit.

Time Value of Money Tools

Money is the basic unit of measure used in finance. But, there is a timing element or attribute to the value of money; money held today has greater value than money to be received in the future. Thus, there is a time value of money. This lesson considers the concepts and determinations of the value of money under different assumptions as to time. Each assumption as to time (or timing) is explained and illustrated graphically.

I. Overview

A. Virtually every area of financial management requires understanding and using time value of money concepts. While money is the unit of measure used in financial management, all money does not have the same value, in large part due to the time value associated with money. Simply put, money currently held is worth more than money to be received in the future. In order to analyze investment proposals and other opportunities, money (or dollars) that relate to different points in (or periods of time) must be adjusted to comparable values. This is accomplished by converting all dollars to their current or present value, or to a common future value. The concepts and calculations for making these conversions are covered here. Six major circumstances will be presented.

1. Present value now of an amount to be received (or paid) at some single future date.
2. Future value at some future date of a single amount invested now.
3. Present value now of an ordinary annuity to be received over some future time period.
4. Future value at some future time of an ordinary annuity invested over some future time period.
5. Present value now of an annuity due to be received over some future time period.
6. Future value at some future time of an annuity due invested over some future time period.

B. A timeline graphic will illustrate the concept underlying each of these circumstances. The calculation of each value will be demonstrated using assumed facts and excerpts from relevant time value tables.

II. Present Value of a Single Amount

A. Present value now of an amount to be received (or paid) at some single future date -- This calculation determines the value now (at the present) of a single amount to be received at some single future date. Obviously, since a dollar held now is worth more than a dollar to be received in the future, the present value of an amount is less than the future value of that amount.

B. Illustration -- To illustrate, assume $50,000 is to be received 5 years in the future. What is the present (current) value of the future $50,000? Graphically, the circumstances can be shown as:

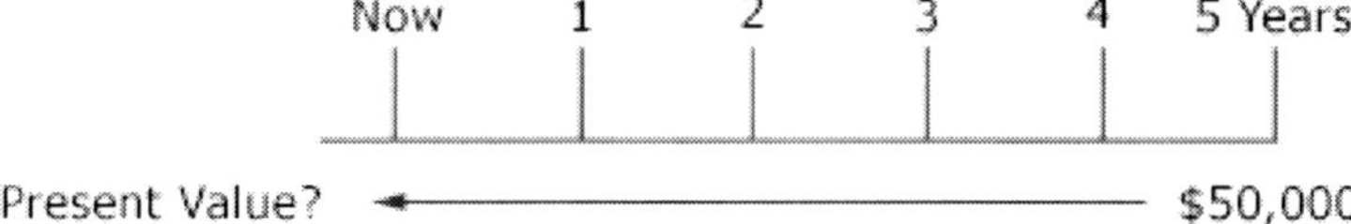

C. The future value (principal) is $50,000 and the number of periods is 5 years. In order to determine the present value, a discount (or interest) rate must be used. That rate measures the time value attached to money by the entity. Assume the appropriate rate is 6% and the related present value of $1.00 table shows the following for 5 periods:

Rate	2%	4%	6%	8%	10%
5 Periods	.906	.822	.747	.681	.621

D. The appropriate discount factor for 5 periods at 6% is .747. Therefore, the present value (PV) of $50,000 to be received in 5 years would be calculated as:

PV = $50,000 x .747 = $37,350

1. Or, $50,000 to be received in 5 years with a discount rate of 6% is worth $37,350 now.

E. The calculation of present value of a single future amount frequently is used in assessing investment opportunities for which a portion of the cash flows relate to a single amount to be received (or paid) in the future. For example, it would be used to determine the present value of the disposal value of an asset when disposal will occur in the future (e.g. the end of the life of the project).

III. Future Value of a Single Amount

A. **Future value at some future date of a single amount invested now --** This calculation determines the value at some future date of a single amount invested now. The future value is the amount that will have accumulated as of some future date as a result of earning interest on the amount invested at the present and, over multiple periods, the compounding of interest (that is, earning interest on interest). Obviously, as a result of interest earned, the future value will be greater than the present value of the investment.

B. **Illustration --** To illustrate, assume $50,000 invested now will earn 6% annual interest compounded annually. What is the future value of the investment at the end of five years? Graphically, the circumstances can be shown as:

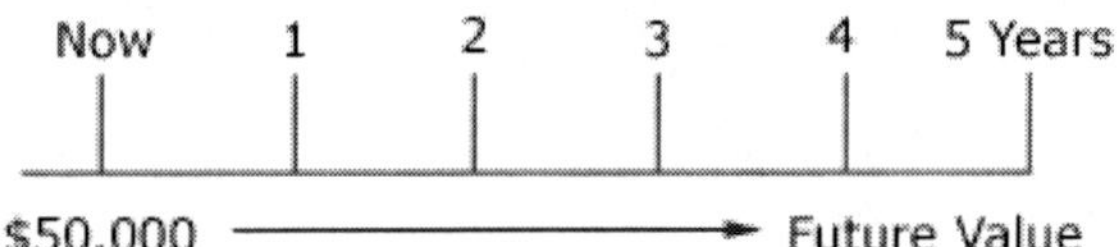

C. The present value (principal) is $50,000 and the number of periods is 5 years. The principal will earn 6% per year compounded annually. The related future value of $1.00 table shows the following for 5 periods:

Rate	2%	4%	6%	8%	10%
5 Periods	1.104	1.217	1.338	1.469	1.611

D. The appropriate future value factor for 5 periods at 6% is 1.338. Therefore, the future value (FV) of $50,000 invested for 5 years at 6% compounded annually would be calculated as:

FV = $50,000 x 1.338 = $66,900

1. Or, $50,000 invested now for 5 years at 6% compounded annually would accumulate to $66,900.

E. In those situations where interest compounds more often than once a year, the number of periods used is the number of compounding periods and the interest rate is the annual rate divided by the number of compounding periods within each year. For example, if interest in the above example is compounded quarterly, the number of periods is 20 (5 years x 4 quarters) and the related rate is 1.5% (6%/4 quarters = 1.5% per quarter).

IV. Present Value of an Ordinary Annuity (Also called an "Annuity in Arrears")

A. Present value now of an ordinary annuity to be received over some future time period -- This calculation determines the value now (at the present) of a series of equal amounts to be received (or paid) at equal intervals over some future period of time. An annuity is, by definition, a series of equal dollar amounts. An ordinary annuity (as compared to an annuity due) means that the series of equal amounts is received (or paid) at the end of each period. In an annuity due the series of equal amounts is received (or paid) at the beginning of each period. The present value of the series of amounts to be received (or paid) in the future will be less than the sum of the future nominal values of those amounts.

B. Illustration -- To illustrate, assume $5,000 is to be received at the end of each of the next 5 years. What is the present value of the $25,000 to be received over the next 5 years? Graphically, the circumstances can be shown as:

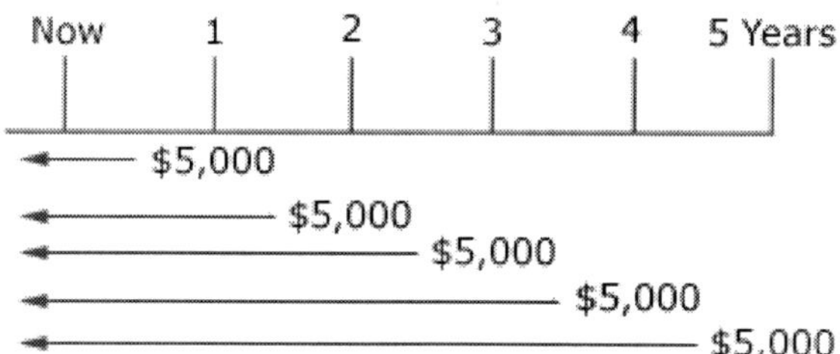

Present Value?

C. The annuity is $5,000 and the number of periods is 5 years. Assume the appropriate discount rate (interest rate) is 6% and the related present value of an ordinary annuity of $1.00 table shows the following for 5 periods:

Rate	2%	4%	6%	8%	10%
5 Periods	4.713	4.452	4.212	3.993	3.791

D. The appropriate discount factor for 5 periods at 6% is 4.212. Therefore, the present value (PV) of a 5-year, $5,000 ordinary annuity discount at 6% would be calculated as:

PV = $5,000 x 4.212 = $21,060

1. Or, $5,000 to be received at the end of each of the next five years discounted at 6% is worth $21,060 now.

E. The calculation of the present value of an annuity is used frequently in assessing investment opportunities for which a series of equal amounts of revenue, cost, and/or cost savings are expected over some future period.

V. Future Value of an Ordinary Annuity

A. **Future value at some future time of an ordinary annuity invested over some future time period --** This calculation determines the value at some future date of a series of equal amounts to be paid (or received) at equal intervals over some future period. As an ordinary annuity, the series of equal amounts will be paid (or received) at the end of each period. The future value of the annuity will be greater than the sum of the series of payments (or receipts) as a result of interest earned on each payment (or receipt).

B. **Illustration --** To illustrate, assume $5,000 is to be paid at the end of each of the next 5 years and will earn interest at 6% compounded annually. What is the future value of the series of payments at the end of 5 years? Graphically, the circumstances can be shown as:

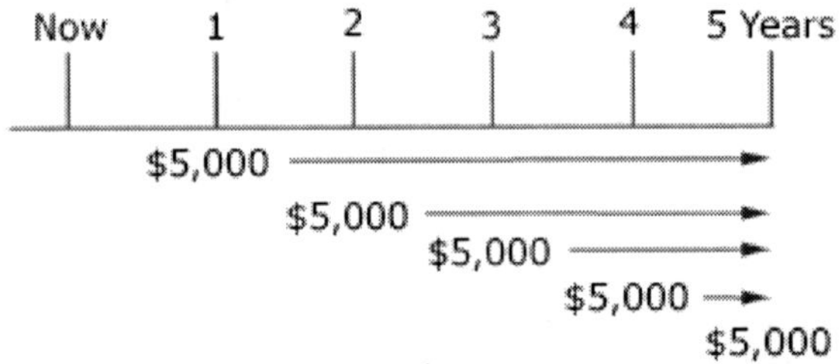

C. The annuity is $5,000 and the number of periods is 5 years. Each payment will earn 6% compounded annually. Thus, for example, the first payment made at the end of the first year will earn 6% compounded for each of the next four years. The related future value of an ordinary annuity of $1.00 table shows the following for 5 periods:

Rate	2%	4%	6%	8%	10%
5 Periods	5.204	5.416	5.637	5.867	6.105

D. The appropriate future value factor for 5 periods at 6% is 5.637. Therefore, the future value (FV) of a 5-year, $5,000 ordinary annuity at 6% would be calculated as:

FV = $5,000 x 5.637 = $28,185

1. Or, $5,000 deposited at the end of each of the next five years earning 6% compounded annually would accumulate to $28,185.

VI. Present Value of an Annuity Due (Also called Annuity in Advance)

A. **Present value now of an annuity due to be received over some future time period** -- (Also called Annuity in Advance) In an annuity due, the series of equal amounts is received (or paid) at the beginning of each period, whereas in an ordinary annuity the series of equal amounts is received (or paid) at the end of each period. The relationship between the two types of annuities is shown in the following illustration:

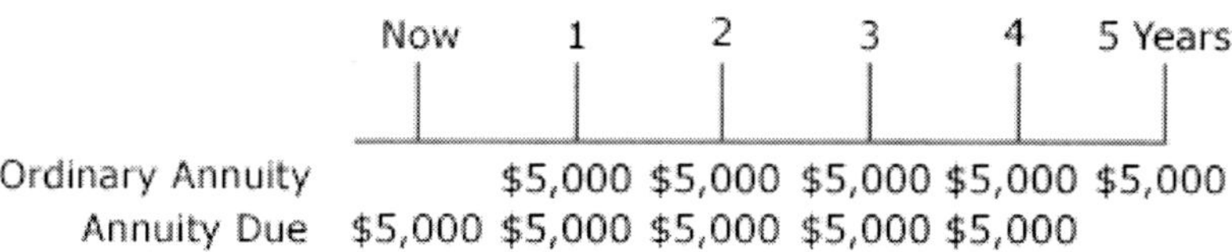

B. While each annuity is $5,000 for 5 years, the annuity due will result in a greater present value than an ordinary annuity because the first amount does not have to be discounted-its present value is $5,000. Similarly, when the future value is computed, each amount in an annuity due compounds for one additional period than in an ordinary annuity, resulting in a greater future value for an annuity due.

C. The calculation of the present value of an annuity due determines the value now (at the present) of a series of equal amounts to be received (or paid) at equal intervals over some future period of time with the amounts received (or paid) at the beginning of each period. The present value of the series of amounts to be received in the future will be less than the sum of the nominal future values of those amounts.

D. **Illustration --** To illustrate, assume $5,000 is to be received at the beginning of each of the next 5 years, with the first amount received now. What is the present value of the $25,000 to be received now and over the next 4 years? Graphically, the circumstances can be shown as:

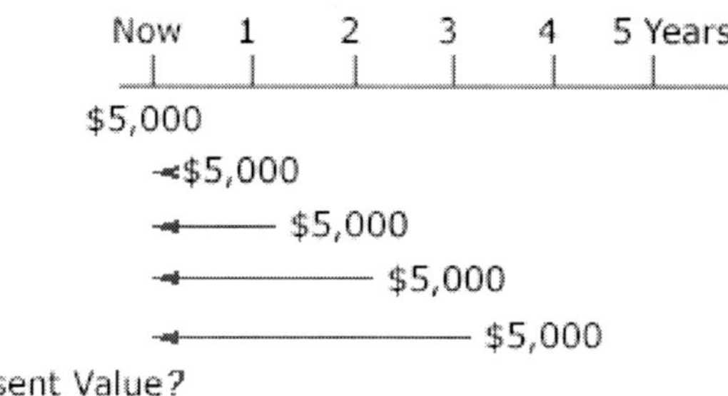

E. The annuity is $5,000 and the number of periods is 5 years. Assume the appropriate discount rate is 6% and the related present value of an ordinary annuity of $1.00 table shows the following for 4 periods and 5 periods:

Rate	2%	4%	6%	8%	10%
4 Periods	3.808	3.630	3.465	3.312	3.170
5 Periods	4.713	4.452	4.212	3.993	3.791

F. Notice that this is the present value table for an ordinary annuity, not an annuity due, and that present value factors are given for both 4 periods and 5 periods. If a present value table for an annuity due were given, you would simply use the appropriate present value factor for the number of time periods and the discount rate, as we have done in all prior illustrations. However, if only a present value table for an ordinary annuity is given, the present value of an annuity due can be determined. (Prior CPA Exams have required candidates to use an ordinary annuity table values to solve for an annuity due amount).

G. Since, as described and illustrated above, an annuity due involves the first payment (or receipt) occurring at the present, that payment does not have to be discounted. Therefore, the number of payments to be discounted is one less than the number of payments in the annuity and the number of periods is one less. For an annuity of 5 payments, with the first one now, only 4 payments must be discounted over 4 periods to get the present value. So, we can use the present value factor for 4 periods (3.465) and add 1.000 for the payment that is already at the present value. Our present value factor would be 3.465 + 1.000 = 4.465 and the present value (PV) of a 5 period, $5,000 annuity due at 6% would be calculated as:

PV = $5,000 x 4.465 = $22,325

1. Or, $5,000 to be received at the beginning of each of the next 5 years, starting now, discounted at 6% is worth $22,325 now.

H. The present value of an annuity due (and annuities due, in general) is often used in accounting as well as in financial management. For example, the determination of the present value of minimum lease payments, with the first payment due at the signing of the lease, would require an annuity due calculation.

VII. Future Value of an Annuity Due

Note:
The present value and future value concepts and calculations covered in this section will be used in subsequent sections in carrying out various financial management analysis and decision-making.

A. Future value at some future time of an annuity due invested over some future time period -- The calculation of the future value of an annuity due determines the value at some future date of a series of equal amounts to be paid (or received) at equal intervals over some future period of time with the amounts paid (or received) at the beginning of each period. The future value will be greater than the sum of the series of amounts as a result of interest earned on each amount. Because the first amount is paid (or received) at the start of the annuity, the amount of interest earned and the amount at the end of the annuity will be greater than the future value of an ordinary annuity.

B. Illustration -- To illustrate, assume $5,000 is to be paid at the beginning of each of the next 5 years, with the first amount paid now. What is the future value of the $25,000 to be paid starting now and over the next 4 years? Graphically, the circumstances can be shown as:

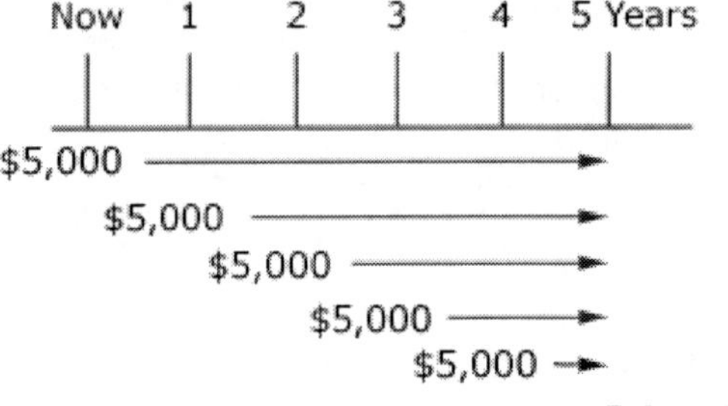

C. The annuity is $5,000 and the number of periods is 5 years. Assume the appropriate interest rate is 6% and the related future value of an ordinary annuity of $1.00 table shows the following for 5 periods and 6 periods:

Rate	2%	4%	6%	8%	10%
5 Periods	5.204	5.416	5.637	5.867	6.105
6 Periods	6.308	6.633	6.975	7.335	7.716

D. Notice that this is the future value table for an ordinary annuity, not an annuity due, and that future value factors are given for both 5 periods and 6 periods. Since an annuity due involves the first payment (or receipt) occurring at the present, that payment earns an additional period of interest. Therefore, the number of periods that interest is earned is one more than in an ordinary annuity. Thus, for an annuity of 5 payments, with the first one now, we can use the ordinary annuity for 6 periods (6.975) and subtract 1.000 for the fact that the annuity is for 5 periods. Our future value would be 6.975 - 1.000 = 5.975 and the future value (FV) of a 5 period, $5,000 annuity due at 6% would be calculated as follows:

FV = $5,000 x 5.975 = $29,875

1. Or, $5,000 to be paid (or received) at the beginning of each of the next 5 years, starting now, at 6% would accumulate to $29,875. (Recall that the future value of a comparable ordinary annuity was $28,185).

Interest Rate Concepts & Calculations

Simply put, interest is rent for the use of money. Interest rate is an expression of the price or cost for the use of money. A number of interest and interest rate concepts are used in accounting and finance. This lesson considers interest and interest rate concepts and calculations.

I. **Overview --** Interest is the money paid for the use of money. From the point of view of the borrower, it is the cost of borrowed funds; from the point of view of the lender, it is the revenue earned for lending money to another. It compensates the lender for deferring use of the funds and for the various risks inherent in making the loan. The greater the perceived risk in an investment or other undertaking, the greater the expected rate of return, or interest rate.

II. **Interest is expressed as a percentage rate --** Almost always expressed as an annual percentage rate, which is applied to the principal and/or other amount to determine the dollar amount of interest. Depending on the contract in a particular situation, the rate may be fixed, variable, or a combination.

   A. **Fixed Rate --** The percentage rate of interest does not change over the life of the loan or parts of that life. For example, in a 30-year, fixed rate mortgage, the interest rate does not change over the 30-year life of the mortgage, regardless of the changes in rates in the market during that period.

   B. **Variable Rate --** The percentage rate of interest can change over the life of the loan or part of that life. Generally, a change in the rate is triggered by a change in the general level of interest in the economy as measured by a macroeconomic indicator, such as the prime rate of interest. (The prime rate of interest is the rate banks charge to their most credit worthy borrowers). For example, in a 15-year adjustable rate mortgage, the interest rate may be related to changes in the prime rate of interest. If the prime rate goes up or down, so also would the rate on the mortgage.

   C. **Variable-to-Fixed Rate or Fixed-to-Variable Rate --** Though less common, some loans charge one kind of rate, say variable, for a portion of the life of the loan, and a different kind of rate, say fixed, for another portion of the life of the loan. For example, a 25-year mortgage may have an adjustable rate for the first 7 years, after which it carries a fixed rate.

III. **Interest and Interest Rate Concepts**

   A. While an interest rate states the cost of the use of money, not all statements of interest rate are comparable, primarily due to the effects of compounding. The remainder of this section identifies and shows the calculation of a number of different interest and interest rate concepts, including:

      1. Stated interest rate;
      2. Simple interest;
      3. Compound interest;
      4. Effective interest rate;
      5. Annual percentage rate;
      6. Effective annual percentage rate.

   B. Understanding these interest and interest rate concepts is important to both accounting and financial management.

1. **Stated Interest Rate --** The stated interest rate (also called the nominal or quoted interest rate) is the annual rate specified in the loan agreement or comparable contract; it does not take into account the compounding effects of frequency of payments or the effects of inflation.

Example:
The coupon rate of interest on a bond is the stated rate of interest for that bond. If the bond coupon rate is 6%, with interest paid semiannually, the stated rate of interest is 6%, even though the effective rate will be higher because interest is paid 2 times during a year.

   a. Nominal interest rate - as contrasted with real interest rate, also refers to the rate of interest before taking into account the effects of inflation.

   b. Real interest rate - as contrasted with nominal interest rate, refers to the rate of interest after taking into account the effects of inflation on the value of funds. The calculation of the real interest rate (RIR) is:

RIR = Nominal Interest Rate - Inflation Rate

Example:
Assume a one-year investment instrument that pays a stated (nominal) rate of interest of 8%. During the year inflation is 3%. The real interest rate (RIR) is:

RIR = 8% - 3% = 5%

So, while the nominal interest rate is 8%, because of inflation the real interest rate is 5%.

2. **Simple Interest --** Simple interest is interest computed on the original principal only; there is not compounding in interest computation. (See Compound Interest, below.)

Example:
Assume a two-year, $2,000 note that provides for 6% simple interest with principal and interest to be paid at the end of the two year period. The basic interest expression provides:

Interest = Principal x Rate x Time, or
= P x R x T, or
= $2,000 x .06 x 2 years = $240

Thus, at the end of the second year the borrower would repay $2,000 principal + $240 interest = $2,240.

3. **Compound Interest --** Compound interest provides that interest is paid not only on the principal, but also on any amount of accumulated unpaid interest. Compound interest pays interest on interest; simple interest does not.

Example:

Assume the two year, $2,000 note that provides 6% interest in the prior example, but terms of the note provide that interest is compounded annually with repayment at the end of the two-year period.

Interest Year 1 = I = P x R x T = $2,000 x .06 x 1 =	$120.00
Interest Year 2 = I = ($2,000 + $120) x .06 x 1 =	127.20
=	$247.20

Thus, at the end of the second year the borrower would repay $2,000 principal + $247.20 interest = $2,247.20. As a result of paying interest on the first (1st) year's interest, the total interest is $7.20 more than under simple interest.

a. The above calculation can be done using the formula for future value (FV) of $1.00:

$FVn = P(1 + R)^n$

Where: P = Principal

R = Interest rate per year

n = Number of years

Substituting with the facts above:

$FVn = \$2000(1 + .06)^2$

$FVn = \$2000(1.06)^2$

$FVn = \$2,000(1.1236)$

FVn = $2,247.20 = $2,000 principal + 247.20 interest

b. Compound interest and future value of $1.00 calculations are performed in the same manner. Both account for interest being paid on accumulated interest. For multiple period calculations either the formula above or a future value of $1.00 table can be used.

4. **Effective Interest --** The effective interest rate is the annual interest rate implicit in the relationship between the net proceeds from a loan and the dollar cost of the loan.

Example:
Assume the facts above, which were a two-year, $2,000 note with 6% interest. We saw that if the contract provided for simple interest, the dollar amount of interest was:

I = P x R x T = $2,000 x .06 x 2 = $240

The effective rate (EI) is 6%, which can be shown as the relationship between the cost ($240) and the proceeds ($2,000), or:

EI = ($240/$2,000)/2 years

EI = .12/2 = .06

Assume the contract provides the same terms, except that the note will be discounted. In that case, the proceeds are:

$2,000 - $240 = $1,760

The effective rate of interest (EI) is now:

EI = ($240/$1,760)/2 years

EI = 13.64/2 = .0682

   a. In addition to discounting, such items as origination fees, compensating balances, and installment payments will cause the effective rate to be different from the stated rate of interest.

5. **Annual Percentage Rate --** The annual percentage rate (APR) is the annualized effective interest rate without compounding on loans that are for a fraction of a year. It is computed as the effective interest rate for the fraction of a year multiplied by the number of time fractions in a year (e.g., 2 if semiannual, 4 if quarterly, and 12 if monthly).

Example:
Assume the facts above, which were a $2,000 note with 6% interest, but assume that the note is for 90 days (3 months = 1 quarter) and the note is discounted. The interest, proceeds, effective interest rate, and annual percentage rate will be:

I = P x R x T

I = $2,000 x .06 x 90/360

I = $2,000 x .06 x .25 = $30

Proceeds = $2,000 - $30 = $1,970

Effective Interest = $30/$1,970 = 1.52%

Annual Percentage Rate = 1.52% x 4 quarters = 6.08%

Thus, while the stated rate is 6.00%, the annual percentage rate (APR) is 6.08%. Recall that the annual percentage rate (APR) is the required basis for interest rate disclosure in the U.S.

6. **Effective Annual Percentage Rate --** The effective annual percentage rate, also called the annual percentage yield, is the annual percentage rate with compounding on loans that are for a fraction of a year. As discussed under compounding, the assumption is that interest is paid on interest that would accumulate for each period during the year. The formula for computing the effective annual percentage rate (EAPR) is:

$EAPR = (1+I / p)^{p}-1$

Where: I = Annual (nominal) interest rate

p = Number of periods in the year

Example:
Assume the facts above, which were a 90-day, $2,000 note with a 6% interest rate. Substituting, the EAPR would be:

$EAPR = (1+.06 / 4)^{4} - 1 = (1+.015)^{4} - 1 = (.1015)^{4} - 1$

Thus, while the annual percentage rate is 6.08%, the effective annual percentage rate is 6.136%, due to the assumed compounding within the year.

Capital Budgeting

Introduction and Project Risk

Capital budgeting is concerned with the acquisition and financing of long-term (or capital) asset investments. Making capital budgeting decisions involves assessing both the risks inherent in long-term undertakings and the likely rewards (or returns) to be derived from those undertakings. This lesson defines and describes capital budgeting and considers the nature and role of risk and reward in the capital budgeting process.

I. Capital Budgeting

A. In order to be successful in a competitive environment, an entity must have a more or less continuous stream of new undertakings or projects. Identifying and implementing profitable projects is essential if a firm is to grow and survive in the long run. This section is concerned with the kinds of decisions involved in considering new undertakings or projects, the risk-reward relationship inherent in new undertakings.

B. Capital budgeting is the process of measuring, evaluating, and selecting long-term investment opportunities. These opportunities are typically in the form of projects or programs being considered by a firm and almost always would involve significant cost and extend over many periods. Depending on the entity, such projects may include the routine acquisition of new property, plant, and equipment, changing a production process, adding new products or services, establishing new locations, or other similar undertakings. All of the various kinds of projects and programs undertaken by an entity over time largely determine its current resources and operations, as well as its on-going success or failure. Therefore, effective capital budgeting is essential to every successful organization.

II. Project Risk and Reward Considerations

A. Inherent in every project considered are elements of risk and reward. Risk is the possibility of loss or other unfavorable results that derives from the uncertainty implicit in future outcomes.

B. Definition of Risk

1. Risk is defined in technical models in terms of the deviation of actual returns from expected returns. (A number of technical risk and return models are used to measure market risk, especially as it applies to securities investments, including the capital asset pricing model, the arbitrage pricing model, the multifactor model, and the regression model.) The risks associated with investment in a project or similar undertaking result from a number of uncertainties, some of which are specific to the undertaking and some of which relate more to the larger market (macroeconomic) environment. A particular project may be at risk from the following:

   a. Incomplete or incorrect analysis of the project, including failure to incorporate revenue or cost elements or misestimation of those elements.

   b. Unanticipated actions of customers, suppliers, and competitors, including changing prices of resources, and the advent of new technology.

   c. Unanticipated changes in laws, regulations, or other political changes.

   d. Unanticipated macroeconomic changes, including changes in interest rates, inflation/deflation rates, tax rates, and currency exchange rates.

C. Reducing Risk

1. For a large firm, certain risks which are associated with individual projects are mitigated by having a large number of diverse projects (a portfolio of projects) which span multiple periods. In effect, having a diverse portfolio of projects reduces the aggregate risk to the firm in much the same manner that diversification of securities holdings reduces the risk in a securities investment portfolio. The reduced risk that results from a large, diverse portfolio of projects results because:
   a. With a large number of projects, each individual project accounts for a relatively small percentage of total undertakings, thus any unexpected outcome will have only a small impact on the total firm results.
   b. With a large number of diverse projects, the unfavorable outcomes experienced by some projects are more likely to be offset by favorable outcomes experienced by other projects.
2. On the other hand, certain risks are likely to impact most projects in the same manner.

Example:
The risk associated with an increase in interest rates would apply similarly to all long-term projects. An unanticipated increase in interest rates would tend to result in lower returns from all long-term projects. In most cases, risks which derive from the macroeconomic environment cannot be reduced by project diversification.

3. Identifying and assessing the risks inherent in a project, especially those risks, which are not reduced by diversification, are essential in determining an appropriate expected reward (or return) from a project. The expected return on a project must be sufficient to cover the expected net cost of the project and provide a profit sufficient to meet the returns demanded by those who provide the firm's capital-creditors and shareholders. Just as the return demanded by those who provide capital will vary with the perceived risk associated with their investment in the firm, so also will the expected return required on projects vary with the perceived risk associated with each project considered by the firm.

D. The Risk-Reward Relationship

1. The risk-reward relationship is familiar: the greater the perceived risk, the greater the expected reward. Thus, the relationship between risk and reward is positive and can be shown graphically as:

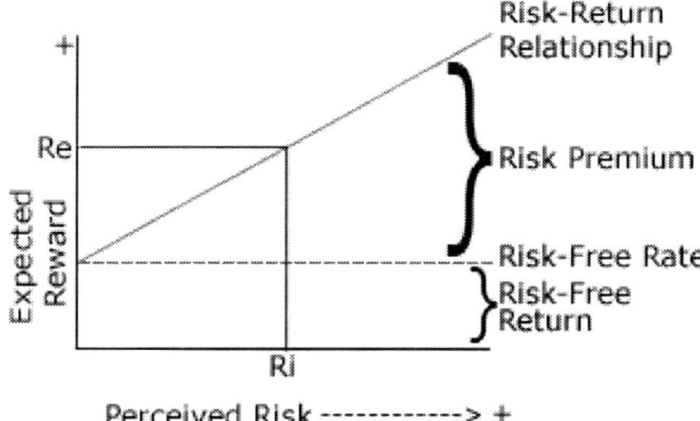

2. As the above graph shows, there is a risk-free rate of return expected on every investment. This rate reflects the reward expected for the deferred current consumption that results from making an investment. In the U.S., the risk-free rate of return normally is measured by the rates on U.S. Treasury securities (bills and notes). Investors or firms could earn the rates paid on these securities without incurring the risk associated with commercial securities or with project undertakings. The return expected above the risk-free rate, called the risk premium, depends on the perceived risk inherent in an investment opportunity-securities, projects, or other. In the graph above, if the level of risk is perceived to be Ri (Risk) on the horizontal axis, the expected return is Re (Return) on the vertical axis. At higher levels of expected risk, a higher return would be expected, and at lower levels of expected risk, a lower return would be expected.

3. **The relationship between a firm's projects and the sources of the firm's capital** that funds those projects provides a basis for establishing the rate of return required on its project undertakings. The interrelationship between a firm's undertakings and its sources of capital can be illustrated as follows:

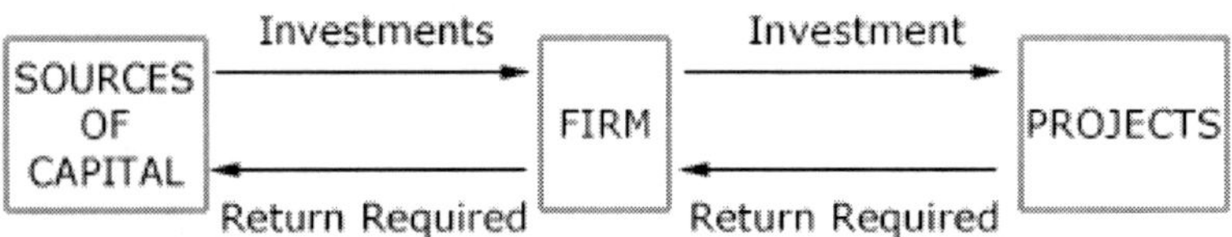

4. As the illustration shows, the rate of return required in order to attract and maintain capital funding determines the rate of return that must be earned on projects by the firm. The rate of return required to attract and maintain capital is the cost of capital to the firm and that cost of capital is the rate the firm must earn on its investment in projects, often called the hurdle rate. Unless a firm is able to earn an adequate rate of return on the aggregate of its undertakings, it cannot attract and maintain capital.

E. Discount Rate

1. As described in the Cost Concepts section, while the cost of capital can be determined for each element of capital (e.g. long-term notes, bonds, preferred stock, common stock, etc.), it is usually appropriate to calculate and use the weighted average cost of capital. Specifically, the cost of capital for each element is weighted by the proportion of total capital provided by each element. The resulting weighted average is the rate of return that a firm must expect to earn on a project it undertakes. In evaluating projects, that rate is called the hurdle rate or discount rate.

Evaluation Techniques

Introduction to Evaluation Techniques

Successful capital investments are essential to the success of a business. Therefore, accurate evaluation of potential capital projects is critical. This lesson identifies the techniques for evaluating and comparing potential capital projects which will be covered in subsequent lessons.

I. The following lessons considers various techniques for evaluating capital budgeting opportunities

A. Six different techniques will be described and illustrated, and the advantages and disadvantages will be summarized. The techniques to be considered are:

1. Payback period approach;
2. Discounted payback period approach;
3. Accounting rate of return approach;
4. Net present value approach;
5. Internal rate of return approach;
6. Profitability Index approach.

B. The first five approaches are used primarily to decide whether to accept or reject a project based on the economic feasibility of the project. The last technique, the profitability index approach, is particularly useful in ranking acceptable projects.

Payback Period Approach

The payback period approach is one of the basic techniques for assessing the economic feasibility of capital projects. This lesson describes and illustrates the use of the payback period approach, and identifies the advantages and disadvantages associated with its use.

I. Payback Period Approach

A. The payback period approach to assessing a capital project determines the number of years (or other periods) needed to recover the initial cash investment in the project and compares the resulting time with a pre-established maximum payback period. If the expected payback period for a project is equal to or less than the pre-established maximum, the project is deemed acceptable; otherwise, it would be considered unacceptable.

B. The following example is used to illustrate this analysis:

1. A firm is considering a project with an initial cash outlay of $250,000 and no residual value. The project is expected to provide five years of new cash flows as follows:

Year 1	$ 50,000
Year 2	75,000
Year 3	75,000
Year 4	75,000
Year 5	25,000
TOTAL	$300,000

2. The firm's maximum payback period is 3 years.

C. Analysis -- With a 3 year maximum payback period, this project would not be acceptable. The total expected cash inflow over the first 3 years of the project is:

Year 1	$ 50,000
Year 2	75,000
Year 3	75,000
TOTAL	$200,000 less than Initial cash outlay $250,000 = Reject

II. Advantages and Disadvantages of the Payback Period Approach -- The payback period method uses expected cash flow, (not expected accounting net income), the cash flows are not discounted, and does not consider the results after the maximum payback period.

A. Advantages

1. Easy to understand and use;

2. Useful in evaluating liquidity of a project;

3. Establishing short maximum period reduces uncertainty.

B. Disadvantages

1. Ignores the time value of money (i.e., present value of the future cash flows);
2. Ignores cash flows received after the payback period;
3. Does not measure total project profitability;
4. Maximum payback period may be arbitrary.

III. Conclusion -- Because of the serious disadvantages associated with the payback period method, its most appropriate use is in preliminary screening of projects or when used in conjunction with other evaluation methods.

Discounted Payback Period Approach

The discounted payback period approach to assessing the economic feasibility of capital projects is a variation of the basic payback period approach that takes the time value of money into account. This lesson describes and illustrates the discounted payback period approach, and identifies the advantages and disadvantages associated with its use.

I. **The discounted payback period method --** Is a variation of the payback period approach that takes the time value of money into account. It does so by discounting the expected future cash flows to their present value and uses the present values to determine the length of time required to recover the initial investment. Because the present value of the cash flows will be less than their future (nominal) values, the discounted payback period will be longer than the undiscounted payback period.

A. Using the facts above and discount factors assuming 6%, the analysis would be:

Year	Cash Flow	PV Factor	PV Amount	Sum of PVs
1	$ 50,000	.943	$ 47,150	$ 47,150
2	75,000	.890	66,750	113,900
3	75,000	.840	63,000	176,900
4	75,000	.792	59,400	236,300
5	25,000	.747	18,675	254,975
TOTALS	$300,000		$254,975	

B. The present value of cash inflows expected over the first 3 years, the maximum payback period for the firm, is $176,900, less than the initial cash outlay of $250,000. Thus, the project would be rejected. Notice that the 3-year cash flows under the undiscounted and discounted payback period methods are different:

Undiscounted	$200,000
Discounted	176900

C. The discounted cash flows would take a longer period to recapture a given initial cash outlay than the undiscounted cash flows.

II. **The advantages and disadvantages of the discounted payback period method --** Are the same as for the undiscounted payback period method, except that the use of time value of money becomes an advantage, not a disadvantage. Like all methods that use time value of money concepts, it is subject to the uncertainty associated with assuming an interest rate applicable to future periods.

Accounting Rate of Return Approach

The accounting rate of return approach uses accounting-based values to assess the economic feasibility of capital projects. This lesson describes and illustrates the accounting rate of return approach, and identifies the advantages and disadvantages associated with its use.

I. Accounting Rate of Return

Definition:

The accounting rate of return (also called the simple rate of return) method: Assesses a project by measuring the expected annual incremental accounting income from the project as a percent of the initial (or average) investment.

A. Expressed as a formula, the accounting rate of return (ARR) would be calculated as:

ARR = (Average Annual Incremental Revenues - Average Annual Incremental Expense) / Initial (or Average) Investment

B. Both incremental revenues and incremental expenses in the numerator are as determined by accrual accounting. If the average amount invested in the project is used in the denominator, rather than the full initial investment, it would be computed as the average book value of the asset over its life.

C. The following assumptions are used to illustrate the analysis, assuming the initial investment is used:

1. A firm is considering a project with an initial cash outlay of $250,000 and no residual value. The project is expected to provide incremental net income (revenues - expenses) over the next five years of the following amounts:

Year 1	$ 12,000
Year 2	18,000
Year 3	26,000
Year 4	24,000
Year 5	20,000
TOTAL	$100,000

2. The average expected incremental net income is: $100,000/5 years = $20,000. Therefore:

APR = $20,000 / $250,000 = 8.0%APR

3. The resulting 8.0% would be the expected annual rate of return on the project. If the average amount invested was used as the denominator, it would be a much lower denominator (depending on the depreciation method used) and the accounting rate of return would be much higher. The determined rate could be compared to a pre-established rate to determine whether or not the project is acceptable.

II. The advantages and disadvantages of the accounting rate of return

A. Advantages

1. Easy to understand and use;
2. Consistent with financial statement values;
3. Considers entire life and results of project.

B. Disadvantages

1. Ignores the time value of money (i.e., present value of future net profits or losses.);
2. Uses accrual accounting values, not cash flows.

Net Present Value Approach

The net present value approach is one of two major methods of assessing the economic feasibility of capital projects that takes into account the time value of money. This lesson describes and illustrates the net present value approach, and identifies the advantages and disadvantages associated with its use.

I. Net Present Value

Definition:

The net present value approach: Assesses projects by comparing the present value of the expected cash flows (revenues or savings) of the project with the initial cash investment in the project.

A. The present value of expected cash flows is determined by discounting those flows to their present value using the firm's cost of capital as the discount rate (also called the hurdle rate). The difference between the resulting present value and the initial cost (which is at present value) is the net present value of the project. If the net present value is zero or positive, the project is deemed economically acceptable; if the net present value is negative, the project is deemed unacceptable.

B. Using the facts above and assuming the firm's cost of capital is 6%, the analysis would be:

Year	Cash Flow	PV Factor	PV Amount	Sum of PVs
1	$ 50,000	.943	$ 47,150	$ 47,150
2	75,000	.890	66,750	113,900
3	75,000	.840	63,000	176,900
4	75,000	.792	59,400	236,300
5	25,000	.747	18,675	254,975
TOTALS	$300,000		$254,975	

C. The present value of (all) cash inflows is $254,975, and the cost of the initial investment in the project is $250,000. Therefore:

PV of Cash Flows	$254,975
Initial Investment	250,000
Net Present Value	$4,975.00

D. Since the net present value of the project is estimated to be $4,975, the project should be accepted. Notice, unlike the prior payback period methods that only consider the results during the maximum payback period, the net present value method considers the entire period (life) of the project.

II. The advantages and disadvantages of the net present value method

A. Advantages

1. Recognizes the time value of money (i.e., present value of the future cash flows);
2. Relates project rate of return to cost of capital;
3. Considers the entire life and results of the project;
4. Easier to compute than the internal rate of return method (the other discounted cash flow method).

B. Disadvantages

1. Requires estimation of cash flows over entire life of the project, which could be very long;
2. Assumes cash flows resulting from new revenues or cost savings are immediately reinvested at the hurdle rate of return.

Internal Rate of Return Approach

Like the net present value approach, the internal rate of return approach takes the time value of money into account in assessing the economic feasibility of capital projects. This lesson describes and illustrates the internal rate of return approach, and identifies the advantages and disadvantages associated with its use.

I. Internal Rate of Return

Definition:

The internal rate of return (also called the time adjusted rate of return) method: Evaluates a project by determining the discount rate that equates the present value of the project's future cash inflows with the present value of the project's cash outflows. The rate so determined is the rate of return earned by the project.

A. Conceptually and mathematically, the internal rate of return method is directly related to the net present value method. Whereas the net present value method uses an assumed discount rate to determine whether or not the present value of a project is positive or not, the internal rate of return computes the discount rate (rate or return) that would make the present value of the project's cash flows equal to zero.

II. Calculation of Internal Rate of Return

A. The calculation of a project's exact internal rate of return is best done with a financial calculator. In the absence of a financial calculator, the determination of the internal rate of return will require interpolation and trial and error.

B. Assuming an even cash flow over the life of a project, the determination of the internal rate of return begins by solving the equation:

Annual Cash Inflow (or Savings) x PV Factor = Investment Cost, or
PV Factor = Investment Cost/Annual Cash Inflow (or Savings)

C. Using the investment cost and expected annual cash inflow, the present value factor can be determined. Next, the resulting present value factor would be related to an interest (discount) rate for the time period of the project. Only by rare coincidence will the exact calculated present value for the number of periods be found on a present value table. Therefore, it will be necessary to interpolate to determine the exact internal rate of return.

III. Illustration -- The following assumptions are used to illustrate the process:

A. A firm is considering a project with an initial cost of $37,500 and no residual value. The project is expected to save the firm $10,000 per year over its 5-year life. The following values were extracted from a present value of an annuity table for 5 periods:

Rate	8%	10%	12%	14%	16%
5 Periods	3.993	3.791	3.605	3.433	3.274

PV Factor = Initial Cost / Annual Savings = $37,500 / $10.000 = 3.750 PV Factor

B. On the annuity table, the present value factor closest to 3.750 is 3.791. Since 3.750 is less than 3.791, but greater than the next listed value, 3.605, the exact internal rate of return is greater than 10%, but less than 12%.

C. That rate can be determined using interpolation as follows:

Interest Rate	Present Value Factors	
10%	3.791	3.791
IRR (?)		3.750
12%	3.605	____
Difference	.186	.041

D. The true internal rate of return is 10% plus .041/.186 of the 2% difference between 10% and 12%. The **calculation** would be:

IRR = 10% + (.041/.186) .02 =

= 10% + (.2204) .02 =

= 10% + .0044 = 10.44% IRR

E. The determination of the internal rate of return is especially difficult when the cash flows from the project are not even over the life of the project. Unless a computer program is used, the calculation of the internal rate of return when all future cash flows are positive but uneven requires a trial and error approach. You begin by picking a likely rate and determine the resulting net present value. If the computed net present value is more or less than zero, the rate used is adjusted iteratively until a zero net present value is found. The corresponding rate used is the internal rate of return. When future cash flows are both positive and negative, the internal rate of return method can result in multiple solutions and it should not be used in that case.

IV. The advantages and disadvantages of the internal rate of return method

A. Advantages

1. Recognizes the time value of money (i.e., present value of the future cash flows);
2. Considers entire life and results of the project.

B. Disadvantages

1. Difficult to compute;
2. Requires estimation of cash flows over entire life of project, which could be very long;
3. Requires all future cash flows be of the same direction, either positive or negative;
4. Assumes cash flows resulting from new revenues or cost savings are immediately reinvested at the project's internal rate of return.

Profitability Index and Ranking

Once economically feasible projects have been identified, acceptable projects need to be ranked in terms of desirability. While the net present value and internal rate of return approaches provide a measure of relative attractiveness, neither takes into account the relative cost of each project. This lesson considers the profitability index, a measure designed to rank projects in terms of economic desirability.

I. The profitability index -- Also called the cost/benefit ratio, provides a way of ranking projects by taking into account both cash flow benefit expected from each project and the cost of each project.

A. The profitability index (PI) determines the benefit to cost ratio of a project (or other investment) by computing the value provided per unit (dollar) of investment in a project.

B. The PI for each project may be computed using either the present value of future cash inflows or the net present value (NPV = net of cash inflows and outflows, including the initial project cost) of a project, with either of these values being divided by the initial project cost.

1. When the present value of future cash flows is used, the PI for each project would be computed as:

PI = PV of Cash Inflows / Project cost

a. A project would be economically feasible (and logically acceptable) only if the PI $\geq$ 1; otherwise, the present value of cash flows would be less than the cost of the project.

b. The resulting percentage index ($\geq$ 1) for each project can be used to rank projects. The higher the percentage, the higher the rank of the project.

2. When the net present value (NPV) is used, the PI for each project would be computed as:

PI = Net Present Value / Project cost

a. A project would be economically feasible if the NPV is zero or positive (present value of expected cash inflows is equal to or greater than the present value of expected outflows). Thus, the resulting PI would be $\geq$ 0, which means the project is providing value at least equal to the discount rate used (e.g., WACC).

b. The resulting percentage index ($\geq$ 0) for each project can be used to rank projects. The higher the percentage, the higher the rank of the project.

II. Illustration

A. The following illustrates the determination of the profitability index (PI) for two projects being considered using assumed values for PV (or, alternately, NPV):

Project A: PV (or NPV) =	$60,000/Initial Cost =	$50,000	= 1.20 PI
Project B: PV (or NPV) =	$110,000/Initial Cost =	$100,000	= 1.10 PI

1. Based just on present values (PV) or net present values (NPV), Project B ($110,000) would be ranked higher than Project A ($50,000), but when the amount of the initial investment is taken into account, Project A has a higher profitability index (PI = 1.20) than Project B (PI = 1.10). That result comes about because of the much lower initial investment cost of Project A.

III. **Summary --** When ranking acceptable capital projects, methods based on discounted values are much better than methods which don't incorporate the time value of money. The net present value method and, especially the profitability index derived using net present value and the initial project cost, generally are preferable to other methods. In the final analysis, however, some degree of subjectivity is likely to enter into deciding which projects will be implemented.

A. Once capital budgeting (project investment) decisions have been made, the impact of these plans must be built into other affected budgets. For example, a planned new project may have implications for sales revenue, production costs, and cash flows, in addition to asset acquisition.

B. Once a project is initiated, it should be monitored frequently to assure that it continues to meet the entity's requirements for acceptability.

Capital Project Ranking Decisions

Because firms have practical limitations on the number of capital projects they can undertake, they will select acceptable projects based on their relative economic value to the firm. This lesson considers the need for ranking capital projects and the appropriateness of each of the evaluation approaches considered in prior lessons as a means of ranking projects.

I. Introduction

A. The section on the Internal Rate of Return Approach considers the evaluation of possible projects to determine whether a project is economically feasible for a firm to undertake. The resulting decision is to either accept or reject a project. Theoretically, a firm and its investors would benefit if the firm pursues all projects that meet its acceptability requirements, especially when the net present value and internal rate of return methods are used. In practice, however, a firm will limit the number of projects undertaken, especially in the short run.

B. This limitation on projects, called capital rationing, may occur for a number of reasons, including:

1. The firm does not have access to sufficient funds to take on all its acceptable projects;
2. The firm may not have sufficient management capacity to take on all its acceptable projects;
3. Firm management may believe market conditions are too unstable to commit to all acceptable projects.

C. When management decides to limit the economically acceptable projects it will undertake, it will select projects based on some ranking of the projects. In addition, project ranking will be used in any case in which projects are mutually exclusive - selecting one, rules out selecting others. For example, if a firm has determined two or more alternative acceptable projects to revamp a production process, only one of these alternatives will be implemented. The project selected should be based on a ranking of projects using established criteria. Use of each of the accept-reject decision approaches described above in making ranking decisions will be discussed. In addition, the use of a profitability index for ranking will be described and illustrated.

II. Payback Period and Ranking --

The limitations inherent in the payback period method of making the project accept-reject decision also limit its usefulness in ranking projects. Recall, the major limitations of this method are its failure to consider the time value of money (It does not discount future cash flows.) and its failure to consider economic affects after the payback period. Therefore, use of the payback period method to rank projects would place them in order of how quickly invested capital would be recovered (measured in nominal dollars), and not their relative economic value to the firm. Relative payback periods may be important, however, when liquidity issues are a major concern to a firm, since the payback period measures how quickly an investment will be recovered.

III. Discounted Payback Period and Ranking --

Like the payback period method, this method evaluates a project based on how quickly an investment will be recovered. Unlike the payback period approach which uses nominal cash flows, the discounted payback period method discounts future cash flows and uses the discounted present value to determine the payback period. Because it uses discounted values it is better than the undiscounted payback period approach, but for ranking purposes it fails to consider the total economic performance of a project. It only measures the outcome up until the initial investment is recovered. Use of this method for ranking would be appropriate only when liquidity issues are a major concern.

IV. Accounting Rate of Return and Ranking -- The accounting rate of return uses estimated future accrual-based net income and the cost of the investment (or average cost of the investment) to develop a rate of return on the investment. Because the computation uses nominal accrual-based net income, and not discounted cash flows, its use in ranking projects would ignore the time value of money and would not take into account the impact of different net incomes earned in different future periods. For example, two projects with the same accounting rate of return, based on average expected net incomes, may have very different timing of those incomes.

V. Net Present Value and Ranking

A. The net present value of a project is derived by discounting future cash flows (or savings) and determining whether or not the resulting present value is more or less than the cost of the investment. If the net present value is zero or positive, the project is economically feasible; if the net present value is negative, the project should be rejected. Because the net present value approach uses discounted cash flows, it provides a means of ranking projects in terms of a comparable dollar value of each project. For example, other things being equal, the project with the highest positive net present value would be ranked first, the second highest positive value ranked second, and so on.

B. While the net present value method enables not only a basis for accepting or rejecting a project, but also a useful ranking of projects, it does not address the issue of differences in initial cost of each project. This issue is addressed by the use of a profitability index, which is described below. Despite this issue, ranking projects by the level of their positive net present values is usually the preferred basis.

VI. Internal Rate of Return and Ranking

A. Like the net present value approach, the internal rate of return method incorporates the present value of future cash flows. Specifically, it determines the rate of return inherent in a project by determining the discount rate that equates the present value of the inflows with the present value of the outflows of the project. And, like the net present value method, the internal rate of return can be used not only to identify acceptable projects, but also to rank them. The project with the highest internal rate of return would be ranked first, the second highest rate next, and so on.

B. Differences between the methodology used in the net present value method and the internal rate of return method, however, can result in different rankings for a given set of projects. These ranking may be different depending on:

1. Project size;
2. Timing of cash flows;
3. Project life-span.

C. While the other methods discussed above are primarily concerned with determining the economic feasibility of capital projects, the profitability index method is primarily intended for use in ranking projects. It does so by taking into account both the net present value of each project and the cost of each project. Specifically, the index results from dividing the net present value of the project by the initial cost of the project. As a result of that division, an index of 1.0 is logically the lowest acceptable outcome. Any value lower than 1.0 would indicate that the project's net present value is less than the initial investment. As values on the profitability index increase, so does the financial attractiveness of the proposed project.

VII. Summary

A. In summary, when ranking acceptable capital projects, methods based on discounted values are much better than methods which don't incorporate the time value of money. The net present value method and, especially the profitability index derived using net present value and the initial project cost, generally are preferable to other methods. In the final analysis, however, some degree of subjectivity is likely to enter into deciding which projects will be implemented.

B. Once capital budgeting (project investment) decisions have been made, the impact of these plans must be built into other affected budgets. For example, a planned new project may have implications for sales revenue, production costs, and cash flows, in addition to asset acquisition. Further, once a project is initiated, it should be monitored frequently to assure that it continues to meet the entity's requirements for acceptability.

Financing Options

Introduction and Financial/Capital Structure

All activities and undertakings of an entity, including capital projects, must be financed. A variety of both short-term and long-term potential sources are available to most firms. This lesson introduces the need for financing and distinguishes between financial and capital structures and the nature of financing provided by each.

I. Introduction

A. Once the projects and activities to be undertaken are decided upon, a firm must separately decide how those undertakings will be financed. This relationship and this requirement exist from the inception of a firm and continue throughout its operating life.

B. This section defines an entity's financial and capital structure, identifies various means of short-term and long-term financing and the advantages and disadvantages of each means of financing, summarizes cost of capital concepts, and outlines guidelines for making appropriate financing decisions in different circumstances.

II. Financial Structure and Capital Structure

A. From an accounting perspective, all items of liabilities and owners' equity are sources of financing an entity's assets, and therefore its operations. While accounts payable and common stock equity may be significantly different in terms of amount, duration, and other characteristics, each is nonetheless a source of funds for carrying out the activities of the entity. The mix of all elements of liabilities and owners' equity constitute a firm's financial structure. The concept of capital structure is less inclusive. It includes only the long-term sources of financing, that is, long-term debt and owners' equity. The elements of and relationships between financial structure and capital structure can be illustrated using a typical balance sheet format:

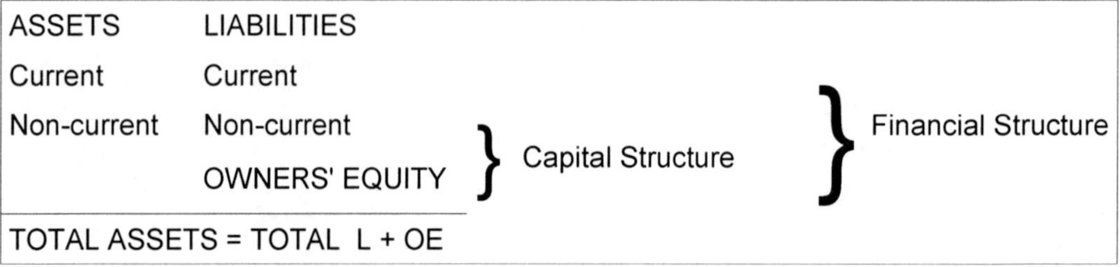

ASSETS	LIABILITIES		
Current	Current		Financial Structure
Non-current	Non-current	Capital Structure	Financial Structure
	OWNERS' EQUITY	Capital Structure	Financial Structure
TOTAL ASSETS = TOTAL L + OE			

B. Thus, financial structure is a more inclusive concept and measure than capital structure. While all elements of financial structure are sources of an entity's financing, only the elements of capital structure provide long-term financing.

Short-term (Working Capital) Financing

Introduction to Short-term Financing

Short-term financing is comprised of sources that provide funding for a period of one year or less. This lesson describes short-term financing and identifies the primary current assets and liabilities used for short-term financing. Each of the current items identified in this lesson is considered in detail in subsequent lessons.

I. Short-term (Working Capital) Financing

A. Like the accounting definition of current liabilities, the concept of short-term financing generally applies to obligations that will become due within one year. Therefore, items which are considered current liabilities also are considered forms of short-term financing. In addition, current assets which can be used to secure financing would be forms of short-term financing. The primary forms of short-term financing would include:

1. Trade accounts payable;
2. Accrued accounts payable (e.g., wages, taxes, etc.);
3. Short-term notes payable;
4. Line of credit, revolving credit and letter of credit;
5. Commercial paper;
6. Pledging accounts receivable;
7. Factoring accounts receivable;
8. Inventory secured loans.

B. Each of these forms of financing is described and discussed in the following lessons.

Payables

Among the most common forms of short-term financing are various payables due within one year or less. This lesson considers three of those, including trade accounts payable, accrued accounts payable, and short-term notes payable. Each is described and the advantages and disadvantages as a form of financing identified.

I. Trade Accounts Payable

A. Financing through trade accounts payable occurs in the normal course of business as a firm routinely buys goods or services from its suppliers. The credit derived from trade accounts normally is not secured, in that no assets are pledged as collateral, but rather depend on the borrowers ability and willingness to pay the obligation when due. Financing certain acquisitions (e.g., supplies and inventory) through trade accounts is a highly flexible source of short-term financing - the level of financing goes up concurrent with the purchase of the goods or service. This sort of financing that occurs automatically in the carrying out of day-to-day operations, as happens with many general short-term payables, is called "spontaneous financing."

B. Often, trade credit is extended with the offer of a cash discount for early payment of an obligation. These offers would be incorporated as part of the credit terms and generally are expressed as a percent of the amount of the obligation. For example, credit terms of "2/10, n/30" offer a 2% discount if the bill is paid within 10 days, otherwise the full amount is due within 30 days. Other discount rates and discount periods are common. The annual effective rate of interest implicit in such cash discount offers shows that effective cash management would take advantage of most cash discount offers. For example, the effective annual percentage rate (APR) of not taking an offer of "2/10,n/30" is almost 37%, calculated as follows using $1.00 as the amount of the obligation:

> APR = Discount Lost / Principal x 1 / Time Fraction of Year
>
> APR = .02 / .98 = 1 / (20 / 360) = .0204 x 360 / 20
>
> APR = .0204 x 18 = 36.73%

C. The principal is the amount that would have been paid if the discount were taken. (Even if $1.00 were used as the principal, the APR would be .02 x 18 = 36.0%.)

D. The advantages and disadvantages of using trade accounts payable for financing can be summarized as:

1. **Advantages**
   - **a.** Ease of use - little legal documentation required;
   - **b.** Flexible - expands and contracts with needs (purchases);
   - **c.** Interest normally not charged;
   - **d.** Unsecured - no assets pledged as collateral;
   - **e.** Discount often offered for early payment.
2. **Disadvantages**
   - **a.** Requires payment in the short term;

b. Higher effective cost if discounts not taken;

c. Use specific - finances only assets acquired through trade accounts.

II. Accrued Accounts Payable

A. Accrued accounts payable result from benefits or cash received for which the related obligation has not been paid yet. Thus, they are very much like trade accounts payable in their financing implications. Common examples are:

1. Salaries and wages payable;

2. Taxes payable;

3. Unearned revenue (collected in advance).

B. To the extent there is a timing difference between when the benefit (or cash) is received and when the related obligation is satisfied, the cost or funds involved provide temporary (short-term) financing to the entity. For example, if salaried employees are paid once a month, they effectively are making a recurring one month loan to the firm which accumulates to the total monthly pay for all salaried employees. (The technical amount would be the average salaries for the month). For a large firm, the resulting amount of financing would be significant. A similar effect occurs from taxes and revenues collected prior to payment or satisfaction of the obligation.

C. The advantages and disadvantages are similar to those for trade accounts payable, including:

1. **Advantages**

a. Ease of use - occurs in the normal course of business;

b. Flexible - expands and contracts with activity;

c. Unsecured - no assets pledged (though taxing authorities have a specific legal claim).

2. **Disadvantages**

a. Requires satisfaction in the short term;

b. Certain sources are use specific - only finances benefits acquired through accrued accounts (e.g., salaries).

III. Short-term Notes Payable

A. Short-term notes payable result from borrowing, usually from a commercial bank, with repayment due in one year or less. These borrowings are typically for a designated purpose, require a promissory note be given, and carry a rate of interest determined by the credit rating of the borrower. Although a promissory note (a legally enforceable promise to pay) is required, short-term notes generally are unsecured, unless the borrower's credit rating dictates the lender require security. The interest rate usually will be expressed as a rate (or points) above the prime rate (or a similar benchmark). For example, the rate may be expressed as "1.00% over prime."

B. In addition to the interest cost associated with short-term notes, the borrower also may be required to maintain a compensating balance with the lending institution. A compensating balance is an amount that the borrower maintains in a demand deposit account with the lender as a condition of the loan (or for other bank services). The amount required to be maintained is usually expressed as a percent of the loan (or other factor) and increases the effective cost of the loan.

C. The advantages and disadvantages of short-term notes for financing purposes are:

1. Advantages

a. Commonly available for creditworthy firms;

b. Flexible - amounts and periods (within one year) can be varied with needs;

c. Unsecured - no assets pledged as collateral;

d. Provides cash.

2. Disadvantages

a. Poor credit rating results in high interest (and possibility of security required);

b. Requires satisfaction in the short term;

c. A required compensating balance increases cost and reduces effective funds available;

d. Refinancing may be necessary.

Stand-by Credit & Commercial Paper

Stand-by credit makes funds available from a lender for a specific amount, usually for a specified period of time, and often to be available under certain conditions. This lesson covers several forms of stand-by credit, including line of credit, revolving credit, and letter of credit. It also covers commercial paper as a form of financing.

I. Line of Credit/Revolving Credit/Letter of Credit

Definition:

A line of credit: Is an informal agreement between a borrower and a financial institution whereby the financial institution agrees to a maximum amount of credit that it will extend to the borrower at any one time.

A. Generally, the agreement is good only for the prospective borrower's fiscal year and, although the agreement is not legally binding on the financial institution, provides the firm reasonable assurance that the agreed upon financing will be available. Like a short-term note, a line of credit is generally unsecured, has an interest rate that is indexed to the prime rate (or other benchmark), and may require a compensating balance. Unlike a short-term note, however, a line of credit usually is not arranged for a specific purpose, but rather for a more general use. For example, it might be "to meet working capital requirements."

Definition:

A revolving credit agreement: Is like a line of credit, but is in the context of a legal agreement between the borrower and the financial institution.

B. Borrowings under such agreements generally are unsecured and have the same interest, maturity, and compensating balance requirements as a line of credit.

Definition:

A letter of credit: Is a conditional commitment by a bank to pay a third party in accordance with specified terms and commitments.

C. For example, payment may be made to the third party (e.g., a supplier) upon submission of proof that goods have been shipped. Use of a letter of credit provides assurance of funding to the third party without the borrowing firm having to pay in advance of shipment of goods. Letters of credit frequently are used in connection with foreign transactions.

D. The advantages and disadvantages of line of credit, revolving credit and letter of credit are:

1. Advantages

a. Commonly available for creditworthy firms;

b. Highly flexible - credit used (debt incurred) only when needed;

c. Unsecured - no assets pledged as collateral;

d. Line of credit and revolving credit provide cash for general use.

2. **Disadvantages**

a. Poor credit rating results in high interest (and possibly security);

b. Typically involve a fee;

c. Requires satisfaction in the short term;

d. A required compensating balance increases cost and reduces effective funds available;

e. Line of credit does not legally obligate the financial institution.

II. Commercial Paper

Definition:

Commercial paper: Is short-term unsecured promissory notes sold by large, highly creditworthy firms as a form of short-term financing.

A. By convention, these notes are for 270 days or less (otherwise, SEC registration is required), with most being for six months or less. Commercial paper may be sold with interest discounted (deducted up front) or to pay interest over the (short) life of the note or at its maturity, and may be sold directly to investors or through a dealer. The effective interest rate typically is less than the cost of borrowing through a commercial bank.

B. The advantages and disadvantages associated with the use of commercial paper for financing are:

1. **Advantages**

a. Interest rate is generally lower than other short-term sources;

b. Larger amount of funds can be obtained through multiple commercial paper notes than would be available through a single financial institution;

c. Compensating balances are not required;

d. Unsecured - no assets are pledged as collateral;

e. Provides cash for general use.

2. **Disadvantages**

a. Only available to most creditworthy firms;

b. Requires satisfaction in the short term, usually of a large amount;

c. Lacks flexibility of extension or other accommodation available in bank loans.

Receivables & Inventory

Certain non-cash current assets can be used as sources of financing for a firm. This lesson considers the ways accounts receivable and inventory can provide financing, either by being converted to cash or serving as security for borrowings.

I. Pledging Accounts Receivable

A. Financing through pledging accounts receivable uses a current asset, trade accounts receivable, as security for short-term borrowings. Specifically, the firm pledges some or all of its accounts receivable as collateral for a short-term loan from a commercial bank or finance company. If the terms of agreement between the firm and the lender provide that all accounts receivable are pledged without regard to or analysis of the collectibility of individual accounts, the lender will lend a smaller portion of the face value of receivables than if only specific accounts with known risk are pledged. For example, a maximum loan of only 70% of receivables may be made when simply all receivables are pledged, but as much as 90% of face value may be loaned on receivables that have been determined to be creditworthy. The rate of interest on loans secured by accounts receivable typically will range from 2% above prime and up. In addition, a fee based on the face value of the receivables usually will be charged.

B. The advantages and disadvantages of using pledged accounts receivable to secure a loan are:

1. Advantages

a. Commonly available;

b. Flexible - as new receivables occur, they are available as security;

c. Compensating balances are not required;

d. Provides cash for general use;

e. Lender may provide billing and collection services.

2. Disadvantages

a. Accounts are committed to lender;

b. Cost may be greater than certain other sources of short-term financing;

c. Requires repayment in the short term.

II. Factoring Accounts Receivable

A. Factoring accounts receivable is the sale of accounts receivable to a commercial bank or other financial institution (called a "factor"). Actual payment to the firm for its accounts receivable may occur at various times between the date of sale and collection of the receivables. The funds received can then be used for financing of other assets or used for other purposes. The terms of the sale may be:

> Without Recourse - the factor bears the risk associated with collectibility (unless fraud is involved).
>
> With Recourse - the factor has recourse against the firm for some or all of the risk associated with uncollectibility.

B. The factor charges a fee (factor's fee) based on the creditworthiness and length of maturity of the receivables, and the extent to which the factor assumes risk of uncollectibility.

C. The advantages and disadvantages of factoring accounts receivable are:

1. **Advantages**

   a. Commonly available;

   b. Flexible: as new accounts receivable occur, they are available for sale;

   c. Compensating balances are not required;

   d. Provides cash for general use;

   e. Buyer generally assumes billing and collection responsibilities.

2. **Disadvantages**

   a. Cost may be greater than certain other sources of short-term financing;

   b. If sold with recourse, firm may have on-going risk;

   c. Sale of their accounts may alienate customers.

III. Inventory Secured Loans

A. With an inventory secured loan a firm pledges all or part of its inventory as collateral for a short-term loan. The amount that can be borrowed depends on the value and marketability of the inventory. Different arrangements for inventory secured loans provide different treatment of the inventory and different levels of security for the lender:

1. **Floating lien agreement --** The borrower gives a lien against all of its inventory to the lender, but retains control of its inventory, which it continuously sells and replaces.
2. **Chattel mortgage agreement --** The borrower gives a lien against specifically identified inventory and retains control of the inventory, but cannot sell it without the lender's approval.
3. **Field warehouse agreement --** The inventory used as collateral remains at the firm's warehouse, but is placed under the control of an independent third-party and held as security.
4. **Terminal warehouse agreement --** The inventory used as collateral is moved to a public warehouse where it is held as security.

B. The cost of using inventory secured loans for financing will depend on several factors, including the nature of the inventory used as collateral, the credit standing of the borrower, and the specific type of security agreement. The typical interest rate is 2% above prime and up, and may involve other fees.

C. The advantages and disadvantages of using inventory to secure short-term financing are similar to those for pledging accounts receivable, and include:

1. **Advantages**

   a. Commonly available for certain inventories (e.g., oil, wheat, etc.);

   b. Flexible - as new inventories are obtained, they are available as security;

   c. Compensating balances are not required;

   d. Provides cash for general use.

2. Disadvantages

- **a.** Pledged inventory may not be available when needed;
- **b.** Cost can be greater than certain other sources of short-term financing;
- **c.** Requires repayment in the short term;
- **d.** Not available for certain inventory.

D. The foregoing section has identified and described the most common forms of short-term financing. Because these forms of financing have to be satisfied in the near term, generally they are not appropriate for financing capital projects. Nevertheless, they provide an important role in the overall financing of a firm's total assets and operations.

Long-Term (Capital) Financing

Introduction to Long-Term Financing

Long-term financing is comprised of sources that provide funding for periods greater than one year and includes both debt and equity instruments. This lesson describes long-term financing and identifies the primary forms of long-term financing. Each of the forms of long-term financing is considered in detail in subsequent lessons.

I. Long-Term (Capital) Financing

A. Long-term financing comprises the sources of funds used by a firm that do not mature within one year. A distinction sometimes is made between intermediate-term and long-term financing. In that case, intermediate-term financing is taken as sources of financing which mature in more than one year but less than ten years, and long-term financing is taken as sources of financing which extend beyond ten years, including shareholders' equity. Since the different sources may overlap those two time periods, the discussion here treats both categories as long term and makes note of the likely term of each source. Further, treating all sources of funding that are not short term as a group is consistent with distinguishing those sources which constitute capital structure (as contrasted with financial structure) of a firm.

B. Because long-term financing provides the major source of funding for most firms and because the length of commitment associated with these sources is by definition for a long period of time, a firm should carefully consider the alternative sources of long-term financing and the relative proportion of each it will employ. The cost associated with each source and the relative dollar amount of each source used will determine the firm's weighted average cost of capital that, as we discussed earlier, will determine which undertakings are economically feasible for the firm to pursue. The primary forms of long-term financing would include:

1. Long-term notes;
2. Financial (Capital) leases;
3. Bonds;
4. Preferred stock;
5. Common stock.

C. Each of these forms of financing is discussed in the following lessons.

Long-term Notes & Financial Leases

Two common forms of long-term debt financing are notes and financial leases. This lesson describes the use of each of these sources and identifies the advantages and disadvantages associated with the use of each.

I. Long-term Notes

A. Long-term notes typically are used for borrowings normally of from one to ten years, but some may be of longer duration. These borrowings usually are repaid in periodic installments over the life of the loan and usually are secured by a mortgage on equipment or real estate. In addition to requiring collateral, long-term notes often contain restrictive covenants that impose restrictions on the borrower so as to reduce the likelihood of default. Such covenants commonly place restrictions on:

1. **Maintaining certain working capital conditions --** For example, maintaining a minimum dollar amount of working capital or a minimum working capital ratio.
2. **Additional incurrence of debt --** For example, requiring lender approval before taking on additional long-term debt, including as might arise through financial leases.
3. **Frequency and nature of financial information --** For example, requiring the borrower to provide periodic financial statements and related disclosures, perhaps with an audit report.
4. **Management changes --** For example, requiring lender approval before certain changes in key personnel are made.

B. The cost of financing through use of a long-term note will depend on a number of factors, including the general level of interest in the market, the creditworthiness of the firm borrowing and the nature and value of any collateral, and will be expressed as a function of the prime interest rate (or other benchmark). Therefore, during the life of the note, the rate of interest will fluctuate as the prime rate changes.

C. The advantages and disadvantages associated with the use of long-term notes include:

1. **Advantages**
   - **a.** Commonly available for creditworthy firms;
   - **b.** Provides long-term financing, often with periodic repayment.
2. **Disadvantages**
   - **a.** Poor credit rating results in higher interest, greater security requirements, and more restrictive covenants;
   - **b.** Violation of restrictive covenants triggers serious consequences, including technical default.

II. Financial Leases

A. Leasing, rather than buying, is an alternative way of financing the acquisition of certain assets. When leasing is an option for acquiring assets in a capital budgeting project, evaluation of the project has to take into account the different costs associated with each alternative for financing the project - buying and leasing. Therefore, the analysis would need to determine:

1. Whether or not the proposed project is economically feasible if assets are purchased; and

2. Whether or not the proposed project is economically feasible if assets are leased.

B. Several possible outcomes of the analysis are possible:

1. **Reject** -- If neither analysis shows that the project is economically feasible, the project would be rejected.

2. **Purchase** -- The project should be accepted using asset purchase if:

a. The traditional capital budgeting analysis (e.g., net present value using the cost of capital) shows the project to be economically feasible, but the leasing-based analysis does not.

b. Both analyses show the project to be economically feasible, but the traditional purchase analysis shows a better "return."

3. **Lease** -- The project should be accepted using asset leasing if:

a. The leasing-based analysis shows the project to be economically feasible, but the traditional capital budgeting analysis does not.

b. Both analyses show the project to be economically feasible, but the leasing-based analysis shows a better "return."

C. **In analyzing the alternatives**, leasing may be the better option as a result of lower cost of leasing. That is, the lessor can provide the asset at a lower cost than if the lessee purchased the asset. This may occur because the lessor has efficiencies, lower interest rates, or tax advantages that the lessee does not have. In addition to being justified on a strictly economic basis, leasing is sometimes used for more subjective reasons, including flexibility and convenience.

D. If leasing is to be used, from a financial management perspective, the lease would be considered a **financial lease**, as opposed to an operating lease. While the classifications used in finance (financial and operating) are similar to the concepts of capital leases and operating leases used in accounting, there are some differences. A financial lease is a legally enforceable, noncancelable contract under which the lessee commits to making a series of payments to the owner of the asset (lessor) for use of the asset over the period of the lease. Thus, for financial analysis purposes, whether or not the lease is, in effect, a sale - the concept underlying the designation for capital lease in accounting - is not relevant. Practically, however, both categories (financial and capital) reflect the same consequence for financing - the use of an asset is acquired at the present with the cost being incurred over multiple future periods. (In both finance and accounting, operating leases are considered more like renting than a means of financing asset acquisition and are not particularly relevant here).

E. In finance, leases are described as being **net leases** or **net-net leases** to identify which costs of the asset are the responsibility of the lessee. In a net lease, the lessee assumes the cost associated with ownership during the period of the lease. Normally, these costs are referred to in accounting as executory costs and include maintenance, taxes, and insurance. In a net-net lease, the lessee is responsible for not only the executory costs, but also a pre-established residual value. The particular nature - lease, net lease, or net-net lease - will affect the cost of the lease to the lessee and, therefore, the viability and benefits of leasing.

F. The advantages and disadvantages associated with leasing are:

1. **Advantages**

a. Limited immediate cash outlay;

b. Possible lower cost than purchasing, resulting primarily from lessor efficiencies, lower interest rates, or tax savings, some of which are "passed on" to the lessee;

c. The resulting debt (lease payment) is specific to the amount needed;

d. Possibility of scheduling payments to coincide with cash flows;

e. No (or fewer) restrictive agreements than incurring certain other debt.

2. **Disadvantages**

a. Not all assets are commonly available for lease;

b. Lease financing is asset specific - funds are not available for general use;

c. Lease terms may prove different than the period of asset usefulness;

d. Often chosen for reasons other than economic justification.

Bonds

One of the most common forms of obtaining long-term debt financing for large corporations is through the issuance of bonds, which can provide large amounts of funding for long periods of time. This lesson defines and describes bonds, bond characteristics, bond valuation, and bond yields. It concludes with a summary of the advantages and disadvantages associated with the use of bonds for financing purposes.

I. Introduction

Definition:

Bonds: Are long-term promissory notes wherein the borrower, in return for buyers'/lenders' funds, promises to pay the bondholders a fixed amount of interest each year and to repay the face value of the note at maturity.

A. While most bonds have some common characteristics, there are differences between certain kinds of bonds. Common characteristics include:

1. **Indenture** -- the bond contract;
2. **Par value or face value** -- the "principal" that will be returned at maturity, most commonly $1,000 per bond;
3. **Coupon rate of interest** -- the annual interest rate printed on the bond and paid on par value;
4. **Maturity** -- the time at which the issuer repays the par value to the bondholders.

II. A major difference in bonds is whether or not the bond issue is secured by collateral

Definitions:

Debenture bonds: Are unsecured; no specific asset is designated as collateral. These bonds are considered to have more risk and, therefore, must provide a greater return than secured bonds.

Secured bonds: Have specific assets (e.g., machinery and equipment) designated as collateral for the bonds.

Mortgage bonds: Are secured by a lien on real property (e.g., land and building).

III. Bond Values

A. Because a very large number of bonds, each with a par value of (say) $1,000, can be issued, very large sums can be raised through bond issues. While the par value of each bond may be $1,000, the cash proceeds received upon issuing the bonds will depend on the relationship between the coupon interest rate (on the face of the bond) and investors' required rate of return when the bonds are issued. The investors' required rate of return would be based primarily on the return available from other investment opportunities in the market with comparable perceived risk (i.e., the investors' opportunity cost). If the investors' required rate - the market rate - is more than the coupon rate, the bonds will sell at less that par (i.e., at a discount); if the market rate is less than the coupon rate, the bonds will sell at more than par (i.e., at a premium).

B. The determination of a bond's selling price at issue and the determination of a bond's value during its life is a function of the present value of its future cash flows. Bonds have two cash flows:

1. **Periodic interest --** discounted as the present value of an annuity;
2. **Maturity face value --** discounted as the present value of a single amount.

C. Both cash flows would be discounted using the market (investors') required rate of return at the time, which reflects the market's assessment of the risk inherent in the bond issue and rates available through other comparable investments.

IV. Bond Yields

A. Two measures of rates associated with bonds are noteworthy, current yield and yield to maturity.

Definition:

Current Yield: Is the ratio of annual interest payments to the current market price of the bond. Assuming a $1,000, 6% bond currently selling for $900, the current yield (CY) would be computes as:

CY = Annual Coupon Interest / Current Market Price

CY = ($1,000 x .06) / $900 = $60 / $900 = 6.67

a. Thus, while the coupon rate is 6%, the current yield based on the current price is 6.67%. As the market price of the bonds changes, so too will the current yield.

Definition:

Yield to Maturity (also called the Expected Rate of Return): Is the rate of return required by investors as implied by the current market price of the bonds.

b. Changes in the market price of an outstanding bond reflect changes in the rate of return expected on those bonds. Determining the yield to maturity is done by determining the discount rate that equates the present value of future cash flows from the bond issue with the current price of the bonds. That rate is the rate of return currently expected by bondholders. The process of determining that rate is identical to the process of determining the internal rate of return on a capital project. In the absence of a financial calculator or computer, the process is one of trial and error, and interpolation using present value tables.

c. As the bondholders' current expected rate of return, the yield to maturity is an important measure of the firm's current cost of debt capital.

V. Changes in Interest -- Because **changes in the market rate of interest** cause the price of bonds to change inversely (i.e., as market rates of interest go up, the value of bonds goes down, and vice versa), investors in bonds face a market rate risk. Further, that risk is greater the longer the term of the bonds because of the longer holding period of the fixed interest rate. Thus, a 20-year bond would have a higher interest rate risk than a 10-year bond, and a firm would have to pay a somewhat higher rate if interest for that risk difference.

VI. Advantages and disadvantages associated with the use of bonds for financing purposes

A. Advantages

1. A source of large sums of capital;
2. Does not dilute ownership or earnings per share;
3. Interest payments are tax deductible.

B. Disadvantages

1. Required periodic interest payments-default can result in bankruptcy;
2. Required principal repayment at maturity-default can result in bankruptcy;
3. May require security and/or have restrictive covenants.

Preferred Stock

Two types of equity instruments are commonly used for long-term financing - preferred stock and common stock. As the term implies, preferred stock offers "preferences" to shareholders that are not provided to common shareholders. This lesson considers the characteristics of preferred stock, the valuation of and returns on preferred stock, and the advantages and disadvantages associated with the use of preferred stock for financing purposes.

I. Preferred Stock

A. Although preferred stock grants an ownership interest in the firm, it is frequently described as having characteristics of both bonds and common stock.

1. It is like bonds in that the dividend amount, like interest, is limited in amount and generally does not have voting rights.

2. It is **like common stock** in that it:

a. Grants ownership interest;

b. Has no maturity date;

c. Does not require dividends be paid;

d. Dividends paid are not an expense and are not deductible.

3. Unlike common stock, for which there are few variations in features, preferred stock may have a variety of characteristics, including:

a. A firm can have different classes or types of preferred stock with different characteristics and different preferences.

b. Cumulative/Noncumulative feature to distinguish whether or not dividends not paid in any year accumulate and must be paid before common dividends are paid.

c. Participating/Nonparticipating feature to distinguish whether or not preferred shareholders can receive dividends in excess of the stated preference rate.

d. Protective provisions to protect preferred shareholders' interest. For example, the right to vote under certain circumstances or the requirement for a preferred stock sinking fund.

e. Convertible/Nonconvertible feature to distinguish whether or not preferred stock shareholders can exchange preferred stock for common stock according to a specified exchange rate.

f. Call provision which gives the firm the right to buy back the preferred stock, normally at a premium.

II. Preferred Stock Values

A. Because of its preference claim to dividends, for financial valuation and analytical purposes preferred stock is treated very much like bonds. Like bonds, the value of preferred stock is the present value of expected future cash flows. Whereas bonds have two forms of future cash flows, interest and principal at maturity, preferred stock has only one primary stream of future cash flows, dividends. Further, while bonds have a maturity, preferred stock may be outstanding indefinitely. Therefore, the elements used to estimate the value of preferred stock are:

1. Estimated future annual dividends;
2. Discount rate in the form of investors' required rate of return;
3. An assumption that the dividend stream will exist in perpetuity.

B. Using the assumed elements, the theoretical value of a share of preferred stock (PSV) can be calculated as:

PSV = Annual Dividend / Required rate of Return

C. For example, if the annual dividend is $4.00 and preferred investors expect an 8% return, the implied value of the preferred stock would be:

PSV = $4.00 /.08 = $50.00

III. Preferred Stock Rate of Return

A. Like bondholders, preferred stockholders have a rate of return they expect to earn on their investment. That currently expected rate of return can be derived using two directly determinable elements:

1. Annual dividend;
2. Market price.

B. Using these elements, the expected rate of return (PSER) can be calculated as:

PSER = Annual Dividend / Market Price

C. Assuming an annual dividend of $4.00 and a current market price of $52.00, the calculation would be:

PSER = $4.00 / $52.00 = .077 = 7.7%

D. Thus, based on the current market price, the currently expected rate of return on the preferred stock is 7.7%.

E. Since the annual dividend is "fixed" and the market price will change to reflect changes in market perceptions of the stock, the expected rate of return reflects the rate investors currently require to invest in the stock. That rate is a measure of the firm's current cost of preferred stock capital.

IV. Advantages and disadvantages -- associated with the use of preferred stock for financing include

A. Advantages

1. No legally required periodic payments; default cannot result from failure to pay dividends;
2. Generally a lower cost of capital than common stock;
3. Generally does not bestow voting rights;
4. No maturity date;
5. No security required.

B. Disadvantages

1. Dividend expectations are high;
2. Dividend payments are not tax deductible;
3. If triggered, protective provisions may be onerous;
4. Generally, a higher cost of capital than bonds.

Common Stock

Common stock is the basic form of long-term equity financing for corporations. This lesson considers the characteristics of common stock, the valuation and returns on common stock, and the advantages and disadvantages associated with the use of common stock for financing purposes.

I. Common Stock Characteristics

A. Common stock represents the basic ownership interest in a corporation. Unlike preferred stock, the characteristics of common stock are fairly uniform. While it is possible in some jurisdictions to have more than one class of common stock with different rights, regulatory and other requirements virtually preclude more than one class of common stock. Characteristics of common stock include:

1. **Limited liability --** common shareholders' liability is limited to their investment.
2. **Residual claim to income and assets --** common shareholders' claim to income and assets on liquidation comes after the claims of creditors and preferred shareholders.
3. **Right to vote --** for directors, auditors and changes to the corporate charter. A temporary power of attorney, called a proxy, can be used to delegate that right.
4. **Preemptive right --** the right of first refusal to acquire a proportionate share of any new common stock issued.

B. The fact that common shareholders have only a residual claim to income (and assets on liquidation) adds an element of risk, often referred to as financial risk, for the common shareholder. While the common shareholders are entitled to all income remaining after other capital sources (creditors and preferred shareholders) have received interest and dividends, they bear the risk of weak earnings. As a consequence, the cost of common stock capital is usually higher than that of either bonds or preferred stock.

II. Common Stock Values

A. As with other sources of capital, the value of common stock is the present value of expected cash flows; for common stockholders that is expected dividends and stock price appreciation. Thus, if an assumption is made that a share of common stock is to be acquired and held for only one year, the current value of that share should be the sum of:

1. Present value of dividends expected during the one year holding period discounted at the investor's required rate of return;
2. Present value of the expected stock market price at the end of the one year holding period discounted at the investor's required rate of return.

B. When considering an investment to be made for multiple holding periods, expectations about future dividends, and especially about future stock market prices, become much less certain. One way that uncertainty is addressed in financial analysis is by assuming that dividends grow at a constant rate indefinitely. The constant growth in dividends is assumed to incorporate both dividends distributed and growth in stock value. Under that assumption, the current value of common stock (CSV) can be computed as:

CSV = Dividend in 1st Year / (Required Rate of Return - Growth Rate)

Example:
Assume an expected dividend of $2.10, an expected indefinite dividend growth of 5% annually and a required rate of return of 8%, the resulting value of the common stock would be:

CSV = $2.10 / (8% - 5%) = $2.10 / .03 = $70.00

III. Common Stock Returns

A. Under the assumption that dividends are expected to grow at a constant rate indefinitely into the future and that the stock market price is reflected by that dividend growth rate, the expected rate of return (CSER) for a prospective current investor (marginal investor) can be computed as:

CSER = (Dividend in 1st Year / Market Price) + Growth Rate

Example:
Assume an expected dividend of $2.10, a growth rate of 5% and a current market price of $70.00, the calculation would be:

CSER = ($2.10 / $70.00) + .05

CSER = 03 + .05 = .08 = 8%

Thus, the marginal investor with a required rate of return of 8% would be willing to pay $70.00 per share, the current market price of the stock. This rate of return is the current cost of capital through common stock financing. In addition, since common stockholders have a residual claim to income, and retained earnings is largely residual income, this rate of return also reflects the implicit cost of internal financing - that is, the cost of using retained earnings, rather than distributing them in the form of dividends.

IV. Advantages and disadvantages -- associated with the use of common stock financing include

A. Advantages

1. No legally required periodic payments. Default cannot result from failure to pay dividends;
2. No maturity date;
3. No security required.

B. Disadvantages

1. Generally a higher cost of capital than other sources;
2. Dividends paid are not tax deductible;
3. Additional shares issued dilute ownership and earnings.

Cost of Capital & Financing Strategies

Capital structure consists of long-term sources of financing. Each of those sources has a cost associated with its use. A number of factors determine the cost of each element of capital. This lesson summarizes factors which enter into that determination and identifies guidelines for appropriate financing strategies.

I. Cost of Capital - Summary Concepts and Relationships

A. Long-term financing is provided by those sources of capital funding that do not mature within one year. Thus, these sources include long-term notes, financial leases, bonds, preferred stock and common stock (including retained earnings), as well as variations (hybrids) of these kinds of securities. Although computed differently, the cost of obtaining capital from each of these sources is the rate of return that each source requires, which is based on the returns available from other comparable investments in the market - the investors' opportunity cost. While the cost of each element of capital will be somewhat unique for each firm, some general relationships which influence these costs can be identified:

1. **Macroeconomic conditions --** includes market condition and expectations concerning economic factors such as interest rates, tax rates, and inflation/deflation rates. Increasing interest rates, tax rates and inflation, or expectation thereof, will result in a higher cost of capital.
2. **Past performance of the firm --** reflects management's operating and financial decisions and the riskiness associated with those decisions. The greater the inferred risk inherent in past performance, the higher the risk premium required and, therefore, the cost of capital.
3. **Amount of financing --** recognizes that the larger the absolute amount of financing sought, the higher the cost of capital.
4. **Relative level of debt financing --** recognizes that the higher the proportion of financing sought through debt, as opposed to equity, the higher the cost of capital.
5. **Debt maturity --** recognizes that the longer the maturity of debt, the higher the cost of capital. The longer the debt, the greater the risk of interest rate changes, thus, lenders charge a maturity premium for that risk.
6. **Debt security --** recognizes that the greater the value of collateral relative to the amount of debt, the lower the interest rate, or cost of capital.
7. **Returns --** Rates of return earned historically by investors on various forms of investment provide insight into the relative average cost of each element of capital over long periods of time. For example, one study (Ibbotson & Sinquefield) shows the following long-run annual rates of return:

Security Type	Annual Rate of Return
Long-term Corporate Bonds	5.9%
Common Stock	12.3
Common Stock-Small Firms	17.6

8. Since preferred stock has characteristics of both bonds and common stock, the rate of return on preferred stock reasonably could be expected to be greater than that of bonds, but less than that of common stock.

II. Financing Strategies

A. At any point in time, a firm's historic financing strategy is evident in its balance sheet. The assets show the results of the firm's accumulated investment in projects and other undertakings, and the liabilities and shareholders' equity sections show how the firm's undertakings have been financed. For any new undertaking the firm generally will have several alternative means of financing it. Although the best financing alternative will depend on all the facts and circumstances existing at the time, certain guidelines for appropriate financing strategy exist. These guidelines include:

1. **Hedging principle of financing --** This guideline (also called the principle of self-liquidating debt) holds that long-term or permanent investments in assets should be financed with long-term or permanent sources of capital and short-term needs should be financed with short-term sources of financing. Thus, long-term assets (e.g., property, plant, and equipment, among others) and permanent amounts of current assets (e.g., level of accounts receivable and inventory generally on-hand) should be financed with long-term debt or equity. Conversely, temporary investments in assets (e.g., a temporary increase in inventory to meet seasonal demand) should be financed with temporary sources of financing. **The objective of this principle is to match cash flows from assets with the cash requirements need to satisfy the related financing.**

2. **Optimum capital structure objective --** This guideline seeks to minimize a firm's aggregate cost of permanent (long-term) capital financing by using an optimum (or satisfying) mix of debt and equity components. Since a corporation will have common stock, a major issue is how much debt financing it should use relative to its equity financing. As noted above, long-term debt financing is less costly than common stock financing. (This is logical if for no other reason than that the tax shield resulting from debt expense-interest-is tax deductible, while the cost of common stock-dividends-is not.) Therefore, firms will be motivated to use increasing amounts of long-term debt for financing, the concept of financial leverage. At some level of relative debt, however, the increased risk of default associated with the debt will result in debt investors demanding such a high return (default premium) that the cost of debt will be greater than the cost of common stock. **The objective in structuring the firm's capital mix is to determine the set or sets of capital sources that result in the lowest composite cost of capital for the firm.**

3. **Business risk constraint --** This guideline recognizes that a firm with higher variability in its operating results should limit the extent to which it uses debt financing (i.e., financial leverage). Business risk derives from the uncertainty inherent in the nature of the operations of the business and would be affected by such things as macroeconomic conditions, degree of competition, size and diversification, and operating leverage, among others. This risk is measured in terms of the variability of a firm's expected operating earnings (earnings before interest and taxes, known as EBIT). The higher the variation, the greater the risk. **Firms with higher business risk have an increased chance that operating results may cause default on fixed obligations and, therefore, should use less debt financing than a firm with steady operating results.**

4. **Tax rate benefit effect --** This guideline recognizes that, other things being equal, the higher the tax rate of a firm, the greater the benefit of debt financing. Because the cost of debt-that is, interest-is tax deductible, it generates a tax benefit. **Therefore, the higher the tax rate faced by a firm, the greater the amount of tax saved from the use of debt financing compared to using equity financing.**

Note:
These guidelines should be taken into account in deciding the nature and mix of resources used by a firm in financing it projects and operations. This section has considered the major options available to a firm for financing its capital projects and its on-going operations. It has considered the nature of a firm's financial and capital structure, the short-term and long-term sources, and cost of financing available and the advantages and disadvantages of each. Finally, guidelines for an effective financing strategy have been identified and described.

Working Capital Management

Introduction

As described in earlier lessons, working capital components - current assets and current liabilities - are sources of short-term financing. Effective management of those working capital elements not only optimizes that financing role, but also enhances operating functions of a firm. This lesson defines and describes working capital, the objectives of working capital management and identifies elements of working capital to be considered in detail in subsequent lessons.

I. Working Capital

> **Definition:**
>
> *Working capital (also called Net Working Capital)*: Is the difference between a firm's current assets and its current liabilities. Expressed in formula fashion it is: Working Capital = Current Assets - Current Liabilities

II. Current assets and current liabilities -- Are considered short-term balance sheet elements, defined for purposes here as:

> **Definitions:**
>
> *Current Assets*: Cash and other resources expected to be converted to cash, sold, or consumed within one year.
>
> *Current Liabilities*: Obligations due to be settled within one year.

III. Definitions -- While these definitions are consistent with those used in accounting and the included individual assets and obligations existing at any point in time are considered short term, the amounts committed to current assets, and the financing provided by current liabilities will each include an amount that is permanent in nature. As an example, although inventory is likely to turn over and fluctuate during the year, there will always be some minimum amount of resources invested in inventory. Similarly, trade accounts payable will be paid and new ones incurred during the year, but there is some minimum amount of financing provided by trade payables throughout the year. These minimum amounts are permanent uses (assets) and sources (liabilities) of financing.

IV. Objective -- The **objective** in managing working capital is to maintain adequate working capital so as to:

- **A. Meet on-going operating and financial needs** of the firm, for example:
  1. **Inventory --** To meet production requirements;
  2. **Cash --** To meet obligations as they come due.
- **B. Not over invest** in net working capital (assets) which provide low returns or increase costs, for example:
  1. **Excess idle cash --** Which has a low rate of return, if any;
  2. **Excess accounts receivable --** Which don't earn interest;
  3. **Excess inventory --** Which incurs storage costs and risks becoming obsolete.

V. **Management of net working capital --** Provides another illustration of the trade-off between risk and reward in financial management. Sufficient net working capital must be maintained to avoid the risk of interrupting operations and the ability to meet current obligations, but over investment in net working capital reduces the rewards which could be recognized by the firm through investment in assets with greater returns.

  A. The following sections discuss the management of the **major elements of working capital** :

    1. Cash;
    2. Marketable securities;
    3. Accounts receivable;
    4. Inventories;
    5. Current liabilities.

  B. The focus is on current assets because of their differences and because the use of current liabilities as a means of short-term financing was discussed in the earlier section on Financing Options. Nevertheless, a summary discussion of the management of current liabilities will conclude this section.

Cash Management

Because cash is pervasive in carrying out business activities, strategies for the management of cash are essential to the short-term stability of a firm and to its long-term prosperity. This lesson describes a number of techniques which can be used to accelerate the collection of cash and to control the outflow of cash, the central objectives of cash management.

I. Introduction to Cash Management

> **Definition:**
>
> *Cash, the most liquid of assets,*: Is considered to consist of all currency, coins and other demand instruments (checks, money orders, etc.) held either on-hand (e.g., day's receipts, change fund, petty cash fund, etc.) or in demand deposit accounts with financial institutions.

A. Because cash (per se) provides little or no return (and will lose real value during inflation), firms seek to maintain a minimum cash balance consistent with meeting its debt and other obligations as they come due. Holding too much cash will result in loss of return to the firm.

II. Basis -- The basis for determining a firm's cash needs is its cash budget, which shows expected cash receipts and disbursements for each budget period. If the projected cash balance is higher than the needed amount, management can plan to make investments or pay down existing debt. On the other hand, if a cash shortage is projected, management can either reduce cash requirements, make plans to borrow, or otherwise plan for the shortfall. In order to monitor these cash balances, large firms prepare daily cash reports so that excess cash can be invested and cash shortages provided for. Because management projections of the amount and timing of cash inflows and outflows may prove incorrect, firms must invest in some amount of cash to hedge that uncertainty.

III. Cash -- Within the context of its target cash balance firms will seek to accelerate cash inflows and defer cash outflows in order to have cash available for a longer period so that it can be invested in higher return projects or undertakings. For example, the claim to cash reflected by accounts receivable does not provide the return to the firm that would result from collecting the account and investing the cash in inventory or a capital undertaking.

IV. Accelerating and Controlling Cash Inflows

A. The time between when a firm establishes a claim to cash (e.g., as a result of providing goods or services) and when that cash is available to the firm to reinvest should be as short as possible. As noted above, a claim to cash, whether in the debtor's accounts payable or en route to the firm's bank account, does not provide a return to the firm. Therefore, the firm should establish policies and procedures to reduce this time period, and to simultaneously provide security of the cash.

B. Efforts to encourage prompt payment by debtors will be discussed in the next section on Accounts Receivable Management. Here we will be concerned with reducing the time from when a customer initiates payment until the cash is available for use by the receiving firm, a time period commonly referred to as float. This period of float may be reduced by:

1. **Lock-box System --** Under a lock-box collection system, the firm leases post office boxes in areas where it has a high volume of payments through the mail. Customers remit payment to those post office boxes ("locked boxes"). The firm's bank collects the remittances from the lock-boxes and processes and deposits the checks directly to the firm's account(s). The bank then notifies the firm of the sources and amounts collected so that the firm can update it cash and receivables accounts. A lock-box arrangement may reduce the float from 7 (or more) days to 2 or 3 days, depending on the circumstances.
   - **a.** The resulting benefits are:
     - **i.** Cash is available for use sooner than it would be otherwise.
     - **ii.** The firm's handling of collections is reduced considerably, resulting in less cost and greater security.
     - **iii.** Reduced likelihood of dishonored checks and earlier identification of those that are dishonored.
   - **b.** Firms with a high volume of receipts by mail should investigate the use of a lock-box system.
2. **Preauthorized Checks --** As the title implies, under this arrangement cash is collected through checks that are authorized in advance. Such an arrangement would be appropriate for a firm to consider when its customers pay a fixed amount each period for many periods.
   - **a.** The general process would involve:
     - **i.** Customer's authorization and indemnification agreement with the firm's bank.
     - **ii.** Firm builds database with needed information.
     - **iii.** Each period the firm prepares an electronic file and deposit slip and sends them to the bank.
     - **iv.** Bank prints checks and deposits funds to firm's account, and processes checks through clearing system, as usual.
   - **b.** The use of preauthorized checks has several significant advantages:
     - **i.** Cash is available for use sooner and the amount is highly predictable.
     - **ii.** The firm's handling of collection is reduced considerably, resulting in less cost and greater security than a lock-box arrangement.
     - **iii.** Customers may appreciate not having to deal with periodic bills.
3. **Concentration Banking --** Concentration banking is used to accelerate the flow of cash to a firm's principal bank. That flow is achieved by having customers remit payment and company units make deposits to banks close to their locations. The funds collected in the multiple local bank accounts are transferred regularly, and often automatically, to the firm's account in its primary (or concentration) bank. The benefits of concentration banking are similar to those resulting from lock box arrangement and, in fact, a lock box system can incorporate concentration banking. The benefits of concentration banking include:
   - **a.** Cash being available for use sooner than it would be otherwise.
   - **b.** Excess cash from multiple locations flow to a single account (or bank) for better control and use.
   - **c.** Arrangements can be made with the concentration bank to automatically invest cash in excess of needed amounts.

4. **Depository Transfer Checks/Official Bank Checks**

   a. Depository transfer checks, also called official bank checks, are used to transfer funds between a firm's accounts. Depository transfer checks are unsigned, non-negotiable, and payable only to an account of the firm. For example, in a manual system, at the time a unit of the firm makes a deposit at a local bank, it also prepares and sends a depository transfer check to its principal (and perhaps, concentration) bank. The receiving bank deposits the funds to the firm's account and processes the depository check back to the local bank where funds were deposited by the firm's unit.

   b. As an alternative to traditional processing of depository transfer checks, an automated system exists which transmits the deposit information electronically to the principal bank where the actual check is prepared and processed, and the funds deposited to the firm's account. Under either the traditional or the automated process, funds normally are not available for the firm to use until the depository transfer check actually clears the local bank.

   c. Using depository transfer checks is an efficient way of transferring funds between a firm's banks, especially when an automated transfer system is used. Depository transfer checks may be used in conjunction with a lock-box and/or concentration banking arrangement(s).

5. **Wire Transfers**

   a. Wire transfer is an electronic means of transferring funds between banks. The Federal Reserve Bank Wire System and a private wire service operate in the U.S. Because it is a relatively expensive method of transferring funds, wire transfers should be used only for large transfers, for example, as a means of moving large sums in a concentration banking arrangement. (See also Electronic Funds Transfer.)

   b. This subsection has described procedures a firm can use to speed-up its collection of cash or the transfer cash between the firm's banks. The basic purpose of such procedures is to make cash available sooner so that it can be put to work earning a return. The next subsection looks at ways the payment of cash can be deferred and controlled.

V. **Deferring and Controlling Cash Outflows --** The central objectives of deferring and controlling cash outflows is to make cash available to the firm for a longer period and to control cash disbursements. Several methods are identified and described.

A. **Managing the Purchases/Payment Process**

1. This topic recognizes that certain things can be done to conserve cash before obligations are incurred, as well as after they are incurred. The following would be included:

   a. Establish and use charge accounts rather than paying cash.

   b. Select suppliers that provide generous deferred payment terms.

   c. Do not pay bills before they are due, except to take advantage of discounts offered.

   d. Stretch payments, which involves making payments after the established due date. This would be appropriate where it is customary in the industry and where there are no adverse financial affects or where impairment of credit rating would not result.

B. Remote Disbursing -- Remote disbursing is intended to increase the float on checks used to pay obligations. By increasing the float, cash is available longer to the paying firm. It is accomplished by establishing checking accounts in remote locations and paying bills with checks drawn on those accounts. Therefore, even when the entity being paid receives the payment check in a timely manner, it takes longer for the check to clear the account of the paying firm. Thus, it has use of the funds for a longer period of time.

C. Zero Balance Accounts

1. The use of zero balance accounts is based on an agreement between the firm and a bank under which the firm has accounts with no real balance. Under one arrangement, checks written on these accounts are processed as usual, resulting in overdrawn accounts, but by agreement with the bank these overdrafts are covered automatically, usually at the end of each day, by transfers from a master account. Thus, at the end of each day, these accounts have no balance.
2. Under a different application of zero balance accounts, after a firm determines an amount to be paid from an account - for example, the monthly payroll - an amount equal to the payments is deposited into the account. Therefore, the account has no real balance since any outstanding checks are exactly equal to the account balance.
3. The benefits of zero balance accounts include:
   a. Near elimination of excess cash balances in those accounts.
   b. Very little administration required, e.g. monitoring and reconciling accounts.
   c. Possible increase in payment float through use of zero balance accounts in remote banks.

D. Payment through Draft -- Using payment through drafts a firm prepares a legal instrument, called a draft, in lieu of a check. Drafts, unlike checks, are not drawn on a bank, but on a demand deposit of the firm. The drafts are returned to the firm's bank through the banking system and paid by the firm's bank after being approved by the issuing firm. While payment through drafts may increase cash disbursement float, its prime benefit is the control that is maintained over the disbursements.

E. Electronic Funds Transfers (EFTs) -- As the title implies, an electronic funds transfer is an electronic means of transferring funds similar to wire transfer, but used in a broader context. Rather than payments occurring through the use of checks or drafts, payments are initiated and processed based on the transfer of computer files between entities.

Example:
A company prepares a file of payments to vendors with all applicable information and transmits the file electronically to its bank. The bank then reduces the firm's account and forwards the payments electronically through the Automated Clearinghouse (ACH) system, which routes payments electronically to the accounts of individual vendors.

1. **The advantages of electronic funds transfers include**
   a. Drastically reduced float, so firms can defer payments until they are due and still ensure payments are received when due.

b. Much of the administration can be routine and integrated with a firm's larger accounting and information system, thus reducing cost and errors.

c. Very low transaction fee costs, especially when compared to traditional check writing and mailing.

VI. **This subsection --** Has looked at ways the outflow of cash can be deferred and better controlled so that cash is available for use longer than it would be otherwise and so that lower cost and better security are provided in the management of cash. The next section looks at the management of marketable securities, a separate item of working capital.

Short-term Securities Management

Cash in excess of immediate needs should be "put to work" by investing it so as to earn a return. Appropriate short-term investment securities must be selected in a prudent manner so as not to put the firm's cash position at risk. This lesson describes the objective in choosing short-term investments and identifies a variety of instruments that may be suitable.

I. **Temporary excess cash --** When a firm has temporary excess cash, it should invest those funds so as to earn a return greater than would be provided by "idle cash." Because the funds so invested will be needed in the near term to satisfy obligations or to invest in planned undertakings, management must be prudent in the use of such investments. The following considerations will be of major concern in selecting short-term investments:

   A. **Safety of Principal --** Investments should have little risk of default by the issuer. Default risk is a measure of the likelihood that the issuer will not be able to make future interest and/or principal payments to a security holder. Temporary investments should be in securities with a low risk of default, U.S. Treasury issues, for example.

   B. **Price Stability --** Investments should not be subject to market price declines that would result in significant losses if the securities were to be sold for cash. Investments in most debt instruments have an associated interest rate risk, the risk that derives from the relationship between the rate of interest paid by a security and the changing rate of interest in the market. Specifically, the market value of an existing debt instrument varies inversely with changes in the market rate of interest. Thus, the interest rate risk is that the market rate of interest will increase, resulting in a decrease in the market value of an investment. If that investment were sold, it would incur a loss and, as a result, less cash would be available. This risk is mitigated by investing in securities that mature over short periods.

   C. **Marketability/Liquidity --** Investments should be in instruments that have a ready market for converting securities to cash (i.e., liquidating the securities) without incurring undue cost. Thus, securities that are thinly traded (e.g., closely held) or which have high cost of premature conversion (e.g., some certificates of deposit) should be avoided.

II. **Other Factors --** That may enter into the short-term investment decision, but are usually of much less concern, include:

   A. Taxability;

   B. Diversification;

   C. Cost of administering.

III. **Opportunities --** A variety of opportunities are available for short-term investments in what is referred to as the money market. The primary investments in the money market include:

   A. **U.S. Treasury Bills --** These direct obligations of the U.S, Government are considered to be virtually risk-free, can be acquired in increments of $5,000 with a minimum $10,000 investment, have maturities of 3-months (91 days), 6-months (182 days), and 1-year (365 days), and are periodically available directly through the Federal Reserve Banks and continuously available in the secondary market. U.S. Treasury Bills provide:

      1. Safety of principal;

      2. Price stability if held to (short) maturity;

      3. Marketability/liquidity.

B. **Federal Agency Securities**

1. These securities are obligations of a federal government agency (such as the Federal National Mortgage Association-"Fannie Mae," Federal Home Loan Bank, Federal Land Bank, and others) that are the responsibility of the agency; these securities are not backed by the good faith and credit of the federal government. As a consequence, these securities are perceived as having slightly more risk than Treasury obligations.
2. In addition, they are not as marketable as Treasury obligations. Therefore, the securities of these agencies have slightly higher yields to compensate for the higher default risk and lower marketability. These securities are offered in various denominations and with a wide range of maturities. The secondary market for these securities is good (while the secondary market for Treasury obligations is excellent).

C. **Negotiable Certificates of Deposit --** These securities are issued by banks in return for a fixed time deposit with the bank. The securities pay a fixed rate of interest and are available in a variety of denominations and maturities. Unlike conventional certificates of deposit, negotiable certificates of deposit can be bought and sold in a secondary market. Therefore, if a holder needs cash before maturity, rather than incurring an interest penalty by "cashing in" the certificate, it can be sold in the secondary market at little or no penalty. These securities offer a high safety of principal and relative short-term stability, but somewhat less marketability than Treasury or federal agency obligations.

D. **Bankers' Acceptances --** A banker's acceptance is a draft (or order to pay) drawn on a specific bank by a firm which has an account with the bank. If the bank accepts the draft, it becomes a negotiable debt instrument of the bank that is available for investment. The primary use of bankers' acceptances is in the financing of foreign transactions. Bankers' acceptances are issued in denominations that relate to the value of the transaction for which the acceptance was made. Maturities typically are from 30 days to 180 days. Because acceptances have a higher risk and less marketability than Treasury or Federal agency obligations, they have a higher yield than those securities.

E. **Commercial Paper --** Commercial paper is short-term unsecured promissory notes issued by large, established firms with high credit ratings. Commercial paper is available in a variety of denominations, either directly from the issuing firm or dealers, and can be purchased with maturities from a few days up to 270 days. The secondary market for commercial paper is very limited, usually restricted to dealers in the paper. Because of the lack of marketability, commercial paper provides a yield greater than other short-term instruments with comparable risk, but usually still less than the prime rate of interest.

F. **Repurchase Agreements (Repos)**

1. In a repurchase agreement the firm makes an investment (a loan) and simultaneously enters into a commitment to resell the security at the original contract price plus an agreed interest income for the holding period. These agreements are usually for large denominations and have maturities specified in each agreement. The yield available is usually less than available on Treasury Bills, but may offer advantages of maturity and very short-liquidity.
2. The major benefits of investing in repurchase agreements are:
   a. The time of the agreement (maturity) can be adjusted to any length, including as short as 1 day.
   b. Since the agreement provides for resale of the investment at the original price (plus interest), the risk of market price declines is avoided.
3. These benefits make repurchase agreements a viable investment option, especially for very short-term uses of excess cash.

IV. The foregoing section -- Describes the principal instruments for short-term investments in the U.S., including:

> **Note:**
> Other alternatives are available, including short-term tax-exempt securities, money market mutual funds and foreign securities. A firm with excess cash will need to consider the relative characteristics of each opportunity in view of the firm's investment criteria for safety, liquidity, and yield.

A. U.S. Treasury Bills;

B. Federal Agency Securities;

C. Negotiable Certificates of Deposit;

D. Bankers' Acceptances;

E. Commercial Paper;

F. Repurchase Agreements.

Accounts Receivable Management

Accounts receivable result from a decision to sell goods or services on credit. Management of the resulting receivables requires the adoption of a set of credit and collection policies. This lesson describes the role of accounts receivable and the decisions and processes needed to manage those receivables.

I. Accounts Receivable

A. For many businesses, accounts receivable account for a significant portion of current assets, and in some cases up to 25% of total assets. For these firms, effective management of accounts receivable is essential not only for profitability, but also for viability. For any firm that sells goods or services on account, how it manages its credit and collection process plays a role in the firm's success (or failure).

B. From an accounting perspective, accounts receivable management is concerned with the conditions leading to the recognition of receivables (the debit) and the process that results in eliminating the receivable (the credit). Therefore, this lesson will consider:

1. Establishing general terms of credit;
2. Determining customer creditworthiness and setting credit limits;
3. Collecting accounts receivable.

II. Establishing General Terms of Credit -- If sales are to be made on credit, the firm must establish the general terms under which such sales will be made. To a certain extent, for competitive reasons the terms of sale adopted by a firm will need to approximate terms established in its industry. Specific terms of sale decisions to be made include:

A. Total Credit Period -- Establishes the maximum period for which credit is extended. Typical industry practice reflects that the length of the credit period relates to the "durability" of goods sold. For example, firms that sell perishable goods (e.g., fresh produce) typically have a shorter credit period than firms that sell more durable goods. This credit period establishes the length of time the firm is expected to finance its sales on credit and for which it must, in turn, have financing.

B. Discount Terms for Early Payment -- If a discount is to be offered for early payment of accounts, the discount rate and period must be decided. The combination of the discount rate and period will determine the effective interest rate associated with the discount offered which, in turn, will determine the effectiveness of the discount policy. As we saw in the earlier discussion of trade accounts payable, the effective interest rate on cash discounts not taken usually are significant. For example:

> 2/10, n/30 = 2% discount if paid within 10 days = 36.7% APR
>
> 5/10, n/30 = 5% discount if paid within 10 days = 94.74% APR

1. The rate and period a firm economically can offer depends on the margin realized on its sales and its cost of financing its accounts receivable. Practically, the rate and period will need to be competitive with other firms in the industry.

C. Penalty for Late Payment -- Determines the penalty to be assessed if customers don't pay by the final due date, including the length of any "stretch" period before the penalty applies. The penalty at least should cover the cost of financing the accounts receivable.

D. **Nature of Credit Sales Documentation --** Determines the form of documentation to be required from customers at the time they purchase on account. The most common arrangement is to sell on an open account, that is, an implicit contract documented only by a receipt signed by the buyer. If the amount being charged is very large or if the buyer's credit is suspect, a firm will likely require more formal documentation, such as a commercial draft. If foreign sales are to be made, appropriate processes will have to be decided upon.

III. Determining Customer Credit Worthiness and Setting Credit Limits

A. The decisions here are to determine whether or not a customer can buy on account and, if so, what maximum amount can be charged. In making these decisions it is critical to recognize that the objective is to maximize profits, not to minimize credit losses. A policy that is too stringent will result in failing to make sales that would be paid, resulting in lower losses on accounts receivable, but also resulting in lost revenues.

B. When a customer is considered for credit, there are two major approaches to determining both whether or not to grant credit and at what level:

   1. **Credit-rating Service --** A number of firms are in the business of assessing the creditworthiness of individuals and businesses, including Equifax, Experian, TransUnion, and Dun and Bradstreet. Reports from these agencies provide considerable information about a potential credit customer, including a score that reflects relative creditworthiness. Such scores can be used in both making the credit decision and in establishing a credit limit. Other sources of information about prospective credit customers include trade associations, banks, and chambers of commerce, among others.

   2. **Financial Analysis --** In some cases, a firm may undertake its own analysis of a prospective credit customer. Since this can be an expensive undertaking, it is typically done only by large firms and in special circumstances where the seller wants a more direct understanding of the prospective credit customer. The analysis would rely on information from outside sources, but would incorporate the firm's own analysis, including financial ratio development from the prospect's financial information. Since the consideration is whether or not to extend short-term credit, the focus of the analysis will be on the prospect's short-term debt paying ability.

C. Once credit-granting decisions have been made and credit sales have occurred, the final area of accounts receivable management is collection.

IV. Collecting Accounts Receivable

A. The most significant risk faced in selling on credit is that a sale will be made, but not collected. Even with the best of screening processes, a business that sells on account can expect some loss from non-collection. The objective is to keep that post-sale loss to a minimum. To accomplish this, a firm must monitor its accounts receivable and take action where appropriate.

   1. **Monitoring Accounts Receivable --** Collection management needs to monitor accounts receivable both in the aggregate and individually. Assessment of total accounts receivable is done with averages and ratios, including:

      a. Average collection period;

      b. Day's sales in accounts receivable;

      c. Accounts receivable turnover;

      d. Accounts receivable to current or total assets;

      e. Bad debt to sales.

      f. (See the later lessons on Ratio Analysis for Financial Management.)

2. Individual accounts receivable can be assessed using an aging of accounts receivable schedule. Such a schedule shows for each credit customer the amount owed by how long the amount has been due. A typical schedule would take the form:

	Not Due	30-Days Over	60-Days Over	90-Days Over...	Totals
Customer A	$	$	$	$	$

   a. Since the probability of not collecting increases with the age of an amount due, overdue accounts need to be pursued promptly.

3. **Collection Action --** When accounts are overdue, effective management requires action be taken, including:

   a. Prompt "past due" billing;

   b. Dunning letters with increasingly serious demands;

   c. Use of collection agency.

4. These actions are not without a financial and, probably, a goodwill cost. Therefore, each case may need to be decided based on the amount involved and other considerations.

Inventory Management

Inventory plays a role in the operation of manufacturing, retail and most service businesses. Management of the inventory asset is central to these businesses. This lesson identifies and describes alternative inventory systems and presents certain quantitative techniques that can be used to help manage inventory.

I. Central Issue

A. The central issue in inventory management is to determine and maintain an optimum investment in all inventories. For a manufacturing firm that includes raw materials, work-in-process, and finished goods; for a retail firm that is goods for resale. As with other aspects of financial management, inventory management involves a risk-reward trade-off. In this case, the trade-off is between over investing in inventory so as to avoid shortages and incurring excessive cost, and under investing in inventory to save cost, but incurring the risk of shortages.

B. Two general approaches to our systems of inventory management are currently common in the U.S., the traditional materials requirement planning system and the just-in-time inventory system.

II. Traditional Materials Requirement Planning (MRP) System -- This approach to manufacturing and inventory management has been predominant in the U.S. since the 1960, though in many firms it has been replaced by just-in-time systems in recent years. It is characterized by:

A. Supply Push -- Goods are produced in anticipation of there being a demand for the goods. Therefore, the characteristics of the product available to the end user have already been decided-colors, features, sizes, etc.

B. Inventory Buffers -- Because production is in anticipation of sales, inventories are maintained at every level in the process as buffers against unexpected increased demand. If demand is less than production, finished goods inventory accumulates.

C. Production Characteristics -- MRP is based on long set-up times and long production runs; it is not flexible. It uses specialized labor and function-specific equipment.

D. Supplier/Purchases Characteristics -- Relationships with suppliers are impersonal and purchases are made through bids accepted from many suppliers, with the low bid usually accepted, regardless of the supplier's location. Purchases are normally made in large lots that are greater than immediately needed.

E. Quality Management -- Quality standards are set at an acceptable level, allowing for a certain level of defects.

F. Accounting Issues -- Traditional cost accounting is used with emphasis on job order and processing cost approaches. Multiple inventory accounts are used. Accounting involves complex cost accumulation and allocations, including setting standards, allocating costs, and variance analysis and reporting.

III. Just-in-Time Inventory (JIT) Inventory System

A. This approach to manufacturing and inventory management originated in the Japanese auto industry (Toyota) and has been widely adopted in recent years to improve production and, especially, inventory management. As the term implies, the basis of the system is obtaining (supply side) and delivering (sell side) inventory just as or only when it is needed. It is characterized by:

1. **Demand Pull --** Goods are produced only when there is an end user demand. Goods are produced with the characteristics desired by the customer and in the quantity demanded.
2. **Inventory Reduction --** The customers' demand pulls inventory through the production process in that each stage produces only what is needed by the next stage and outside purchases are made only as needed. Thus, excess raw materials, work-in-process and, ideally, finished goods inventories are greatly reduced or eliminated.
3. **Production Characteristics --** Production occurs in work centers or cells in which the full set of operations to produce a product are carried out. Workers are trained to operate multiple pieces of equipment and robots are used where feasible. Each work center functions like a mini-factory.
4. **Supplier/Purchases Characteristics --** Close working relationships are developed with a limited number of suppliers to help coordinate operating interrelationships and to help assure timely delivery of quality inputs. Physical distance between supply source and production facilities is minimized. Goods are purchased only in the quantity needed to meet production demand and entered directly in the production process
5. **Quality Management --** Because inventory is squeezed out of every stage of the production process, inputs to the process must be high quality, otherwise a defective input likely would stop production. Therefore, there must be total control of quality of inputs. This is accomplished by working closely with suppliers to insure quality in their production process, as well as implementing quality practices within its own processes.
6. **Accounting Issues --** JIT uses simplified cost accounting. It eliminates or combines inventory accounts because inventory is reduced or eliminated. Many more accounts are considered direct cost (e.g., material handling, equipment depreciation, and repairs and maintenance), thus reducing amounts allocated on a somewhat arbitrary basis. The accounting focuses less on variance analysis and more on aggregate measures, including days inventory on hand, return on assets, lead-time, and others.
7. **Summary --** In summary, just-in-time inventory systems and related production processes provide the following financial benefits:
    - **a.** Reduced investment in inventory;
    - **b.** Lower cost of inventory transportation, warehousing, insurance, property taxes, and other related costs;
    - **c.** Reduced lead time in replenishing product inputs;
    - **d.** Lower cost of defects;
    - **e.** Less complex and more relevant accounting and performance measures.

B. While just-in-time inventory and related production processes can provide significant benefits for many firms, the concepts and practices cannot be used by every firm and will not be appropriate for all processes of some firms. Firms that use a traditional materials requirement planning system or similar large lot production systems will be particularly concerned with the economic order quantity and the appropriate reorder point.

IV. Economic Order Quantity

A. There is a trade-off between inventory ordering cost and inventory carrying cost. Specifically, the larger the quantity ordered, the lower the cost of ordering (e.g., clerical, transportation, handling, etc.), but the higher the carrying cost (e.g., warehousing, insurance, property taxes, financing costs, etc.). Determining the order size that will minimize total inventory cost is solved using the economic order quantity model. The basis for the model is recognizing that:

Total inventory cost = Total order cost + Total carrying cost

1. Further:

Total order cost =	Number of orders	x Per order cost
or, =	(Total units for period/order size)	x Per order cost
or, =	T/Q	x O
Total carrying cost =	Average Inventory	x Per unit carrying cost
or, =	(Order size/2)	x Per unit carrying cost
or, =	Q/2	x C

2. Therefore:

Total inventory cost = (T / X) x O + (Q / 2) x C

3. By rearranging to solve for Q, the economic order quantity (EOQ), we get:

$$EOQ = \sqrt{\frac{2\ TO}{C}}$$

4. To illustrate the application of this equation, assume the following for a firm's production period:

Total Demand for Input X = 10,000 units

Per Order Cost = \$100

Per Unit Carrying Cost = \$2.00

$$EOQ = \sqrt{\frac{2 \times 10{,}000 \times 100}{2}} = \sqrt{\frac{2{,}000{,}000}{2}} = \sqrt{1{,}000{,}000} =$$

EOQ = 1,000

5. Therefore, the firm should order in lot sizes of 1,000 units to minimize its total cost of inventory acquisition.

B. The following assumptions are inherent in the economic order quantity model:

1. Demand is constant during the period;
2. Unit cost and carrying cost are constant during the period;
3. Delivery is instantaneous (or a safety stock is maintained).

C. To the extent these assumptions do not hold, formula modifications will need to be made.

V. Reorder Point

A. This analysis is concerned with determining the inventory quantity at which goods should be reordered. In a traditional materials requirement planning system, inputs tend to be acquired periodically and in large lots which are used over a long production period. At some remaining quantity new inputs must be ordered so as to be available before the current inventory runs out; that quantity is the reorder point.

B. The quantity at which inventory is reordered must be sufficient to continue production until the new order is delivered-the delivery time stock. In addition, a safety stock is usually maintained to hedge against unforeseen events (e.g. unexpected usage or unusual defects). Therefore, the reorder point can be expressed as:

Reorder Point = Delivery time stock + Safety stock

C. To illustrate the application of this equation, assume the following for a firm:

Example:
Annual Usage Equally Over a 50 Week Year = 300,000 units
Delivery Time = 2 weeks
Safety Stock = 1,000 units

The weekly usage is: 300,000/50 weeks = 6,000 per week

Therefore, the reorder point (RP) is:

RP = 6,000 per week x 2 weeks = 12,000 + 1,000 safety = 13,000 units

When the stock drops to 13,000 units, inventory should be reordered.

VI. Inventory management and control -- Can be facilitated by the use of certain ratios, including:

A. Inventory turnover;

B. Number of days' sales in inventory.

C. See the later lessons on Ratio Analysis for Financial Management.

Current Liabilities Management

Major current liabilities including trade accounts payable, accrued accounts payable, and short-term notes, were discussed at length in the section on Short-term (Working Capital) Financing. As was noted there, current liabilities are forms of short-term financing which implicitly must be satisfied (paid or restructured) in the short term, usually using current assets. The material presented earlier will not be repeated here, but some brief comments will summarize that material.

I. Current Liabilities

A. Major current liabilities including trade accounts payable, accrued accounts payable, and short-term notes, were discussed at length in the section on Short-term (Working Capital) Financing. As was noted there, current liabilities are forms of short-term financing which implicitly must be satisfied (paid or restructured) in the short term, usually using current assets.

B. The material presented earlier will not be repeated here, but some brief comments will summarize that material.

1. **Short-term liabilities --** most appropriately incurred in connection with assets which will generate cash in the short term to repay the liability. This is the essence of the principle of self-liquidating debt, also called the hedging principle of financing.
2. **Permanent Amount of Financing --** Just as some amount of current assets is a permanent use of financing, some amount of current liabilities provides a permanent amount of financing. For example, to the extent a minimum balance always remains in trade accounts payable, that minimum amount is a form of permanent financing.
3. **Short-Term Borrowing --** Generally, short-term borrowing does not require collateral and does not impose restrictive covenants.
4. **Early Payment --** Discounts offered for early payment of trade accounts payable are usually significant, many with an effective annual interest rate of over 30%, and should be taken if possible.
5. **Effective Cost of Borrowing --** If current liabilities (e.g. short-term notes, line of credit, etc.) require maintaining a compensating balance (greater than any balance that would otherwise be maintained with the institution), the effective cost of borrowing is greater than the stated cost.
6. **Stand-by Financing --** A line of credit provides an effective means of arranging "stand-by" financing. The credit is prearranged and can be used when needed, thus reducing the cost associated with any idle borrowing.

II. Prior lessons -- Have considered management of the major elements (or accounts) which comprise working capital, including management of:

A. Cash;

B. Marketable securities;

C. Trade accounts receivable;

D. Inventories;

E. Current liabilities.

III. The focus -- Has been on the financial management of these elements, not the accounting for them. The general object is to manage all of these elements so as to maximize the firm's use of resources and thereby increase its profitability.

Ratio Analysis for Financial Management

Introduction

Ratios and related measures can be used to analyze financial and other information. These ratios and measures quantify relationships between financial and operating items to provide important summary indicators about a firm which are useful to financial management and others. This lesson defines ratio analysis and points out some important concepts related to the use of ratios. Subsequent lessons cover the ratios and measures most commonly used and which are specified in the Content Specifications as appropriate for the BEC section of the CPA Examination.

I. **Ratio analysis**

> **Definition:**
>
> *Ratio Analysis*: Is the development of quantitative relationships between various elements of a firm's financial and other information.

II. **Ratio analysis --** Enables comparisons over time for a firm, across firms (especially within the same industry), and facilitates identifying operating and financial strengths and weaknesses of a firm.

III. **Ratio Analysis Concepts --** The following concepts are helpful in understanding and using ratio analysis and similar measures:

A. The names given to ratios and other measures usually indicate the elements to be used in the analysis.

> **Example:**
> Debt to Equity ratio = Total **Debt** (Liabilities) / Owner's **Equity**

B. The name given to ratios frequently indicates the quantitative function to be performed. The terms "to" and "on" indicate to divide the first item described by the second item described.

> **Example:**
> Debt to Equity ratio = Divide Debt by Equity
>
> Return on Assets = Divide Net Income (the Return) by Assets

C. When using a balance sheet value with an income statement value, you must get the average balance for the balance sheet value. The income statement value is for the year; the balance sheet values are for points in time. Therefore, you need to average the balance sheet items.

Example:
Accounts Receivable Turnover = (Net) Credit Sales / Average (Net) Accounts Receivable (e.g., Beginning + Ending/2)

IV. Ratios and measures -- Can be grouped according to the major purpose or type of measure being analyzed. The major purposes or types of measures analyzed in the following lessons are:

- **A.** Liquidity/Solvency;
- **B.** Operational Activity;
- **C.** Profitability;
- **D.** Equity/Investment Leverage.

Liquidity Measures

This lesson considers ratios and measures which assess the liquidity of a firm. Each measure is described and the method of calculation illustrated.

I. Liquidity Measures

Definition:

Liquidity (also known as Solvency): Measures the ability of the firm to pay its obligations as they become due.

A. These measures are particularly appropriate for use in managing working capital.

II. Major liquidity measures

A. Working Capital -- Measures the extent to which current assets exceed current liabilities and, thus, are uncommitted in the short term. It is expressed as:

Working Capital = Current Assets - Current Liability

B. Working Capital Ratio -- Measures the quantitative relationship between current assets and current liabilities in terms of the "number of times" current assets can cover current liabilities. It is computed as:

Working Capital Ratio = Current Assets / Current Liabilities

1. Is a widely used measure of the firm's ability to pay its current liabilities.
2. Changes in Current Assets and/or Current Liabilities have determinable affects on the Working Capital Ratio (WCR):
    - **a.** An increase in current assets (alone) increases the WCR;
    - **b.** A decrease in current assets (alone) decreases the WCR;
    - **c.** An increase in current liabilities (alone) decreases the WCR;
    - **d.** A decrease in current liabilities (alone) increases the WCR;
    - **e.** If the WCR equals 1.00, equal increases or equal decreases in current assets and liabilities will not change the WCR; it will remain 1.00;
    - **f.** If the WCR exceeds 1.00 then:
        - **i.** Equal increases in current assets and liabilities decrease the WCR.

Example:
WCR = CA 20,000 / CL 10,000 = 2

WCR = (CA 20,000 + 10,000) / (CL 10,000 + 10,000) = 30,000 / 20,000 = 1.5

ii. Equal decreases in current assets and liabilities increase the WCR.

Example:
WCR = CA 30,000 / CL 20,000 = 1.5

WCR = CA 20,000 / CL 10,000 = 2

g. If the WCR is less than 1.00 then:

i. Equal increases in current assets and liabilities increase the WCR.

Example:
WCR = CA 10,000 / CL 20,000 = .50

WCR = (CA 10,000 + 10,000) / (CL 20,000 + 10,000) = 20,000 / 30,000 = .66

ii. Equal decrease in current assets and liabilities decrease the WCR.

Example:
WCR = 20,000 / 30,000 = .66

WCR = 10,000 / 20,000 = .50

C. Acid-Test Ratio -- (Also known as Quick Ratio) - Measures the quantitative relationship between highly liquid assets and current liabilities in terms of the "number of times" that cash and assets that can be converted quickly to cash cover current liabilities. It is computed as:

Acid Test Ratio = (Cash + (Net) Receivables + Marketable Securities) / Current Liabilities

D. Defensive-Interval Ratio -- Measures the quantitative relationship between highly liquid assets and the average daily use of cash in terms of the number of days that cash and assets that can be quickly converted to cash can support operating costs. It is computed as:

Defensive-Interval Ratio = (Cash + (Net) Receivable + Marketable Securities) / Average Daily Cash Expenditures

E. **Times Interest Earned Ratio --** Measures the ability of current earnings to cover interest payments for a period. It is measured as:

Times Interest Earned Ratio = (Net Income + Interest Expense + Income Tax Expense) / Interest Expense

F. **Times Preferred Dividends Earned Ratio --** Measures the ability of current earnings to cover preferred dividends for a period. It is computed as:

Times Preferred Dividends Earned Ratio = Net Income / Annual Preferred Dividend Obligation

Operational Activity Measures

This lesson considers ratios and measures which assess the operational activities of a firm. Each measure is described and the method of calculation illustrated.

I. **Operational Activity Measures**

> **Definition:**
>
> *Operation Activity Ratios*: Measure the efficiency with which a firm carries out its operating activities.

II. **Included in operational activity ratios --** Are measures that assess the management of accounts receivable and inventory, including:

A. **Accounts Receivable Turnover --** Measures the number of times that accounts receivable turnover (are incurred and collected) during a period. Indicates the quality of credit policies (and the resulting receivables) and the efficiency of collection procedures. It is computed as:

> Accounts Receivable Turnover = (Net) Credit Sales / Average (Net) Accounts Receivable (e.g., Beginning + Ending/2)

1. **Number of Days' Sales in Average Receivables --** Measures the average number of days required to collect receivables; it is a measure of the average age of receivables. It is computed as:

> Number of Days Sales In Average Receivables = 300 or 360 or 365 (or other measure of business days in a year) / Accounts Receivable Turnover (computed in A, above)

2. **Inventory Turnover --** Measures the number of times that inventory turns over (is acquired and sold or used) during a period. Indicates over or under stocking of inventory or obsolete inventory. It is computed as:

> Inventory Turnover = Cost of Goods Sold / Average Inventory (e.g. Beginning + Ending/2)

3. **Number of Days' Supply in Inventory --** Measure the number of days inventory is held before it is sold or used. Indicates the efficiency of general inventory management. It is computed as:

> Number of Days' Supply in Inventory = 300 or 360 or 365 (or other measure of business days in a year) / Inventory Turnover (computed in C, above)

4. **Operating Cycle Length --** Measures the average length of time to invest cash in inventory, convert the inventory to receivables, and collect the receivables; it measures the time to go from cash back to cash. It is computed as:

Number of Days in Operating Cycle = Number of Days' Sales in Average Receivables + Number of Days' Supply in Inventory

Profitability Measures

This lesson considers ratios and measures which assess the profitability of a firm. Each measure is described and the method of calculation illustrated.

I. Profitability Measures

Definition:

Profitability Ratios: Measure aspects of a firm's operating (income/loss) results on a relative basis.

II. Major profitability measures

A. **Gross Profit --** Measures the dollar amount of sales (revenue) after subtracting the cost of goods sold. It is computed as:

Sales (or Revenue) - Cost of Goods Sold = Gross Profit

B. **Gross Profit Margin --** Measures the rate of gross profitability on sales (revenue)-how much (percentage) of each sales dollar that is available to cover expenses and provide a profit. It is computed as:

Gross Profit Margin = Gross Profit / (Net) Sales

C. **(Net) Profit Margin (on Sales) --** Measures the rate of net profitability on sales (revenue)-how much (percentage) of each sales dollar that ends up as net income. It is computed as:

(Net) Profit Margin = Net Income / (Net) Sales

D. **Return on Total Assets OR Return on Investment --** Measures the rate of return on total assets and indicates the efficiency with which invested resources (assets or total equity) are used. It is computed as:

1. **Comments on Numerator** -- When total assets or total investment is used in the denominator, interest expense is added back because either of those measures include the value of debt for which the interest was paid. Similarly, dividends would be added back because they are payments to the stockholders' equity holders.

Return on Total Assets OR Return on Investments = Net Income + (add back) Interest Expense (net of tax effect) + (add back) Dividends / Average total Assets OR Average total Investment (e.g., Beginning + Ending/2)

2. **Comment on Denominator --** Because total assets is equal total investment (by creditors and shareholders), the two denominators provide the same measure of performance. The alternatives (assets or investment) provide perspectives for adjusting the denominator. For example, from the asset perspective, any or all of the following could be deducted from total assets: unproductive assets, assets held for sale, intangible assets, or accumulated depreciation (added back). From the investment perspective, various subsets of debt and/or equity may be used. (See Returns on Owners' Equity and Common Stockholders' Equity (only), below).

Study Tip:
On the exam, information for making adjustments (interest expense, dividends, unproductive assets, etc.) probably will not be given. In that case, simply use Net Income and Average total Assets or Average total Investment.

E. **Return on Owners' (all Stockholders') Equity --** Measures the rate of return (earnings) on all stockholders' investment.

> Return on Owners' Equity = Net Income / Average Stockholders' Equity (e.g., Beginning + Ending / 2)

F. **Return on Common Stockholders' Equity --** Measures the rate of return (earnings) on common stockholders' investment. It is computed as:

> Return on C/S Equity = Net Income - Preferred Dividend (obligation for the period only) / Average Common Stockholders' Equity (e.g. Beginning + Ending / 2)

G. **Residual Income**

1. Measures the excess of an entity's dollar amount of income over the dollar amount of its required return on average investment (based on its hurdle rate of return).
2. The required return on average investment is computed as:

> Required $ Return = Average Invested Capital x Hurdle Rate

3. Residual Income is computed as:

> Residual Income = Net Income - Required $ Return

H. **Economic Value Added (EVA) --** Measures an entity's economic profit (as differentiated from its accounting profit). The determination of accounting profit deducts actual interest expense (cost) on debt, but does not deduct the (imputed) cost of debt and shareholders' equity based on the firm's opportunity cost. EVA uses accounting earnings before deducting interest and deducts from that the dollar value of opportunity cost associated with long-term (L-T) debt and shareholders' equity (SE). The basic formula is:

Note:
Cost of capital or hurdle rate may be used as Opportunity cost.

> EVA = Earnings before interest - [(Opportunity cost) x (L-T debt + SE)]

I. **Earnings Per Share (EPS -- Basic Formula) --** Measures the income earned per (average) share of common stock. Indicates ability to pay dividends to common shareholders. It is computed as:

> EPS (Basic) = Net Income - Preferred Dividends obligation for the period only) / Weighted Average Number of Shares Outstanding

J. Price-Earnings Ratio (P/E Ratio) -- Measures the price of a share of common stock relative to its latest earnings per share. Indicates a measure of how the market values the stock, especially when compared with other stocks. It is also called the "multiple"-how many times EPS is built into the market price of the stock. It is computed as:

P/E Ratio (the "Multiple") = Market Price for a Common Share / Earnings per (Common) Share (EPS)

K. Common Stock Dividends Payout Rate -- Measures the extent (percent) of earnings distributed to common shareholders. It is computed as:

1. Total Basis:

C/S Dividend Payout Rate = Cash Dividends to Common Shareholders / Net Income to Common Shareholder

2. Per Share Basis:

C/S Dividend Payout Rate = Cash Dividends per Common Share / Earnings per Common Share

L. Common Stock Yield -- Measures the rate of return (yield) per share of common stock. It is measured as:

Common Stock Yield = Dividend per Common Share / Market Price per Common Share

Equity/Investment Leverage Measures

This lesson considers ratios and measures which assess the relative equity or investment in a firm. Each measure is described and the method of calculation illustrated.

I. Equity/Investment Leverage Ratios

- **A.** Equity/Investment Leverage Ratios provide measures of relative sources of equity and equity value.

II. Major equity/investment leverage ratios

- **A. Debt to Equity Ratio --** Measures relative amounts of assets provided by creditors and shareholders. It is computed as:

> Debt to Equity Ratio = Total Liabilities / Total Shareholders' Equity

- **B. Owners' Equity Ratio --** Measures the proportion of assets provided by shareholders. It is computed as:

> Owners' Equity Ratio = Shareholders' Equity / Total Assets

- **C. Debt Ratio --** Measures the proportion of assets provided by creditors. Indicates the extent of leverage in funding the entity. It is computed as:

> Debt Ratio = Total Liabilities / Total Assets

- **D. Book Value per Common Stock --** Measures the per share amount of common shareholders' claim to assets. It is computed as:

> Book Value per Common Stock = Common Shareholder's Equity / Number of Outstanding Common Shares

- **E. Book Value per Preferred Share --** Measures the per share amount of preferred shareholders' claim to assets. It is computed as:

> Book Value per P/S = Preferred Shareholders' Equity (including dividends in arrears) / Number of Outstanding Preferred Stock

Risk Concepts - Summary

Throughout this lesson on FINANCIAL MANAGEMENT several concepts of risk have been identified and described. This section summarizes those concepts so that the elements of risk can be better understood and the differences appreciated.

I. **Risk --** Risk is the possibility of loss or other unfavorable outcome that results from the uncertainty in future events. Entities face a variety of different kinds of economic risk as they carry out their operating and financing activities. Many of those kinds of risk have been identified and described in earlier sections. This section summarizes those risks and certain other risks not previously identified.

II. **Business Risk**

   A. This concept refers to the broad, macro-risk a firm faces largely as a result of the relationship between the firm and the environment in which it operates. Thus, the nature and extent of this broad risk factor would be a function of both the nature of the firm and the nature of the environment. The nature of the firm would include the kind of products and services it provides, its cost structure, its financial structure, and all the other elements that make up the total firm, including the specific kinds of risk inherent in the firm. The nature of the environment would include the general economic conditions (e.g. as reflected by business cycles), competition, customer demand, technology, and other major elements of the environment in which the firm operates. The firm's business risk would be embodied in the firm's sensitivity (given its nature) to changes in the general economic environment (given its nature).

   B. The various business risk elements faced by a company are frequently classified into two types, diversifiable and nondiversifiable.

      1. **Diversifiable Risk --** (also called Unsystematic, Firm-Specific or Company-Unique) This is the portion or elements of risk that can be eliminated through diversification of investments. For example, in our discussion of capital budgeting we noted that a firm could mitigate certain risks associated with individual projects by investing in diverse kinds of projects. Similarly, a firm would reduce certain risks associated with its securities investments by diversification of the securities in its portfolio.

      2. **Nondiversifiable Risk --** (also called Systematic or Market-Related) This is the portion or elements of risk that cannot be eliminated through diversification of investments. The factors that constitute nondiversifiable risk usually relate to the general economic and political environment. Examples include changes in the general level of interest, new taxes, and inflation/deflation. Since these broad changes affect all firms, diversification of investments does not tend to reduce the risk associated with these factors of the environment.

   C. In a sense, the concept of business risk is sufficiently broad so as to include virtually all operating risks faced by a firm. In fact, for financial analysis purposes this risk is measured by the expected variability in a firm's earnings, before taking into account its interest and taxes (called EBIT-earnings before interest and taxes). Since EBIT reflects all of a firm's results for a period except its cost of borrowing (interest), it measures the expected consequences of all of a firm's operating activities (except debt financing) and the risk inherent in those activities.

III. Various more specific risks are discussed in the following subsections

A. **Financial Risk --** This is the particular risk faced by the firm's common shareholders that results from the use of debt financing, which requires payment regardless of the firm's operating results, and preferred stock, which requires dividends before returns to common shareholders. The payment of interest reduces earnings available to all shareholders and the payment of preferred dividends reduces the retained earnings available to common shareholders. The existence of these obligations increases the risk to common shareholders that variations in earnings will result in inadequate residual profits to reward common shareholders and could result in insolvency.

B. **Default Risk --** This is the risk associated with the possibility that the issuer of a security will not be able to make future interest payments and/or principal repayment. In the U.S. the lowest uncertainty of future payments-the lowest default risk-is ascribed to U.S. Treasury obligations. They are considered to be free of the risk of default (risk-free) and are used as the benchmark when evaluating the default risk of other securities.

C. **Interest Rate Risk**

1. This is the risk associated with the effects of changes in the market rate of interest on investments. The clearest illustration is provided by the effect of changes in the market rate of interest on long-term debt investments. When debt investments are made, the price paid depends on the market rate of interest for comparable investments at the time. Subsequently, as the market rate of interest changes, so also does the value of the debt investment-they change inversely, i.e., in opposite directions. Therefore, if the market rate goes up, the value of the outstanding debt goes down. A firm (or individual) that invests in debt has the risk that the market rate of interest will go up, causing the value of the debt to go down, which if sold before maturity would result in a loss.

2. A similar risk exists in other business contexts. For example, in using discounted cash flows for capital budgeting decisions, an interest rate is used (the hurdle rate) based on the expected cost of capital to fund the project. If interest rates change causing a higher cost of capital, the real present value will be less than that assumed. A project that was economically feasible under one interest rate assumption may prove to be unacceptable as a result of an increased interest rate.

3. Generally, the longer the period of an interest-based investment, the greater the perceived risk of the investment. Thus, the interest rate risk associated with a three-month Treasury Bill would be less than that of a 20-year bond investment, and the 20-year bond would require a higher interest rate risk premium. Note that Treasury obligations are not interest rate risk-free because the interest rate risk results from the difference between the effective rates paid by an investment and the current rate in the general market.

D. **Inflationary (or Purchasing Power) Risk --** This risk derives from the possibility that a rise in the general price level (inflation) will result in a reduction in the purchasing power of a fixed sum of money. For example, given inflation, the real purchasing power of a future cash flow from a capital project would be less than the nominal purchasing power of that cash flow. Therefore, if inflation was expected to be significant, it may be appropriate to adjust the cash flows and hurdle rate used for the expected inflation.

E. **Liquidation (or Marketability) Risk**

1. This risk derives from the possibility that an asset cannot be readily sold for cash equal to its fair value. Two possible elements are implied:

   a. Inability to sell for cash in the short term; and

   b. Inability to receive fair value in cash for the asset.

2. Mitigating this risk would be especially important when making investments that may need to be converted quickly to cash.

IV. **International Risk --** A firm that has transactions denominated in a foreign currency or that has operations in a foreign country faces additional risks not faced by a firm that does all of its business domestically. Those risks relate to the different political environment and the use of a different (foreign) currency.

A. **Political Risk --** This risk exists to a greater or lesser extent any time a firm has substantive operations in a country other than its home country. Differences in political climate, governmental processes, business culture and ethics, labor relations, market structures, and other factors all add elements of uncertainty and, therefore, risk to the firm.

B. **Currency Exchange Risk --** This risk derives from changes in exchange rates between currencies. As exchange rates change, so also does the home currency value of transactions and balances. Changes will affect firms in two ways:

1. **Foreign Currency Transaction Risk --** This risk results when a transaction is to be settled in a foreign currency and the exchange rate changes between the date the transaction is initiated and when it is settled. For example, assume a U.S. firm buys from a French firm and agrees to pay the French firm in Euros. If the dollar cost of Euros increases between the date the purchase takes place and when the U.S. firm pays its obligation, the U.S. firm will pay more dollars to acquire the required Euros. Both payables and receivables denominated (to be settled) in a foreign currency are subject to the currency exchange risk.
2. **Foreign Currency Investment Risk --** This risk results when a firm has a direct foreign investment. As exchange rates change so also does the home currency value of the foreign investment and its operating results. For example, the dollar value of a foreign subsidiary and its operating results will decrease if the foreign currency weakens against the dollar-the same foreign currency asset value and net income would equal fewer dollars in the parent's balance sheet and income statement.

Information Technology (IT)

Purposes and Types of IT Systems

Role of Information Technology (IT) in the business environment. Over the past forty years, information technology has transformed not just the way firms collect and report the results of business transactions, but the way the firm conducts its business, communicates with both internal and external stakeholders and even the way the firm itself competes in the marketplace. This section provides an overview of the types of systems now available, the manner in which they can be used to support both low-level and high-level activities within the organization, and the processing methodologies employed. On the whole, the information in this section is not as heavily tested as the information in the IT Fundamentals and IT Risks and Controls sections. However, many topics are regularly tested in one or two questions on most exams and several topics - namely ERP systems and computerized transaction processing methodologies - are tested on every exam. Accounting information systems comprise only a small part of an organization's IT system. This section provides a framework for understanding what these other systems are and how they fit together to support the organization's information needs. Be sure to cover enterprise resource planning (ERP) systems thoroughly as it is the most consistently, though not heavily, tested topic in this section.

I. **Purposes of IT systems --** IT systems are often classified according to the types of activities they support.

   A. **Operational systems --** Support the day-to-day activities of the business (purchasing of goods and services, manufacturing activities, sales to customers, cash collections, payroll, etc.)

      1. Are often known as **transaction processing systems (TPS)**.

      2. Operational systems **process both non-financial transactions** (placing orders for goods, accepting an order from a customer, etc.) and **financial transactions** (billing a customer, receiving payment from a customer, paying employees for services rendered).

         a. Financial transactions **generate debit and credit entries** into the accounts.

      3. Accounting systems are transaction processing systems.

   B. **Management Information Systems --** Systems designed to **support routine management** problems based primarily on data from transaction processing systems.

      1. MISs support management of daily operations; management issues in this area consist primarily of well-defined, structured problems.

         a. MISs take planning information (budgets, forecasts, etc.) data and compare it to actual results in periodic management reports (summary reports, variance reports, and exception reports).

      2. **Accounting Information Systems (AIS) --** AIS take the financial data from transaction processing systems and use it to produce financial statements and control reports for management (e.g., accounts receivable aging analysis, product cost reports, etc.); AIS are a **subset of MISs**.

   C. **Decision support systems (DSS) --** Provide information to mid- and upper-level management to assist them in managing non-routine problems and in long-range planning.

1. Unlike MISs, **DSSs frequently include external data** in addition to summarized information from the TPS and include significant analytical and statistical capabilities.
2. **Data driven DSSs --** Process large amounts of data in an endeavor to find relationships and patterns.
    a. **"Data warehousing"** and **"data mining"** systems are common examples of data driven DSSs.
3. **Model driven DSS --** Feed data into a previously constructed model in order to predict outcomes.
4. **Executive support systems (ESS) or strategic support systems (SSS) --** Are a subset of DSS that are especially designed for forecasting and making long-range, strategic decisions; as such, they have a greater emphasis on external data.

D. **Knowledge work systems --** Facilitate the work activities of professional level employees (engineers, accountants, attorneys, etc.) by providing information relevant to their day-to-day activities (e.g., how the company has handled specific types of audit exceptions) and/or by automating some of their routine functions (e.g., computer-aided systems engineering (CASE) packages used by programmers to automated some programming functions).
1. Usually exist separately from operational systems, but can be integrated.
2. **Office automation systems (OAS) --** Provide similar support to clerical level employees.
    a. Include many of the typical programs found on personal computers: word processing, spreadsheets, end-user databases, etc.

E. **Enterprise Resource Planning systems (ERPs) --** ERPs provide transaction processing, management support, and decision-making support in a single, integrated package. By integrating all data and processes of an organization into a unified system, ERPs attempt to eliminate many of the problems faced by organizations when they attempt to consolidate information from operations in multiple departments, regions, or divisions.
1. Goals of ERP systems:
    a. **Global visibility --** The integration of all data maintained by the organization into a single database; once the data is in a single database, it is available to anyone who is authorized to see it.
    b. **Cost reductions --** Long run systems maintenance costs are reducing by eliminating the costs associated with maintaining multiple systems.
    c. **Employee empowerment --** Global visibility of information improves lower level communication and decision making by making all relevant data available to the employee; this empowers the employee and, in turn, makes the organization more agile and better able to compete in a volatile business environment.
    d. **"Best practices" --** ERP systems processes are based on analysis of the most successful businesses in their industry; by adopting the ERP system, the organization automatically benefits from the implementation of these "best practices."

2. **Components of an ERP system --** ERP systems are typically purchased in modules (i.e., Sales, Logistics, Planning, Financial Reporting, etc.); ERP vendors have designed their systems to be purchased as a unit, that is from a "single source;" however, many organization pick and choose ERP modules from several vendors according to their perception of how well the ERP model fits with their company's way of doing business, a practice dubbed "best of breed."
    a. **Online transaction processing system (OLTP) --** The modules which comprise the core business functions: sales, production, purchasing, payroll, financial reporting, etc. These functions collect the operational data for the organization and provide the fundamental motivation for the purchase of an ERP.
    b. **Online analytical processing system (OLAP) --** Incorporates data warehouse and data mining capabilities within the ERP.
3. **ERP system architecture --** ERP systems are typically implemented using a **client/server network** configuration; although early implementations generally utilized proprietary LAN and WAN technologies, current implementations often utilize Internet-based connections.
    a. ERPs may use **two-tiered** or **three-tiered architectures** (see IT Fundamentals); because of the concentration of programs and data on a single system, three-tiered architecture is preferred.

II. **Types of IT systems --** IT systems can also be identified by the way that data is captured and processed.

A. **Flat file systems --** early IT systems used flat file technology. Flat files are characterized by:

1. **Independent programs and data sets --** Each application develops its own set of data and processing programs; data sharing across applications is accomplished through creation of separate programs which select data records from one application and reformats them so that the data can be incorporated into another application.
2. High degrees of **data redundancy** (multiple instances of the same piece of information; data redundancy can lead to data inconsistency - different values for the same piece of information).
3. Difficulty in achieving **cross functional reporting** (combining of information from multiple applications in a single report, for example, a report which combines gender and ethnicity information from the personnel system with hours worked from the payroll system).

B. **Database systems --** Data from related applications is pooled together in a set of logically related files (the database) which can be accessed by multiple applications through a database management system (DBMS); organizational database systems may exhibit a high level of integration (relatively few, large databases) or a low level of integration (relatively more, smaller databases); the higher the level of integration, the less data redundancy found within the organization and the easier it is to achieve cross-functional reporting.

1. Database systems are discussed in greater detail in the IT Fundamentals section.

C. **Knowledge Management (KM) --** A variety of practices which are designed to electronically capture and disseminate information throughout the organization. Knowledge management practices are intended to lead to the achievement of specific outcomes such as shared intelligence, improved performance, competitive advantage, or higher levels of innovation. Knowledge management includes:

1. **Knowledge base (or knowledgebase) --** A special type of database designed for retrieval of knowledge; it provides the means to collect and organize the information and develop relationships among information components.

2. **Expert systems (knowledge-based systems) --** A computer program that contains subject-specific knowledge derived from experts; the system consists of a set of rules that are used to analyze information provided by the user of the system; based on the information provided, the system then recommends a course of action.

3. **Data warehouse --** A database designed to archive an organization's operational transactions (sales, purchases, production, payroll, etc.) over a period of years; external data that might be correlated with these transactions such as economic indicators, stock prices, exchange rates, market share, political issues, weather conditions, etc. can also be incorporated into the data warehouse; data mining techniques - the process of performing statistical analysis and automatically searching for patterns in large volumes of data - can then be used to identify patterns and relationships among the data elements.

   a. **Data mart --** A specialized version of a data warehouse that contains data that is pre-configured to meet the needs of specific departments; companies often support multiple data marts within their organization.

   b. Terms associated with data warehouses:

      i. **Drill down --** The ability to move from summary information to more granular information (i.e., viewing an accounts receivable customer balance and drilling down to the invoices and payments which resulted in that balance).

      ii. **Slicing and dicing --** The ability to view a single data item in multiple dimensions; for example, the sale of VCRs might be viewed by product, by region, by time period, by company, etc.

E-Business and E-Commerce

This section provides an overview of the types of business conducted on the internet and a few of the enabling technologies that support internet based business transactions. Two topics in this section - electronic data interchange (EDI) and electronic funds transfer (EFT) systems - are tested on almost every exam and so should be studied carefully. It is also important to be able to distinguish between the terms associated with e-business: B2B vs. B2C, e-business vs. e-commerce, CRM vs. SCM, etc.

I. Definitions

Definition:

E-business: E-business is the generic name given to any business process that relies on electronic dissemination of information or on automated transaction processing.

A. E-business can be conducted within the organization as well as between the organization and its trading partners. Most e-business is conducted via the Internet using Web-based technologies, but other processing modes are also included.

Definition:

E-commerce: E-commerce is a narrower term used to refer to transactions between the organization and its trading partners.

B. **Business-to-business (B2B) e-commerce --** Involves electronic processing of transactions between businesses and includes electronic data interchange (EDI), supply chain management (SCM) and electronic funds transfer (EFT).

C. **Business-to-consumer (B2C) e-commerce --** Involves selling goods and services directly to consumers, almost always using the Internet and web-based technology. B2C e-commerce relies heavily on intermediaries or brokers to facilitate the sales transaction.

D. Some of the more pervasive types of e-business and e-commerce are discussed below.

II. Types of e-business

A. **Customer relationship management (CRM) --** Technologies used to manage relationships with clients; both biographic and transaction information about existing and potential customers is collected and stored in a database; the CRM provides tools to analyze the information and develop personalized marketing plans for individual customers.

B. **Electronic Data Interchange (EDI) --** EDI is computer-to-computer exchange of business data (e.g., purchase orders, confirmations, invoices, etc.) in structured formats that allow direct processing of the data by the receiving system; EDI reduces handling costs and speeds transaction processing compared to traditional paper-based processing.

1. EDI requires that **all transactions be submitted in a specified format**; translation software is required to convert transaction data from internal company data format to EDI format and vice versa.

   a. The most common specification in the United States is the American National Standards Institute format **ANSI X.12**; internationally, the United Nations EDI for Administration, Commerce and Transport (**UN/EDIFACT**) format is the dominant standard.

2. EDI can be implemented using direct links between the trading partners, through communication intermediaries (called "service bureaus"), through VANs, or over the Internet.

   a. Despite increased interest in web-based EDI using an XML based standard (RosettaNet is the leading contender for this standard), the **vast majority of EDI transactions are still processed through value added networks.**

      i. The **well-established audit trails, controls, and security** provided for EDI transactions by VAN are the principal reasons for their continued popularity.

3. **EDI costs include**

   a. **Costs of change** -- Costs associated with locating new business partners who support EDI processing; legal costs associated with modifying and negotiating trading contracts with new and existing business partners and with the communications provider; costs of changing internal policies and procedures to support the new processing model (process reengineering) and employee training;

   b. **Hardware costs** -- Often additional hardware such as communications equipment, improved servers, etc. is required;

   c. Costs of **translation software**;

   d. **Cost of data transmission**;

   e. Costs of **security, audit**, and **control procedures**.

C. **Electronic Funds Transfer (EFT)** -- A technology for transferring money from one bank account directly to another without the use of paper money or checks; EFT substantially reduces the time and expense required to process checks and credit transactions.

1. Typical examples of EFT services include:

   a. **Retail payments** -- Such as credit cards, often initiated from POS terminals;

   b. **Direct Deposit** -- Of payroll payments directly into the employee's bank account;

   c. **Automated teller machine (ATM) transactions**

   d. **Non-consumer check collection** -- Through the Federal Reserve wire transfer system.

2. **EFT service** -- Typically provided by a third party vendor who acts as the intermediary between the company and the banking system:

   a. Transactions are processed by the bank through the Automated Clearing House (ACH) network, the secure transfer system that connects all U.S. financial institutions.

3. **EFT security** -- Provided through various types of **data encryption** as transaction information is transferred from the client to the payment server, from the merchant to the payment server, and between the client and merchant

4. **Token-based payment systems --** Such as electronic cash, smart cards (cash cards), and online payment systems (e.g., PayPal) behave similarly to EFT, but are governed by a different set of rules

    a. Token-based payment systems can offer anonymity since the cards do not have to be directly connected to a named user.

5. **Electronic wallets --** Are not payment systems, but are simply programs that allow the user to manage their existing credit cards, user names, passwords, and address information in a easy-to-use, centralized location.

D. **Supply chain management (SCM) --** The process of planning, implementing, and controlling the operations of the supply chain: the process of transforming raw materials into a finished product and delivering that product to the consumer. Supply chain management incorporates all activities from the purchase and storage of raw materials, through the production process, into finished goods through to the point-of-consumption.

System Development & Implementation

The systems development life cycle provides a structured approach to developing, implementing, and maintaining computerized information systems. The area is regularly, though lightly, tested on the exam. Exam questions in this area tend to focus on identification of the steps in the systems development life cycle and on the activities performed within each of the steps.

I. **Developing a computer system --** This is a task that requires communication and coordination among multiple groups of people with very different points of view and priorities. Without a clear-cut plan for defining, developing, testing, and implementing the system, it is perilously easy to end up with a system that fails to meet its objectives and must be scrapped. The systems development life cycle is designed to provide this plan.

II. **Purpose of the systems development life cycle (SDLC) method --** The systems development life cycle provides a structured approach to the process of systems development by:

   A. Identifying the players in the development process and defining their responsibilities;

   B. Establishing a series of activities that must be performed in order to arrive at the expected result;

   C. Requiring project review and approval at critical points throughout the development process.

III. **Parties involved in the SDLC method --** It is critical that each party involved in the development process thoroughly reviews the system and signs off to indicate approval at each stage of development. This helps to ensure that the system will perform as expected and will be accepted by the end users.

   A. **IT steering committee** -- Members of the committee are selected from functional areas across the organization, including the IT department; the committee's principal duty is to approve and prioritize systems proposals for development.

   B. **Lead systems analyst** -- The manager of the programming team:

      1. Usually responsible for all direct contact with the end user;

      2. Often responsible for developing the overall programming logic and functionality.

   C. **Application programmers --** The team of programmers who, under direction of the lead analyst are responsible for writing and testing the program.

   D. **End users --** The employees who will use the program to accomplish their tasks:

      1. Responsible for identifying the problem to be addressed and approving the proposed solution to the problem

IV. **Steps in, and Risks to, the SDLC method --** Riskier systems development projects use newer technologies or have a poorly defined (i.e., sketchy) design structure. In the SDLC method, program development proceeds through an orderly series of steps. At the end of each step, all of the involved parties (typically the lead systems analyst, the end user, and a representative from the IT administration or the IT steering committee) sign a report of activities completed in that step to indicate their review and approval. The seven steps in the SDLC method are: (please note that there are several variations of the seven steps in common use.)

   A. **Planning and Feasibility Study --** When an application proposal is submitted for consideration, it is evaluated from three respects:

1. **Technical feasibility --** Is it possible to implement a successful solution given the limits currently faced by the IT department?
2. **Economic feasibility --** Even if the application can be developed, should it be developed? Are the potential benefits greater that the anticipated cost?
3. **Operational feasibility --** Given the status of other systems and people within the organization, how well will the proposed system work?
   a. Once feasibility has been established, a **project plan** is developed; the project plan establishes:
      i. **Critical success factors --** The things that the project must complete in order to succeed;
      ii. **Project scope --** A high level view of what the project will accomplish;
      iii. **Project milestones and responsibilities --** The major steps in the process, the timing of those steps, and identification of the individuals responsible for each step.

B. **Analysis --** During this phase the systems analysts work with end users to understand the business process and document the requirements of the system; the collaboration of IT personnel and end users to define the system is known as joint application development (JAD).

1. **Requirements definition --** The requirements definition formally identifies the things that the system must accomplish; it serves as the framework for system design and development.
   a. All parties sign off on the requirements definition to signify their agreement with the project's goals and processes.

C. **Design --** In the design phase, the technical specifications of the system are established; the design specification has two primary components:

1. **Technical architecture specification --** Identifies the hardware, systems software, and networking technology on which the system will run;
2. **Systems model --** Uses graphical models (flowcharts, etc.) to describe the interaction of systems processes and components; defines the interface between the user and the system by creating menu and screen formats for the entire system.

D. **Development --** During this phase, programmers use the systems design specifications to develop the program and data files:

1. The hardware and IT infrastructure identified during the design phase is purchased during the development phase;
2. The development process must be carefully monitored to ensure compatibility among all systems components as correction of errors becomes much more costly after this phase.

E. **Testing --** The system is evaluated to determine whether it meets the specifications identified in the requirements definition:

1. Testing procedures must project expected results and **compare actual results with expectations:**
   a. Test items should confirm correct handling of **both correct data and data that includes errors.**
2. Testing most be performed at multiple levels to ensure correct intra- and inter-system operation:

a. **Individual processing unit** -- Provides assurance that each piece of the system works properly;

b. **System testing** -- Provides assurance that all of the system modules work together;

c. **Inter-system testing** -- Provides assurance that the system interfaces correctly with related systems;

d. **User acceptance testing** -- Provides assurance that the system can accomplish its stated objectives with the business environment.

F. **Implementation** -- Before the new system is moved into production, existing data must be often be converted to the new system format and users must be trained on the new system; implementation of the new system may occur in one of several ways:

1. **Parallel implementation** -- The new system and the old system are run concurrently until it is clear that the new system is working properly:

   a. Is the safest strategy as it affords a fall-back position in case the new system encounters problems;

   b. Is only used in highly sensitive implementations because of the expense of maintaining both systems.

2. **"Cold turkey" or "plunge" or "big bang" implementation** -- The old system is dropped and the new system put in place all at once:

   a. As the names imply, this is the riskiest strategy: a "sink or swim" approach;

   b. Should only be used for very simple systems or when there is no other viable alternative.

3. **Phased implementation** -- Instead of implementing the complete system across the entire organization, the system is divided into modules that are brought on line one or two at a time:

   a. The slower pace of implementation allows more time for users to adjust to the new system and significantly reduces the opportunity for problems.

4. **Pilot implementation** -- Similar to phased implementation, except rather than dividing the system into modules, the users are divided into smaller groups and are trained on the new system one group at a time:

   a. Slows the pace of implementation to make it more manageable;

   b. Creates a core group of users that understand the new system and can provide support for new users as they come on board.

G. **Maintenance** -- Monitoring the system to ensure that it is working properly and updating the programs and/or procedures to reflect changing needs:

1. **User support groups and help desks** -- Provide forums for maintaining the system at high performance levels and for identifying problems and the need for changes;

2. All updates and additions to the system should be subject to the same structured development process as the original program.

Transaction Processing in a Computerized Environment

Questions about transaction processing have appeared on the CPA exam for many years (even pre-dating the creation of the BEC section of the exam) and remain one of the most consistently tested areas in the IT section today. This section begins with a review of the manual accounting cycle and goes on to discuss batch processing, online and real-time processing, point-of-sale systems, and centralized vs. decentralized processing. You are likely to find questions on your exam from each one of these areas so be sure to cover the material thoroughly.

I. **Transaction Processing** -- This section reviews manual transaction processing then describes the similarities and differences between the steps in manual and computerized transaction processing. Many of the documents, validation techniques, and processing procedures used in manual accounting systems carry over to computerized transaction processing systems.

II. **Manual processing of accounting information** -- The steps in the classic manual accounting process model are as follows:

   A. A business transaction occurs and is captured on a source document;

   B. Data from the source document is recorded chronologically in a journal (journalizing):

      1. The journal records the complete accounting transaction - both the debit and the credit.

   C. Individual debits and credits are copied from the journal to the ledgers (posting); all transactions are posted to the general ledger and many are also posted to a subsidiary ledger:

      1. **The general ledger** -- Classifies transactions by financial statement accounts (cash, inventory, accounts payable, sales revenue, supplies expense, etc.);

      2. **The subsidiary ledgers (subledgers)** -- Classify transactions by alternative accounts (e.g., customer accounts, vendor accounts, product accounts). Not all transactions are posted to subledgers: each subledger corresponds to a single general ledger account and only transactions that affect that account are posted in the subledger. Examples of subledgers include:

         a. **A/R Subledger** -- Classifies A/R transactions (credit sales and customer payments) by Customer;

         b. **A/P Subledger** -- Classified A/P transactions (credit purchases and payments to vendors) by Vendor;

         c. **Inventory Subledger** -- Classifies Inventory transactions (product purchases and product sales) by Product.

   D. The ledgers are used to produce summarized account reports:

      1. The general ledger produces the trial balance and financial statements;

      2. The subsidiary ledgers produce reports consistent with their content (customer a/r balances, vendor a/p balances, etc.).

III. **Computerized processing of accounting information** -- Most computerized accounting systems process transactions in roughly the same manner as manual systems: transaction data is first captured and recorded chronologically; it is then reclassified and summarized by account; finally, the account summaries are used to produce financial statements and other reports. The files used to record this information correspond roughly to journals and ledgers.

A. **Data entry/data capture --** When a transaction occurs, the data may be manually recorded on a physical source document and then keyed into the system or it may be captured electronically using automated data capture equipment such as bar code readers.

   1. The transaction data is recorded in a **transaction file**:

      a. **Transaction files --** In a computerized environment are equivalent to journals in a manual environment;

      b. **Transaction files are temporary files --** Data in the transaction files is periodically purged from the system to improve system performance.

B. **Master file update --** Data from the transaction files is used to update account balances in the master files. For example, the data from recording a utilities bill payment would be used to increase the balance of the Utilities Expense account and decrease the balance of the Cash account in the general ledger master file.

   1. **Master files** are used to maintain transaction totals by account:

      a. **Master files --** In a computerized environment are equivalent to ledgers in a manual environment;

      b. The general ledger and the subsidiary ledgers are all examples of master files;

      c. Master files are **permanent files**: the individual account balances change as transactions are processed but the accounts and master files themselves are never deleted.

C. **System output --** The master file account balances are used to produce most reports.

   1. The general ledger master file is used to produce the financial statements.

IV. **Processing Methodologies --** Processing methodology refers to the way computerized systems capture data and update the master file. Two principal methods are employed:

A. **Batch processing --** Batch processing is a periodic transaction processing method in which transactions are processed in groups:

   1. Input documents are **collected and grouped** by type of transaction. These groups are called **"batches."** Batches are **processed periodically** (i.e., daily, weekly, monthly, etc.);

   2. Batch processing is accomplished in four steps:

Step 1:	**data entry:** the transactions data is manually keyed (usually) and recorded in a transactions file
Step 2:	**preliminary edits:** the transaction file data is run through an **edit program** that checks the data for completeness and accuracy; invalid transactions are corrected and re-entered.
Step 3:	**sorting:** the edited transaction file records are **sorted into the same order as the master file**
Step 4:	**master file update:** the individual debits and credits are used to update the related account balance in the general ledger master file and, if appropriate, in the subsidiary ledger master file

3. **Batch controls --** One or more batch control totals is usually calculated for each batch. (See IT Risks and Controls for a detailed discussion of batch control totals.)
   a. The manually calculated batch control total is compared to computer generated batch control totals as the batch moves through update process.
   b. Differences between the two control totals indicate a processing error.
4. Batch processing is a **sequential processing method** - transactions are sorted in order to match the master file being updated.
   a. In some situations, sequential transaction processing can dramatically improve transaction processing efficiency.
5. **Time lags --** Are an inherent part of batch processing: there is always a time delay between the time the transaction occurs, the time that the transaction is recorded, and the time that the master file is updated. Thus, under batch processing:
   a. The accounting records are not always current; and
   b. Detection of transaction errors is delayed.
6. Batch processing is appropriate when:
   a. Transactions occur periodically (e.g., one a week, once a month, etc.);
   b. A significant portion of the master file records will be updated;
   c. Transactions are independent (e.g., no other time-critical activities depend on the transaction in question).

B. **On-line, real-time (OLRT) processing --** OLRT is a continuous, immediate transaction processing method in which transactions are processed individually as they occur.

1. In OLRT processing, transactions are entered and the master files updated as transactions occur.
   a. Require the use random access devices such as magnetic disk drives in order to process transactions.
2. Each transaction goes through all processing steps (data entry, data edit, and master file update) before the next transaction is processed. Thus, under OLRT processing:
   a. The accounting records are always current;
   b. Detection of transaction errors is immediate.
3. Because transactions are processed as they occur, OLRT systems generally require a networked computer system to permit data entered at many locations to update a common set of master files; this means that OLRT systems are more expensive to operate than batch systems
4. OLRT systems are desirable whenever:
   a. It is critical to have very current information;
   b. Transactions are continuous and interdependent as, for example, when a sales order is received: sales orders are received continuously and, once approved, cause other activities to occur (picking the goods in the warehouse, shipping the goods to the customer, invoicing the customer);
   c. Transactions are infrequent and few in number. (Batch processing is only cost effective when a significant number of transactions must be processed.)

C. **Point-of-sale (POS) systems --** POS systems are one of the most commonly encountered data capture systems in the marketplace today. POS systems combine on-line, real-time processing with automated data capture technology, resulting in a system that is highly accurate, reliable, and timely.

1. POS systems usually consist of a special purpose computer that is connected to or integrated with an **electronic cash register**:
    a. Each individual POS system is generally **networked to a central computer** that maintains a database of the products available for sale as well as the financial accounting data.
2. POS systems use **scanners** to capture data encoded on **product bar codes**:
    a. Use of scanners provides dramatic increases in **processing efficiency** and **transactions accuracy**.
3. The transaction detail and immediacy of the transaction information facilitates:
    a. Just-in-time inventory management;
    b. Cash flow management;
    c. Integration of marketing efforts.

V. **Centralized, decentralized, and distributed systems --** Organizations with multiple locations must address the problem of consolidating data from the individual locations.

A. **Centralized systems --** Maintain all data and perform all data processing at a central location; remote users may access the centralized data files via a telecommunications channel, but all of the processing is still performed at the central location.

1. **Advantages --** Of centralized systems include:
    a. Better data security once it is received at the central location;
    b. Consistency in processing.
2. **Disadvantages --** Of centralized systems include:
    a. **High cost of transmitting --** Large numbers of detailed transactions;
    b. **Input/output bottlenecks --** At high traffic times (end of period;)
    c. **Inability to respond in a timely manner --** To information requests from remote locations.

B. **Decentralized systems --** Allow each location to maintain its own processing system and data files. In decentralized systems most of the transaction processing is accomplished at the regional office and summarized data is sent to the central office. For example, in payroll processing, the regional offices calculate time worked, gross pay, deductions, and net pay for each employee and transmit totals for salary expense, deductions payable, and cash paid to the central database.

1. **Advantages --** Of decentralized systems include:
    a. Realization of **substantial cost savings** by reducing the volume of data that must be transmitted to the central location;
    b. Reduction of processing power and data storage needs at the central site;
    c. Elimination of input/output bottlenecks;
    d. Better responsiveness to local information needs.

2. **Disadvantages --** Of decentralized systems include:

    a. Greater potential for security violations because there are more sites to control;

    b. Cost of installing and maintaining equipment in multiple locations.

C. **Distributed database systems --** Are so named because rather than maintaining a centralized or master database at a central location, the database is distributed across the locations according to their needs. (Methods of distributing the database are discussed in the database section of IT Fundamentals.)

1. **Advantages --** Of distributed database systems include:

    a. Better communications among the remote locations because they must all be connected to each other in order to distribute the database;

    b. More current and complete information;

    c. Reduction or elimination of the need to maintain a large, expensive central processing center.

2. **Disadvantages --** Of distributed database systems include the disadvantages associated with decentralized systems in general and:

    a. Cost of establishing communications among remote locations;

    b. Conflicts among the locations when accessing and updating shared data.

IT Fundamentals

Computer Data and Hardware

This section looks at IT system components, from the program and data files that are used to convey instructions and information to the communications infrastructure that allows the Internet to deliver that information all over the world. Computer data and computer hardware are the foundation on which the IT system is built and their testing on the exam reflects that: at least one or two questions covering material from this section appear on every exam. In particular, be sure that you understand the terminology related to the different types of computer data, the components of the CPU and the characteristics of the various types of secondary storage devices. ***Note:*** *The material in this section is heavily tested on every exam.*

I. **Computer Data --** All information and instructions used in IT systems are conveyed using binary code: a series of zeros and ones. This section looks at how the zeros and ones are strung together to create meaning.

A. **Bit (binary digit) --** An individual zero or one; the smallest piece of information that can be represented.

B. **Byte --** A group of (usually) 8 bits that are used to represent alphabetic and numeric characters and other symbols (3, g, X, ?, etc.). Several coding systems are used to assign specific bytes to characters; ASCII and EBCIDIC are the two most commonly used coding systems. Each system defines the sequence of zeros and ones that represent each character.

C. **Field --** A group of characters (bytes) that identify a characteristic of an entity. A data value is a specific value found in a field. Fields can consist of a single character (Y, N) but usually consist of a group of characters. Each field is defined as a specific data type. Date, Text and Number are common data types.

Entity	Field	Data Value	Data Type
Invoice	Invoice Number	4837	numeric
Customer	Street Address	1034 Rose Ave.	alpha-numeric or text
Product	Sale Price	$13.95	currency

The data type determines how programs will treat the characters entered into the field;

In a database environment, fields are also known as attributes.

D. **Record --** A group of related fields (or attributes) that describe an individual instance of an entity (a specific invoice, a particular customer, an individual product);

E. **File --** A collection of records for one specific entity (an Invoice File, a Customer File, a Product File).

1. In a database environment, files are also known as tables.

F. **Database --** A set of logically related files.

CPA exam questions sometimes ask you to order data elements by size.
The following data hierarchy displays these relationships:

Files: *are composed of*

Records: *are composed of*

Fields: *are composed of*

Data values: *are composed of*

Bytes (characters): *are composed of*

Bits: *the smallest storage element in a computer system.*

II. **Computer Hardware --** Includes the physical equipment in your computer and the equipment that your computer uses to connect to other computers or computer networks. Computer hardware falls into four principal classifications:

A. **Central Processing Unit (CPU) --** The CPU is the control center of the computer system. It has three principal components:

1. **Control Unit --** Interprets program instructions;
2. **Arithmetic Logic Unit (ALU) --** Performs arithmetic calculations;
3. **Primary storage (main memory) --** Stores programs and data until they while they are being used. It is divided into two main parts:
   a. **Random access memory (RAM) --** Stores data temporarily while it is being processed;
   b. **Read-only memory (ROM) --** Used to permanently store the data needed to power on the computer; includes portions of the operating system:
      i. ROM may be programmable (one time only) and is then known as Programmable Read-Only Memory (PROM);
      ii. ROM may also be erasable-programmable (may be programmed multiple times) and is then known as Erasable Programmable Read-Only Memory (EPROM).
4. **Additionally**, there are **two forms of memory** used directly by the CPU:
   a. **Registers --** Very small pieces of memory which are used to hold instructions and processing results as the CPU is executing a program instruction;
   b. **Cache memory --** Very fast and easily accessed memory which is used to store frequently/recently used program instructions and data; cache memory speeds up processing since the computer no longer has to go to RAM to retrieve data and/or program instructions.
5. **Virtual memory --** A methodology that extends the processing capacity of a computer system by using secondary storage devices (see below) to temporarily hold portions of a program not currently needed by the processor; the program is broken up into sections called pages; pages that are not currently needed to perform processing functions are stored on disk (the "virtual" memory); when needed, they are brought into RAM.
6. **Parallel processing --** Many modern computers use several microprocessors to perform the functions of a CPU rather than a single processor; the use of multiple processors to perform the basic interpretation and execution of program instructions is called parallel processing.

B. Secondary storage devices -- Provide permanent storage for programs and data; depending on the way the devices are set up, they can either be online (the data on the device is available for immediate access by the CPU) or offline (the device is stored in an area where the data is not accessible to the CPU).

1. **Magnetic disks --** Are random access devices: data can be stored on and retrieved from the disk in any order; this is the most efficient way to store and retrieve individual records; magnetic disks are the most commonly used form of secondary storage.

   a. Data on magnetic disks is **organized in concentric circles** called **tracks**;

   b. The disk as a whole is divided into **pie-shaped wedges** called **sectors**;

   c. When **multiple disks are stacked and fastened together** to form a single unit called a **disk pack.**

      i. The column of tracks extending from the top most disk through the bottom disk is called a **cylinder**. (For example, the fourth track on all of the disks in a disk pack would comprise a cylinder.)

   d. Several techniques are used to access data stored on random access devices:

      i. **Direct access --** The primary record key (PRK - the unique identifier for each record; for business transactions, the PRK is often a document number or account code) is equivalent to the disk address; to access the record, the computer simply retrieves the record at the location specified by the PRK; this technique is the fastest retrieval method but is difficult to implement in a business environment and so is seldom used in business systems.

      ii. **Hashed access --** A mathematical algorithm is used to translate the primary record key into a disk address; this method is almost as fast as direct access but, like direct access, is difficult to implement in a business environment.

      iii. **Indexed access --** A separate index file is established that lists the primary record key of each record and its disk address; to retrieve a record, the system looks up the PRK in the index, identifies the disk address and then retrieves the record; this technique, though somewhat slower than direct or hashed access, is extremely flexible and is the most common method of data retrieval in business systems.

      iv. **Indexed Sequential Access Method (ISAM) --** It is possible to store data on a disk in sequential order rather than random order; a number of business transactions can be processed more efficiently when stored sequentially; when data is stored sequentially on a disk, an index is usually created so that it is possible to find individual records directly without reading through the entire sequence of records; files that are stored on a disk in this manner are called **Indexed Sequential Access Method files (ISAM)**: Indexed - because individual records can be individually accessed through an index file; *Sequential* - because the records can be processed as a group in PRK order; and *Access Method* - because the focus of the method is on data retrieval.

2. **Magnetic tape --** Magnetic tape is a **sequential access device**: data is stored in order of the primary record key (i.e., document number, customer number, inventory number, etc.) and must also be retrieved sequentially; although once used for transaction processing, this medium is now **used mostly for archiving data**.

a. Because it is not possible to access a specific record stored on magnetic tape without reading through all the records between the current position on the tape and the desired position, accessing a specific record stored on magnetic tape is significantly slower than accessing a specific record stored on a magnetic disk. (Think of the difference between finding a particular song stored on a CD compared to a song stored on a cassette tape.)

b. Slow access speed makes tape **impractical for online**, real-time systems which need to retrieve individual transactions quickly; however, it's low cost makes it a practical choice for storing archived data which is not accessed frequently.

3. **Optical disks --** Use laser technology to "burn" data on the disk (although some rewritable disks use magnetic technology to record data); in general, read-only and write-once optical disks are a more stable storage medium than magnetic disks; optical disks, like magnetic disks are random access devices; there are several different types of optical disks:

   a. **Compact disks (CDs) --** Medium capacity (approximately 700M) devices; may be read-only (CD-ROM), recordable or "write once, read many" (CD-R) or rewritable - may be written to many times (CD-RW).

   b. **Digital video disks (DVDs) --** High capacity (approximately 4.7 G) devices; like CDs, they may be read-only, recordable or rewritable (DVD-ROM, DVD-R or DVD-RW, respectively)

4. **Flash drives --** (Also known as jump drives or thumb drives) - Are very small, portable devices that can store anywhere from 500 M of data to over several gigabytes of data; the term "drive" is a bit of a misnomer as there are no moving parts to "drive;" rather, the memory in a flash drive is similar to the RAM used as primary storage for your CPU.

   a. Flash drives are usually connected to your computer using one of its Universal Serial Bus (USB) ports.

5. **Redundant Array of Independent (or Inexpensive) Disks (RAID) --** A technology that uses a group of disk drives under control of a single system to record data on multiple disks; because this recording occurs in real time (i.e., on an on-going basis) the system essentially creates a backup of each transaction as soon as it is recorded; RAID technology improves system fault tolerance (the ability of the system to continue operation when part of the system fails) and, since data can be retrieved from multiple disks simultaneously, facilitates data retrieval.

C. **Peripherals --** Devices that transfer data to or from the CPU but do not take part in processing data; Peripherals are commonly known as input and output devices (I/O devices).

1. **Input devices --** Instruct the CPU and supply data to be processed:

   a. **Keyboard, mouse, trackball --** Commonly used end-user input devices;

   b. **Touch-screen technology --** Frequently used in commercial environments because it makes the data entry process much more intuitive;

   c. **Microphones and voice recognition technology --** Popular user interface for use in automated phone systems;

   d. **Point of Sale (POS) scanners --** Used in a variety of retail and commercial environments to identify products;

   e. **Magnetic Ink Character Recognition (MICR) devices --** Used extensively by the banking industry to read magnetic ink characters on checks;

f. **Optical Character Recognition (OCR) devices --** A scanning devices used in conjunction with a software program to read typed and/or handwritten data.

2. **Output devices --** Transfer data from the processing unit to other formats:

   a. **Printers, plotters --** Provide paper output;

   b. **Monitors, flat panel displays, CRT (Cathode Ray Tube) displays --** All refer to commonly used forms of visual output;

   c. **Speakers, voice output communication aids (VOCAs) --** Provide auditory output; in the case of VOCAs, digital data is converted into speech.

D. **Classification of computing systems --** Computers are often placed into categories according to their processing capacity and the way in which they are used.

1. **Supercomputers --** Computers at the leading edge of processing capacity; their definition is constantly changing as the supercomputer of today often becomes the personal computer of tomorrow; currently supercomputers are characterized by the use of **parallel processing**: the **use of multiple processors** - often hundreds of processors - as if they were a single unit **in computer clusters**. (Groups of loosely connected computers designed to spread processing workload.)

   a. Supercomputers are generally used for calculation-intensive scientific applications such as weather forecasting and climate research, biological and physical simulations, cryptology, etc.

2. **Mainframe computers --** Computers used by commercial organizations to support mission critical tasks such as sales and order processing, inventory management and e-commerce applications; unlike supercomputers, which tend to support processor-intensive activities (i.e., a small number of highly complex calculations), mainframe computers tend to be input/output (I/O) intensive (i.e. a very large numbers of simple transactions); mainframes frequently support thousands of users at a single point in time.

   a. Since mainframe computers are critical to the daily operations, they must have an extremely high degree of reliability and availability.

3. **Microcomputers or Personal Computers (PCs) --** Comprise an extremely diverse group of devices ranging from handheld personal digital assistants (PDAs) through desktop machines that can serve as components in large, networked environments; some of the more common classifications, based primarily on processing power and use, include:

   a. **Fat clients (or thick clients) --** A personal computer that is connected to a network; fat clients perform their own processing functions and can store some or all of their programs and data;

   b. **Thin clients --** A "stripped down" personal computer that is connected to a network; thin clients do not have file storage capability and have only limited processing capability - they serve primarily as devices to access network resources; thin clients are favored by many network administrators because they provide less opportunity for the introduction of viruses and other system threats;

   c. **Workstations --** High-performance desktop computers that are connected to a network and used by individual end-users to perform specific tasks;

   d. **Servers --** Computers which have been configured to provide resources to the network; common types of servers include print servers, file servers and web servers; unlike workstations, servers are not used directly by individual end-users but are accessed by many end-users through the network.

Computer Software

Computer software provides the interface between the computer user and the computer hardware - the CPU, printers, disk drives, keyboards, monitors, etc. Without software, the computer hardware could not perform any of the tasks we depend on it to do. Computer software is created using a variety programming languages. The language used to create the software often depends on the function the software is expected to perform - from the applications software that allows us to play games, write papers and perform calculations to the systems software that controls the hardware. Computer software is tested very regularly on the exam, although not usually very deeply. Most questions involve defining a term or identifying its characteristics. Popular areas for testing include the functions and characteristics of operating systems and the classification of programming languages into 5th generation languages, 4th generation languages, etc.

I. **Three Categories** -- Computer software is divided into three categories

II. **Systems software** -- Consists of the programs that run the computer and support system management operations. Several of the most frequently encountered types of systems software are discussed below.

   A. **The operating system** -- Provides the **interface between the user and the computer hardware**. It defines the commands can be issued and how they are issued (e.g., typing in a command, pointing at an icon and clicking, issuing a verbal command).

      1. The operating system also performs basic systems management tasks including:

         a. Controlling and allocating memory;

         b. Prioritizing and scheduling system requests;

         c. Controlling input and output devices;

         d. Managing file systems.

      2. Other operating system characteristics include:

         a. **Multitasking (or multiprogramming)** -- Allows the user to run multiple programs (i.e., a word processor, a spreadsheet and a computer game) or complete multiple tasks (i.e., printing a document, copying a file and playing a video) simultaneously or at least gives the appearance of running simultaneously: the operating system actually runs only one task at a time but constantly switches between tasks; most modern operating system are multi-tasking.

         b. **Multiprocessing** -- Allows the system to control multiple CPUs on a single computer system;

         c. **Multi-user capabilities** -- Allows the system to operate in a networked environment and communicate with other devices on the network.

      3. Some common operating systems are listed below; all systems listed are multi-tasking and can be set up to support multi-user environments:

         a. **Microsoft Windows** -- The standard operating system for most personal computers;

b. **Unix/Linux --** A widely used operating system that works on a variety of platforms (personal computers, servers, workstations); Linux is the open source (available at no cost; developed and maintained by its end users) version of Unix;

c. **Mac OS X --** The current version of the operating system used on Macintosh computers.

B. **Database management systems (DBMS) --** Control the storage and retrieval of data maintained in a database. The DBMS acts as an intermediary or middleware between the operating system and the application programs used by end users to update and access the data. The DBMS maintains the referential integrity of the data.

1. The DBMS provides the following "sub-languages" to allow the user to store and retrieve data:

a. **Data definition language (DDL) --** Used to create tables and fields of information within the fields;

b. **Data manipulation language (DML) --** Used to add, update and delete data;

c. **Data query language (DQL) --** Used to extract information from the database.

2. **Network operating systems (NOS) --** Control the traffic on a network, controls access to network resources such as files and printers and performs administrative functions for the network, including maintaining network security.

III. **Programming languages --** All software is created through the use of a programming language. Programming languages are comprised of a **set of instructions** and a **syntax** that determines how the instructions can be put together to control behavior of the computer.

A. Most programming languages used today are either "third generation" or "fourth generation" languages, however, all programming languages must ultimately be reduced to "first generation" or **binary language** in which all instructions are represented by a series of zeros and ones ("on" and "off"): binary symbols (0s and 1s) are the only symbols that processors can recognize and interpret.

1. **Machine language (also known as object code) --** Is comprised of "instructions" composed entirely of binary digits (0s and 1s); machine language is **first generation language (1GL)**.

2. **Assembler language --** Is one step removed from machine language; assembler languages use more easily understood mnemonic codes to represent the actual machine language instructions (e.g., the instruction to zero out a register (0001100 in machine language) would be represented by the mnemonic ZEROREG); assembler code must be translated into machine code in order to be used to control the computer; assembler language is **second generation language (2GL)**.

3. **Job control language (JCL) --** Is the language used on many mainframe computers (e.g., IBM) to control how and when programs should be run and to coordinate the resources (e.g., data, access to sub-routines) needed by the programs.

4. **Procedural language --** Uses "English-like" commands which make programs easier to understand and, in general, faster to write than 1st or 2nd generation languages. Procedural languages are also know as **third generation languages (3GL)**. COBOL, Pascal, Basic, C, C++ and Java are all examples of procedural language.

a. Programs written in the procedural language are known as source code. Source code must be then converted into object code (binary code) in order to be used by the computer. The conversion is accomplished by one of two means:

   i. **Compiled into object code --** Compilation creates a permanent, compiled version of the program which may be run many times. or,

   ii. **Interpreted into object code --** Interpretation translates the source code and executes it immediately but does not save a permanent version of the translation, consequently the code must be interpreted each time the program is run.

5. **Non-procedural or "problem-oriented" languages --** Are even more "English-like" than third generation languages: that is, they require even less knowledge of programming syntax and data structure. In fact, many non-procedural languages can be used by a knowledgeable end-user, thus negating the need for programming assistance from a programmer. Non-procedural languages are known as **fourth generation languages (4GL)**.

   a. Examples of 4GLs include:

      i. **Query languages (Structured Query Language (SQL), Query-by-Example (QBE) --** Permit an end-user to extract data from a database using either very simple instructions (SQL) or by using a drag-and-drop graphical interface (QBE);

      ii. **Report generators --** re included with most database management systems and allow a user to design a report in a graphical environment rather than having to program the alignment and spacing of the various report; sections.

      iii. **Forms generators --** Used by programmers to significantly reduce the time required to generate data entry screens and forms;

      iv. **Data analysis programs --** Allow the user to perform sophisticated statistical analysis; examples include SAS and SPSS.

   b. 4GLs are designed to reduce the time and cost of software development.

6. **Visual or graphical program development environments --** Generate source code for 3rd of 4th generation languages such as Java or Basic. Graphical environments speed program development because there programmers do not have to actually write the code and consequently there are fewer errors in the resulting programs. Visual or graphical program languages are known as **fifth generation languages (5GL)**.

7. **Object-oriented programming (OOP) --** OOP languages are organized around "objects" and data rather than "actions" and logic. Traditional programming languages focus on the sequence of activities that we perform on data: input the data, process the data (e.g., use it to modify existing data and/or store the new data), output the data. The data is a result of the processing logic. Object-oriented programming flips this point of view and focuses instead on the object itself: each object can be viewed as an independent entity with a specified set of characteristics (data values) and a specified set of capabilities.

   a. An object represents a **specific instance of a class** of objects. For example:

      i. "Copying machine" is an object belonging to a class called "Equipment;"

      ii. "Toyota Prius" is an object belonging to a class called "Vehicles."

b. Objects have several characteristics that make them very powerful and flexible:

   i. **Inheritance --** Classes of objects can be broken down into sub-classes; subclasses "inherit" characteristics and capabilities from their class; for example, if the Vehicle class was broken down into a subclasses of SUVs, Trucks, Hybrids, etc. the subclass objects would have similar characteristics to the objects of the main class (e.g., engine size, body type, fuel efficiency, etc.) but would also be able to add their own unique characteristics.

   ii. **Polymorphism --** The **ability of behavior to vary** based on the conditions in which the behavior is invoked. For example, if a copying machine is being depreciated using double-declining balance depreciation and a desk is being depreciated using straight-line depreciation, the behavior "depreciate" would evoke a different response for the copying machine object and the desk object.

   iii. **Encapsulation --** Limits the amount of detail one object shares with other objects.

c. Object oriented programming capabilities have been integrated into several well-known languages (C++, Java); OOP is particularly popular for computer game development.

8. **Mark-up or "tagging" languages --** Markup languages combine text and "extra information" about the text: the tag. Depending on the markup language, the tag may indicate how to display the text (e.g., centered, bold, red font) or may identify the text as a specific type of item (e.g., a book title, an author, a publisher). Markup languages can be used to support a wide variety of activities.

   a. **HTML (HyperText Markup Language) --** The best-known markup language, HTML is used to create web pages. HTML tags, like most other tags, are codes that are enclosed in brackets and are used in pairs - a beginning tag and an ending tag. For example, in the following text:

```
<c>This Text Should be Centered</c>
```

   b. The <c> tag marks the beginning of a text string that should be centered. The </c> tag marks the end of the text that should be centered. Other tags may identify structural components (headings, numbered items, bulleted text) and **hyperlinks - text that links the current document to other documents** available on the web.

   c. **XML (eXtensible Markup Language) --** XML is a general-purpose markup language that is often used as a specification or meta-language for the creation of special purpose markup languages. XML's "extensible" characteristic allows users to "extend" the language by creating new tags to support specialized applications. A common use of XML is to facilitate electronic communication of information between organizations or systems. For example, an XML variant facilitates communication of news items between news gathering organizations and news consumers. Specialized tags are used to identify the news classification, headline, date and time and body of the news item, etc. The item can then be distributed to recipients across a wide variety of platforms.

   d. **XBRL (eXtensible Business Reporting Language) --** XBRL is an XML variant that is used to describe business transactions. The specification is being developed by an international consortium of regulatory bodies, accounting firms, industry representatives and software producers. In the United States, the SEC now accepts corporate filings using XBRL.

i. XBRL is based on a standardized set of **taxonomies** (classification systems) that identify individual reporting elements as well as the relationships between elements. For example, the XBRL taxonomy identifies a class of accounts called assets and specifies tags within that class that identify individual accounts such as cash, accounts receivable, inventory and equipment.

ii. XBRL, when fully developed, will provide a **common format for communicating financial information** between businesses and their trading partners, regulatory agencies and the broader financial community **independent of their software and processing technologies**

iii. XBRL is expected to dramatically improve the availability and usefulness of financial information by:

1. Providing a standardized means of comparison among companies;
2. Permitting rapid dissemination of accounting information (one of the requirements of Sarbanes-Oaxley);
3. Making investment information more easily obtained and analyzed by investors.

IV. **Application software --** Encompasses the diverse group of end-user programs that are used to accomplish a specific objectives. Application software can be generic (word processors, spreadsheets, databases) or can be custom developed for a specific application (ex.: a marketing information system for a clothing designer). Application software may be purchased "off the shelf" or developed internally.

A. **Enterprise software --** Refers to the broad classes of application software used to support business activities (sales and marketing systems, accounting systems, human resource management systems, etc.).

B. **Artificial Intelligence (AI) --** Refers to systems designed to make decisions in relatively unstructured environments. Unlike traditional computing systems AI systems are characterized by **learning** (the acquisition of information and rules for using the information), **reasoning** (using the rules to reach approximate or definite conclusions), and **self-correction**.

1. **Expert systems --** A subclass of AI systems frequently used in business. Expert systems are used in relatively structured decision environments and include the following components:

   a. **Knowledge database --** The set of rules used for making decisions;

   b. **Domain database --** A set of facts relevant to the decisions to be made;

   c. **Inference engine --** Uses rules from the knowledge database and facts from the domain database together with information provided by the user to arrive at a decision or conclusion; information engines use **heuristics ("rules of thumb" or decision-making shortcuts** that typically result in viable, though not necessarily optimal, decisions.) to find solutions to problems.

2. **Neural networks --** A system of programs and data structures designed to recognize patterns in large quantities of data; neural networks use feedback from previous decisions to learn and adapt.

   a. **Fuzzy logic --** Is used in neural networks and other AI systems to make decisions when there is no absolute "true" or "false" response to a question; fuzzy logic systems can make decisions based on "degrees of truth" and imprecise measures (small, thin, low, etc.).

Databases

The two principal choices for storing data are independent, "flat" files or databases. Databases offer significant advantages over independent data files, including elimination of redundant information and simplified data extraction and reporting, especially cross-functional reporting. The vast majority of business and accounting data is maintained in databases rather than flat files. Database concepts and terminology are tested regularly on the exam but are usually tested at a relatively low level of difficulty. Identification questions about the languages used to create and maintain a database (DDL, DML and DQL) are common as are questions about the differences between the relational and hierarchical database models.

Definition:

Database System: A **database** is a **set of logically related files**. Most business data is highly inter-related and consequently most business data is stored in databases.

I. Overview

A. The following independent flat files could easily be brought together into a database (relationships are represented by arrows):

Customer File<==>Sales Invoice File<==>Product File<==>Purchase Order File<==>Vendor File

B. Bringing the independent files together into a database reduces the amount of redundant (repetitious) data in the system and greatly facilitates data retrieval and reporting.

C. Databases are characterized by the way the data relationships are established and the way the database is implemented across the organization.

II. Database models -- Depending on the database model, related records may be linked together in several different ways.

A. Hierarchical or tree model -- This model can represent 1:1 and 1:M relationships but **cannot represent M:M relationships**; relationships in hierarchical databases are **one-directional**, always moving from the 1 side of the relationship to the Many side of the relationship; records in a hierarchical database are linked using **physical (address) pointers**.

1. Disadvantages of the hierarchical model:

   a. When **data sets are volatile** (e.g., when there are many new records, changes to old records) **the physical pointers demand heavy processing overhead**; consequently, hierarchical systems tend to run slowly in this type of environment.

   b. The inability to correctly represent M:M relationships creates data redundancy whenever M:M relationships exist within the system.

2. Advantages of the hierarchical model: The use of physical pointers makes **data retrieval very simple and efficient**; for this reason, **data warehouses often use the hierarchical model**.

B. **Network model --** Similar to the Hierarchical model, the Network model uses physical pointers to implement relationships; however, the network model is **bi-directional** and **can represent M:M relationships**; unfortunately, the **processing overhead** associated with the bi-directional points is **so great** that this network model is too slow to be competitive.

C. **Relational model --** In the relational model, relationships between records are established by using the **primary record key** (a field that uniquely identifies each transaction) to **logically link records together**. The link is created by **including the primary record key** from one record as a field in the related record. The linking field is called a **foreign key**. The relational model can represent 1:1, 1:M and M:M relationships.

1. Data is retrieved from the database using **relational algebra** - a procedural query language that allows users to extract information from the database; the principal operators used in relational algebra are:

    a. **Select --** Creates a **subset (or selection) of records** from one file (or table) that meet the specified criteria.

    b. **Join --** Pulls **data from two files (or tables) together** based on a shared data value(s).

    c. **Project --** creates a new table **made up of only selected fields (or columns) of data** from the original table or file.

2. Disadvantages of the relational model:

    a. Relational algebra is not an efficient way of extracting information from the database; when the database files are extremely large, these inefficiencies may **slow database response time** down to unacceptable levels.

3. Advantages of the relational model:

    a. The use of logical links, instead of physical pointers, **significantly reduces processing overhead** when data is added, deleted, or updated making the relational model ideal for recording data in business systems.

    b. Since the relational model supports 1:1, 1:M, and M:M relationships, there is very **little data redundancy** in the system.

III. Terminology and concepts associated with the databases

A. **Normalization --** The process of organizing data in tables so that data redundancy is eliminated and each table presents information about a single entity or relationship.

B. **Schema --** A view of the **logical and physical relationships** that make up the database; **sub-schemas** are views of a **portion of the database**, frequently, what an individual user would see in order to do his job; sub-schemas are also known as **user views**.

C. **Data dictionary --** A listing of all of the data fields found in the database; some data dictionaries also identify forms, queries, and reports that use each field.

D. **Referential integrity --** This ensures that **relationships expressed between two entities are valid**; for example, if there is a relationship between invoices and customers and Invoice #1020 is related to Customer #405, referential integrity verifies that Customer #405 exists before the relationships is established.

IV. Database management system -- A "middle-ware" program that interacts with the database application and the operating system to define the database, enter transactions into the database, and extract information from the database; the DBMS uses three special languages to accomplish these. objectives:

A. **Data definition language (DDL) --** This allows the user to define the tables and fields and the relationships among the tables. Example commands in the DDL include CREATE, DROP, and ALTER. These commands relate to fields or tables (but not records).

B. **Data manipulation language (DML) --** This allows the user to add new records, delete old records, and to update existing records. Example commands include UPDATE, INSERT, and DELETE. These commands relate to records but not to fields or tables.

C. **Data query language (DQL) --** This allows the user to extract information from the database; most relational databases use **structured query language (SQL)** to extract the data; some systems provide a graphic interface that essentially allows the user to "drag and drop" fields into a query grid to create a query; these products are usually called **Query-By-Example (QBE).**

V. **Distributed databases --** A single database frequently needs to be used by individuals in different locations. For example, a school with multiple campuses needs to have student information available at all campuses. Although it is possible to create direct connection from all of the campuses to a single central database, the data communications costs and increases in processing time when all the campuses try to access the central database usually make this choice prohibitive. Instead, the database is physically duplicated so that it can be distributed to multiple users: this is a **distributed database**. A distributed database can be set up in one of several ways depending on the nature of the database and the data usage:

A. **Replication --** A **complete copy of the database** is made and is installed on the remote system;

1. Replication is the best choice when there is **considerable overlap in the set of records** needed by each location (this would be the case in the school example, if students commonly took courses on several different campuses);

2. Replicated databases must periodically be **synchronized** so that the updates are reflected on all of the systems;

B. **Partition --** The database is **broken into parts** based on who needs access to specific data items;

1. Partitioning is the best choice when there is **little overlap in the data needed at each location** (in the school example, this would be the case if students usually took all of their courses at a single campus);

2. When a location needs data that is stored at a different site, the location must use remote access to update the data.

C. **Record-locking --** This is used in distributed databases to **prevent multiple users from attempting to simultaneously update the same record**;

1. **Deadlock** - A condition that can occur if multiple users, in the process of updating two different records, **need access to the same information in order to complete** their updates: processing for both transactions stops until one of the updates is canceled (reversed).

VI. **Object-oriented database management systems (OODBMSs) --** Have the ability to store complex information ("objects") in a database environment instead of limiting data to text;

A. In true OODBMSs, the data has all the characteristics of the objects found in Object-Oriented Programming (encapsulation, inheritance, etc.);

B. While true OODBMSs are not in wide-spread use, many **relational databases have been upgraded to include some objects**, notably email addresses, hyperlinks and graphics.

Computer Networks 1

Computer networks permit communications between computers that are separated by a few feet or by thousands of miles. This section discusses the different types of networks that are used to complete these connections, their components and their characteristics. Most CPA exams will have two or three questions on computer networks. These questions can cover a wide variety of topics included in this section and, while some questions are relatively simple, some of the questions can be complex. Although students with strong IT backgrounds may be able to answer these questions, most students find them very difficult even after studying the material. Though additional studying may improve performance in these students, since the question topics are difficult to predict and since there is likely to be only one truly difficult questions, the additional study time might be better spent on other topics

I. **Computer networks and data communications --** At it's most minimal implementation, a computer network consists of two computing devices connected by some type of communications channel which the devices can use to exchange data; most networks are substantially larger than this but the principal is the same: a communications channel is established which allows computers (and similar devices) to exchange data and share resources (software, hardware, data) among other computers on the network.

II. **Components of a network**

  A. **Nodes --** Any device connected to the network is a node:

    1. **Client --** A node, usually a microcomputer, which is used by end users; it uses network resources but does not usually supply resources to the network;

    2. **Server --** A node dedicated to providing services or resources to the rest of the network (e.g., a file server maintains centralized application and data files, a print server provides access to high quality printers, etc.); servers are not generally used by end-users.

  B. **Transmissions media --** The communication link between nodes on the network; it may be one of several types of wired or wireless media. Local Area Networks (LANs) use dedicated communications lines (i.e., used only by the network); Wide Area Networks (WANs) use public or shared communications lines (i.e., telephone lines, television cables, etc.)

    1. **Wired communications media**

      a. **Twisted pair --** Traditionally used for phone connections, twisted pair is the slowest, least secure (e.g., easy to tap) and most subject to interference of all the wired media; recent modifications have however, improved performance significantly; lowest cost media;

      b. **Coaxial cable --** Similar to the cable used for television, coaxial cable is faster, more secure and less subject to interference than twisted pair but has a slightly higher cost;

      c. **Fiber optic cable --** Extremely fast and secure, fiber optic cable communications are based on light pulses instead of electrical impulses; because of this they are not subject to electrical interference and the signal does not degrade over long distances; more expensive to purchase and to install.

2. **Wireless communications media**

   a. **Microwave transmission --** May use a combination of terrestrial microwave and/or satellite microwave transmission; used primarily by WANs;

   b. **Wi-Fi or spread-spectrum radio transmission --** Depending on power levels may be used for relatively large networks serving hundreds of users or for small home networks; found in LAN environments but frequently used to provide access to WANs; Wi-Fi connections are generally slower than wired systems using coaxial (Ethernet) cable or fiber optic cable;

   c. **Bluetooth --** Uses the same radio frequencies as Wi-Fi, but with lower power consumption resulting in a weaker connection; used to provide a direct communications link between two devices (i.e., a PDA and a computer, a computer and a printer, etc.);

   d. **Digital cellular (Cellular Digital Packet Data or CDPD) --** Allows transmission of data over the cell phone network; used by WANs.

C. **Network Interface Card (NIC) --** A circuit board and software installed on each node of the network that allows it to connect to the communications media and communicate over the network; also known as a network adapter card.

   1. Each type of transmissions media requires a specific network interface card.

D. **Network operating system --** Controls communication over the network and access to network resources:

   1. **Peer-to-Peer systems --** All nodes share in communications management; no central controller (server) is required; these systems are relatively simple and inexpensive to implement; used by LANs;

   2. **Client/Server systems --** A central machine (the server) presides as the mediator of communication on the network and grants access to network resources; client machines are users of network resources but also perform data processing functions; used by LANs:

      a. **Two-tier architecture --** A client-server system in which there are only two principal types of entities: clients and servers; in these systems, most of the data processing takes place on the client;

      b. **Three-tier architecture --** A client-server system in which there are two types of servers: **application servers**, which are responsible for providing application software to the client and which perform much of the actual data processing, and **database servers**, which store the data needed for the applications; provides better input/output (I/O) than two-tiered architecture because the processing load is split across the two servers.

   3. **Hierarchical operating systems --** Use a centralized control point generally referred to as the host computer; the host not only manages communications and access to resources but often performs most of the data processing as well; nodes connected to these systems often function as dumb terminals: they are able to send and receiving information but do not actually process the data; used by WANs.

E. **Communications devices --** Allow networks to open themselves up to other networks and to remote access:

   1. **Modems --** Translate digital data from the computer into the analog format needed on most dial-up telephone line connections; used by WANs;

   2. **Multiplexers --** Take multiple communications lines on the network and consolidate them so that they can be sent on a single, faster line; used by WANs;

3. **Concentrators --** Similar to multiplexers, take multiple inputs and consolidate them into a single output; unlike multiplexers, they perform additional error checking and validation functions; used by WANs;
4. **Bridges --** Communications devices that connect similar networks together; used by WANs and LANs;
5. **Routers --** Essentially smart bridges: not only do they transmit data but they are also able to determine the fastest route for to get to your destination; used by WANs and LANs;
6. **Gateways --** Communications devices that let you connect dissimilar networks (i.e., LANs and WANs); used by WANs.

Computer Networks 2

Computer networks 2 includes four topics: (1) network topologies, i.e., the ways in which nodes in a network are physically connected, (2) types of networks, i.e., the geographical reach and some related network characteristics, (3) the internet, i.e., a client-server based "network of networks," (4) private networks, which include (4a) intranets (i.e., within-organization), (4b) extranets (i.e., outside organization), and (4c) virtual private networks (VPNs), which are a flexible, cost-effective means of securely accessing a network.

I. **Network topologies** -- The network topology describes the way nodes on the network are physically connected to each other.

A. **Star topology** -- Nodes are connected through a large central computer known as the host; the host computer has direct connections to the end-user computers, typically desktop or laptop PCs however, there are no direct connections between the end-user machines: all communications must go through the host computer:

1. This topology is popular for mainframe computing and other applications where many users need access to the same data: the data resides on the host computer and is easily accessible by all end users;
2. Star topologies can be used by LANs or WANs.

B. **Ring topology** -- Each node on the network is connected to two other nodes, creating a ring; this configuration eliminates the central site and confers equal status on all the nodes:

1. Peer-to-peer network operating systems in which each machine shares in the management of network communications are frequently used for ring topologies, although client-server systems can also be used;
2. Because each node is connected to two other nodes, adding or removing a node from the network can be time-consuming and costly;
3. Communications on ring topologies are frequently managed by a technique called token-passing (in fact, early ring networks were called "token ring networks") in which a signal or "token" is continuously passed around the network; when a node wants to communicate, it attaches its message to the token and marks it "busy;"
4. Ring topologies can be used only for LANs.

C. **Bus topology** -- A single communications line, the "bus," is strung between a terminus (end-point) and the server node that controls the network; end-user nodes connect to the bus at the point that is most convenient for them:

1. Client-server network operating systems in which processing is shared between the client (end-user) machines and the server, though the server provides most of the network management, are often used for bus networks; however, peer-to-peer systems are also possible in this configuration;
2. Bus topologies are generally less costly to install and maintain than ring topologies; Ethernet networks, an extremely common type of LAN, are usually implemented using bus topologies;
3. Communications on a bus are often controlled by a protocol called CSMA-CD (Carrier Sense Multiple Access with Collision Detection) in which a machine simply listens for communications on the bus and, if the line is free, sends its message.

D. **Tree topology --** A larger and fast bus line is used to pull small star networks together on a single, faster network; tree topology is essentially a bus topology in which the "nodes" connected to the bus are actually LANs on their own.

II. **Types of networks --** Networks are frequently characterized by the way that the network is constructed and managed and by the network's geographic reach. Two broad types are recognized: Local Area Networks (LANs) and Wide Area Networks (WANs).

A. **Local area networks (LANs) --** Local area networks were so named because they were originally confined to very limited geographic areas (a floor of a building, a building or possibly a couple of buildings in very close proximity to each other). With the advent of relatively inexpensive fiber optic cable, local area networks can extend for many miles. For example, many urban school districts have local area networks that connect all of the schools in the district. However, LANs are still distinguished from WANs in several ways:

1. **Communications channels --** LANs typically use **dedicated communication channels**. That is, the connections between nodes are not used for any purpose other than LAN communication;

2. **Network control --** Most LANs use either **peer-to-peer systems** (usually relatively small networks) or **client server** systems (larger networks); they seldom use hierarchical systems;

3. **Users** -- Although LANs can offer public access through connections to other networks and the internet, most LANs **serve a very limited audience** - typically the members of the organization that operates the LAN (the company, the school, the household, etc.);

B. **Wide area networks (WANs) --** Although WANs can vary dramatically in geographic area, most WANs are national or international in scope. They can also be distinguished from LANs by the communications channels that they employ and their network control systems:

1. **Communications channels** -- In order to achieve the requisite geographic reach, WANs usually employ **shared public communications channels** (fiber optic, terrestrial microwave, satellite) for at least some part of their communications channel;

2. **Network control --** Most WANs use **hierarchical control systems** to manage access to centralized information resources.

3. **Value Added Networks (VANs) --** VANs are privately owned WANs that are primarily **used to facilitate Electronic Data Interchange** (EDI - see E-commerce). VANs **provide additional services beyond standard data transmission** such as automatic error detection, protocol conversion, and message storing and forwarding services.

a. VANs typically use batch processing: messages are separated by vendor, batched together, and then transmitted to their specific destinations; VANs frequently send messages at night when line traffic is lower; this periodic processing can cause significant data transfer delays.

b. VANs charge a fixed fee plus a fee per transaction and can be prohibitively expensive for smaller companies.

III. **The Internet** -- Is a "network of networks": a global network of millions of interconnected computers and computer networks. The Internet has been called the world's largest client-server network. The thousands of different clients and servers are able to communicate because they all use a common protocol: **TCP/IP - Transmission Control Protocol / Internet Protocol**.

A. End-user access to the Internet is provided by **Internet Service Providers (ISPs)** who either provide direct connections to the **Internet backbone** (a collection of extremely high speed, high capacity communications lines that are joined together at network access points) or connect to larger ISPs that ultimately provide that connection.

B. **A number of different protocols and services co-exist on the Internet** including the World Wide Web (**WWW** or the Web), e-mail services (Simple Mail Transfer Protocol - **SMTP** or Internet Message Access Protocol - **IMAP**), file transfer services (File Transfer Protocol or **FTP**) and instant messaging (**IM**).

C. **Intranets and extranets --** Intranets and extranets are private (e.g., limited access) networks built using Internet protocols. Because of this, users can access network resources through their web browser rather than a proprietary interface. This substantially reduces both training time for users and system development time for programmers. For these reasons intranets and extranets are rapidly replacing traditional proprietary LANs and WANs:

1. **Intranets --** Are available only to members of the organization (business, school, association); intranets are often used to connect geographically separate LANs within a company;
2. **Extranets --** Are intranets that are opened up to permit associates (company suppliers, customers, business partners, etc.) to access data that is relevant to them.

D. **Virtual private networks (VPNs) --** Provide a means for remote users or networks to securely access a corporate network (usually a LAN) via the Internet; VPN programs accomplish this by first authenticating the user on the system (e.g., requesting and verifying a user name and password) and then creating a secure connection with the LAN called a VPN tunnel.

1. Virtual private networks are a more cost effective and flexible means of providing secure remote access than other alternatives such as leased lines.

IT Risks and Controls

Risks and Controls in Computer-based Accounting Information Systems

Although manual and computer-based systems share many of the same control objectives, the risks encountered in computer-based systems are different than those encountered in manual systems. This section describes the control goals and risks associated with computer-based systems and several of the models used to design and evaluate internal controls in computer-based systems. Though the control models themselves are not usually directly tested on the CPA exam, the control characteristics and classifications used in the models are frequently included as part of control questions. It is particularly important to understand the preventive-detective-corrective control model and the general control-application control model.

I. Overview of Risk and Internal Control

A. The Institute of Internal Auditors provides the following definition:

> **Definition:**
>
> *Internal Control*: Any action taken... to manage risk and increase the likelihood that established objectives and goals will be achieved.

1. In other words, internal controls can only be understood in the context of the objectives and goals of the firm.
2. **Control Objectives --** A number of accounting pronouncements (SAS 78, SAS 94, among others) have identified the following as general objectives of internal controls:
    - **a. Safeguard assets** of the firm;
    - **b. Promote efficiency** of the firm's operations;
    - **c. Measure compliance** with management's prescribed policies and procedures;
    - **d. Ensure accuracy and reliability** of accounting records and information:
        - **i.** Identify and **record all valid transactions;**
        - **ii.** Provide **timely** information in appropriate detail to permit proper classification and financial reporting;
        - **iii.** Accurately measure the **financial value of transactions**; and
        - **iv.** Accurately records transactions in the **time period** in which they occurred.
3. **Risks in Computer-based systems --** Though the risks faced by any individual organization depend on the business activities and environment of that specific organization, SAS 94, *The Effect of Information Technology on the Auditor's Consideration of Internal Control in a Financial Statement Audit*, identifies the following general risks associated with computerized accounting systems:
    - **a.** Reliance on faulty systems or programs;
    - **b.** Unauthorized access to data leading to destruction or wrongful changes, inaccurate recording of transactions, or recording of false or unauthorized transactions;

c. Unauthorized changes in master files, systems, or programs;

d. Failure to make necessary changes in systems or programs;

e. Inappropriate manual intervention;

f. Loss of data.

B. All organizations using computer-based systems face these risks. The significance of each risk and the degree of control necessary to mitigate the risk varies from organization to organization.

II. **Comparison of Risks in Manual vs. Computer-based Transaction Processing Systems --** Although the objectives of controls in manual and computer-based systems are the same, the risks present in the two systems differ; consequently, the control procedures necessary to mitigate these risks also differ. Some of the distinctions between manual and computerized systems are summarized below:

A. **Segregation of duties --** A fundamental control in manual systems, the segregation of transaction authorization, custody of assets, and transaction recording ensures that no one person has the ability to misappropriate assets and cover up the misappropriation via an accounting entry. In a computerized environment, transaction processing often results in the **combination of functions which are normally separated** in a manual environment. For example, when cash receipts are processed by a cashier, the cash deposit, the cash receipts journal, and the A/R subsidiary ledger are (usually) all updated by a single entry. In a manual environment, at least two of these functions would normally be segregated.

1. In these instances, it is the **computer program itself that provides a compensating control**. Continuing with the cash receipts example: in a manual system, when the same person that records the cash receipt and prepares the bank deposit also updates the customer's account in the accounts receivable ledger, lapping (posting Customer A's payment to Customer B's account to cover up the earlier theft of the Customer B's payment) is possible. In an automated system, the computer program prevents this fraud by ensuring that the same customer is identified with the cash receipt, the bank deposit, and the accounts receivable posting.

B. **Disappearing audit trail --** Manual systems depend heavily a paper audit trail to ensure that transactions are properly authorized and that all transactions are processed. In general, physical (paper) audit trails are substantially reduced in a computerized environment, particularly in on-line, real-time systems. (In batch systems, source documents still exist and provide an excellent audit trail.)

1. **Electronic audit trails --** Can be created by maintaining a file of all of the transactions processed by the system (transaction log file), including the user name of the individual who processed the transaction; when properly maintained, electronic audit trails are **as effective as paper-based audit trails**.

C. **Uniform transaction processing --** Because computer programs process data the same way every time, processing consistency is improved in a computerized environment as compared to a manual environment and "clerical" errors (i.e., random arithmetic errors, missed postings, etc.) are virtually eliminated.

1. In a computerized environment, however, there is an increased potential for "systemic" errors, such as errors in programming logic. For example, if a programmer inadvertently entered a sales tax rate of 14% instead of 1.4%, all of the sales transactions would be affected by the error. Proper controls over program development and implementation help prevent these types of errors.

D. **Computer initiated transactions --** Many computerized systems gain efficiency by automatically generating transactions when specified conditions occur. For example, the system may automatically generate a purchase order for a product with the quantity on hand falls below the reorder point. Automated transactions are not subject to the same types of authorization that are found in manual transactions and may not be as well documented.

1. Automated transactions should be regularly reported and reviewed. Care should be taken to identify transactions that are more frequent or in larger amounts than a predetermined standard.

E. **Potential for increased errors and irregularities --** Several characteristics of computerized processing act to increase the likelihood that fraud may occur and remain undetected for long periods of time.

1. Opportunity for **remote access to data** in networked environments increases the likelihood of unauthorized access;
2. **Concentration of information** in computerized systems means that, if system security is breached, the potential for damage is much greater than in manual systems;
3. Decreased human involvement in transaction processing results in **decreased opportunities for observation**;
4. Errors or fraud may occur in the **design or maintenance of application programs**.

F. **Potential for increased management review --** Computer-based systems increase the availability of raw data and afford more opportunity to perform analytical reviews and produce management reports. Audit procedures are frequently built into the application programs themselves (embedded audit modules) and provide for continuous monitoring of transactions.

1. The opportunities for increased reporting and review of processing statistics can mitigate the additional risks associated with computerized processing.

III. **Types of Controls --** The control models discussed below represent different ways of looking at what is essentially the same set of controls. It is common for organizations to use multiple models to develop and review their controls as evaluating risks and controls from different points of view helps to ensure that all risks have been considered and that controls have been deployed in an effective and cost-efficient manner.

A. **Preventive, detective, and corrective control model --** This model has a long history in the internal control literature and is well integrated into audit procedures. The focus of the model is on the **timing of the control relative to the potential error:** that is, *when* the controls are applied. A well-controlled system has a balance of preventive and detective controls and has a corrective control in place for every detective control.

1. **Preventive controls - "before the fact" controls --** Preventive controls attempt to **stop an error or irregularity before it occurs**. They tend to be "passive" controls, that is, once they are in place they simply need to be activated to be effective. Examples of preventive controls include locks on buildings and doors, use of user names and password to gain access to computer resources, and building segregation of duties into the organizational structure.
2. **Detective controls - "after the fact" controls --** Detective controls attempt to **detect an error after it has occurred**. They tend to be "active" controls, that is, they must be continually performed in order to be effective. Examples of detective controls include data entry edits (checks for missing data, values that are too large or too small, etc.), reconciliation of accounting records to physical assets (bank

Study Tip:
The dual nature of such controls can make it difficult to properly categorize a control as preventive or detective. In these instances, candidates should attempt to distinguish the fundamental, underlying nature of the control from its secondary effects.

reconciliations, inventory counts), and tests of transactions to determine whether they comply with management's policies and procedures (audits).

a. Effective detective controls, when known to the relevant constituency, often **take on preventive characteristics**. For example, surveillance cameras are fundamentally detective controls: they are designed to detect the commission of an unauthorized act. However, when it is known that surveillance cameras are in use, they can also serve to prevent unauthorized acts. The decrease in the number of drivers running red lights when drivers know that surveillance cameras are installed on traffic signals is a current example of this phenomenon.

3. **Corrective controls are always paired with detective controls** -- They attempt to reverse the effects of the observed error or irregularity. Examples of corrective controls include maintenance of backup files, disaster recovery plans, and insurance.

B. **Feedback and feed-forward controls --** Feedback and feed-forward controls focus on changing inputs or processes to promote desirable outcomes by comparing actual results (feedback) or projected results (feed-forward) to a predetermined standard.

1. **Feedback controls --** Evaluate the results of a process and, if the results are undesirable, adjust the process to correct the results; most detective controls are examples of feedback controls.

2. **Feed-forward controls --** Project future results based on current and past information and, if the future results are undesirable, change the inputs to the system to prevent the outcome. Many inventory ordering systems are essentially feed-forward controls: the system projects product sales over the relevant time period, identifies the current inventory level, and orders inventory sufficient to fulfill the sales demand.

C. **General Controls and Application Controls --** This control model has been incorporated into many control models, including auditing standards (SAS 55, SAS 78, SAS 95), the COSO model, and the COBIT model (see below). The focus of the model is on the functional area of the control: that is, *where* the control is applied rather than *when* it is applied. The model divides information processing controls into two categories: General Controls and Application Controls:

1. **General controls --** General controls are controls over the computing environment as a whole. General controls apply to all computerized functions, not just accounting functions. General controls help ensure that data integrity is maintained.

a. Examples of general controls include restricting physical access to computer resources, production and storage of backup files, and performing background checks of computer services personnel.

2. **Application controls --** Application controls are controls over **data input, data processing, and data output** activities. Application controls are designed to ensure the accuracy, completeness, and validity of transaction processing. As such, application controls have a relatively narrow focus on those accounting applications that are involved with data entry, update, and reporting.

a. Examples of application controls includes checks to ensure that input data is complete and properly formatted (e.g., dates, dollar amounts), that account numbers are valid, and that values are reasonable (e.g., that we don't sell quantities that are greater than the quantity currently in inventory).

IV. Internal Control Models

A. Several models of internal control in computer-based environments have been developed over the past 20-25 years. In general, these control models share the same fundamental control objectives or goals (securing data and equipment from unauthorized access, providing timely, reliable information, etc.) While early models utilized a controls-based approach to designing and evaluating internal control systems, newer models use a risk-based approach that takes into account the organization's strategic goals and objectives.

1. **Committee of Sponsoring Organizations (COSO) model --** The Committee of Sponsoring Organizations was formed in 1987 to develop an integrated internal control model. It is comprised of five organizations: the AICPA, the Institute of Internal Auditors, the Institute of Management Accountants, the American Accounting Association, and the Financial Executives Institute. Since the issuance of the initial framework in 1992, the COSO model has been widely accepted by business and is incorporated into the management structure of many organizations.

2. The original COSO framework identified five components which could be used to describe and evaluate an organization's internal control system:

   a. **Control environment --** Management's philosophy towards controls, organizational structure, system of authority and responsibility, personnel practices, policies and procedures;

   b. **Risk assessment --** Evaluation of the risk inherent in the organization's line(s) of business and methods of operating;

   c. **Information and communications --** The transaction processing and reporting system; in order to be of benefit, information must be reliable and timely;

   d. **Monitoring --** In order to ensure the ongoing reliability of information, it is necessary to monitor and test the system and its data;

   e. **Control activities --** The policies and procedures put in place to ensure that management's objectives are met.

Study Tip:
Though the COSO framework in its entirety has not been tested, questions regarding the characteristics of several of the framework's components, most notably the control environment, have appeared on the exam.

3. **COSO Enterprise-Risk Management (ERM) model --** In 2004, the original COSO model was expanded to enable the user to view internal controls within the broader context of the entity's overall strategies and goals. The ERM model expands the number of control components from five to eight and incorporates a multi-dimensional viewpoint by adding organizational objectives and organizational levels to the control framework:

   a. **Organizational objectives --** Organizational objectives can impact the design and implementation of control systems. For example, an organization that wants to foster creativity and independence may not want to implement rigid work schedule rules.

   b. Evaluating controls without understanding the organizational goals that the controls should support can lead to inappropriate conclusions. Consequently, the ERM model specifically includes corporate objectives as part of the control structure. Four types of objectives are considered:

      i. **Strategic objectives --** High level goals that support the overall mission of the organization;

      ii. **Operations objectives --** Goals that deal with the day-to-day operating activities of the organization (i.e., sales activities, warehousing, manufacturing, etc.);

iii. **Reporting objectives --** Information system goals dealing with the accuracy, completeness, timeliness, and reliability of internal and external reporting;

iv. **Compliance objectives --** Goals designed to ensure that the organization meets all legal and regulatory requirements.

c. **Organizational levels --** Because risks and objectives differ from one level of an organization to another, four business levels are included in the model:

i. Entity-level;

ii. Division;

iii. Subsidiary;

iv. Business unit.

d. **Additional control components --** The ERM model adds three additional components to the five components of internal control specified by the original model (control environment (Control environment is changed to "internal" environment in the ERM model), risk assessment, information and communication, monitoring, and control activities):

i. **Objective setting --** Ensures that the company establishes objectives at each of the four specified levels (strategic, operational, reporting, and compliance);

ii. **Event Identification --** Events that might affect - either positively or negatively - the organization's ability to meet its objectives;

iii. **Risk Response --** Depending on management's appetite for risk, observed risks may be either **avoided, reduced, shared, or accepted.**

Study Tip:
Though there is no evidence that CPA exam questions have been asked in this area, the COSO ERM model will likely receive attention from the examiners in the future.

e. By incorporating a multi-dimensional viewpoint, the ERM model significantly enhances an organization's ability to evaluate and assess its portfolio of controls and ensure that they are aligned with the company's objectives and risk appetite.

4. **Control Objectives for Information and related Technology (COBIT) Framework --** COBIT is a widely used international standard for identifying best practices in IT security and control. The COBIT framework is organized around three components:

a. **Domains and processes --** The IT function is divided into four domains within which 34 basic IT processes reside:

i. Planning and Organization;

ii. Acquisition and Implementation;

iii. Delivery and Support;

iv. Monitoring.

b. **Information criteria --** In order to be of value to the organization, data must have the following criteria:

i. Effectiveness;

ii. Efficiency;

iii. Confidentiality;

iv. Integrity;

v. Availability;

vi. Compliance;

vii. Reliability.

c. **IT resources --** Identifies the physical resources that comprise the IT system:

i. People;

ii. Applications;

iii. Technology;

iv. Facilities;

v. Data.

d. There are over 300 generic COBIT control objectives associated with the 34 basic IT processes.

Study Tip:
To date, it does not appear that COBIT has been directly tested on the CPA exam so there is not a pressing need for a more detailed understanding of the model. However, given the broad application of the COBIT framework in practice, it is likely that questions about it will appear on the CPA exam at some point in the future.

Controls Related to People

The principal controls over IT personnel have to do with the organizational structure of the IT department and the procedures used to hire, evaluate, and terminate IT personnel. The organizational structure of the IT department and job descriptions and responsibilities of the individuals within the department are frequently tested on the CPA exam.

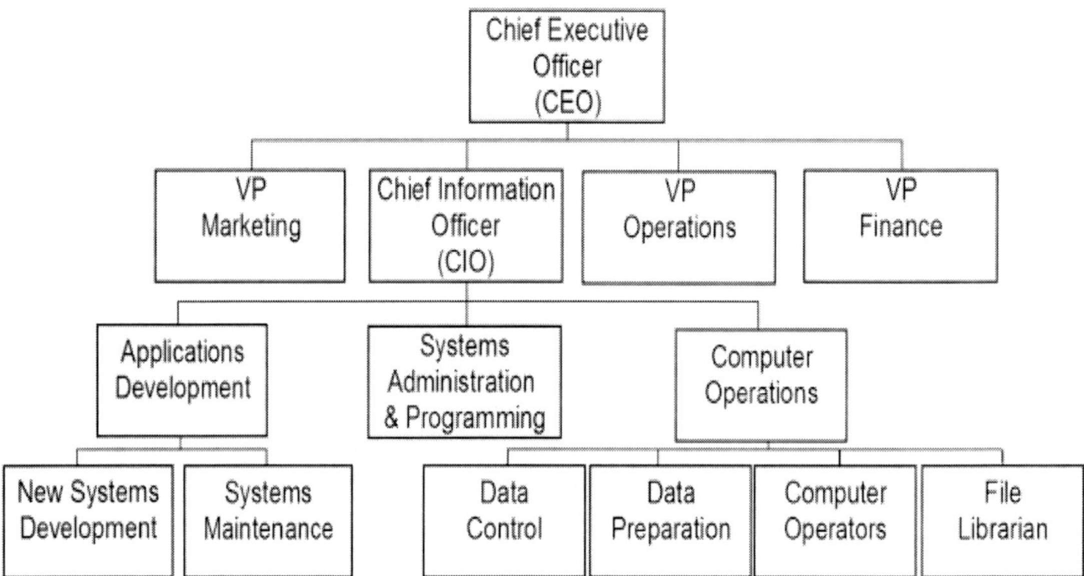

I. **Organizational structure in the Information Technology (IT) Department --** There are three main functional areas within the IT Department:

   A. Applications Development;

   B. Systems Administration and Programming;

   C. Computer Operations.

II. **Segregation of Functions --** The functions in each of these areas must be strictly segregated within the IT Department. Without proper segregation of these functions, the effectiveness of additional controls is compromised.

   A. Applications Development -- This department is responsible for creating new end-user computer applications and for maintaining existing applications.

   1. Systems analysts -- Are responsible for analyzing and designing computer systems; systems analysts generally lead a team of programmers who complete the actual coding for the system; they also work with end users to define the problem and identify the appropriate solution.

   2. Application programmers -- Work under the direction of the systems analyst to write the actual programs that process data and produce reports.

   3. All new program development and maintenance of existing programs is completed in a "test" environment using copies of live data and existing programs rather than in the "live" production environment.

Study Tip:
The controls listed in this section are all **general controls:** controls over the IT department as a whole. The majority of the controls are also **preventive controls**. For example, the segregation of duties inherent in the organizational structure of the IT department prevents employees from making unauthorized changes to program and data files; personnel hiring policies prevent the organization from hiring an individual that doesn't meet management's specifications, etc.

B. **Systems Administration and Programming --** This department is responsible for maintaining the computer hardware and computing infrastructure and is also responsible for granting access to system resources.

1. **System administrators --** Database administrator, network administrator, and web administrators are responsible for management activities associated with the system they control. In particular, they are responsible for granting access to their system resources, usually by means of user names and passwords. For example, the Database Administrator controls access to the various database fields, forms, and reports; the Network Administrator manages system performance and controls access to the network resources, etc. System administrators, by virtue of the influence they wield, **must not be permitted to participate directly in operations** of these systems.

2. **System Programmers --** Maintain the various operating systems and related hardware. For example, they are responsible for updating the system for new software releases and installing new hardware. Because their jobs require that they be in direct contact with the production programs and data, it is imperative that they are **not permitted to have access to information about application programs or data files**.

C. **Computer Operations --** This department is responsible for the day-to-day operations of the computer system including receipt of batch input to the system, conversion of the data to electronic media, scheduling computer activities, running programs, printing and distributing reports, running system backups, and maintaining the program and data files in a secure environment. The breadth of the responsibilities in this department requires that operations within the department include their own segregation of duties.

1. **Data control --** This position is controls the flow of all documents into and out of Computer Operations; for batch processing, schedules batches through data entry and editing, monitors processing, and ensures that batch totals are reconciled; data control should not access the data, equipment, or programs.

2. **Data entry clerk (data conversion operator) --** Keys handwritten or printed records to convert them into electronic media; traditionally part of the central IT function, networked systems now permit data entry in most end-user locations; the data entry clerk should not be responsible for reconciling batch totals and should not be able to run programs or access system output.

3. **Computer operators --** Responsible for operating the computer: loading program and data files, running the programs, and producing output. Computer operators should not enter data into the system or reconcile control totals for the data they process. (That job belongs to Data Control.)

4. **File librarian --** Files and data that are not online are usually stored in a secure environment called the **File Library**; the File Librarian is responsible for maintaining control over the files, checking them in and out only as necessary to support scheduled jobs. The file librarian should not have access to any of the operating equipment or data (unless it has been checked into the library).

D. Functions in these three areas should be **strictly segregated**. In particular:

1. **Computer operators --** Should never be allowed to become programmers;

2. **Systems programmers --** Should never have access to application program documentation;

3. **Data administrators --** Should never have access to computer operations ("live" data);

4. **Application programmers and systems analysts --** Should not have access to computer operations ("live" data);

5. **Application programmers and systems analysts --** Should not control access to data, programs, or computer resources.

III. **Personnel policies and procedures --** The competence, loyalty, and integrity of its employees are among one of an organization's most valuable assets. Appropriate personnel policies are critical in hiring and retaining quality employees.

A. **Hiring practices --** Applicants should complete detailed employment applications and formal, in-depth employment interviews prior to hiring. When appropriate, specific education and experience standards should be imposed. All applicants should undergo thorough background checks and verification of academic degrees, work experience, and professional certifications, as well as searches for any criminal records.

B. **Evaluation --** Employees should be evaluated on a regular basis. The evaluation process should provide clear feedback on the employee's overall performance as well as specific strengths and weaknesses. To the extent that there are weaknesses, it is important to provide guidance on how performance can be improved.

C. **Termination --** Though a clearly specified set of procedures should be invoked whenever any employee leaves the organization, regardless of whether the departure is voluntary or involuntary, it is especially important to be careful and thorough when dealing with involuntary terminations. In involuntary terminations, the employee's user name and keycard should be disabled prior to notification of the termination in order to prevent any attempt to destroy company property. After notification, the terminated employee should be accompanied at all times until escorted out of the building.

Control over IT Facilities

Control over IT facilities involves the safeguarding of the computer equipment, programs, and data. It begins with the provision of an appropriate operating environment for the computer equipment and goes on to provide protection from unauthorized physical access to the hardware and software, and controls that allow the system to recover if problems are detected. Of the controls listed in this section, data backup procedures and disaster recovery plans are the most frequently tested on the CPA exam.

Study Tip:
The controls listed in this section are all **general controls**: controls over the IT department as a whole. Some of the controls are **preventive controls**. For example, restricting access to the IT department prevents unauthorized individuals from gaining physical access to the system. Controls relating to program and data backup files and disaster recovery plans are **corrective controls**: controls that are designed to help correct and recover from previously detected problems.

I. **IT facilities --** Include computer hardware (CPUs, disk and tape drives, printers, communications devices, etc.), software (program files), and data files, as well as the computing infrastructure (network communication media and devices) and the rooms and buildings in which they reside. Control over IT facilities involves safeguarding equipment, programs, and data from physical damage.

II. **Physical location --** Computer operations should be located in facilities which are safe from fire, flood, climate variations (heat, humidity), and unauthorized access.

   A. The computer room should be climate controlled so as not to be subject to excess heat and humidity, which can damage equipment and data files; needless to say, there should be no windows that open in the computer room.

   B. Fire suppression systems appropriate for electrical fires (halon or a similar chemical suppressor - not water!) should be installed and checked periodically.

   C. Adequacy of power and backup power systems should be evaluated at least one a year.

III. **Physical access --** To the computer facility in general should be restricted; access to program and data files and to the computer hardware should be subject to further restrictions.

   A. **Access to the computer operations areas --** Should be restricted to those directly involved in operations. Authorized individuals should be required to wear identification badges. Physical access is secured by locks, keypad devices, access card readers, security personnel, and surveillance devices.

      1. **Social engineering --** Is a set of techniques used by attackers to fool employees into giving them access to information resources.

         a. Physical access to the system can be gained by a technique known as **piggybacking** in which an unauthorized user slips into a restricted area with an authorized user, using the authorized user's entry credentials to gain access.

   B. **Data stored on magnetic disks and tapes --** Should be protected by:

      1. **External labels --** Used by computer operators to visually identify the disk;

      2. **Internal labels ("header" and "trailer" records) --** Read by the processing program to determine the identity of the data file;

      3. **File protection rings or locks --** Physically prevent the media from being overwritten;

      4. **Setting file attributes --** Logically restrict the ability of the user to read, write, update, and/or delete records in a file.

   C. **Programs and data files --** Should be physically secured and under the control of a file librarian in order to protect the programs and data from unauthorized modification.

IV. Back-up procedures -- Are formal plans for making and retaining back-up copies of data files that can be used to recover from equipment failures, power failures, and data processing errors. At least one archive should be maintained in an off-site location, so that recovery is possible even when a major disaster occurs.

A. Businesses rely extensively on the concept of **"redundant backups"** - Having multiple backup copies which means that if one backup fails or if the problem occurred prior to the last backup, the company need not rely on a single archived copy: there are usually several more versions of the data to choose from.

B. Backup procedures vary in part depending on the type of processing employed:

1. **"Grandfather, father, son" system --** A traditional term used to refer to a three "generation" backup procedure: the "son" is the newest version of the file; the "father" is one generation back in time, the "grandfather" is two generations back in time; "grandfather, father, son" methodology was associated with batch processing in a magnetic tape environment where a new master file (the "son") was created when the old master file (the "father") was updated.

2. **Checkpoint and restart --** Common to batch processing, a checkpoint is a point in data processing where the accuracy of the processing can be verified; backups are maintained during the update process so that, if a problem is detected, it is only necessary to return to the backup at the previous checkpoint instead of returning to the beginning of transaction processing.

3. **Rollback and recovery --** Common to online, real-time processing; all transactions are written to a transaction log when they are processed; periodic "snapshots" are taken of the master file; when a problem is detected, the recovery manager program, starts with the snapshot of the master file and reprocesses all transactions that have occurred since the snapshot was taken.

C. Network capabilities can be used to provide continuous backup capabilities; such backup facilities are necessary to create fault tolerant systems (systems that continue to operate properly despite the failure of some components) and high-availability clusters - HACs: (Computer clusters that are designed to improve the availability of services - used extensively in e-commerce environments where services must be continuously available.)

1. **Remote backup service (online backup service) --** A service that provides users with an online system for backing up and storing computer files. Remote backup has several advantages over traditional backup methodologies: the task of creating and maintaining backup files is removed from the IT department's responsibilities; the backups are maintained off site; some services can operate continuously, backing up each transaction as it occurs.

2. **Storage Area Networks (SANs) --** Can be used to replicate data from multiple sites; data stored on a SAN is then immediately available without the need to recover it; this enables a more effective disaster recovery process.

3. **Mirroring --** The maintenance of an exact copy of a data set to provide multiple sources of the same information; mirrored sites are most frequently used in e-commerce for load balancing - distributing excess demand from the primary site to the mirrored.

V. Disaster recovery plans (DRPs)

A. These are plans for continuing operations in the event of destruction of not only program and data files but also of the transaction processing facilities. In addition to backup data files, DRPs must **identify mission critical tasks** and ensure that processing for these tasks can continue with virtually no interruptions.

B. Disaster Recovery Plans are frequently classified by the types of backup facilities maintained and the time required to resume processing:

1. **Cold site ("empty shell") --** An off-site location that has all the electrical connections and other physical requirements for data processing, but does not have the actual equipment or files. Cold sites often require one to three days to be made operational. A cold site is the least expensive type of alternative processing facility available to the organization.
2. **Warm site --** A location where the business can relocate to after the disaster that is already stocked with computer hardware similar to that of the original site, but does not contain backed up copies of data and information.
3. **Hot site --** An off-site location that is completely equipped to immediately take over the company's data processing; all equipment plus backup copies of essential data files and programs are also usually maintained at this location: enables the business to relocate with minimal losses to normal operations - typically within a few hours. A hot site is one of the most expensive facilities to maintain.

Control over Data

Once data is successfully entered into the system, a variety of controls are necessary to ensure that any subsequent access and changes to the data are authorized. Data controls limit access to data to authorized users and ensure the security and integrity of the data transmissions.

I. **Data Control** -- Control over data includes control of logical access to data through user authentication and application program authorizations as well as through encryption and hardware controls.

II. **Hardware controls** -- Are controls built into the computer equipment to ensure that data is transmitted and processed accurately. These controls operate automatically and require no user interaction unless a problem is detected.

A. **Parity check (parity bit)** -- A 0 or 1 included in a byte of information which makes the sum of bits either odd or even; For example, using odd parity, the parity check bit for this byte of data:

> 001101
>
> is zero because the sum of the digits in the byte is 3, an odd number.
>
> Had the bit been as follows:
>
> 101101
>
> the sum of the digits would be 4 and the parity bit would have been 1.

Study Tip:
Hardware controls are regularly tested on the CPA exam - usually in simple, identification questions. With the exception of boundary protection controls, the hardware controls listed are examples of **detective controls** since they operate to detect problems that have already occurred during data transmission. Boundary protection controls are preventive controls.

B. **Read after write check** -- Verifies that data was written correctly to disk by reading what was just written and comparing it to the source.

C. **Echo check** -- Verifies that transmission between devices is accurate by "echoing back" the received transmission from the receiving device to the sending unit.

D. **Diagnostic routines** -- Program utilities that check the internal operations of hardware components.

E. **Boundary protection** -- When multiple programs and/or users are running simultaneously and sharing the same resource (usually the primary memory of a CPU), boundary protection protects program instructions and data from one program from being overwritten by program instructions and/or data from another program

III. **Logical access controls** -- Though controlling physical access to program and data files is a fundamental concern in any IT system, controlling logical access to IT resources - that is, controlling electronic access to data via internal and external networks - is a much larger concern. The primary controls over logical access involve **user authentication** and **user authorization.**

A. **User authentication** -- The first step in controlling logical access to data is to establish user identification. This is normally accomplished by creating a user name for each authorized user and associating the user name with a unique identifier.

1. The identifier is typically based on:

a. Something the user *knows* (passwords, personal identification numbers (PINs);

   b. Something the user *has* (smart card, ID badges);

   c. A *physical characteristic* of the user (fingerprints, voice prints).

2. **Passwords --** Need to be "strong" to be useful; a strong password:

   a. Is usually at least eight characters long;

   b. Must include upper and lower case letters, at least one numeral and at least one special character;

   c. Is subject to a password policy that requires changing the password at least once per year.

3. **Security tokens --** Include devices which provide "one-time" passwords that must be input by the user and as well as "smart cards" that contain additional user identification information and must be read by an input device.

   a. **"One-time" passwords --** Used to strengthen the standard password by requiring access to a physical device which displays a new "one-time password" every 30-60 seconds (the "one time" password is derived from an algorithm which usually involves the date and time); the user enters this password along with the traditional user name and password; once received, the computer independently recalculates the "password"; if the entered value and computed value are the same, the computer then recognizes the individual.

   b. **Smart cards and identification badges --** Have **identification information embedded on a magnetic strip on the card** and require the use of additional hardware (a card reader) to read the data into the system. Depending on the system, the user may only need to swipe the card to log onto the system or may need to key in other information in order to log on.

4. **Biometric controls --** A physical characteristic is used to gain access instead of a password; common choices for biometric controls include fingerprint or thumbprint, retina patterns, and voice print patterns; biometric controls can be **very reliable**, but generally require special input equipment.

5. **Multi-factor authentication --** Since all authentication techniques are individually subject to failure, many organizations require multi-factor authentication procedures - the use of several separate authentication procedures at one time (e.g., user name, password, one-time password and fingerprint). Redundant authentication procedures significantly enhance the authentication process.

6. **Social engineering --** (see Control over Data) - Can also be used to gain logical access to the system by convincing employees to provide user names and passwords to the system. These deceptive requests for information may be delivered verbally or through email.

   a. **Phishing --** Is the name given to deceptive requests for information delivered via email. The recipient of the email is asked to either respond to the email or visit a web site and provide authentication information.

B. **Authorization controls --** Once a user has been authenticated, the resources available to the user are determined by entries in an authorization matrix. The **authorization matrix** specifies each **user's access rights** to programs, data entry screens, and reports. The authorization matrix contains a row for each user and columns for each resource available on the system. There are usually several levels of access for each resource, as shown below:

UserName	GLR83	GLE83	ARN66	ARN67
cls56	N	N	A	R
NMeyer	A	A	N	N
olsen332	R	R	X	R
jparker	X	X	R	R

N = No access
R = Read access only
A = Add, Read
U = Update, Read
X = Add, Update, Delete, Read

Study Tip:
Authentication, authorization and data encryption controls are examples of general controls. They are all also examples of preventive controls. All three types of controls are tested regularly, though not heavily, on the CPA exam.

IV. **Data encryption --** Data encryption is used to protect sensitive data during transmission over networks and when stored on disk. Though data encryption can be an extremely effective tool for providing data security and privacy, the encryption and decryption process can incur large amounts of processing overhead, which can slow system throughput considerably. For this reason, data encryption tends to be used only when the data is most vulnerable, for example, during transmission over external networks. Only the most sensitive stored data is encrypted. See Controls over Technology for details about encryption technology.

Control over Applications

Control over applications begins with controls over application program development and implementation (general controls) and continues through controls over the use of the program to capture, process, and/or report transactions (application controls). Application controls are heavily tested on the CPA exam.

I. **Control over application programs --** Is achieved through three principal types of controls:

   A. Controls over the application program development process;

   B. Controls over the application program library;

   C. Controls over operation of the application program.

II. **Systems Development Life-Cycle (SDLC)**

> **Definition:**
>
> *Systems Development Life-Cycle*: A structured process designed to ensure that the completed system is cost-effective and meets the needs of the end users.

   A. SDLC helps accomplish these objectives by 1) **establishing detailed definitions and expectations** up front and 2) by **requiring approval** by all involved parties at each stage of the development process. The steps in the process and some of the activities included in each step are listed below: (Note: there are minor variations in the definitions of these steps depending on the reference source.)

      1. **Feasibility Analysis (planning) --** A high-level view of the system is presented and evaluated by a cross-functional team; the team considers the goals and objectives of the system, the projected cost of the system, and other competing opportunities and makes a recommendation to go forward with the project as defined, go forward with a modified approach or put the project on hold.

      2. **Systems Analysis --** The system definition is refined and expanded to include cost and development time estimates; a more detailed definition of system inputs and outputs is prepared, hardware specifications are prepared.

      3. **Systems Design --** The system functions are defined in detail: screens and reports are designed, processing logic is outlined, data structures are defined.

      4. **Systems Development --** The elements identified in the Design processes are programmed.

      5. **Systems Implementation --** The system is tested, users are trained, data from the old system is converted to the new system formats; the source code is migrated from the test environment to the production environment. There are several choices as to how the system implementation takes place:

         a. The system may be **implemented all at once**, "cold turkey," and the previous system scrapped; this is the simplest but most dangerous and disruptive type of implementation as the entire organization is changing their way of processing and there is no backup system in place.

b. **Parallel implementation --** The old system and the new system are both run together for a period of time ranging from a few weeks to a few months; this effectively creates a backup for the new system.

c. **Phased-in implementation --** The new system is broken up into component parts and each part is implemented separately; this system implementation is the least disruptive of all the styles.

6. **Systems Maintenance --** Once the system is up and running, it will need to be modified periodically to encompass changes in data inputs or outputs, changes in the way the data should be processed, changes in computing platform, etc.

III. **Source Program Library Management System (SPLMS) --** Source code programs are normally maintained in a library under secure storage (the Source Program Library - SPL); when new programs are developed or old programs modified, the SPLMS manages the migration from the Application Development Test Environment to the active Production Library. The SPLMS ensures that only valid changes are made to the system by checking for all necessary authorizations and, for program modifications, by comparing the new source code to the old source code. Only after the program has been verified, is it allowed to migrate to the SPL.

A. Once in the SPL, the code is compiled and linked to the necessary components. The resulting object code (machine code) is stored in the **Production Load Library**.

B. Authorized versions of major programs should be maintained in a secure, off-site location. (The external auditor frequently maintains these files.)

IV. **Documentation --** Four levels of documentation should be maintained; documentation at each level generally consists of flowcharts and narrative description.

A. **Systems documentation --** Provides an **overview of the program and data files, processing logic** and interactions with each other programs and systems; consists of narrative descriptions and flowcharts; used primarily by systems developers; can be useful to auditors.

B. **Program documentation --** Provides a **detailed analysis of the input data, the program logic, and the data output**; consists of program flowcharts, source code listings, record layouts, etc.; used primarily by programmers; **program documentation is an important resource if the original programmer is not available** and there are questions about the program.

> **Study Tip:**
> All of the preceding controls are **general controls** and are also **preventive controls**. They are tested regularly, but lightly, on the CPA exam.

C. **Operator documentation (also called the "run manual") --** Provides information necessary to execute the program such as the required equipment, data files and computer supplies, execution commands, error messages, verification procedures and expected output; used exclusively by the computer operators.

D. **User documentation --** Describes the system from the point of view of the end user; provides instructions on how and when to submit data and request reports, procedures for verifying the accuracy of the data and correcting errors.

V. **Application Controls**

A. Application controls focus on the accuracy, validity, and completeness of data processing in specific application programs. Application controls are generally placed in one of three categories:

1. **Input controls --** Control over the data entry process;

2. **Processing controls --** Control over the master file update process;

3. **Output controls --** Control over the production of reports.

B. Processing methodology (batch processing vs. online, real-time processing) can impact the selection of application controls as not all controls will work with both batch and online, real-time processing systems.

Study Tip:
When answering questions about application controls, be sure to pay close attention to the processing methodology as that is a determining factor in choosing the correct answer.

1. **Input controls --** (Also known as programmed controls, edit checks, or automated controls) - Ensure that the transactions entered into the system meet the following control objectives:

   a. **Valid --** All transactions are appropriately authorized; no fictitious transactions are present; no duplicate transactions are included;

   b. **Complete --** All transactions have been captured; there are no missing transactions;

   c. **Accurate --** All data has been correctly transcribed, all account codes are valid; all data fields are present; all data values are appropriate.

2. There are more input controls than there are processing and output controls combined. This is due in part to the importance of correct input data: if the data is not input correctly, then all subsequent uses of the data are compromised. This concept is captured succinctly in the acronym GIGO: garbage in, garbage out. The abundance of input controls is also due to the fact that most errors occur at the input phase: the processing and output phases are largely controlled by computer programs that, when properly developed and tested, are not susceptible to errors.

3. Following is a list of the most frequently used input controls:

   a. **Missing data check --** he simplest type of test available: checks only to see that something has been entered into the field.

   b. **Field check (data type/data format check) --** Verifies that the data entered is of an acceptable type - alphabetic, numeric, a certain number of characters, etc.

   c. **Limit test --** Checks to see that a numeric field does not exceed a specified value; for example, the number of hours worked per week isn't greater than 60; There are several variations of limit tests:

      i. **Range tests --** Validate both upper and lower limits; for example, the price per gallon cannot be less than $4.00 or greater than $10.00;

      ii. **Sign tests --** Verify that numeric data has the appropriate sign (positive or negative); for example, the quantity purchased cannot be negative.

   d. **Valid code test (validity test) --** Checks to make sure that each account code entered into the system is a valid (existing) code; this control does not ensure that the code is *correct*, merely that it exists; in database environments, this is known as referential integrity.

   e. **Check digit --** Designed to ensure that each account code entered into the system is **both valid and correct**. The check digit is a number that is created by applying an arithmetic algorithm to the digits of a numeric account code. The algorithm yields a single digit that is appended to the end of the code. Whenever the account code (including check digit) is entered, the computer recalculates the check digit and compares the calculated check digit to the digit entered. If the digits fail to match, then there must be an error in the code and processing is halted.

      i. Check digits are one of the most reliable methods available for ensuring that the correct code has been entered.

f. **Reasonableness check (logic test) --** Checks to see that data in two or more fields is consistent. For example, a Rate of Pay value of "$3,500" and a Pay Period value of "Hourly" may both be valid values for the fields when the fields are viewed independently; however, the combination (an hourly pay rate of $3,500) is not valid.

g. **Sequence check --** Verifies that all items in a numerical sequence (check numbers, invoice numbers, etc.) are present. It is the most commonly used control for processing completeness.

h. **Key verification --** The re-keying of critical data in the transaction, followed by a comparison of the two keyings. For example, in a batch environment, one operator keys in all of the data for the transactions and a second operator re-keys all of the account codes and amounts. The computer compares the results and reports any differences. Key verification is generally found in batch systems, but can be used in online real-time environments as well. (Consider the process required to change a password: enter the old password, enter the new password, and then re-enter the new password.)

i. **Closed loop verification --** Helps ensure that a valid and correct account code has been entered; after the code is entered, this system looks up and displays additional information about the selected code. For example, the operator enters a customer code and the system displays the customer's name and address. This technique is only available in online real-time systems.

j. **Batch control totals --** Manually calculated totals of various fields of the documents in a batch. Batch totals are compared to computer-calculated totals and are used to ensure the accuracy and completeness of data entry. Batch control totals are available, of course, only for batch processing systems.

   i. **Financial totals --** Totals of a currency field that result in meaningful totals, such as the dollar amounts of checks. (Note that the total of the hourly rates of pay for all employees is not a financial total because the summation is not meaningful.)

   ii. **Hash totals --** Totals of a field, usually an account code field, for which the total has no logical meaning, such as a total of customer account numbers in a batch of invoices.

   iii. **Record counts --** Count of the number of documents in a batch or the number of lines on the documents in a batch.

k. **Preprinted forms and preformatted screens --** Reduce the likelihood of data entry errors by organizing input data in a logical manner: when the position and alignment of data fields on a data entry screens matches the organization of the fields on the source document, data entry is faster and there are fewer errors.

l. **Default values --** Pre-supplied data values for a field when that value can be reasonably predicted; for example, when entering sales data, the sales order date is usually the current date; fields using default values generate fewer errors than other fields.

m. **Automated data capture --** Use of automated equipment such as bar code scanners to reduce the amount of manual data entry; reducing human involvement reduces the number of errors in the system.

4. **Processing controls --** Controls that are designed to ensure that master file updates are completed accurately and completely. They also serve to detect unauthorized transactions entered into the system and maintain data integrity.

a. **Run-to-Run Controls --** Use batch figures to monitor the batch as it moves from one programmed procedure (run) to another; totals of processed transactions are reconciled to batch totals - any difference indicates an error.

b. **Internal labels ("header" and "trailer" records) --** Used primarily in batch processing, electronic file identification allows the update program to determine that the correct file is being used for the update process.

c. **Audit Trail Controls --** Each transaction is written to a transaction log as it is processed; the transaction logs become an electronic audit trail that allows the transaction to be traced through each stage of processing; electronic transaction logs constitute the principal audit trail for online, real-time systems.

5. **Output controls --** Ensure that computer reports are **accurate** and are **distributed only as authorized**.

   a. **Spooling (print queue) controls --** Jobs sent to a printer that cannot be printed immediately are spooled - stored temporarily on disk - while waiting to be printed; access to this temporary storage must be controlled in order to prevent unauthorized access to the files.

   b. **Disposal of aborted print jobs --** Reports are sometimes damaged during the printing or bursting (separation of continuous feed paper along perforation lines) process; since the damaged reports may contain sensitive data, they should be disposed of using secure disposal techniques.

   c. **Distribution of reports --** Data control is responsible for ensuring that reports are maintained in a secure environment prior to distribution and that only authorized recipients receive the reports; a Distribution Log is generally maintained to record transfer of the reports to the recipients.

   d. **End user controls --** Supplement the Information Systems department controls by independently performing checks of processing totals and reconciling report totals to separately maintained records.

Control over Technology

The rapid growth of internet-based technologies has opened up a remarkable wave of opportunities for businesses but has brought with it a host of new risks. This section looks at some of the more common risks associated with these technologies and the controls designed to control these risks. This risks and controls in this rapidly changing area are regularly tested on the CPA exam. There is no "standard" question in this area: some are simple, definitional questions while others require significant sophistication and depth of understanding - often a much deeper level of understanding than that possessed by the typical candidate. If the latter type of question is encountered, most candidates should simply make an educated guess and move on

I. **Changes in technology --** and changes in the way technology is used within the organization bring changes to the risks faced by organizations and the controls they use to mitigate those risks. In particular, the growth e-commerce and other internet-based technologies in recent years have brought about significant changes in the IT risks faced by many organizations. These additional risks derive from two principal sources: 1) **the use of the internet** as the communications provider and 2) e-commerce which frequently involves interaction between entities that have no prior contracts or agreements with each other. These additional problems center on:

   A. Establishment of **identity and authenticity**;

   B. **Privacy and security** of information; and

   C. **Affecting a secure exchange** of money for goods and services provided.

II. **Problems associated with identity and authenticity --** Unauthorized access to IT resources is a primary concern of most organizations. Remote access to the IT system dramatically increases the risk of unauthorized access and the techniques used to gain access change on an almost daily basis. The following techniques are commonly experienced by many organizations:

   A. **Packet sniffing --** Programs called packet sniffers capture packets of data as they move across a computer network; packet sniffing has legitimate uses to monitor network performance or troubleshoot problems with network communications, however, it is **often used by hackers to capture user names and passwords, IP addresses, and other information** that can help the hacker break into the network; packet sniffing a computer network is similar to wire tapping a phone line.

   B. **Session hijacking and masquerading --** Masquerading occurs when an attacker **identifies an IP address** (usually through packet sniffing) and then attempts to use that address to gain access to the network; if the masquerade is successful then the hacker has hijacked the session: gained access to the session under the guise of another user.

   C. **Malicious software (malware) --** Programs that exploit system and user vulnerabilities to gain access to the computer; there are many types of malware:

      1. **Virus --** An unauthorized program, usually introduced through an email attachment, which copies itself to files in the users system; these programs may actively damage data or they may be benign.

      2. **Worm --** Similar to viruses except that worms attempt to replicate themselves across multiple computer systems; they generally try to accomplish this by activating the system's email client and sending multiple emails.

3. **Trojan horse --** A malicious program hidden inside a seemingly benign file; Trojan horses are frequently used to insert back doors into a system (see below).
4. **Back door --** A software program that allows an unauthorized user to gain access to the system by side-stepping the normal logon procedures; back doors were once commonly used by programmers to facilitate access to systems under development.
5. **Logic bomb --** An unauthorized program which is planted in the system; the logic bomb lies dormant until the occurrence of a specified event or time (e.g., a specific date, the elimination of an employee from "active employee" status, etc.).

D. **Password crackers --** Once a user name has been identified, password cracking software can be used to generate a large number of potential passwords and use them to try to gain access.

1. When weak password controls are in use, (i.e., passwords that have less than 8 characters, that use one letter case, do not require use of numbers or special symbols), password cracker programs are extremely effective.

III. **Denial of service attacks --** Rather than attempting to gain unauthorized access to IT resources, some attackers threaten the system by attempting to **prevent legitimate users from gaining access to the system**. These attacks, called denial of service attacks, are perpetrated by **hanging up the server with a flood of incomplete access requests**.

A. Denial of service attacks take advantage of the three-part system handshake used to establish a connection to the network: 1) the user sends a request to log on to the network; 2) the system responds with an acknowledgment and permission to log on; 3) the user sends a response that completes the login request.

B. During the period of time between the systems acknowledgment and the user's final response, the server holds a communication port open for the user; in a denial of service attack, the hacker fails to send the final response causing the system to hold the connection open until it finally passes a time threshold and allows the connection to drop.

C. As the hacker floods the system with thousands of incomplete connection requests, all connections are ultimately held by the hacker, thus completing the denial of service.

D. Denial of service attacks may come from single hackers or may come from multiple sources; oftentimes the sources are unwitting participants in the attack, having been unknowing victims of Trojan horse or logic bomb attacks.

IV. **Preventing and detecting unauthorized access --** Though no control system can completely eliminate risk, risks can be significantly reduced through employment of appropriate policies and procedures. The following tools are commonly used to prevent or detect unauthorized access to the IT system.

A. **Access controls --** Strong access controls are the foundation of an effective control system:

1. **User names --** Users should only be granted access to the services that they need to do their work;
2. **Passwords --** Only "strong" passwords should be permitted; "one-time" passwords and/or biometric passwords should be used to strengthen the password system. (See IT Risks and Controls for details.)

B. Firewalls -- In simplest terms, a firewall is a combination of hardware (usually) and software that reviews network traffic and filters communications based on rules specified by the system administrator. Data packets that do not comply with the communication rules are blocked. Decisions about whether to allow or block individual data packets are usually based on the packet's source and destination addresses, the type of resources requested, the communications ports used, and the contents of the data packet. Most organizations use several types of firewalls:

1. **Network firewalls --** Network firewalls perform relatively low-level filtering of data packets based primarily on data packet header information such as source and destination IP addresses and communications ports.
   a. Block transmissions which fail to comply with the rules expressed in the **access control list** - the data communications rules established by the system administrator.
   b. Network firewalls differ from **boundary routers**, which can perform the same functions, because they usually perform **stateful packet filtering**; stateful packet filtering maintains a table of all active internet connections and determines whether the current data packet is consistent with the state of the connection.
   c. Because they don't examine the data packet contents, network firewalls are **very fast.**
   d. Data which passes through the network firewall is forwarded to the application firewall.
2. **Application firewalls --** Application firewalls perform more sophisticated inspection of data packets than network firewalls. As the name implies, application firewalls are established for specific applications.
   a. Application firewalls offer additional protection by controlling the execution of files or the handling of data by specific applications, preventing the program from gaining unauthorized access to the system.
   b. Application firewalls can perform **deep packet inspection** (examination of the contents of body of the data packet), which **enhances security but slows processing.**
   c. Application firewalls can be highly customized to the specific computing environment.
3. **Personal firewalls --** Are software-based firewalls set up on individual end-user computers to block unwanted traffic; while they offer some protection for individual users, they are not sophisticated enough to provide protection to large computing environments.

C. Virus detection and spyware detection software -- A variety of programs are available to detect and/or eliminate various types of malware from computer systems; such software should be **installed on all computers** and **run in active mode** (e.g., always operational, online, real-time) so that the system is constantly being screened for malware and so that the software is always updated with the latest malware signatures.

D. Intrusion detection systems (IDS) -- Actively gather and analyze information from various areas within a computer or a network to identify possible security breaches, which include both intrusions (attacks from outside the organization) and misuse (attacks from within the organization).

1. Intrusion detection systems are capable of alerting management to the presence of a threat and of taking direct action to eliminate the threat.

2. Like anti-virus and anti-spyware software, intrusion detection systems are being constantly updated to reflect changing threats to system security.

V. Controlling problems associated with privacy and security

A. **Encryption --** Can be used to provide both privacy (protection of data against unauthorized access) and authentication (user identification).

B. In general, encryption technology uses a mathematical algorithm to translate **cleartext (plaintext)** - text that can be read and understood - into **ciphertext** (text which has been mathematically scrambled so that its meaning cannot be determined).

1. **Symmetric encryption --** (Single-key encryption or private key encryption) - Symmetric encryption uses a single algorithm to encrypt and decrypt the text. The sender uses the encryption algorithm to create the ciphertext and sends the encrypted text to the recipient; the sender must also let the recipient know which algorithm was used to encrypt the text; the recipient then uses the same algorithm (essentially running it in reverse) to decrypt the text.

   a. Although the ciphertext created with symmetric encryption can be very secure, the symmetric encryption methodology itself is inherently insecure because the sender must always find a way to let the recipient know which encryption algorithm to use.

2. **Asymmetric encryption --** (public/private-key encryption) - Uses two paired encryption algorithms to encrypt and decrypt the text: if the public key is used to encrypt the text, the private key must be used to decrypt the text; conversely, if the private key is used to encrypt the text, the public key must be used to decrypt the text.

   a. To acquire a public/private key pair, the user applies to a **certificate authority** (CA); the CA registers the public key on its server and sends the private key to the user; when someone wants to communicate securely with the user, they access the public key from the CA server, encrypt the message and send it to the user; the user then uses the private key to decrypt the message; the transmission is secure because only the private key can decrypt the message and only the user has access to the private key.

VI. Facilitating secure exchanges -- E-commerce can only take place in an environment in which there is a high degree of certainty regarding the identity of the trading partners and the reliability of the transaction data. Electronic identification methodologies and secure transmission technology are designed to provide such an environment.

A. **Digital signatures --** Digital signatures use public/private key pair technology to **provide authentication of the sender**. The authentication process is based on the private key: because the private key is known only to the user, it can be used as a means of identifying the sender as follows:

1. The sender creates a digest of the message (A digest can be viewed as a mathematically created abbreviation for the message.) and uses his private key to encrypt it;
2. This is the **digital signature** and provides the basis for authentication;
3. The sender then uses the recipient's public key to encrypt the message and the digital signature and sends the message;
4. The recipient decrypts the message and digital signature with his private key and his system then prepares a digest of the message received, which should be identical to the original digest;
5. The recipient then uses the sender's public key to decrypt the digital signature, producing the digest of the original message;

6. The system compares the two digests: if they are identical, the recipient has assurance that 1) the sender is who he claims to be and 2) the message has not been tampered with during transmission;

7. The weakness in digital signatures lies in the fact that the public/private key pair can be acquired without any verification that the applicant is who he says he is.

B. **Digital certificate --** For transactions that require a high degree of assurance, a digital certificate provides legally recognized electronic identification; the certificate is based on public/private key technology, just like the digital signature; the difference is that the holder of the certificate must submit identification when requesting the certificate and the certificate authority completes a background check to verify the identity before issuing the certificate.

C. **Secure Internet transmissions protocols --** Sensitive data sent via the Internet is usually secured by one of two encryption protocols: **SSL** (Secure Sockets Layer) or **S-HTTP** (Secure Hypertext Transport Protocol).

1. **Consumer purchases made via the Internet --** Are usually encrypted using **SET** (Secure Electronic Transactions) protocol; the SET protocol is used by the merchant intermediary to securely transmit the payment information and to authenticate the identities of the trading partners.

Control over End-User Computing and Small Business Environments

End-user computing and small business environments provide control challenges because of the lack of specialized staff to provide oversight and control over the computing resources. In general, control in these environments is improved by heightening awareness of the risks, developing and adhering to standards of operation, and by engaging outside assistance to compensate for the missing controls whenever possible. Risks and controls in end-user and small business environments are lightly tested on the CPA exam.

I. **End-user computing --** The creation, implementation, and control of systems by the user of the system and small businesses exhibit characteristics that make them much more difficult to control than systems operating in larger, traditional IT environments. These systems therefore carry a higher level of risk. Though these risks cannot be completely eliminated, strong compensating controls can provide substantial improvements in security and control.

II. **Characteristics of small business environments**

   A. **Microcomputers** are used almost exclusively;

   B. There is **no centralized Information Technology department** to provide a focus of control; and

   C. Because there are too few individuals to provide for segregation of duties (in end-user environments, there is usually only a single individual) **incompatible functions are frequently combined.**

III. **Specific risks and controls**

   A. **Physical access --** Because personal computers are often found in openly available areas, care should be taken to make sure that doors are locked when offices are open and that removable storage devices (diskettes, CDs, DVDs, flash drives, etc.) are stored in secure locations.

   B. **Logical access --** All machines should require a user name and password in order to access the system and should be set to automatically log out of the system when they have not been used for a period of time; networked systems should protect all network available resources from unauthorized access.

   C. **Data backup procedures --** Company-wide standards for backing up files should be established and enforced; if possible, this process should be centralized and automated through a network; off-site backups must be maintained on an on-going basis.

   D. **Program development and implementation --** User-developed programs - which include spreadsheets and databases - should be subject to third party review and testing to ensure that they operate as expected; copies of the authorized versions of these programs should be separately cataloged and maintained in a secure location.

   E. **Data entry and report production --** Since it is common for a single individual to be responsible for all aspects of a transaction, all work should be regularly reviewed by an independent third party.

IV. **In general --** As many standard IT controls as possible should be integrated into the end-user or small business environment. When possible, additional supervision and/or review should be implemented as a compensating control.

Information Technology Glossary

Term	Definition/Change
Batch Processing	A data entry technique in which items to be processed are collected into groups of similar items and periodically submitted to data entry. Batch processing is efficient and relatively inexpensive, but the processing lag time it introduces means that system data is not always current.
Control group	Independent department with Information Systems responsible for logging in all input to the system, monitoring data processing procedures, and distributing output.
Control totals	Manually calculated totals of significant data fields in the documents of a batch; counts of the number of lines and/or documents in a batch. Control totals are reconciled to computer calculated totals and are used to ensure accuracy and completeness of data entry.
Corrective controls	Paired with detective controls, they attempt to reverse the effects of the error or irregularity which has been detected. Examples of corrective controls include maintenance of backup files, disaster recovery plans, and insurance.
Database Management System (DBMS)	The program that manages the interface between application programs such as accounts receivable update, payroll time card processing,
Decision tables	A type of documentation that depicts logical relationships of a processing system by identifying the decision points and processing alternatives
Detective controls	"After the fact" controls designed to detect an error after it has occurred (though preferably before it is used to update the database or appears in reports). Examples of detective controls include data entry edits (field checks, limit tests, etc.) and reconciliation of batch control totals.
Documentation	Descriptions of a program's input, processing, and output provided in overview (**system documentation**) and in detail (**programming documentation**) as well as instructions for running the program (**run manuals, operations documentation**) and for reconciling the processing results (**user documentation**); presented in a combination of flowcharts, decision tables, and narrative.
Encryption	the process of coding data so that it cannot be understood without the correct decryption algorithm.

External labels	A tag placed on data storage media (floppy disks, magnetic tape, CDs, etc.) designed to prevent inadvertent use of the wrong file.
File Server	In a Local Area Network, a computer that provides centralized access to program and data files
Firewall	A firewall consists of hardware, or software, or both, that help detect security problems and enforce security policies on a computer system. A firewall is like a door with a lock for a computer system.
General Controls	Broad-based, pervasive controls that define how programs and data are created, stored, and used, and how reports are produced; apply equally to all computerized functions; designed to ensure the security, effectiveness (correctness, timeliness), and efficiency of data processing.
Grandfather-Father-Son File Security Control	A technique used to maintain redundant backup copies (three "generations") of data files; backup files are used to recover from systems failures in which data files are destroyed.
Hash Totals	In batch processing, the summation of a field in source documents that has no inherent meaning (e.g., in a payroll system, the sum of employees' social security numbers) but which can be used to control for accuracy and completeness of data entry and processing.
Internal Label (Header and Trailer Labels)	Descriptive information stored at the beginning and end of a file that identifies the file, the number of records in the file, and provides data enabling detection of processing errors.
Password strength	The capacity of a password to resist attempts to learn or "crack" it, typically by the use of nefarious automated password cracking software.
Preventive Controls	"Before the fact" controls designed to stop an error or irregularity from occurring. Examples of preventive controls include locks on building and doors, password protected access to files, and segregation of duties.
Random Access	Data storage devices that permit direct access to an individual data item. Magnetic disks (hard disks and floppy disks), CD-ROMs, and DVD disks all provide random access. Contrast with magnetic tape which provides only sequential access.
Server	Computer or other device on a network which only provides resources to the network and is not available (normally) to individual users; examples include print servers, file servers, and communications servers. Contrast with a **workstation**.
Trojan horse	A malicious program that is hidden inside a seemingly benign file.
Workstations (Terminals)	Computers or terminals ("computers" without processing capabilities; can only send and receive information) on a network on which users can perform work. Contrast with a server, which only provides resources for the network and is not available (normally) to individual users.

Planning and Measurement

Cost Measurement and Assignment

Introduction

I. **The identification and assignment of costs is the foundation of management accounting --** Once costs are assigned, costs and revenues can be projected and budgets can be created; when budgets are established, actual results can be compared to expected results and the variances can be evaluated; once the variances are understood, they can be used to modify the business plan and to reward performance.

II. **Heavily Tested --** Given their importance, it should come as no surprise that the topics in this section are some of the most consistently and heavily tested areas in planning and measurement. It is essential for the candidate to have a strong grasp of the terms, relationships, and methodologies discussed in this section as much of the material in subsequent sections depends on a thorough understanding of these topics.

Manufacturing Costs

Understanding the different methods of identifying and classifying costs, how the methods relate to each other, and how costs flow through the accounting system is fundamental to understanding managerial accounting. The terms and concepts in this section are tested directly on every CPA exam and are essential to your understanding of other topics in this subject area.

I. Cost Terminology

A. Two fundamental cost classifications exist with a manufacturing organization: product costs and period costs.

1. **Product costs --** Can be associated with the production of specific revenues (i.e., cost of goods sold). They generally attach to physical product units and are expensed in the period in which the goods are sold. Product costs are also known as **inventoriable** costs or **manufacturing** costs.
2. **Period costs --** Cannot be matched with specific revenues (i.e., accountant's salary) and are expensed in the period incurred. These costs are also called **selling and administrative** costs.

B. This division of costs can be seen in the format of the income statement:

Net Sales	
- Cost of Goods Sold	***(product costs)***
= Gross Profit	
-Selling & Administrative Expenses	***(period costs)***
= Net Profit(Loss)	

II. Manufacturing (or inventoriable) costs --
Include all costs associated with the manufacturing of a product split. Manufacturing costs are split into the "three factors of production:"

A. Direct Material -- The cost of significant raw materials and components that are directly incorporated in the finished product. For example, direct material costs of a leather briefcase include cost of leather (raw material) as well as buckles and zippers (purchased components).

1. The cost of "normal" spoilage or scrap is included as part of the direct material costs; "normal" scrap is waste that is unavoidable in the manufacturing process. For example, when manufacturing clothing, it is never possible to use all of the material: there is always some material that is wasted no matter how close together the pattern pieces are laid on the fabric. This is "normal" waste and is included in the cost of the direct materials.

B. Direct Labor -- The wages and salaries paid for work that directly converts raw materials into a finished product. Continuing with our leather briefcase example, the direct labor costs associated with the manufacture of a leather briefcase include wages paid to workers who cut the leather, finish the leather, and sew the briefcase.

1. Just as normal scrap is included in the direct materials cost, so is "normal" downtime included as a direct labor cost. For example, the cost of worker breaks, training classes, etc.

C. **Factory Overhead --** The cost of labor and supplies that are necessary to support the production process but are not easily traceable to the finished product. Factory overhead associated with production of a leather briefcase includes salaries paid to the production line supervisors, wages paid to mechanics who maintain the equipment, wages paid to custodians who maintain the factory, thread used to sew the briefcase together, electricity used to power the equipment and provide light to the factory, and depreciation on the factory building and equipment.

1. Factory overhead can be **variable** (the total cost changes with the quantity produced) or **fixed** (the total cost remains the same regardless of the quantity produced (within reasonable limits). In the example above, the cost of thread is variable overhead because the more briefcases produced, the more thread used; the depreciation on the factory building is fixed because the depreciation stays the same regardless of how many briefcases are produced.
2. In highly automated manufacturing environments direct labor costs are frequently so insignificant a part of total production costs they are not separately tracked but simply added to factory overhead costs.

III. **Other manufacturing cost classifications --** Several other ways of classifying costs are tested on the CPA exam.

A. **Direct Costs and Indirect Costs --** This classification looks at the behavior of the cost in regards to how it is traced to the product:

- 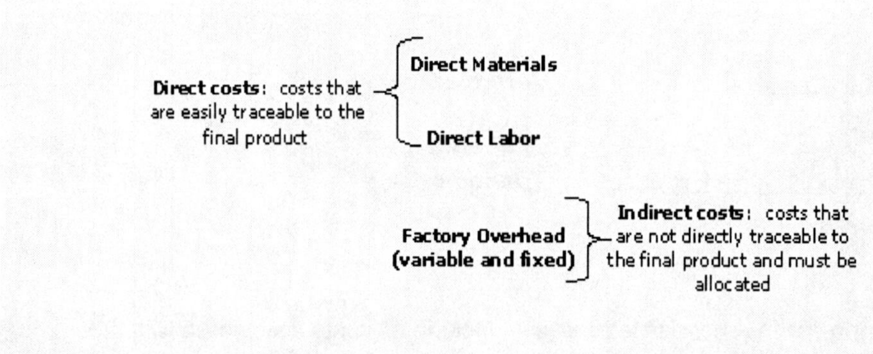

B. **Direct Costs --** (Also known as *prime costs*) Are costs that can be associated with specific units of production. Direct materials are actually incorporated in the product. Direct labor is comprised of the salary costs of workers who fabricate the product.

1. Direct costs are controllable by management.

C. **Indirect Costs --** Are necessary costs of the manufacturing process that cannot easily be identified to specific units. Indirect costs are also known as overhead. Indirect materials include custodial and maintenance supplies, depreciation, and scrap. Indirect labor includes salaries for supervisors, custodians, and maintenance and repair personnel. Indirect costs **can be either variable** (supplies) **or fixed** (depreciation).

1. Variable indirect costs are controllable by management; fixed indirect costs are usually uncontrollable by management.
2. Note that the distinction between direct and indirect costs is often one of convenience. Traditional cost allocation classifies many costs as indirect because they are insignificant or difficult to allocate to products. For example, the cost of thread used to sew a briefcase together could be calculated and assigned to the briefcase as a direct cost. However, because the cost of the thread is so

insignificant, it is usually treated as an indirect cost and allocated to each briefcase on some other basis. Alternative allocation methods such as Activity-Based Costing look at costs more critically and attempt to assign them directly to products: **costs that were previously classified as indirect costs become direct costs**. These methods produce more precisely costed products, which facilitates better pricing decisions.

D. **Prime Costs and Conversion Costs --** These overlapping cost classifications are frequently tested on the exam. As explained above, **"prime costs"** is another term for "direct costs" - significant costs that can be directly associated with the product. **Conversion costs** are the costs necessary to convert raw materials into finished goods: Direct Labor costs plus Factory Overhead costs.

> **Study Tip:**
> Direct labor is included as a prime cost and as a conversion cost. This overlap in classifications is frequently tested on the exam.

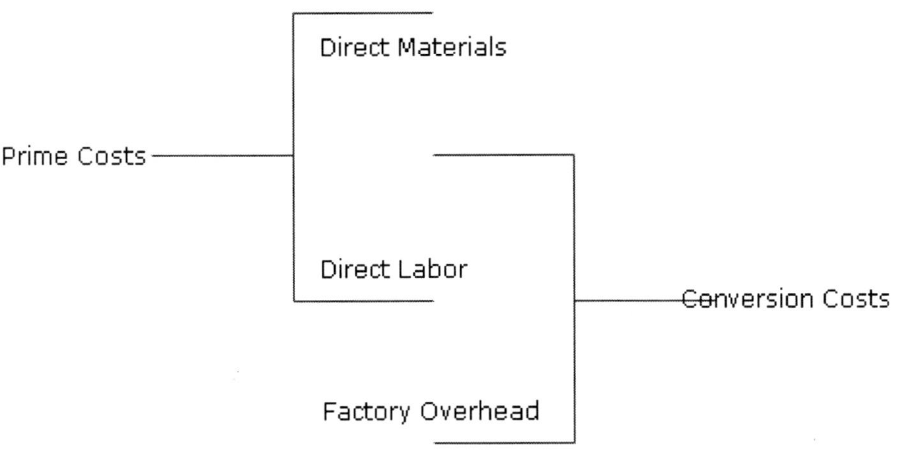

E. **Value-added Costs and Non-value-added Costs**

1. **Value-added costs --** Are product costs that enhance the value of the product in the eyes of the consumer. Most direct costs are value-added costs. Continuing with the briefcase example, the leather that the briefcase is made of and the labor required to cut the pieces and sew them together are value-added costs.
2. **Nonvalue-added costs --** Are costs that could be eliminated without deterioration of product quality, performance, or perceived value to the consumer. Many nonvalue-added costs are essential to production and cannot be completely eliminated. For example, oiling the machine that is used to sew the briefcase together is a nonvalue-added cost from the customer's viewpoint. However, if the machine wasn't oiled, sooner or later it would stop sewing. Oiling the machine is an essential, but nonvalue-added, cost. **Most, though not all, overhead costs are nonvalue-added costs**. For example, the thread used to sew the briefcase together is usually an overhead cost, but most consumers would see it as a value-added cost.

IV. **Overhead Allocation --** Since overhead costs are not directly associated with specific units of production, an estimated overhead amount is applied to production based on a predetermined formula. Actual overhead costs are accumulated separately. At the end of the period, the applied overhead is compared to the actual overhead and an entry is made to adjust any difference.

A. **Predetermined Overhead Application Rate --** The first step in applying overhead is to calculate the rate that will be used to apply overhead to production. The rate is based on an estimated overhead amount, which is applied to some measure of activity -- units produced, machine hours, direct labor hours, etc. The measure of activity should have some plausible relationship to the overhead charges. For example, if most of the overhead is related to maintenance costs of machinery, then machine hours would be a likely candidate.

> **Study Tip:**
> Estimated amounts based on **currently attainable standards** are always used for this formula - *not* **historical, ideal, or theoretical amounts**. This is a frequently tested concept on the CPA exam.

1. The formula for developing the overhead rate is:

estimated total overhead costs / **estimated** normal activity volume

2. The result of this calculation is the **Overhead Application Rate** (or **Overhead Allocation Rate**). The Overhead Allocation Rate is normally established prior to the beginning of the period. That is, it is a predetermined rate.

B. **Applied Overhead --** The amount of estimated overhead charged to production. Applied overhead is calculated by multiplying the predetermined overhead rate times the actual number of activity units used in production (direct labor hours, machine hours, etc).

1. Applied overhead is included in the cost of work in process by the following entry:

DR: Work in Process	XXX	
CR: Factory Overhead Applied		XXX

C. **Actual Overhead --** The amount actually paid for overhead expenses. These costs are initially charged to the specific expense account (i.e., supplies inventory, utilities, maintenance, supervision, etc.) and to the Factory Overhead Control account. For example:

DR: Factory Overhead Control Utilities Expense	XXX	
CR: Accounts Payable		XXX

D. **Closing out the Overhead Accounts --** At the end of the period the Factory Overhead Control account (which contains the actual overhead costs) and the Factory Overhead Applied account (which contains the overhead costs that were applied to production using the Predetermined Overhead Rate) are closed out.

1. For example, assume that the actual overhead costs were $50,000 and the overhead costs applied to production were also $50,000. The following entry would close (zero out) the overhead accounts:

DR: Factory Overhead Applied	$50,000	
CR: Factory Overhead Control		$50,000

2. Of course, it is unusual for the estimated overhead applied to production and the actual overhead costs to be equal. Usually there are differences between the amount of applied overhead and the amount of actual overhead.

   a. **Immaterial differences** between the two amounts are usually **allocated to Cost of Goods Sold**.

   b. If the **difference** *is* **material**, it should be **prorated to Work in Process, Finished Goods, and Cost of Goods Sold** based on their respective ending balances.

3. The treatment of material differences between actual and applied overhead is commonly tested on the exam.

E. **Overapplied Factory Overhead --** When more overhead costs are applied to products than are actually incurred, factory overhead is said to be overapplied. When the accounts are closed at the end of the period, overapplied overhead reduces Cost of Goods Sold.

Question:
Priceless Products incurs $20,000 in actual overhead costs during the period. Using their predetermined overhead allocation formula, Priceless applied $21,000 to products as overhead costs, resulting in $1,000 of overapplied overhead. Priceless regards this amount as immaterial and charges over/underapplied overhead to Cost of Goods Sold at the end of the period when the accounts are closed. How will this entry affect Cost of Goods?

Answer:
Cost of Goods Sold will decrease when the accounts are closed:

DR: Factory Overhead Applied	$21,000	
CR: Factory Overhead Control		$20,000
CR: Cost of Goods Sold		$1,000

F. **Underapplied Factory Overhead --** When more overhead costs are actually incurred during the period than are applied to products, factory overhead is said to be underapplied. When the accounts are closed at the end of the period, underapplied overhead increases Cost of Goods Sold.

Question:
Cost Conscious Products incurs $10,000 in actual overhead costs during the period. Using their predetermined overhead allocation formula, Cost Conscious applied $9,500 to products as overhead costs. If Cost Conscious charges over/underapplied overhead to Cost of Goods Sold at the end of the period when the accounts are closed, how will this affect Cost of Goods?

Answer:
Cost of Goods Sold will increase when the accounts are closed:

DR: Factory Overhead Applied	$9,500	
DR: Cost of Goods Sold	$500	
CR: Factory Overhead Control		$10,000

V. Spoilage and Scrap

A. Some spoilage and scrap may be **normal** - That is, it is unavoidable as part of the manufacturing process. Normal spoilage is included with other costs as an inventoriable product cost.

B. Spoilage and scrap may also be **abnormal**, such as when it is due to carelessness or inefficiency. Abnormal spoilage is separated and deducted as a period expense in the calculation of net income.

1. **Responsibility for scrap --** Normal spoilage is part of the production process and is therefore an uncontrollable cost. Abnormal spoilage is due to production inefficiencies and is a controllable cost. Since managers should only be held responsible for controllable costs, managers should be held responsible for abnormal spoilage, but not for normal spoilage.

2. **Sale of scrap --** Any monies received from the sale of scrap are used to reduce factory overhead, and thereby reduce Cost of Goods Sold.

Study Tip:
Be sure that you thoroughly understand the account analysis formats used in this example. The examiners frequently make these questions more difficult by giving you the Cost of Goods Sold or Cost of Goods Manufactured and asking you for one of the intermediate amounts (e.g. the Ending WIP Inventory value or the Direct Labor added during the period). If you understand the format of the analysis, these types of questions are easy to answer by simply filling in the blanks and solving for the unknowns.

VI. **Flow of Costs and Inventory Valuation --** Companies use one of several cost flow assumptions (LIFO, FIFO, weighted average) to assign inventory costs to ending inventory and cost of goods sold. For retail companies who buy products for re-sale, this is a fairly straightforward process. For manufacturing companies, however, the addition of raw materials inventory and work in process inventory makes the process more complex.

A. **Wholesale and Retail Organizations --** Since these organizations purchase the items that they sell, their inventory calculations are relatively simple. Under the periodic inventory method, inventory is counted at the end of the period and valued, typically using FIFO, LIFO, or weighted average cost flow assumptions. The ending inventory valuation is then subtracted from Goods Available for Sale (the value of the beginning inventory plus purchases) to determine Cost of Goods Sold:

+	Beginning Inventory	
+	Purchases (net)	
=	Goods Available for Sale	
-	Ending Inventory	*reported on the B.S.*
=	Cost of Goods Sold	*appears as a line item on the I.S.*

1. This analysis format, which is sometimes called "account analysis" format because it allows you to analyze the debits and credits of any account, is essentially the same format as is used for the Schedule of Cost of Goods Sold.

B. **Manufacturing Organizations**

1. Manufacturing organizations maintain three inventories instead of one:

   a. Raw Materials;

   b. Work in Process;

   c. Finished Goods.

2. Costs flow from Raw Materials Inventory through Work in Process Inventory and into Finished Goods Inventory. As items are sold, costs flow from Finished Goods Inventory into Cost of Goods Sold. The ending balances of the three inventories are added together and reported as a single line item on the Balance Sheet. Cost of Goods Sold appears as a line item on the Income Statement. The analysis of the three inventory accounts is shown on two schedules:

Schedule	*Inventory Accounts Analyzed*
Cost of Goods Manufactured	Raw Materials and Work-in-Process
Cost of Goods Sold	Finished Goods

C. Schedule of Cost of Goods Manufactured -- This schedule calculates the dollar value of the goods that were completed during the period and transferred to finished goods. It is primarily an analysis of the Work-In-Process account (beginning balance + total manufacturing costs - ending balance = cost of goods manufactured), but it is sometimes complicated by calculations related to the Direct Materials Inventory. The basic format is as follows:

+	Beg. Value WIP	
+	Current Period Additions:	
	+ Direct Materials*	
	+ Direct Labor	
	<u>+ Overhead</u>	
-	<u>End. Value WIP</u>	
=	Cost of Goods Manufactured	-->to additions to Finished Goods Inventory

*The current period direct materials costs are calculated by analyzing the Direct Materials Inventory account:

+	Beg. Direct Materials	
+	<u>Purchases (net)</u>	
=	Direct Materials Available for Use	
-	<u>Ending Direct Materials</u>	
=	Direct Materials Used	-->to Direct Materials line on schedule of cost of goods manufactured

D. Schedule of Cost of Goods Sold - This schedule is produced by analyzing the Finished Goods Inventory. It calculates the Cost of Goods Sold:

	Beginning Finished Goods	-->from the Schedule of CGM
+	<u>Cost of Goods Manufactured</u>	
	Goods Available for Sale	
-	<u>Ending Finished Goods</u>	
=	Cost of Goods Sold	-->appears as a line item on the I.S.

Example:

Kingman Enterprises produces custom period furniture for Victorian homes. The following information is available concerning Kingman's production activities during the past quarter:

Inventory	Beg. Value	Purchases/Additions	End. Value
Direct Materials	$120,000	$800,000	$100,000
Work-in-Process	$180,000	Direct Materials: ??? Direct Labor: $120,000 Overhead Applied: $700,000	$120,000
Finished Goods	$250,000	Cost of Goods Manufactured: ???	$350,000

Given this information, calculate the Cost of Goods Manufactured and the Cost of Goods Sold.

Step 1: Calculate the raw materials used during the period:

+ Beg. Direct Materials	+ $120,000
+ Purchases (net)	+ $800,000
= Materials Available for Use	+ $920,000
- Ending Direct Materials	- $100,000
= Direct Materials Used	= $820,000

Step 2: Calculate the cost of goods manufactured:

+ Beginning Value WIP		$180,000
+ Current Period Additions:		
+ Direct Materials used	+ $820,000	
+ Direct Labor	+ $120,000	
+ Overhead Applied	+ $700,000	
		$1,640,000
= Total Manufacturing Costs		$1,820,000
- Ending Value WIP		$120,000
= Cost of Goods Manufactured		$1,700,000

Step 3: Calculate the cost of goods sold:

Beginning Finished Goods	+ $250,000
+ Cost of Goods Manufactured	+ $1,700,000
Goods Available for Sale	= $1,950,000
- Ending Finished Goods	- $350,000
= Cost of Goods Sold	= $1,600,000

Cost Behavior Patterns

Cost behavior patterns allow us to predict how costs change in response to changes in production or sales. A thorough understanding of cost behavior is necessary in order to perform cost-volume-profit analysis and to prepare production and sales budgets. Cost behavior is consistently tested on the CPA exam - both directly and as part of other topics.

I. Costs

A. By analyzing the way costs behave when production and/or sales volume change, we can predict total costs and estimate profit. However, very few costs behave consistently across a wide range of production or sales volumes: at some point, economies or diseconomies of scale will cause the cost behavior to change. Because of this, all discussions of cost behavior must take place within the concept of a relevant range. A **relevant range** is a range of production volumes where:

1. **Total** fixed costs remain constant;
2. **Unit** variable costs remain constant;
3. **Unit** sales price remains constant.

B. All cost behavior patterns are valid only within a relevant range. We will discuss the concept of a relevant range in more detail in conjunction with cost-volume-profit analysis.

II. Fixed vs. Variable Costs

A. Costs can be separated into two principal behavior patterns.

1. **Fixed costs --** Remain constant in total regardless of production volume. Because of this, **fixed costs** *per unit* **vary** - increasing when production decreases and decreasing when production increases.
2. **Variable costs --** Vary in total, in direct proportion to changes in production volume. **Variable costs** *per unit* **remain constant** regardless of production volume.

B. **Total cost --** Is the sum of fixed costs and variable costs. As such, total costs take on characteristics from both component costs: **total costs per unit vary** with changes in production because fixed costs per unit vary with changes in production; **total costs in total vary** with changes in production because variable costs vary in total with changes in production.

Exam Hint: Many CPA exam questions ask about the relationship between fixed costs, variable costs and total costs and changes in production volume. The examiners frequently use the fact that the unit cost relationships and total cost relationships are different to confuse the candidate. For example, a question about fixed costs, which remain constant *in total* over changes in production volume, will ask if the fixed cost *per unit* remains constant when production volume changes. The following matrix may help keep these relationships straight:

Behavior when production volume changes:

	Unit Costs	**Total Costs**
Fixed Costs	Vary	Constant
Variable Costs	Constant	Vary
Total Costs	Vary	Vary

Question:
Stanford Machining planned production of 180,000 units this year. Fixed costs were estimated to be $220,000; total variable costs were estimated to be $540,000. Actual production was 150,000. How would you expect the total fixed costs and total variable costs to change because of the change in production volume? What about the unit fixed costs and unit variable costs?

Answer:
Total fixed costs and *unit* variable costs would not change because of the change in production volume (see matrix above). *Unit* fixed costs would increase from $1.22 (220,000/180,000) to $1.47 (220,000/150,000) and total variable costs would decrease from $540,000 to $450,000 ((540,000/180,000) * 150,000).

III. Other Cost Classifications -- Many costs exhibit both fixed and variable cost characteristics.

A. Step-Variable costs -- Remain constant in *total* over a small range of production levels, but vary with larger changes in production volume. Supervisory salaries, utility costs, and shipping costs often behave in this fashion.

B. Mixed costs (also known as semi-variable costs) -- Have a fixed component and a variable component. The variable component causes them to vary in total with changes in volume. The fixed component, however, prevents them from varying in direct proportion to the change in volume.

Example:
Carpenter Corporation leases a copier from a local office supply company. Under the contract, Carpenter pays a base fee of $800 per month for the copier and an additional $0.015 for each copy over 50,000 per month. This is a mixed cost with an $800 fixed cost and a variable cost of $0.015 for the additional copies.

IV. Predicting Costs

A. High-Low Method

1. When predicting the behavior of a total cost or a mixed cost, the High-Low Method provides a rough estimate of the fixed cost and the variable cost components. Although a more precise cost prediction can be obtained using regression analysis, the high-low method provides a quick, easy cost estimate.

2. The basic concept underlying this method is that when total manufacturing costs change in response to changes in production volume, the changes are, by definition, caused by variable costs.

    a. By calculating the change in total costs between two production volume extremes (the high value and the low value), the total change in variable costs can be isolated.

    b. The unit variable cost can then be determined by dividing the change in total costs by the difference in units produced.

Study Tip:
Although the High-Low Method typically receives little emphasis in academic studies of managerial accounting, it is one of the more consistently covered topics on the CPA exam.

c. Once the unit variable cost is determined, total fixed costs can be identified by calculating the total variable cost at a specified production volume (e.g. multiply unit variable cost times the number of units produced) and subtracting it from the total cost.

B. **Using the high-low method --** To identify fixed and variable cost components using the high-low method:

1. From the range of production volumes presented, select the period with the highest production and the period with the lowest production;
2. **Note --** Do not use highest and lowest *costs* - Always **use** *production volume* ;
3. Calculate the **difference in units produced** at the highest and the lowest levels of production;
4. Calculate the **difference in costs** at the highest and the lowest levels of production;
5. **Divide the difference in costs by the difference in units --** This is your estimated variable cost per unit;
6. Find total variable costs by multiplying the **estimated variable cost per unit by the actual number of units produced** at either the high or the low level of production;
7. Subtract the **total variable costs from the total cost** to determine fixed costs;
8. You can now estimate total costs at any production level by multiplying the production in units times the variable cost per unit and adding it to the total fixed costs.

Example:
Milkenson Industries reported the following production volumes and costs:

Production	Cost
150,000 units	$375,000
225,000 units	$525,000

What are the fixed and variable costs of production for 250,000 units?

Steps:1-4: ($525,000 - $375,000) / (225,000 - 150,000) = $2.00 variable cost per unit

Steps:4-5: $375,000 - ($2.00 * 150,000 units) = $75,000 fixed costs

or

$525,000 - ($2.00 * 225,000 units) = $75,000 fixed costs

Steps:5-7: ($2.00 * 250,000 units) + $75,000 = $575,000 total costs

Answer: $500,000 variable costs and $75,000 fixed costs

Activity-based Costing

By more precisely identifying costs with their underlying causes and assigning them to products accordingly, activity-based costing offers a significant improvement over traditional costing methods. In the process of doing this, it dramatically changes the way we look at costs and the way we allocate them to products. Activity-based costing is tested regularly on the CPA exam, but it is tested almost exclusively from a conceptual point of view: questions that ask for the calculation or allocation of costs are rare.

I. Costing

A. Activity-based costing is a method of assigning overhead (indirect) costs to products. It is an alternative to the traditional, volume-based approach of accumulating large amounts of overhead in a single pool and assigning the costs across all products based on the labor dollars, labor hours, or some other generic allocation base. The volume-based approach, while simple, does not accurately reflect the true relationship between the products produced and the costs incurred and systematically over-assigns costs to some products and under-assigns costs to others.

B. By closely focusing on the causes of costs, ABC is better able to identify the cost of an activity and to more accurately associate activities with the products that require them. This has the potential to significantly improve the accuracy of the resulting product cost. Improved costing accuracy leads to improved pricing and other decisions that depend on the accuracy of costs. In addition, managers can potentially improve their understanding of processes and how they consume resources.

II. Activity-Based Costing Terminology

Activities - procedures that comprise work.

Cost drivers - measures that are closely correlated with the way an activity accumulates costs; for example, the cost driver for production line set up costs might be the number of machines that have to be set up; cost drivers are the basis by which costs are assigned to products (traditionally direct labor hours, machine hours, occupancy percentages, etc.).

Cost center - an area where costs are accumulated and then distributed to products, for example accounts payable, product design, and marketing.

Cost pools - a group of costs that are associated with a specific cost center.

Value-added activities - processes that contribute to the product's ultimate value; includes items such as design and packaging in addition to direct conversion of direct materials into finished goods.

Nonvalue-added activities - processes that do not contribute to the product's value; includes items such as moving materials and more obvious activities such as rework; cost reductions can be achieved by reducing or eliminating nonvalue-added activities.

III. Activity-Based Costing Characteristics

A. Activity-based costing begins by identifying activities. Activities form the building blocks of an ABC system because activities consume resources. Activities are commonly grouped into one of four categories:

1. **Unit level activities --** Activities that must be performed for every product unit; for example, using a machine to polish a silver tray; boxing up an item for delivery;
2. **Batch level activities --** Activities that must be performed for each batch of products produced; examples include setting up the production equipment for the batch and running random quality inspections of items in the batch;
3. **Product sustaining level activities --** Activities that are necessary to support the product line as a whole such as advertising and engineering activities;
4. **Facility (general operations) level activities --** Activities that are necessary to support the plant that produces the products; for example, plant manager salaries, property taxes, and insurance.

B. Once activities have been identified, overhead costs are assigned to them. The costs assigned to a particular activity comprise an activity cost pool. The next step is to identify cost drivers that can be used to allocate the costs to products. When the cost pools created in an ABC system are compared to the cost pools created in a traditional, volume-based costing system, ABC results in a larger number of smaller cost pools that can be more closely aligned to products.

IV. Effects of Adoption of Activity-based Costing

A. Because of the way activity-based costing identifies and allocates costs, organizations that adopt activity-based costing tend to have:

1. More **precise measures of cost;**
2. More **cost pools;**
3. More **allocation bases** (e.g., multiple causes for costs to occur).

B. Activity-based costing can be used:

1. With **job order** and **process costing** systems;
2. With **standard costing** and **variance analysis**;
3. For **service businesses** as well as manufacturers.

C. In general, compared to traditional, volume-based costing, activity-based costing tends to shift costs away from high volume, simple products to lower volume, complex products.

Study Tip:
The items listed in the Effects of the Adoption of Activity-Based Costing are the most heavily tested concepts in activity-based costing.

Absorption & Direct Costing

Absorption costing and direct costing are the two most commonly used alternatives for assigning costs to inventory and reporting income for a manufacturing firm. The difference between the two methods turns on whether fixed costs are assigned to products or whether they are written off in the period in which they are incurred. Absorption and direct costing are fairly light areas on the CPA exam, but the questions that do appear on the exam can be time consuming unless the candidate is properly prepared.

I. Two methods

A. Absorption and direct costing are two methods of assigning manufacturing costs to inventory.

> **Definitions:**
>
> *Absorption costing*: Assigns all three factors of production (direct material, direct labor, and both fixed and variable manufacturing overhead) to inventory.
>
> *Direct costing*: (Also known as variable costing) Assigns only variable manufacturing costs (direct material, direct labor, but only variable manufacturing overhead) to inventory.

1. Absorption costing is required for external reporting purposes. This is currently true for both external financial reporting and reporting to the IRS.
2. Direct costing is frequently used for internal decision making but *cannot* be used for external reporting.

II. Income Statement Cost Classifications

A. A manufacturing company's income statement typically displays two types of costs: product costs and period costs (or, alternatively, **manufacturing costs** and **selling and administrative costs**). To highlight the differences between absorption costing and direct costing, these two cost categories are **further decomposed into two additional groups** depending on whether the costs are **variable** or **fixed**.

1. **Variable manufacturing costs**
   - **a.** Direct material - Materials that are feasibly traceable to the final product;
   - **b.** Direct labor - Wages paid to employees involved in the primary conversion of direct materials to finished goods;
   - **c.** Variable factory overhead - Variable manufacturing costs other than direct material and direct labor (e.g., supplies, utilities, repairs, etc.).
2. **Fixed manufacturing costs**
   - **a.** Fixed Factory Overhead: Fixed manufacturing costs (e.g., depreciation on factory buildings and equipment, manufacturing supervisory salaries and wages, property taxes and insurance on the factory, etc.).
3. **Variable selling and administrative costs**
   - **a.** Selling costs: freight out, sales commissions, etc.;
   - **b.** Administrative costs: office supplies, office utilities, advertising, etc.

4. **Fixed selling and administrative costs**
   - a. Selling costs: salesmen salaries, depreciation on sales-related equipment, etc.;
   - b. Administrative costs: officer's salaries; depreciation, property taxes, and insurance on office building, etc.

B. The principal difference between the absorption model and the direct costing model rests on **which costs are assigned to products**:

1. The **absorption** model assigns **all manufacturing costs** to products;
2. The **direct** model assigns **only variable manufacturing costs** to products.

C. The following graphic details the distribution of costs under each method. Notice that the manufacturing overhead costs are split into a variable and a fixed component and that under direct costing, while the variable overhead is included as a product cost, the fixed overhead is not:

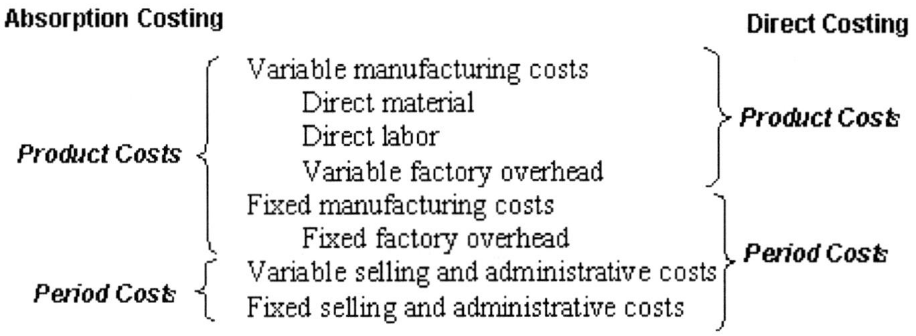

Absorption Costing		Direct Costing
Product Costs	Variable manufacturing costs	*Product Costs*
Product Costs	Direct material	*Product Costs*
Product Costs	Direct labor	*Product Costs*
Product Costs	Variable factory overhead	*Product Costs*
Product Costs	Fixed manufacturing costs	*Period Costs*
Product Costs	Fixed factory overhead	*Period Costs*
Period Costs	Variable selling and administrative costs	*Period Costs*
Period Costs	Fixed selling and administrative costs	*Period Costs*

Example:

Clark Corp. reported the following manufacturing costs.

Direct materials and direct labor	$700,000
Other variable manufacturing costs	100,000
Depreciation of factory building and manufacturing equipment	80,000
Other fixed manufacturing overhead	18,000

Based on this information, determine the product (inventoriable) costs under absorption costing and direct costing.

Product Costs	Absorption Costing	Direct Costing
Direct materials and direct labor	$700,000	$700,000
Other variable manufacturing costs	100,000	100,000
Depreciation of factory building and manufacturing equipment	80,000	
Other fixed manufacturing overhead	18,000	
Total inventoriable costs	$898,000	$800,000

III. Income Statement Format

Study Tip:
Remember that GAAP requires the use of absorption costing for inventory valuation and income determination for external reporting. Direct costing can only be used for internal reporting.

A. Income statements can be prepared using full absorption and direct costing; the methods use different terminology and have different formats.

B. **Absorption costing income statement --** The absorption costing income statement lists its product costs, including the fixed manufacturing costs, "above the line" and subtracts the product costs from Sales to calculate Gross Margin.

+ Sales		
- Variable Manufacturing Costs	--->	*for units sold*
- Fixed Manufacturing Costs	--->	*for units sold*
= Gross Margin		
- Variable Selling and Administrative		
- Fixed Selling and Administrative		
= Operating Income		

C. Characteristics of the absorption costing model:

1. **Cost of Goods Sold --** Includes all manufacturing expenses:

CGS = Variable Manufacturing expenses + Fixed Manufacturing expenses

2. **Gross Margin --** Is calculated as:

Gross Margin = Sales - Cost of Goods Sold

Note:
All selling and administrative costs are treated as period costs regardless of whether the absorption or variable costing methods are used.

3. **Treatment of fixed manufacturing costs --** Fixed manufacturing overhead is allocated to each item produced. This means that if we produce more than we sell, a portion of the fixed manufacturing costs is capitalized and is included on the Balance Sheet as part of Inventory.

4. **Period expenses --** Both variable and fixed selling and administrative costs are treated as period expenses.

D. **Direct costing income statement**

1. The direct costing income statement lists its product costs - direct material, direct labor, and variable factory overhead - plus the variable selling and administrative expenses "above the line" and subtracts the total variable expenses from Sales to calculate the Contribution Margin; fixed manufacturing costs are listed "below the line" and, along with the fixed selling and administrative expenses, are treated as period expenses:

Sales		
- Variable Manufacturing Costs	--->	*only for* **units sold**
- Variable Selling and Administrative Costs		
= Contribution Margin		
- Fixed Manufacturing Costs	--->	*for all* **units** *produced*
- Fixed Selling and Administrative		
= Operating Income		

Study Tip:
Although variable selling and administrative costs are listed "above the line" along with the variable manufacturing costs (direct material, direct labor, variable manufacturing overhead) and are subtracted from sales to arrive at the contribution margin, the **variable selling and administrative costs are *not* product costs** and **are not considered part of Cost of Goods Sold**. Instead, they are always **recognized as a period cost** and are completely expensed each period.

2. Characteristics of the direct costing model:
   a. **Cost of Goods Sold --** Includes only variable manufacturing costs.

CGS = Variable manufacturing costs

   b. **Contribution Margin --** Is calculated by deducting all variable costs from the sales revenue:

Contribution Margin = Sales - Variable manufacturing costs - Variable S&A costs

   c. **Treatment of fixed manufacturing costs --** Fixed manufacturing costs (overhead) are expensed in full each period; no fixed manufacturing costs are capitalized.
   d. **Period expenses --** Variable selling and administrative costs - which are shown "above the line" - as well as fixed manufacturing costs and fixed selling and administrative expenses, are treated as period expenses.

Example:

Waylen Manufacturing produced and sold 200,000 espresso makers during the year for $40 each. Manufacturing and selling costs were as follows:

Direct materials and direct labor	$4,000,000
Variable manufacturing overhead	900,000
Fixed manufacturing overhead	200,000
Variable selling costs	500,000
Fixed selling costs	100,000

What was Waylen's contribution margin?

$8,000,000	Sales (200,000 * $40)
-4,000,000	Direct materials and direct labor
- 900,000	Variable manufacturing overhead
- 500,000	Variable selling costs
2,600,000	Contribution margin

What were the inventoriable costs per unit under direct (variable) costing?

$4,000,000	Direct materials and direct labor
+900,000	Variable manufacturing overhead
$4,900,000	Inventoriable (product) costs
/ 200,000	units
= $24.50	per unit

E. **Effect of product costing model on operating income --** Absorption costing and direct costing assign different costs to inventory. Since direct costing does not include fixed manufacturing costs as part of product cost, the **inventory valuation under absorption costing will always be greater than the inventory valuation under direct costing**. From an external reporting point of view, **direct costing** *understates* **assets on the balance sheet**.

Example:

Brown Manufacturing using direct costing for internal reporting. During the current year they reported the following costs related to the production of one million units:

Direct Materials	$500,000
Direct Labor	80,000
Variable Factory Overhead	100,000
Fixed Factory Overhead	120,000

Under direct costing, their unit cost is $0.68:

Unit product cost = ($500,000+$80,000+$100,000)/1,000,000

= $680,000/1,000,000

Under absorption costing their unit cost is $0.80:

Unit product cost = ($500,000+$80,000+$100,000+$120,000/1,000,000

=$800,000/1,000,000

F. Unit costs under absorption costing -- Will always be greater than unit costs under direct costing because absorption costing includes fixed manufacturing overhead as part of the product cost while direct costing does not. Depending on the circumstances, this can create differences in the income reported under the two methods.

1. Because absorption costing and direct costing assign different costs to products, there may be a difference in income reported under the two methods. However, absorption costing and direct costing do not always produce different incomes: **when the number of units sold equals the number of units produced, absorption costing and direct costing produce identical incomes**.
2. The difference between the two measures of income is due to the different treatment of fixed manufacturing costs. Direct costing deducts all fixed manufacturing costs each period when calculating income. Absorption costing assigns fixed manufacturing costs to products and therefore only deducts fixed manufacturing costs when the units are sold.
3. When units sold equal units produced, direct costing and absorption costing both deduct the full amount of fixed manufacturing costs. However, when the number of units sold is different from the number of units produced, direct costing deducts the fixed manufacturing costs for the goods produced during the period to determine income while absorption costing deducts the fixed manufacturing costs related to the units sold during the period.
4. Depending on whether the units sold are greater than or less than the units produced, the fixed manufacturing overhead deducted under absorption costing may be greater or less than the fixed manufacturing overhead deducted under direct costing.
5. The difference can be calculated as:

Difference in income = Change in Inventory Level X Fixed Manufacturing Overhead per Unit

G. In summary:

When:	Then:
Units Sold = Units Produced	Absorption Costing N.I. = Direct Costing N.I.
Units Sold > Units Produced	Absorption Costing N.I. < Direct Costing N.I.
Units Sold < Units Produced	Absorption Costing N.I. > Direct Costing N.I.

IV. Comprehensive Example

Example:
The following facts are assumed in the income statement examples:

Production costs:

Variable Manufacturing Costs:	$40,000
Fixed Manufacturing Costs:	$10,000
Variable Selling & Administrative Costs:	$20,000
Fixed Selling & Administrative Costs:	$10,000

Production volume: 100,000 units

Sales price per unit: $1.00

Sales volume: varies with each example

Income statements when sales equal production (assume 100K units sold):

DIRECT I.S.		ABSORPTION I.S.	
Sales	100k	Sales	100k
Variable manufacturing	40k	Variable manufacturing	40k
Variable selling and admin	20k	Fixed manufacturing	10k
Contribution Margin	40k	Gross Margin	50k
Fixed manufacturing	10k	Variable selling and admin	20k
Fixed selling and admin	10k	Fixed selling and admin	10k
Operating Income	20k	Operating Income	20k

Since sales volume equals production volume, there is no change in inventory and **operating income is equal under both methods**.

Income statements when sales volume is less than production volume (assume 50K units sold):

DIRECT I.S.		ABSORPTION I.S.	
Sales	50k	Sales	50k
Variable manufacturing	20k	Variable manufacturing	20k
Variable selling and admin	10k	Fixed manufacturing	5k
Contribution Margin	20k	Gross Margin	25k
Fixed manufacturing	10k	Variable selling and admin	10k
Fixed selling and admin	10k	Fixed selling and admin	10k
Operating Income	-0-	Operating Income	5k

Since sales volume is less than production volume, inventory levels must increase. Under absorption (full accrual) costing, the units going into inventory include the fixed manufacturing costs. That is, a portion of the fixed manufacturing costs appears on the balance sheet rather than the income statement. Under direct costing, the total fixed manufacturing costs are included on the income statement as a period expense. Therefore, **income under direct costing is smaller than income under absorption costing.**

Income statements when sales volume is greater than production volume (assume 150K units sold):

DIRECT I.S.		ABSORPTION I.S.	
Sales	150k	Sales	150k
Variable manufacturing	60k	Variable manufacturing	60k
Variable selling and admin	30k	Fixed manufacturing	15k
Contribution Margin	60k	Gross Margin	75k
Fixed manufacturing	10k	Variable selling and admin	30k
Fixed selling and admin	10k	Fixed selling and admin	10k
Operating Income	40k	Operating Income	35k

Since sales volume is greater than production volume, inventory levels must decrease. Under absorption (full accrual) costing, the units coming out of inventory include both fixed and variable manufacturing costs. That is, a portion of the fixed manufacturing costs from a prior period is included on the income statement in addition to the fixed manufacturing costs from the current period. Under direct costing, the units coming out of inventory include only the variable manufacturing costs. Only the fixed manufacturing costs for the current period are included on the income statement. Therefore, income under absorption costing is smaller than income under direct (variable) costing.

Job Order & Process Costing

Job order and process costing techniques are designed to support two common manufacturing technologies: 1) the customized, special order manufacturing of individual or small lot items such as custom print jobs, construction of large ships as well as many service activities and 2) large batch or continuous production of homogeneous items such as paper, dog food, and pens. Most exams will have several questions on job order and/or process costing. Many of the job order questions are concerned with identifying cost flows (cost of materials added to production, amount of overhead associated with a particular job, etc.). Process cost questions tend to focus on the calculation of the equivalent units under different cost flow assumptions (e.g. FIFO vs. weighted average).

I. **Introduction --** Job Order Costing is used to accumulate costs related to the production of **large, relatively expensive, heterogeneous (custom ordered) items**. Costing follows the general rules for manufacturing cost flows and is relatively straightforward:

> **Note:**
> Job order costing is compatible with the use of normal costing, standard costing, and variance analysis.

- **A.** Costs are accumulated in individual work-in-process accounts called job order cost sheets the total of which is accounted for in the work-in-process control account;
- **B.** Overhead is applied based on a predetermined overhead rate.
- **C.** When goods are completed, costs flow on to Finished Goods and when sold, cost flow into Cost of Goods Sold.

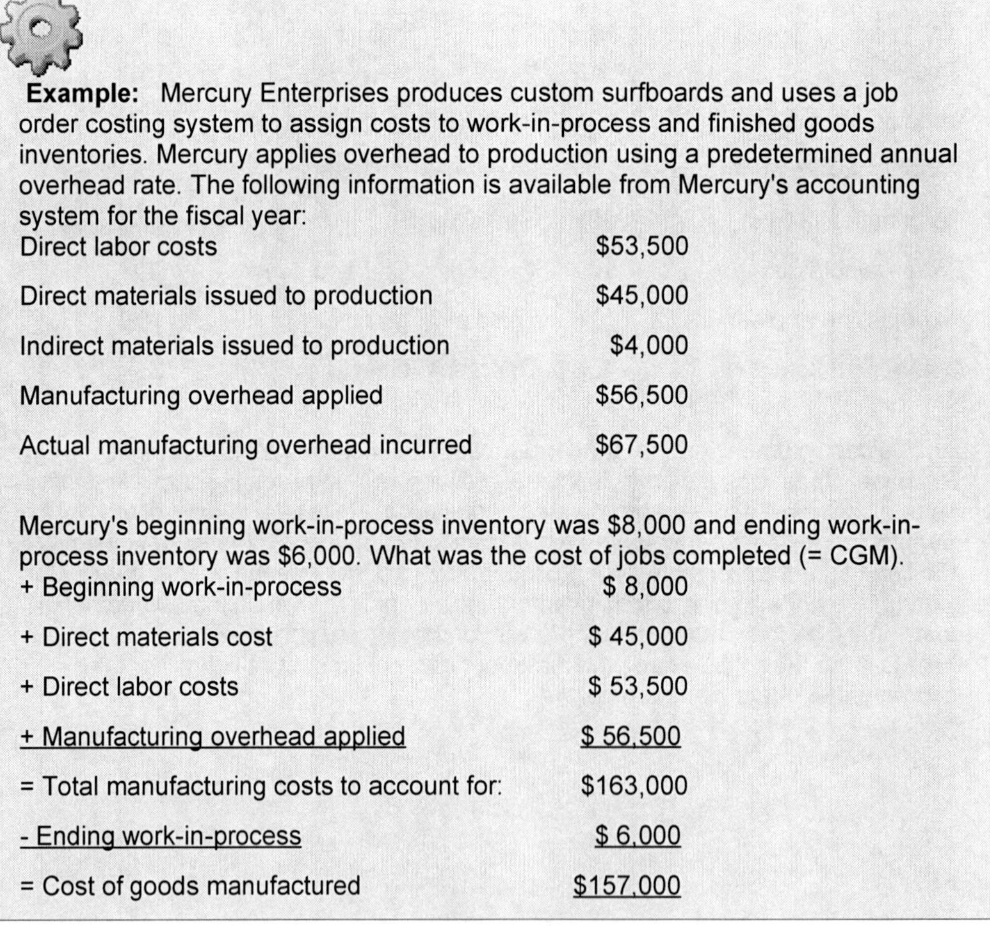

Example: Mercury Enterprises produces custom surfboards and uses a job order costing system to assign costs to work-in-process and finished goods inventories. Mercury applies overhead to production using a predetermined annual overhead rate. The following information is available from Mercury's accounting system for the fiscal year:

Direct labor costs	$53,500
Direct materials issued to production	$45,000
Indirect materials issued to production	$4,000
Manufacturing overhead applied	$56,500
Actual manufacturing overhead incurred	$67,500

Mercury's beginning work-in-process inventory was $8,000 and ending work-in-process inventory was $6,000. What was the cost of jobs completed (= CGM).

+ Beginning work-in-process	$ 8,000
+ Direct materials cost	$ 45,000
+ Direct labor costs	$ 53,500
+ Manufacturing overhead applied	$ 56,500
= Total manufacturing costs to account for:	$163,000
- Ending work-in-process	$ 6,000
= Cost of goods manufactured	$157,000

II. Process Costing -- Process costing is used to accumulate costs for **mass-produced, continuous, homogeneous items which are often small and inexpensive**. Since costs are not accumulated for individual items, the accounting problem becomes one of tracking the number of units moving through the work-in-process into finished goods and allocating the costs incurred to these units on a rational basis. The cost allocation process is complicated because:

A. There may be partially completed items in beginning and ending inventories.

B. Each of the three factors of production (labor, material, and overhead) may be at different levels of completion, making it necessary to perform separate calculations for each factor.

C. Some costs do not occur uniformly across the process; this is particularly true for direct materials. This is why the two categories of the factors of production indicated are typically direct materials and conversion costs (i.e., DL and OH). Direct labor and overhead are normally included together because they are typically uniformly incurred.

D. There are two methods for calculating equivalent units. These are FIFO and weighted average. These methods of calculating equivalent units have nothing to do with the inventory *valuation* methods of FIFO, weighted average, or LIFO.

> **Study Tip:**
> Most of the process costing questions that appear on the exam are theoretical rather than computational. When calculation problems do appear, they usually ask for the equivalent unit calculation only: candidates are seldom asked to complete the inventory valuation.

III. Three-Step Solution Process

A. The following steps walk you all the way through the process of allocating costs to work-in-process and finished goods for a single factor of production. Since the three factors of production - raw materials, labor, and overhead - do not usually accumulate evenly across the production process, the process must be repeated for each of the three factors of production. The three steps are:

B. **Step 1 --** Determine Equivalent Units

1. Identifying the Physical Flow of Units: Clearly identify the physical flow of units. As units move through the production process, each processing department adds material and conversion costs (i.e., labor, and overhead) to work-in-process. As goods move from department to department through the manufacturing process, these costs accumulate.
2. At the beginning of each period, the units in beginning work-in-process are (by definition) only partially complete. The completion rate for beginning WIP inventory reflects the work done "to date," meaning during the prior period. A different percentage of completion is normally associated with each factor of production. During the period, fully-completed units are transferred to the next department or to finished goods. At the end of the period, the units remaining in ending work-in-process are (by definition) at various stages of completion for each factor of production (i.e., direct materials and conversion costs).
3. The following chart summarizes the flow of physical units through a single department's manufacturing process and identifies the percentage of completion of the beginning and ending WIP inventory. For this chart, assume that the following numbers of units and percentage of completion are given:

> **Study Tip:**
> Process costing questions seldom asks the candidate to go past the first step - calculating the equivalent units of production for one factor of production under either FIFO or the weighted-average cost flow assumption.

		Physical Units	*% of Completion*
+	Units in Beg. WIP	+ 20,000	10%
+	Units Added to Production	+ 30,000	---
=	Total Units to Account for	= 50,000	---
-	Units in Ending WIP	- 10,000	50%
=	Units Transferred to Finished Goods	= 40,000	always 100%

> **Note:**
> This analysis follows the same "account analysis" format used to create the Schedule of Cost of Goods Sold and the Schedule of Cost of Goods Manufactured (see Manufacturing Costs).

4. Calculation of Equivalent Units: The term **equivalent units** refers to the **number of whole units that could have been produced** during the period in terms of cost incurred. For example, the cost associated with six units that are 50% complete is equivalent to the cost associated with three units that are 100% complete.

5. Because the units in beginning and ending work-in-process inventory can be at different percentages of completion in terms of cost, **the number of physical units remaining in ending work-in-process inventory and the units transferred to Finished Goods does not reflect the actual work done**. The fraction of work done on the partially completed units in beginning and ending work-in-process must be taken into account.

6. To solve for the equivalent units of production, first multiply the physical units in beginning WIP by 1-% complete and ending work-in-process by their percentage of completion and enter the result in the Equivalent Units column. Units transferred to finished goods are always at 100% completion (if not, they wouldn't be "finished"), so they may be entered in the Equivalent Units column, too. The candidate must use the logic that % of completion indicates work done "this" period. Accordingly, % of completion for beginning WIP reflects work done "last" period, not "this" period. That's why the complement 1-% complete is used for Beginning inventory.

		Physical Units	*% of Completion*	*Equivalent Units*
+	Units in Beg. WIP	+ 20,000	1 - 10%	**+ 18,000**
+	Units Added to Production	+ 30,000	---	+ ???
=	Total Units to Account for	= 50,000	---	= ???
-	Units in Ending WIP	- 10,000	50%	+ 5,000
=	Units Transferred to Finished Goods	= 40,000	always 100%	**= 40,000**

7. After these adjustments are made, solve for the equivalent units to account for and the equivalent units added to production by working from the bottom to the top.

Note:
The "Total Units to Account for" of 45,000 units here is valid for cost computations using the weighted-average method only. FIFO requires an adjustment to achieve current period only results. "Total Units to Account for" related to FIFO requires that equivalent units related to prior period work on beginning inventory be subtracted from total units to account for shown here so that the calculation includes ONLY current period work, i.e. 43,000 = 45,000 - (.1 * 20,000) units.

		Physical Units	*% of Completion*	*Equivalent Units*
+	Units in Beg. WIP	+ 20,000	1 - 10%	+ 18,000
+	Units Added to Production	+ 30,000	---	+ 27,000
=	Total Units to Account for	= 50,000	---	**= 45,000**
-	Units in Ending WIP	- 10,000	50%	- 5,000
=	Units Transferred to Finished Goods	= 40,000	always 100%	= 40,000

Example:

Calculate the equivalent units of production assuming:

Beginning WIP = 2,000 units, 30% complete

Units started during the period = 6,000 units

Units transferred to Finished Goods = 5,000 units

Ending WIP = 3,000 units, 40% complete

Begin by accumulating the physical unit and percentage of completion information:

		Physical Units	*% of Completion*	*Equivalent Units*
+	Units in Beg. WIP	+ 2,000	1 - 30%	???
+	Units Added to Production	+ 6,000	---	???
=	Total Units to Account for	= 8,000	---	???
-	Units in Ending WIP	- 3,000	40%	???
=	Units Transferred to Finished Goods	= 5,000	always 100%	???

Next, multiply the beginning work-in-process by one minus the percentage of completion and ending work-in-process, and units transferred to finished goods by their percentage of completion:

		Physical Units	*% of Completion*	*Equivalent Units*
+	Units in Beg. WIP	+ 2,000	1 - 30%	**+ 1,400**
+	Units Added to Production	+ 6,000	---	+ ???
=	Total Units to Account for	= 8,000	---	= ???
-	Units in Ending WIP	- 3,000	40%	**+ 1,200**
=	Units Transferred to Finished Goods	= 5,000	always 100%	**= 5,000**

Finally, work from the bottom up to solve for the equivalent units to account for and the equivalent units added to production:

		Physical Units	*% of Completion*	*Equivalent Units*
+	Units in Beg. WIP	+ 2,000	1 - 30%	+ 1,400
+	Units Added to Production	+ 6,000	---	+ 4,800
=	Total Units to Account for	= 8,000	---	**= 6,200**
-	Units in Ending WIP	- 3,000	40%	- 1,200
=	Units Transferred to Finished Goods	= 5,000	always 100%	= 5,000

Deciding which equivalent units number to use: The cost flow assumption determines which equivalent units figure to use:

1. Weighted average cost flow: Under the weighted average method, the prior period costs associated with beginning work-in-process inventory are added to the current period costs (including transfer-in costs, if any) and divided by the total equivalent units produced during the period. This yields the average unit cost of production for the period. In the preceding example, the equivalent units produced number is 6,200 units - **the total (equivalent) units to account for**.

2. FIFO cost flow: Under FIFO, the costs and equivalent units associated with prior period work on beginning work-in-process are transferred to finished goods before any current period unit costs are calculated. Then (although not shown above) the current period costs (including transfer-in costs, if any) are divided by the equivalent units added to production ONLY during the current period. This yields the unit cost of production for the current period. In the preceding example, the total equivalent units produced number for FIFO is 5,600 units - **the (equivalent) units added to production during the current period ONLY, i.e. 5,600 = 6,200 - (.3 * 2,000) units**.

Study Tip:
It is extremely important that you know which equivalent units number is used for FIFO cost flow and which equivalent units number is used for weighted average cost flow. Many questions in this area ask only for the equivalent units to use under FIFO or weighted average cost flow.

C. **Step 2** -- Determine the Cost per Equivalent Unit.

1. First determine the total costs to account for; the following costs are usually accumulated during the period:
   a. **Beginning work-in-process costs --** The total costs of production (material, labor, and overhead) that were allocated to the production units during previous periods.
   b. **Transfer-in costs --** The costs of production (material, labor, and overhead) from previous departments that flow with the production items from department to department.
   c. **Current period costs --** The transfer costs and costs of production (material, labor, and overhead) added to the work-in-process during the current period.
   d. **Total costs to account for --** The total of the beginning work-in-process costs, the transfer-in costs, and the current period costs. Total costs must be allocated to ending work-in-process inventory and to finished goods inventory at the end of the period.
2. The cost flow assumption used impacts which costs are used to determine the unit price:
   a. **Weighted average cost flow --** Under the weighted-average cost flow assumption, the **beginning work-in-process inventory costs are added to the current period costs** (including transfer-in costs, if any) before dividing by the equivalent units figure: this process averages the two cost pools together.
   b. **FIFO cost flow --** Under the FIFO cost flow assumption, the costs associated with prior period work on beginning work-in-process inventory are transferred to finished goods in their entirety. The current period (equivalent) unit cost is determined by dividing the **current period costs (including transfer-in costs, if any)** by the equivalent units added to production during CURRENT the period.

Note:
Regardless of the cost flow assumption, all costs must be allocated either to ending work-in-process inventory or to finished goods.

Example:
Assume that the direct labor costs associated with Beginning Work-in-Process inventory were $640. An additional $2,600 in direct labor costs were added during the period.

What is the total cost to be allocated using the Weighted-Average cost flow assumption? $3,240 - the current period costs of $2,600 plus the $640 of costs associated with beginning work-in-process inventory.

What is the total cost to be allocated using the FIFO cost flow assumption? $2,600 - the current period costs; the $640 of costs associated with beginning work-in-process inventory are transferred to finished goods in their entirety.

3. Calculate the cost per equivalent unit. Once the correct equivalent unit number and total costs to allocate have been determined (based on the specified cost flow assumption), calculation of the equivalent unit cost is straightforward: simply divide the cost to be allocated by the equivalent units.

4.

Example:
Continuing with the previous example, the following information has been collected:

Cost Flow Assumption	*Equivalent Units*	*Costs to Allocate*
Weighted Average	6,200	$3,240
FIFO	5,600	$2,600

What is the unit cost using the Weighted-Average cost flow assumption? $0.5226 per unit

What is the unit cost using the FIFO cost flow assumption? $0.4643 per unit

D. **Step 3 --** Determine (a) cost of goods transferred out of WIP and (b) Ending WIP Inventory.

1. Use the cost per equivalent unit to value the work-in-process and finished goods inventories. To allocate costs to work-in-process ending inventory and finished goods, determine the number of equivalent units in each inventory and multiply that number by the cost per equivalent unit. After the costs have been allocated, total them to ensure that they equal the total costs to account for.

Study Tip:
The examiners rarely ask for a complete calculation of costs using the FIFO method. They do, however, ask for the calculation of current period unit cost or for the denominator used in the calculation of current period unit cost (equivalent unit additions for the period).

Example:
Continuing with the previous example, the following information has been collected:

Cost Flow Assumption	***Costs to Allocate***	***Unit Cost***
Weighted Average	$3,240	$0.5226
FIFO	$2,600	$0.4643

	Ending WIP	***Finished Goods***
Equivalent units (from Step 1):	1,200 E.U.	4,400 E.U.

What is the total cost allocated to Ending Work-in-Process inventory and to Finished Goods using the Weighted-Average cost flow assumption?

	Ending WIP	***Finished Goods***
Equivalent units (from Step 1):	1,200	5,000
Unit Cost (from Step 2):	X $0.5226	X $0.5226
Inventory allocations (rounded):	$627	$2,613

Total costs allocated = $3,240

What is the total cost allocated to Ending Work-in-Process inventory and to Finished Goods using the FIFO cost flow assumption?

	Ending WIP	***Finished Goods***
Equivalent units (from Step 1):	1,200	4,400*
Unit Cost (from Step 2):	X $0.4643	X $0.4643
Inventory allocations	$557	$2,043
Beginning WIP Inventory		+ $640
		$2,683

Total costs allocated = $3,240

** 5,000 units transferred to F.G - 600 E.U. associated with Prior Period Beginning WIP inventory*

IV. Normal and Abnormal Spoilage

A. **Normal Spoilage --** occurs as a result of normal operating procedures and cannot be avoided under current technological conditions. Examples include evaporation, shrinkage of material, scrap, and conversion waste. Thus, 100 yards of fabric may *normally* yield only 88 yards of good clothing; and 20 tons of ore may yield only 15 tons of iron.

B. **Abnormal Spoilage --** is the result of an unplanned or accidental event such as an out-of-control process, worker error in production, or some other uncontrollable experience such as a power outage. Under routine conditions, abnormal spoilage is considered avoidable.

C. **Accounting treatment of spoilage --** differs based on whether the spoilage is normal or abnormal. Since normal spoilage is considered unavoidable, its cost is spread over the production of good units. The cost of abnormal spoilage is usually removed from the costing system and treated as a period cost such as other income/expense.

D. **For Job Costing --** unless traceable to a job, the cost of normal spoilage is spread equally across all jobs that are being produced. Spoilage that is caused by the customer may be charged to the customer in the form of additional revenue. For example, a customer ordered custom business cards but decided to add additional phone numbers after the order was complete.

E. **For Process Costing --** the cost of spoilage is typically separately accounted for by process or department. Like job costing treatment, normal spoilage is spread over the good units produced, while abnormal spoilage is removed from the costing system and treated as a period cost (usually other income/expense). However, unique to process costing, the point at which the spoilage occurs can determine how much cost is attributed to spoilage. This can potentially change the amount based on the completion percentage to which costs were already added when the units were determined as ruined. Only the costs added are lost. If the units are 100% complete when they are determined to be ruined then all of the cost of a whole unit is attributed to each. The CPA exam usually treats units as 100% spoiled when removed from production. This simplifies the accounting for the equivalent units.

Joint & By-Product Costing

Joint cost allocation problems occur whenever multiple products are produced from a single manufacturing process. Joint product processes often yield by-products and scrap. Since the allocation of the joint costs is a relatively simple process, CPA exam questions focus on the treatment of by-products and scrap as much as on the joint costing process.

I. **Joint products and by-products are similar --** in that they are both the result of a single manufacturing process that yields multiple products. They both face the accounting problem of allocation of the shared costs of production. Two or more products of *significant sales value* are said to be joint products when they:

   A. Are produced from the same set of raw materials; and

   B. Are not separately identifiable until a *split-off point.*

II. **Joint products frequently receive further processing after the split-off point**

   A. **Split-off --** Is the point at which products manufactured through a common process are differentiated and processed separately.

   B. **Separable costs --** Are additional processing costs incurred beyond the split-off point. Separable costs are attributable to individual products and can be assigned directly.

   C. **Cost Allocation --** Joint costs may be allocated to the joint products in several ways:

      1. **Relative Physical Volume --** Costs are allocated based on the quantity of products produced. The total volume of all products is established (pounds, feet, gallons, etc.), each product's pro-rata share is determined, and the joint costs are allocated based on that proportion.

Question:
Joint costs to be allocated: $300,000

	Volume	Proportion	Allocation
Product A	10,000 gal.	________	________
Product B	30,000 gal.	________	________
Product C	40,000 gal.	________	________

Answer:

	Volume	Proportion	Allocation
Product A	10,000 gal.	12.5%	$37,500
Product B	30,000 gal.	37.5%	$112,500
Product C	40,000 gal.	50.0%	$150,000
TOTAL	80,000 gal.	100.0%	$300,000

2. **Relative Sales Value at Split-Off --** Costs are allocated based on the relative sales values of the products either at split-off or after additional processing. When significant markets exist for the products at the split-off point, the relative sales value of each product at the split-off point can be used to allocate costs.

Question:
Joint costs to be allocated: $200,000

	Relative Value	Proportion	Allocation
Product A	$40,000	______	______
Product B	$10,000	______	______
Product C	$50,000	______	______

Answer:

	Relative Value	Proportion	Allocation
Product A	$40,000	40%	$80,000
Product B	$10,000	10%	$20,000
Product C	$50,000	50%	$100,000
TOTAL	$100,000	100%	$200,000

3. **Net Realizable Value --** Often used when there is no market at split-off, the NRV method uses the ratio of the net realizable value of each product (i.e., final sales value *less any additional separable processing costs* of each product) to the total net realizable value to allocate costs.

Question:
Joint costs to be allocated: $200,000

	Ultimate Sales Value	Add'l Costs Beyond Split	Net Realizable Value	Proportion	Allocation
Product A	$ 25,000	$0	______	______	______
Product B	$135,000	$35,000	______	______	______
Product C	$100,000	$25,000	______	______	______

Answer:

	Ultimate Sales Value	Add'l Costs Beyond Split	Net Realizable Value	Proportion	Allocation
Product A	$ 25,000	$0	$25,000	12.5%	$25,000
Product B	$135,000	$35,000	$100,000	50.0%	$100,000
Product C	$100,000	$25,000	$75,000	37.5%	$75,000

III. By-Products -- By-products differ from joint products in that they have relatively insignificant sales value when compared to the main product(s).

- **A. Costing --** Because of their relatively insignificant sales value, by-products usually are not allocated a share of the joint costs of production. However, when by-products are processed beyond split-off, the additional processing costs are assigned to the by-product. These costs reduce the proceeds ultimately recognized from the sale of the by-product.
- **B. Net proceeds from the sale of by-products --** Are sometimes used to reduce the cost of the main products.
- **C. Proceeds --** May be recognized in several ways:
  1. **Recognize when produced --** The ultimate sales value of the by-product (less any additional costs necessary to sell the by-product) is deducted from the joint cost of the main products *produced* when the by-product is *produced*. This method is preferable as it automatically allocates the cost reductions to Cost of Goods Sold and Ending Inventory.
  2. **Recognize when sold --** When the by-product value is recognized at the time of sale, the net proceeds can be recorded as other revenue, other income, or as a reduction in cost of goods sold.

IV. Scrap -- Scrap is a remnant of the production process which has some, but typically comparatively little recovery value. Scrap is seldom processed beyond the split-off point.

- **A.** The net proceeds from the sale of scrap are used to reduce overhead costs (credit to Factory Overhead Control) or, if material, the sale can be recorded as revenue.

Service Cost Allocation

Service costs come from departments that indirectly support the manufacturing process. They often support other service departments as well. When allocating service costs to production departments, this mutual support becomes problematic. Several methods of allocating service costs exist, but the one usually tested on the CPA exam is the step allocation method. This method, though simple in concept, is computationally intensive, can be very time-consuming, and is a source of frustration to many students. Since the topic is very lightly tested on the exam (perhaps only one question every three or four exams), students who are pressed for time could skim or skip this section without unduly compromising their exam performance.

I. Service Departments and Service Costs

A. Service departments are not directly involved in the manufacturing process, but provide services to departments that are directly involved in the manufacturing process. Custodial services, physical plant maintenance, and personnel are examples of service departments.

B. Since many of the services provided by service departments are essential to the manufacturing process, it is reasonable to attempt to allocate their costs to products. This is accomplished by first allocating the service costs to the production departments. The production departments then allocate their costs, including the costs charged to them by the service departments, to the products.

C. Service cost allocation is complicated by the fact that **service departments frequently provide services to other service departments**. These **reciprocal services** complicate the cost allocation process because when costs are allocated from one service department to another, they create additional cost for the recipient service department, which must then be allocated to other departments, including other service departments.

II. Service Cost Allocation Methods

A. Several methods are used to allocate service costs:

1. **Direct method --** This method **allocates service department costs only to production departments** based on each department's use of the service relative to other *production* departments. This method has the advantage of simplicity but achieves it only at the cost of accuracy. By allocating costs only to production departments, the direct method ignores the sometimes significant reciprocal services that one service department provides for another and potentially distorts the cost allocation.

   a. The direct method is not usually tested on the CPA exam.

2. **Reciprocal method --** This method fully accounts for reciprocal services among service departments by developing a series of equations describing the service departments' relationships with each other and with the production departments. The equations are then solved simultaneously to create a set of equations that can be used to allocate costs. This method has the advantage of accuracy but can be complex to develop and use.

   a. The reciprocal method is not usually tested on the CPA exam.

3. **Step-Down allocation method --** This method allocates service costs to both service departments and production departments but limits the number of reciprocal services that are allocated. As such, the step-down allocation method provides a compromise between the overly-simple direct method and the overly-complex reciprocal method: it is a more accurate method than the direct method but is less accurate than the reciprocal method.

   a. The step-down allocation method is the most common service cost allocation method tested on the CPA exam.

III. Step-Down Allocation Method

A. Under the step-down allocation method, service costs are distributed to other service departments and to production departments in a specified sequence.

Note:
on the CPA exam, dollar value of services provided is often used to determine allocation sequence, with the highest dollar value service department allocated first.

1. The allocation sequence is most often determined by starting with the department that provides the greatest amount of services to other service departments and cascading until all service costs are allocated to production departments.
2. Any type of allocation base can be used to distribute the costs (square footage, materials used, number of employees, etc.) but the allocation base should (ideally) have some relationship to the service provided.
3. With step-down method, once a service department's costs have been allocated, no other costs can be allocated back to it.

Example:
Creekside Construction Products produces modular roof components for the housing industry. It has three service departments and two production departments with costs and allocation base information as shown below:

	Personnel	Janitorial	Maintenance	Cutting	Forming	Total
Costs	$360,000	$210,000	$96,000	$400,000	$534,000	$1,600,000
# employees	120	70	280	630	420	1,520
Square feet	10,000	20,000	40,000	80,000	200,000	350,000
Machine hours	---	---	---	30,000	60,000	90,000

The costs are allocated in the following order:

Personnel - based on the number of employees

Janitorial - based on the square footage

Maintenance - Based on machine hours.

B. **Steps in the allocation process --** The allocation process proceeds as follows:

1. Use the allocation base to determine the percentage of costs to be allocated to the departments.

a. When calculating the allocation percentages, only consider the allocation base units of the departments remaining to receive allocated costs.

b. The total of the allocation percentages should always be 100%.

2. Multiply the costs to be allocated by the allocation base proportional percentage to determine each department's allocation.

a. Sum all of the individual allocations to ensure that the all of the costs have been distributed.

3. Add the newly allocated costs to each service department's previous cost accumulation to determine the total costs to be allocated when processing in the sequence to allocate additional service departments' costs.

C. The steps in the allocation process repeat until all of the service costs have been allocated to production departments.

D. **Solution**

1. **Step 1 - Calculate the allocation percentages**

a. **Personnel --** Allocate to Janitorial, Maintenance, Cutting, and Forming based on number of employees.

Department	Allocation Base Units	Allocation Percentage
Janitorial	70	5%
Maintenance	280	20%
Cutting	630	45%
Forming	420	30%
Total	1,400	100%

b. **Janitorial --** Allocate to Maintenance, Cutting, and Forming based on square footage.

Department	Allocation Base Units	Allocation Percentage
Maintenance	40,000	12.5%
Cutting	80,000	25.0%
Forming	200,000	62.5%
Total	320,000	100%

c. **Maintenance --** Allocate to Cutting and Forming based on machine hours.

Department	Allocation Base Units	Allocation Percentage
Cutting	30,000	1/3
Forming	60,000	2/3
Total	90,000	3/3

2. **Steps 2 and 3 --** Calculate the allocation amounts and add to each department's cumulative costs

	Personnel	Janitorial	Maintenance	Cutting	Forming	Total
Costs	$360,000	$210,000	$96,000	$400,000	$534,000	$1,600,000
Personnel Allocation:		*5%*	*20%*	*45%*	*30%*	*100%*
Allocated Costs	($360,000)	$18,000	$72,000	$162,000	$108,000	Updated Costs
Updated Costs	Updated Costs	$228,000	$168,000	$562,000	$642,000	$1,600,000
Janitorial Allocation:			*12.5%*	*25.0%*	*62.5%*	*100%*
Allocated Costs		($228,000)	$28,500	$57,000	$142,500	$0
Updated Costs	$0	$0	$196,500	$619,000	$784,500	$1,600,000
Maintenance Allocation:				1/3	2/3	3/3
Allocated Costs			($196,500)	$65,500	$131,000	$0
Updated Costs	$0	$0	$0	$684,500	$915,500	$1,600,000

Planning and Control

Introduction

I. **Topics --** The topics in the Planning and Control section include some of the most heavily tested and computationally complex material in the Planning & Measurement section of BEC. Fortunately, these two characteristics do not usually overlap: the most heavily tested topics are not the most computationally complex topics.

II. **Heavily Tested --** The most heavily tested topic in this section is Cost-Volume-Profit (Breakeven) Analysis. Two or three questions on this topic are found on almost every exam. There are usually one or two questions from each of the Budgeting, Forecasting, and Responsibility Accounting topics. The most computationally complex topics in this section are the two variance analysis topics. Overhead variance analysis is tested very lightly - perhaps one question every two or three exams. Sales and direct cost variances (direct material and direct labor variances) are tested more regularly - usually one question per exam - but the questions are typically conceptual and do not require any calculations.

Budgeting

Budgeting is a fundamental tool for planning and control. The budget process produces a series of related budgets that culminate in the master budget, the overall plan of operation for the organization. The budget topics emphasized on the CPA exam are relatively narrow. The difference between static budgets (i.e., a master budget) and flexible budgets is the most consistently tested area. Questions about other types of budgets and occasional detailed questions about budget calculations do appear, but for candidates with limited preparation time a quick review of master budget and flexible budget terminology and of the cash effects of increases and decreases in receivables and payables will probably suffice.

I. **The master budget --** is a comprehensive plan for the overall activities of a company. The master budget is developed for a **specified level of activity**: it is a **static budget** . A static budget is a budget that does not change when actual sales differ from planned sales.

II. **The master budget is composed of several coordinated parts**

   A. **Operating budget --** The operating budget forecasts the results of operations: sales, production expenses, and selling and administrative expenses. The principal budgets found within the operating budget are:

      1. Sales budget;
      2. Production budget;
      3. Production cost budgets (Direct Materials, Labor, and Overhead budgets);
      4. Selling and Administrative Expense budget.

   B. **Financial budget --** The financial budget forecasts cash flows and projects the financial statements that will result from operations. The financial budget consists of the:

      1. Cash budget;
      2. Budgeted (or pro-forma) income statement;
      3. Budgeted (or pro-forma) balance sheet.

   C. **Capital Expenditures budget --** The capital expenditures budget projects expenditures related to the acquisition or construction of capital (fixed) assets. Since acquisition of capital assets often requires an extended planning horizon, the capital expenditures budget often spans multiple fiscal periods.

Study Tip:
To the extent the questions on the CPA exam address specific budgets as opposed to the master budget and the flexible budget, the budgets most frequently tested are the Sales Budget, the Production Budget, and the Cash Budget.

III. **Budgeting Process**

   A. **Operating Budget**

      1. **Sales Forecast --** The budgeting process begins with a **sales forecast**. The sales forecast is based on information obtained from both internal and external sources and provides estimates of sales in dollars and in units. These estimates flow forward to the sales budget.

      2. **Sales Budget --** The sales budget forecasts **planned sales in dollars and in units**, usually on a monthly or quarterly basis. The production budget and many of the items in the selling and administrative expenses budget are based on information from the sales budget.

3. **Production Budget --** The production budget projects the **production quantities needed to support sales and provide for the specified quantity of ending inventory**. Its projections are based on unit sales information from the sales budget, current inventory levels, and desired ending inventory levels. The data from the production budget flows forward to the production costs budgets.
4. **Production Costs Budgets --** A budget is prepared for each of the three factors of production: a **Direct Materials budget, a Labor budget, and an Overhead budget**. The budgets are based on unit production information provided by the Production Budget and, for direct materials, information about current and desired ending inventory levels. The data from the production costs budgets flow forward to the cash budget.
5. **Selling and Administrative Expense Budget --** The selling and administrative expense budget lists the budget expenses for areas outside of manufacturing. Although some items on this budget are tied to the sales budget, most of the information comes from individual department managers as approved by management or by use of the percentage of sales method. The percentage of sales method **determines the expense amount by expressing the expense as a "percentage of sales."** The percentage of sales method is also used in the cash budget to estimate the amount of cash sales.

B. **Financial Budgets**

1. **Cash Budget --** The cash budget projects cash receipts, cash disbursements, and ending cash balance by analyzing:
    a. **Anticipated operating receipts --** Information is derived from the Sales Budget, and from historical information about customer payment characteristics; the principal items of information include:
        i. Cash sales;
        ii. credit sales and accounts receivable collections.
    b. **Anticipated operating expenditures --** Estimates of expenditures are derived from the Production Costs Budgets, the Selling and Administrative Expense Budget and from the company's vendor and employee payment policies; the principal items of information include:
        i. Costs and expenses;
        ii. Purchases on account and accounts payable disbursements.
    c. **Anticipated capital expenditures --** The Capital Expenditures Budget provides information on planned expenditures for capital assets.
2. **Financing and investing activities --** Based on minimum cash balance requirements specified by management, the amount of cash that must be borrowed or may be invested is determined.

Exam Hint: Cash budget questions appear frequently on the exam and often include analysis of the cash effects of increases and/or decreases in receivables and payables. The following matrix summarizes these effects:

Cash Effect of Changes in Receivables and Payables

	Receivables	**Payables**
Decrease	*Cash Increases*	*Cash Decreases*
Increase	*Cash Decreases*	*Cash Increases*

Question:
Browning Company anticipates cash sales of $300,000 and cash expenditures of $220,000 this month. Browning also expects that its Accounts Receivable and Accounts Payable balances will decrease by $50,000 and $40,000, respectively. If Browning's current cash balance is $150,000, what is its projected cash balance at the end of the month?

Answer:

+ Current Cash Balance	+	$150,000
+ Cash Sales	+	$300,000
- Cash Expenditures	-	$220,000
+ Decrease in A/R	+	$50,000
- Decrease in A/P	-	$40,000
= Projected Ending Cash Balance	=	$240,000

3. **Budgeted Financial Statements (Pro-forma Income Statement and Pro-forma Balance Sheet) --** The budgeted financial statements use information from the Operating Budgets, the Cash Budget, and the Capital Expenditures Budget to project the results of operation and financial position at the end of the period.

IV. Production/Purchases Budgets

A. Production/purchases budgets are common to the CPA exam. The following example provides a set of two questions that are the most common to those asked about production and purchase budgets. When illustrating how to solve these problems we use the cost of goods sold/cost of goods manufactured statements. These statements are something that each candidate should already know. If so, then learning new budgeting statement formats are unnecessary.

B. The production budget must be done first. The production budget establishes how many units must be produced to achieve projected sales volume and inventory level targets. These targets can be modeled quantitatively without using costs. This is why in the statement below you see that the "cost" designations have been eliminated (i.e., to reflect only units). Once production volume is established (usually the objective of the production budget question), then the materials budget can be constructed.

C. Once the production budget has been completed, based on the production needed (in units), an appropriate number of material units must be purchased to satisfy the production required. This is the connection between the production budget and the purchases budget and is reflected by the arrows shown on the left side of the statement below.

D. Sometimes these budgets require dollar values that follow the units required to be produced and purchased. This is not a problem if the unit flows have been properly followed. Then all that is required is to value those units based on the costs per unit given in the question data.

Example: In calculating production and purchases budgets, use what you already know. There's no point to creating a new format for the budget that's different from the CGS/CGM format - just find the answer!

Sales budget in units	
January	70
February	90
March	50
April	60

	January	February	March
Beg. Inv – Finished	27	27	
CM = Production	(70)	78	
Goods Available	97	105	
– Ending Inv - Finished	27	15	
Goods Sold	70	90	50
		(.3*90)	(.3*50)
Beg. Inv – Direct	-0-	10	
+ Direct material	150	(156)	
Direct materials	150	166	
– Ending Inv – Direct	10	10	
Direct Materials Used	140	156	
	(70*2)	(78*2)	

Beginning inventory for the year is 27 units. Ending inventory for each month should be 30% of the next month's sales.

a. 106

b. 90

c. **70**

d. 78

How many units of direct material (DM) should the company purchase in February if each FG unit takes 2 units of DM, and they have no beginning inventory in January and they want to maintain an inventory of 10 DM units?

a. 90

b. 106

c. 73

d. **156**

V. Other Budgets and Terms

A. Participative Budgets -- allow subordinates to participate in establishing budget targets. Widely considered a positive behavioral approach, participative budgeting can (1) increase the accuracy of the budget by providing additional information that subordinates bring to the table, and (2) participation can increase perceptions of ownership of the budget targets on behalf of the subordinates.

B. **Strategic Budgeting --** implies a long-range view to planning based on the identification of action plans to achieve the company's goals, and ultimately its mission. Many issues are considered including a comprehensive internal and external analysis, competitive and economic analysis, and an assessment of various types of risk. Note that strategic budgets are easy to detect since terminology is always oriented to the "big-picture" (e.g., long-range, inside and outside the organization, large investments, economics, competitive opportunities/threats, assessment of distinctive competencies, market risks).

> **Note:**
> Strategic budgeting has become a more popular term in recent years. This may increase the likelihood of seeing more questions on this topic on future exams.

C. **A Rolling Budget --** is an incremental budget that adds the current period and drops the oldest period. *Kaizen* (continuous improvement) type companies typically use rolling budgets and de-emphasize past performance in budgeting since results are "expected" to continuously improve.

D. **Zero-Base Budgeting --** is a process of starting over each budget period and justifying each item budgeted. This requires additional work over an incremental approach but may provide more accuracy. This process forces managers to carefully think about their expenditures in hopes of reducing or eliminating the cost of unnecessary items.

E. **Budgetary Slack --** is where managers attempt to build in a cushion for spending and revenue in case targets are not met. The use of slack results in a conservative budget as opposed to the most probable or accurate budget. The risk of managers building slack into their budgets is increased where budget targets are used in evaluation of individual performance and incentive compensation.

VI. Flexible Budget

A. Unlike the master budget, a flexible budget **adjusts revenues and some costs** when actual sales volume is different from planned sales volume. This makes it easier to analyze actual performance because the actual revenues and costs can be compared to the expected revenues and costs at **the actual level of sales activity**. The following adjustments are typical:

1. Revenue is adjusted by multiplying the new quantity times the sales price;
2. Total variable costs are adjusted by multiplying the new quantity times the variable cost per unit;
3. Total fixed costs remain the same as long as volume remains within a relevant range, which is normally the case on CPA exam questions.

Example:

Grenwich's master budget anticipated the following revenues, costs, and net income related to a lawn sprinkler they produce:

Master Budget

Sales (10,000 units @ $15 per unit)	$150,000
Variable manufacturing costs ($5 per unit)	- 50,000
Variable selling & administrative costs ($1 per unit)	- 10,000
Contribution margin	$ 90,000
Fixed manufacturing costs ($2 per unit)	- 20,000
Fixed selling & administrative costs	- 20,000
Operating Income	$ 50,000

If actual sales and production are 12,000 units, what would a flexible budget look like?

Flexible Budget

Sales (12,000 units @ $15 per unit)	$180,000
Variable manufacturing costs ($5 per unit)	- 60,000
Variable selling & administrative costs ($1 per unit)	- 12,000
Contribution margin	$108,000
Fixed manufacturing costs	- 20,000
Fixed selling & administrative costs (total does not change)	- 20,000
Operating Income	$ 68,000

B. **Differences between the flexible budget and the master budget** are known as **sales activity variances** or **volume variances.**

Forecasting Techniques

Forecasting tools assist with the budgeting and planning process by attempting to predict the results of events that occur under uncertain conditions. The fundamental techniques used in this area concern probability theory: expected values, correlation, and regression analysis. The area is consistently tested on the exam - there are usually one or two questions from this topic on every exam. Quantitative questions are sometimes used to test expected value concepts, but questions about correlation and regression occur more frequently and are tested at the conceptual level.

I. Probability and Expected Value

A. Probability analysis is used to determine the likelihood of a specific event occurring when several outcomes are possible. A probability for each outcome is assessed. The probability of a **particular outcome is always between 0 and 1 (never and always)**. The sum of the probabilities associated with the possible outcomes is always 1. (A sum less than one indicates that an outcome has been omitted from the analysis or a probability has been improperly assessed.)

B. The **expected value** is the **long-run average outcome**. Expected value is determined by calculating the **weighted average of the outcomes**: multiply the value of each outcome by its probability and then sum the results.

Study Tip:
Always check to ensure that your probabilities total 100% (or 1, if you're using decimals to represent probabilities). Questions such as this one that state the probability of one event (e.g., the product sells) but do not explicitly mention the second event (e.g., the product doesn't sell) are very common.

Example:
The useful life of a machine is not known, but there is a 20% probability of a 5-year life, a 50% probability of a 6-year life and a 30% probability of a 7-year life. What is the expected life of the machine?

Years Life		Probability		Expected Value
5	X	.2	=	1.0 years
6	X	.5	=	3.0 years
7	X	.3	=	2.1 years
		1		6.1 years expected life

Question:
Gensco Corp. is preparing to develop a new product that requires an investment of $500,000. Gensco believes that if it develops the product there is a 75% chance that it will be able to sell the product to a manufacturer at a profit of $1,000,000. Legal issues are such that if it is unable to sell the product at this price, it will not sell the product at all. What is the expected value of the project?

Answer:

	Profit/Loss	Probability	Expected Value
Profit if product sells:	$1,000,000	75%	$750,000
Loss if product fails to sell	($500,000)	25%	($125,000)
Expected Value		100%	$625,000

II. Joint Probability

A. Joint probability is the probability of an event occurring given that another event has already occurred. The joint probability is determined by multiplying the probability of the first event by the conditional probability of the second event.

B. CPA exam questions often use joint probability calculations to assess the likelihood of a particular combination of events occurring (this technique is frequently used in auditing to assess the likelihood of error occurrence). To calculate the probability of a specific combination of events from a set of event combinations:

1. For each combination of events, multiple the probability of the first event by the conditional probability of the second event;
2. Sum the results for all the event combinations;
3. Divide each result for each event combination by the total of all the event combinations to determine the probability of a particular event combination occurring;
4. Sum the probabilities for each event combination to ensure that the total is 1 (or 100%).

Question:

The following information pertains to three order processing centers operated by the Deming Co.:

Office	Percentage of orders handled	Percentage of errors
Northwest	30%	4%
Central	50%	2%
South	20%	8%

If an error is made, what is the likelihood that it will be made in the Central Office?

Answer:

Office	Percentage of orders handled	Percentage of errors	Combined rate	Divide individual rate by total		Probability of error
Northwest	.30	.04	.012	.012/.038	=	.316
Central	.50	.02	.010	.010/.038	=	.263
South	.20	.08	.016	.016/.038	=	.421
	1.00		.038			1.000

Given that an error is made, there is a 26.3% chance that the error will be at the Central Office.

III. Variance Analysis -- Variance analysis measures the **dispersion of values around the expected value** (the **mean** or **average value**).

A. The **smaller the variance**, the **more tightly clustered** the observations around the expected value.

B. Smaller variances are usually associated with less risk.

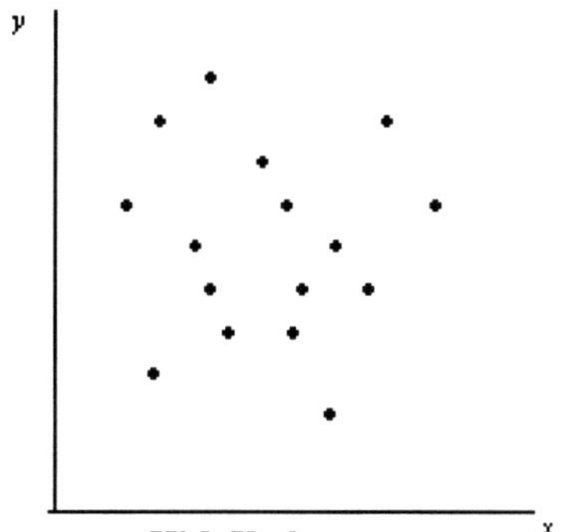

IV. Correlation Analysis

A. Correlation analysis measures the strength of the relationship between two or more variables: a dependent variable (a value that changes in response to changes in related values) and one or more independent variables (values that change, but not in response to changes in other variables in the equation). The **correlation coefficient (R)** measures the **strength of the relationship** between the dependent and independent variable. The correlation coefficient can have **values from -1 to 1** where:

1. 1 indicates perfect positive correlation (as x increases, so does y),
2. -1 indicates perfect negative correlation (as x increases, y decreases), and
3. 0 indicates no correlation (you cannot predict the value of y from the value of x)

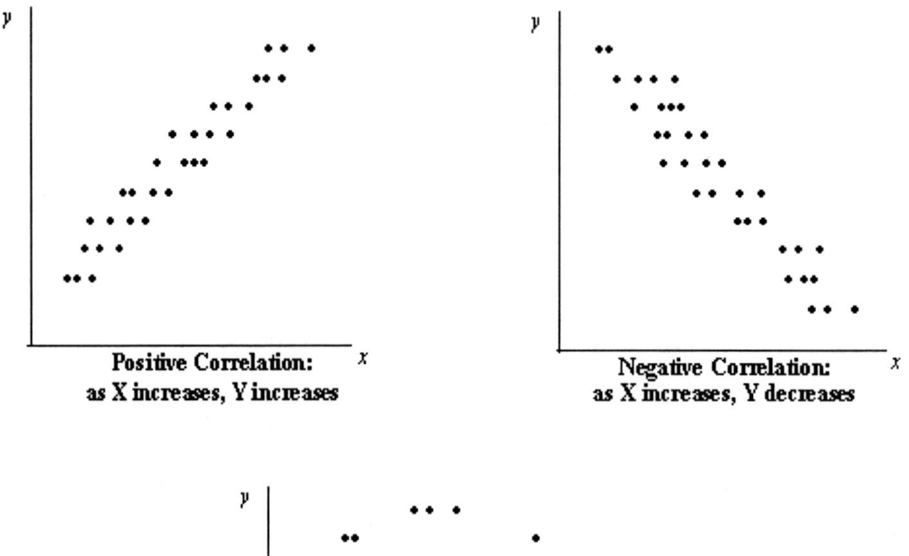

B.

Study Tip:
Be sure to understand the relationship between the Coefficient of Determination (R^2) and the Correlation Coefficient (R). The examiners frequently ask questions about these two measures.

C. The **coefficient of determination (R^2 -- R-squared)** indicates the degree to which the behavior of the independent variable predicts the dependent variable. The coefficient of determination is calculated by squaring the correlation coefficient. R^2 can take on **values from 0 to 1**.

1. The closer R^2 is to 1, the **better the independent variable predicts the behavior of the dependent variable**.

Question:
Bates Company has evaluated two activities for consideration as cost drivers for several manufacturing costs. Regression analysis has produced the following results:

Activity A:		Activity B:	
Y-Intercept:	60	Y-Intercept:	35
B:	4.20	B:	3.5
R^2	.81	R^2	.65

Choose the activity which best predicts the manufacturing costs and construct the regression equation:

Answer:
Activity A with an R^2 of .81 is the best predictor: Y = 60 + 4.2X

V. Regression Analysis

A. Regression analysis predicts the value of one factor (the dependent variable) based on the value of one or more other factors (the independent variables).

1. **Simple Regression --** A regression with one independent variable.
2. **Multiple Regression --** A regression with several independent variables.

B. Linear regression analysis is frequently used in cost accounting to evaluate the strength of the relationship between costs and cost drivers. Regression analysis **does *not* establish cause and effect - it merely indicates a relationship**.

Study Tip:
Regression analysis is a consistently tested area on the CPA exam, with one or two questions appearing on virtually every exam. Questions are not difficult and are usually confined to defining elements in the regression equation and evaluating the significance of values for the Correlation Coefficient (R) and/or the Coefficient of Determination (R^2).

C. Regression Equation -- The relationship between the dependent and independent variables is expressed in the regression equation, which takes the following form:

y = A + Bx

where:

y = dependent variable

A = the y intercept

B = the slope of the line

x = independent variable

1. The regression equation can be shown graphically:

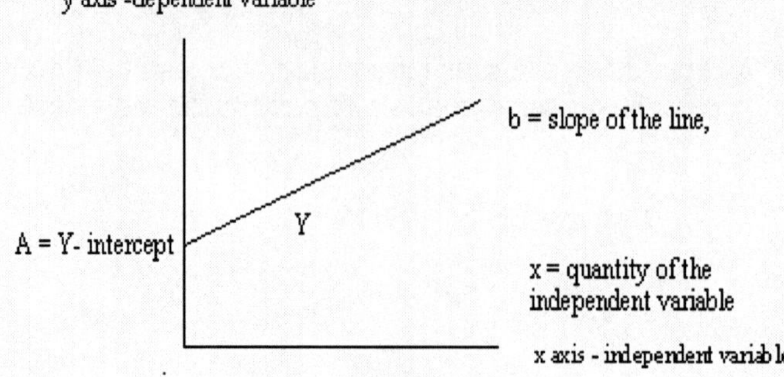

D. **Cost Equation** -- The relationship between fixed costs, variable costs, and total costs can be expressed in the regression equation:

y = A + Bx

where:

y = Total Costs (dependent variable)

A = Fixed Costs (the y intercept)

B = Variable Cost per Unit (the slope of the line)

x = Number of Units (independent variable)

OR

Total Costs = Fixed Costs + (Variable Cost Per Unit * Number of Units)

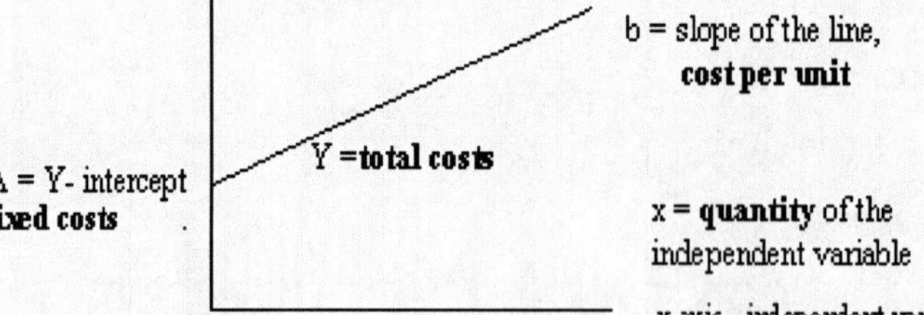

Breakeven Analysis

Cost-volume-profit analysis - also known as breakeven analysis - uses the concepts of cost behavior to determine the sales revenues, quantities, or prices necessary to achieve a specified level of profitability. Cost-volume-profit analysis is one of the most consistently and heavily tested areas in the Planning and Measurement section of the CPA exam. Fortunately, virtually all quantitative questions in this area can be answered using one of the two contribution margin approach formulas discussed in this section. Be sure to memorize and practice using these two formulas!

I. Cost-Volume-Profit (Breakeven) Analysis

A. Breakeven is defined as the sales level at which sales revenues exactly offset total costs, both fixed and variable. Note that total costs include period costs (selling and administrative costs) as well as product (manufacturing) costs. The breakeven point is usually expressed in sales units or in sales dollars.

B. **Basic formula --** This formula provides the definition of breakeven. All other formulas can be derived from this basic formula.

(Quantity X Sales Price) = Fixed Costs + (Quantity X Variable Costs per unit)

C. It is, however, generally more difficult to use than the contribution margin approach formulas discussed below and is not recommended for use on CPA exam questions.

II. Using the Contribution Margin per Unit Approach to Calculate Breakeven in Units

A. The contribution margin represents the **portion of revenues which are available to cover fixed costs**. It is calculated as follows :

Sales Revenue - Variable Costs = Contribution Margin

B. The contribution margin can be expressed on a per unit basis:

Sales Price per Unit - Variable Costs per Unit = Contribution Margin per Unit

C. Since the contribution margin per unit represents the amount that the sale of an individual unit contributes to covering fixed costs, it provides an easy way to calculate the number of units necessary to break even:

Example:
Consider an item with a unit sales price of $1.50 and a variable cost per unit of $1.00. The unit contribution margin is $0.50 per unit ($1.50 - $1.00). If fixed costs are $5,000, then we know that we have to sell 10,000 units in order to cover fixed costs and break even ($5,000 / $0.50)

The following formula expresses this relationship:

Breakeven Point in Units = Total Fixed Costs / Contribution Margin per Unit

Study Tip:
CPA exam questions frequently require you to calculate the unit sales price and variable costs by dividing total sales revenue and total variable costs by the number of units sold. If you are given total dollars, be sure to look for the number of units sold. You may also need to separately identify total variable costs and fixed costs.

Question:
Markson Corporation posted sales of $2,000,000 on a sales volume of 50,000 units. Total costs were $1,700,000, of which $800,000 were fixed costs. What is the breakeven point in units?

Answer:

Sales price per unit:$2,000,000 / 50,000 =	+ $40
Variable cost per unit:($1,700,000 - 800,000) / 50,000	= $18
Contribution margin per unit	= $22

Breakeven point in units:$800,000 / $22 = 36,364 units

III. Using the Contribution Margin per Unit Approach to Calculate Breakeven in Sales Dollars

A. If unit information is available, breakeven point in sales dollars can easily be calculated by calculating the breakeven point in units and then multiplying the number of units by the sales price per unit.

Question:
Parker Corporation sells a product for $15. Variable costs per unit are $5. Fixed costs are $700,000. What is Parker's breakeven point in sales dollars?

Answer:
Contribution margin per unit: $15 - $5 = $10

Breakeven point in units = $700,000/ $10 = 70,000 units

Breakeven point in sales dollars = 70,000 * $15 = $1,050,000

IV. Using the Contribution Margin Ratio Approach to Calculate Breakeven in Sales Dollars

A. Sometimes no unit sales price or unit variable cost information is available. In these cases, it is not possible to calculate the breakeven point in units. It is, however, still possible to calculate the breakeven point in sales dollars, but a slightly different approach must be used.

B. When no unit information is available, but total sales revenue, total variable costs, and total fixed costs are known, the breakeven point in sales dollars can be determined by calculating the contribution margin ratio. The contribution margin ratio represents the **percentage of each sales dollar that is available to cover fixed costs.**

C. For example, if total sales are $100 and variable costs are $40, then the contribution margin is $60. This means that for every $100 of sales, $60 is available to cover fixed costs.

D. If we **express the contribution margin as a ratio (or percentage) of sales dollars**, then we can say that 60% ($60/$100) of each sales dollar is available to cover fixed costs. If total fixed costs are $300, then we can calculate the number of sales dollars necessary to cover fixed costs and break even as:

(Breakeven Sales * 60%) - $300 fixed costs=	$0
Breakeven Sales * 60%=	$300
Breakeven Sales=	$300 / .60
Breakeven Sales=	$500

E. To check to see if the answer is correct, verify that when variable costs and fixed costs are deducted from Breakeven Sales, the Net Income is zero:

+ Breakeven Sales	+	$500	100%
- Variable Costs	-	$200	40%
= Contribution Margin	=	$300	60%
- Fixed Costs	-	$300	
= Net Income	=	$0	

F. The contribution margin per unit formula used to calculate breakeven in units can be modified to calculate breakeven in sales dollars using the contribution margin ratio as follows:

Breakeven Point in Sales Dollars = Total Fixed Costs / Contribution Margin Ratio

...where

Contribution Margin Ratio = Contribution Margin / Sales Revenue

Question:
Given the following facts, calculate breakeven in sales dollars:

Sales Revenue: $120,000
Variable Costs: $90,000
Fixed Costs: $40,000

Answer:

Breakeven Point in Sales Dollars = $40,000 : 25% *

Breakeven Point in Sales Dollars = $160,000

....where

* Contribution Margin Ratio = $120,000 - $90,000 : $120,000

= $30,000 :$120,000

=25%

V. An alternative way of looking at the contribution margin ratio

A. Although the calculations are the same, many people find that using common-size income statement format to calculate the contribution margin ratio makes it easier to solve these questions. The common size format was shown in the initial example in this section and is repeated below:

+ Breakeven Sales+	$500	100%
- Variable Costs-	$200	40%
= Contribution Margin=	$300	60%

B. The common size format expresses variable costs and the contribution margin as a percentage of sales. Sales is always 100%. When using this technique, you calculate the variable costs as a percentage of sales and then subtract to find the contribution margin as a percentage of sales - the contribution margin ratio.

Study Tip:
As mentioned in the introduction to this section, virtually all breakeven questions involving calculations can be solved by using one of the two formulas using the contribution margin approach:
Breakeven Units = Fixed Costs / Contribution Margin per Unit
Breakeven in Sales Dollars = Fixed Costs / Contribution Margin Ratio

C. Consider the following question: If sales are $750,000 and variable costs are $300,000, what is the contribution margin ratio? Start by setting up the common size income statement format and calculate the contribution margin:

	Amount	**%**
+ Sales +	$750	100%
- Variable Costs -	$300	???%
= Contribution Margin =	$450	???%

Next, calculate variable costs as a percentage of sales:

	Amount	**%**	
+ Sales +	$750	100%	
- Variable Costs -	$300	**40%**_	<= $300 / $750
= Contribution Margin =	$450	???%	

And then subtract to calculate the contribution margin as a percentage of sale - the contribution margin ratio:

	Amount	**%**
+ Sales +	$750	100%
- Variable Costs -	$300	40%
= Contribution Margin =	$450	**60%**

You can then use the contribution margin ratio in the breakeven sales dollars formula to calculate breakeven.

Question:
Martin Brothers has sales of $400,000, variable costs of $80,000, and fixed costs of $20,000. What is Martin Brothers' breakeven point in sales dollars?

Answer:
First, use the common size format to solve for the contribution margin ratio:

	Amount	%
+ Sales +	$400	100%
- Variable Costs -	80	20%
= Contribution Margin =	$320	**80%**

Next, use the formula for breakeven in sales dollars to calculate breakeven sales:

$$\text{Breakeven Point in Sales Dollars} = \frac{\$20{,}000}{80\%}$$

Breakeven Point in Sales Dollars = $25,000

D. Since there are always questions on breakeven analysis on the exam, be sure that you know these formulas!

VI. Complicating Issues

A. The examiners sometimes add additional factors to complicate breakeven questions and ask conceptual questions about breakeven.

B. **Targeted Profit** -- When a targeted profit beyond breakeven is specified, simply add this amount to the fixed cost in the numerator. You can think about the contribution margin on the denominator as having to *cover* all items in the numerator. This is exactly the same formula as breakeven, but at the breakeven level there is no profit (i.e. only fixed costs are covered by CM).

Sales in Units = (Fixed Costs + **Targeted Profit**) / Contribution Margin per Unit

1. The difference between budgeted or actual sales (in units or in dollars) and breakeven sales (in units or in dollars) is known as the margin of safety.

Question:
Bexar Enterprises sells a piece of equipment for $1,000 per unit. Variable costs per unit are $500. If total fixed costs are $10,000 and Bexar wants to earn a profit of $200,000, what amount of unit sales is needed to reach this targeted profit ?

Answer:

$$\text{Breakeven in Units} = \frac{\$10{,}000 + \$200{,}000}{\$1{,}000 - \$500} = \frac{\$210{,}000}{\$500} = 420 \text{ units}$$

C. **Underlying assumptions --** In order to perform breakeven analysis, certain assumptions must hold true. First of all, for breakeven analysis to be relevant and useful, the analysis must be restricted to a relevant range of activity, so that model assumptions are at least approximately satisfied, namely: **fixed costs, unit variable costs, and price must behave as constants**. In addition:

1. All **relationships are linear** (Note: this is why there are always straight lines, never curved lines, on breakeven charts.)
2. When multiple products are sold, the **product mix remains constant** (Note: this is not a restrictive assumption of the model, but this condition is widely assumed in practice for problems on the CPA exam.)
3. There are **no changes in inventory levels**, that is, the number of units sold equals the number of units produced.
   a. **Total costs can be divided** into a **fixed** component and a component that is **variable** with respect to the level of output.
   b. **Volume** is the **only driver** of costs and revenues.
   c. The model applies to operating income (i.e., the CVP model is a **before-tax model**).

Note:
Again, Assumptions are relevant since they only apply to a relevant range (the volume over which assumptions of the model are expected to be valid, and the volume over which operations are reasonably expected to take place).

VII. Graphic Interpretations

A. Exam questions occasionally include diagrams of the behavior of individual costs, revenues and costs, and even budgeted revenues and costs. Candidates are usually required to identify lines, areas, or points on the graphs (e.g., fixed costs, breakeven point, profits, losses, etc.) or explain the causes or effects of changes in lines (e.g., what caused a change in the slope of the total costs line, what is the significance of a flatter revenue line, etc.)

B. The breakeven chart shown below is familiar to most candidates and is sometimes used on the CPA exam.

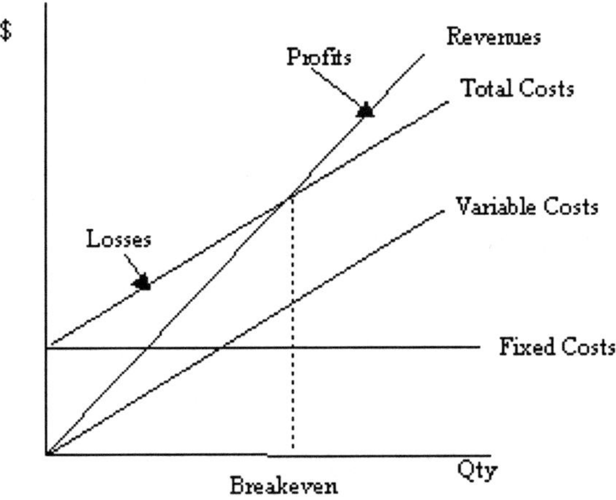

Standard Breakeven Chart

C. The following variation on the breakeven chart is frequently used on the CPA exam. This chart eliminates the separate display of a fixed costs line. Fixed costs are represented by the difference between Total Costs and Variable Costs, which is, by definition, fixed costs:

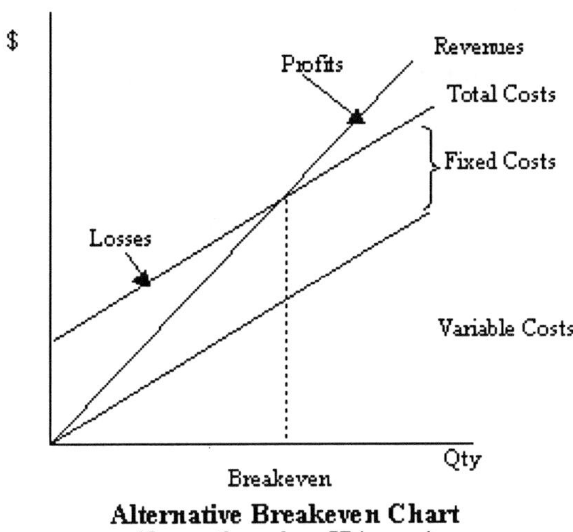

Alternative Breakeven Chart
(frequently used on CPA exam)

D. Volume-Profit Chart

Study Tip:
For problems involving taxes and after-tax income - Remember: The CVP model is a *before-tax* or operating income-based model. If you remember this, conversion to after-tax or net income is easy. Merely perform the necessary calculations while using operating income and then convert to after-tax as required.

Study Tip:
The CPA exam has often tested CVP by requiring the candidate to determine the breakeven point or income after changing one of the variables involved. Often questions will change something and ask you to determine the effect on those. The effect on income (i.e., increase or decrease) is almost always opposite that of the effect on the breakeven point. The only exception to that is where the only change that is made involves and increase or decrease in quantity. In this instance, income will go up or down but the breakeven point will remain the same.

1. Another variation of the breakeven chart graphs Profits (Revenues less Variable Costs and Fixed Costs) instead of separately graphing Revenues, Fixed Costs, Variable Costs, and Total Costs. In this graph, **the slope of the Profit line is equal to the Contribution Margin**: for each unit sold, income increases by the amount of the contribution margin per unit.

2. When no units are sold, the loss is equal to fixed costs. As units are sold, losses decrease by the contribution margin times the number of units sold. At the point where the Profit line crosses the x-axis, profits are zero: this is the breakeven point.

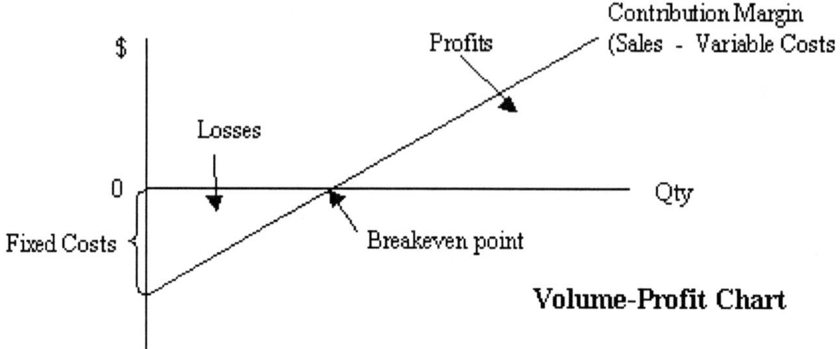

Volume-Profit Chart

3. A few additional observations about the volume-profit chart:
   a. The flatter the line, the smaller the contribution margin per unit.
   b. When comparing profit lines for multiple years and assuming that the sales price has not changed, variable costs per unit for the steeper line are less than variable costs per unit for the flatter line. (Steeper lines indicate larger contribution margins; if the sales price is constant, then variable costs must be relatively smaller.)
   c. Changes in the profit line's y-intercept indicate changes in fixed costs.

Sales & Direct Cost Variance Analysis

Standard costing and variance analysis is usually a very light area on the CPA exam. There are typically one or two questions per exam and, more often then not, the questions are theoretical rather than computational. However, one out of every four or five exams will have a set of four or five questions in this area, most of which are computational so you cannot afford to neglect this area.

I. Types of Standards

A. Standards are predetermined or targeted costs. Standards are similar to budgeted amounts stated on a per unit basis, but standards differ from budgets in that they actually appear in general ledger accounts, while budgeted amounts do not. Standards are developed for each factor of production (materials, labor, and overhead) and usually fit into one of two broad categories:

1. **Ideal/theoretical standards --** Ideal standards **presume perfect efficiency and 100% capacity.**
   a. *Not useful* **for control purposes** as they are not practically attainable.
2. **Currently attainable standards --** Currently attainable standards are based on **higher than average levels of efficiency**, but are clearly achievable
   a. Typically used for employee motivation, product costing, and budgeting.

B. Some other concepts about variances:

1. Standards are *not* **only based on historical performance** as this may incorporate past periods' inefficiencies.
2. Standards may be used **by service organizations as well as manufacturing organizations**. They may be used in **both process costing and job-order costing** environments.
3. Standards **may be used to value inventories** (raw materials, WIP, FG) and **Cost of Goods Sold** as long as they:
   a. Are based on currently attainable performance; and
   b. Do not result in significant variances.
4. Variances may also be calculated for sales revenues. Sales variances are based on the **budgeted or planned sales price**.

> **Study Tip:**
> Be sure that you understand these conceptual issues as at least half of the variance questions on the CPA exam are directed towards the prior points.

II. Variance Calculations

A. Variance analysis analyzes the difference between standard costs and actual costs. When standard costs are used to value inventories, the variance must be written off:

1. **Non-significant variances --** Write off to **CGS**;
2. **Significant variances --** Allocate to ending work-in-process, finished goods, and cost of goods sold.

B. Variance analysis divides the difference between actual costs and standard costs into two parts:

1. Differences due to the **cost of the resource** (price per pound, labor rate per hour, etc.);

2. Differences due to the **quantity used** (gallons, pounds, feet, labor hours, etc.).

Note:
The following method of calculating variances offers an extremely effective and efficient approach to solving variance questions on the CPA exam. It is, however, quite different from the approach found in most academic texts and courses. This traditional approach to variance analysis is shown at the end of this section.

C. These variances are given different names depending on the factor of production:

	Differences in Cost	Differences in Quantity
Materials	Price Variance*	Usage Variance
Labor	Rate Variance	Efficiency Variance**

*Price variances are often considered to be the responsibility of the purchasing department and separated from the goods before they enter the production process

**Although different terminology is sometimes used, price and rate variances are equivalent concepts as are usage and efficiency variances.

D. Variance calculation is a two step process:

1. Calculate the differences in rates, quantities, and total cost (rate X quantity);

2. Use the differences in rates and quantities to calculate the variances.

III. **Step 1: Calculating the differences --** When calculating cost variances, it is best to use the following format:

+ Standard Amount

<u>- Actual Amount</u>

= Difference/Variance

A. When *cost* variances are calculated in this manner, **negative numbers indicate unfavorable variances and positive numbers indicate favorable variances**.

Example:
Mills Company used 80 hours of labor at a cost of $15 per hour to complete 40 steel doors. Based on the company's labor standards for the door, they should have used 85 hours of labor at a cost of $13 per hour to complete the 40 doors. Which of the following correctly states the nature of the variances?

	Efficiency Variance	Rate Variance	Total Variance
A.	Favorable	Favorable	Favorable
B.	Favorable	Unfavorable	Favorable
C.	Unfavorable	Favorable	Unfavorable
D.	Favorable	Unfavorable	Unfavorable

Answer:

	Quantity		Rate		Total
+ Standard Amount	85	X	$13	=	$1105
- Actual Amount*	80	X	$15	=	$1200
= Difference/Variance	5		($2)		($95)

D is the correct answer:

The positive difference in quantities allowed indicates a favorable quantity variance

The negative difference in rates indicates an unfavorable rate variance

The negative difference in the total cost indicates an overall unfavorable variance in total

B. **A note about the standard quantity --** The "standard quantity" is the **"standard quantity allowed for actual production."** For example, if the standard amount of aluminum required to produce a sheet of siding is 2 lbs. and 50 pieces of siding are produced, then the "standard quantity allowed for actual production" is 100 lbs.

IV. **Step 2: Calculating the variances --** The differences in rate and quantity are used to calculate the price/rate variance and the usage/efficiency variance as follows:

Price/rate variance = Difference in Rates X Actual Quantity

Usage/efficiency variance = Difference in Quantities X Standard Rate

Example:
Standard materials usage and cost for one unit of Product A is 6 lbs. at $2.00 per lb. Actual units produced were 20 units; 100 lbs. of raw material at a total cost of $225 were used in production. Calculate the materials price and usage variances for Product A.

Answer:

Price/rate variance = ($2.25 - $2.00) 100 lbs. = $25.00 Unfavorable

Usage/efficiency variance = (100 lbs. - 120 lbs.) $2.00 = $40.00 favorable

Standard Quantity Allowed for Actual Production = 6 lbs. X 20 units = 120 lbs.

Note that the $2.25 actual price was not given in the problem, but was derived from the two related numbers, which were given: 100 lbs. actual quantity used and total price of $225.00

Study Tip:
Although in this instance we have calculated the rate and efficiency variances together, when the labor rate is not controllable by production supervisors, the rate variance is frequently removed prior to production and assigned to the department responsible for setting the rate, usually personnel.

A. **Checking your work --** Notice that the total variance calculated in the analysis format by subtracting total actual costs from total standard costs ($240.00 - $225.00 = $15.00) is the same as the total variance calculated by summing the usage variance and the price variance ($40.00 + ($25.00) = $15.00). When these two independently calculated totals are the same, you can be relatively certain that your calculations are accurate.

Example:
Standard labor for one unit is 2 hours at $14.50 per hour. Actual units produced were 15 units; actual labor charges were 40 hours at $14.10 per hour. Calculate the labor rate and efficiency variances for Product A.

Answer:

Rate variance = ($14.10 - $14.50) 40 hrs. = $16.00 Favorable

Efficiency variance = (40 lbs. ??? 30 lbs.) $14.50 = $145.00 Unfavorable

Standard Quantity Allowed for Actual Production = 2 hrs. X 15 units = 30 hrs.

Study Tip:
Although in this instance we have calculated the price and usage variances together, when price is not controllable by production supervisors, the price variance is frequently removed prior to production and assigned to the department responsible for setting the price, usually purchasing, or personnel (labor rate variances).

V. Complicating Factors -- Multiple choice questions on the CPA exam will sometimes complicate these calculations by providing partial information about the standard and actual figures and the related variances. You must use your knowledge of the relationships among these figures to work backwards and provide the answer to the question. Using the format suggested above simplifies these calculations substantially.

Example:

Jim Bishop Cabinetry Co.'s records show the following data on labor cost:

Actual rate paid	$14.20 per hour
Standard rate	$14.00 per hour
Standard hours allowed	1,000 hours
Labor efficiency variance	$798.00 unfavorable

What were the actual hours worked?

Answer:

Solving for the unknown in the efficiency variance formula provides the difference between the standard and actual quantity used:

Efficiency Variance: Difference in Quantities= ($798.00) / $14.00 = (57) hours

This difference is substituted back into the analysis format and used to derive the number of actual hours used:

Since (AQ - SQA) SP, (AQ -1,000 hrs.) $14. Since the labor efficiency variance is unfavorable, that requires that AQ is higher than SQ. Thus, AQ must be SQA of 1,000 hrs. plus 57 hours = 1,057.

VI. Traditional Variance Analysis Format

A. As previously mentioned, most managerial accounting textbooks use a different tool to assist in variance analysis. The tool below should be familiar to most candidates:

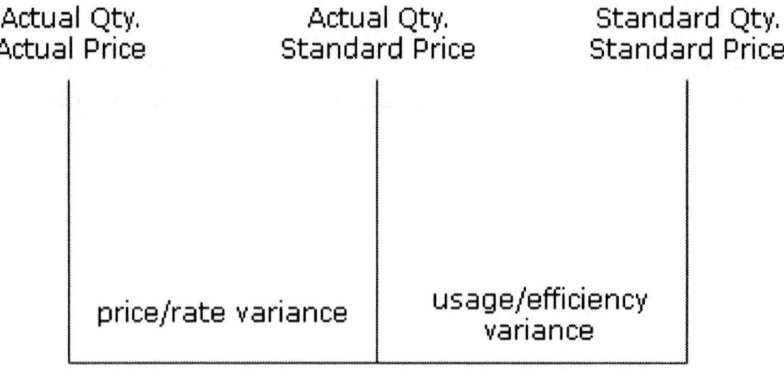

B. The formulas implicit in this model can be stated separately and purely mathematical formulas can be derived to isolate the variances:

Price/rate variance	= (AQ * AP) - (AQ *SP)
	= AQ (AP - SP)
Usage/efficiency variance	= (AQ *SP) - (SQ - SP)
	= SP (AQ - SQ)
Total variance	**= (AQ * AP) - (SQ *SP)**

AQ = Actual quantity

AP = Actual price

SQ = Standard quantity

SP = Standard price

C. This analysis format takes a different approach to organizing the data, but the concept is the same:

1. Use the analysis tool to organize the data provided in the problem. Then, use the relationships implied by the analysis tool to calculate the variances.

D. For illustration, we can solve one of the previous examples using this method:

Example:
Standard labor for one unit is 2 hours at $14.50 per hour. Actual units produced were 15 units; actual labor charges were 40 hours at $14.10 per hour. Calculate the labor rate and efficiency variances for Product A.

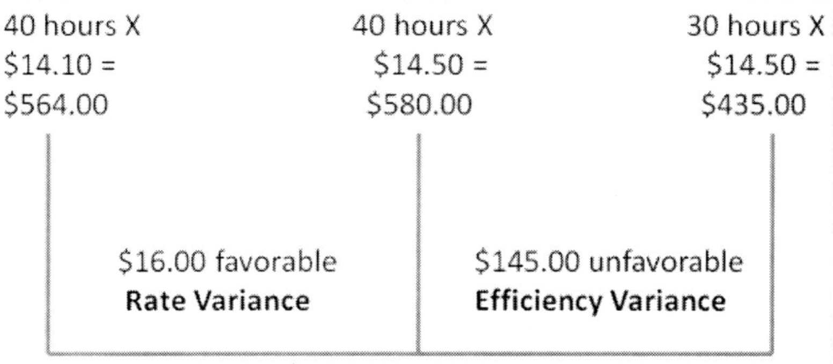

Rate variance = 40 ($14.10 - $14.50)
= 40 (-$0.40)
= ($16.00) favorable

Efficiency variance = $14.50 (40 - 30)
= $14.50 (10)
= $145.00 unfavorable

Total variance = ($40 * $14.10) - (30 * $14.50)
= $564.00 - $435.00
= $129.00 unfavorable

Notice that this technique produces answers identical to the answers derived using the previous model. Use whichever technique works best for you.

VII. Analyzing Sales Variances

A. Though not frequently tested on the exam, occasional questions about sales variances do sometimes appear. Analysis of sales variances can be handled in the same manner as cost variances as long as the following points are observed:

1. **Budgeted or planned sales --** Quantities and prices are used instead of "standard" quantities and prices.
2. **Sales variances work backwards --** When compared to cost variances, that is:
    a. When actual prices are greater than planned prices, favorable variances result (e.g., it's good for people to pay more than you had planned).

   b. When actual quantities sold are greater than planned quantities sold, favorable variances result (e.g., it's good to sell more than you had planned).

3. **Sales variances** -- Use slightly different names:
   a. **Sales price variance** -- Difference in Prices X Actual Quantity Sold
   b. **Sales quantity variance** -- Difference in Units X Planned Unit Price.

Example:
Mercury Corp.'s master budget showed planned sales revenue of $400,000 on sales of 100,000 units. Actual sales were 90,000 at $4.50 per unit. What was Mercury's sales price, sales quantity, and total sales variance?

Answer:

Sales price variance = ($4.50 - $4.00) 90,000 units = $45,000 Favorable

Sales quantity variance = (90,000 units ??? 100,000 units) $4.00 = $40,000 Unfavorable

Total variance = $45,000 Favorable - $40,000 Unfavorable = $5,000 Favorable

Overhead Variance Analysis

Analysis of indirect cost variances (overhead) is more complex than analysis of direct cost variances (material and labor). Most students find it to be a very difficult area of study. Fortunately, there are relatively few overhead variance questions on the CPA exam and when they do occur, they tend to be conceptual questions.

I. Introduction

A. The process of analyzing overhead variances is substantially more difficult than analyzing variances related to direct materials and direct labor because:

1. Some overhead varies with production volume while other overhead is fixed; because of this, separate variances must be calculated for **variable overhead and for fixed overhead**.
2. Fixed overhead is applied to production based on a specified cost driver; if actual usage of the cost driver differs from planned, **applied overhead costs will change solely as a result of changes in cost driver consumption** (i.e., the variance does not represent true changes in overhead).
3. While some overhead costs are **controllable** by the production manager, other overhead costs are **uncontrollable** except in the very long run (e.g., depreciation on factory buildings).

B. Recall that both variable and fixed overhead are applied to production based on a single **predetermined overhead application rate**:

> Overhead application rate = (budgeted variable overhead + budgeted fixed overhead) / (budgeted units of the allocation base)

C. Traditionally, the allocation base is a cost driver that is under the control of the production manager (i.e., direct labor hours). If, however, the allocation base is not under the control of the production manager, the **production manager cannot be responsible for overhead variances due solely to the choice of the allocation base**.

D. Variable overhead varies with production volume. It includes indirect costs such as machine supplies, electricity needed for production processes, and incidental manufacturing costs (i.e., the thread used for sewing garments or the screws used in the construction of a piece of furniture). Because the behavior of variable overhead is similar to the behavior of direct manufacturing costs (material and labor), the analysis format used to analyze direct costs can be applied to variable indirect costs:

Study Tip:
Overhead variances are a fairly light area on the CPA exam. When questions do appear, they are most often conceptual questions about controllability (e.g., which variances is the supervisor actually responsible for) rather than computational questions.

Question:
What are the variable overhead variances for the following?

Bennington City Manufacturing allocates overhead to production based on machine hours. The following information is available regarding its variable overhead for the current quarter:

Variable overhead rate per machine hour:	$0.25
Standard machine hours per unit:	3 hours
Planned production	1,500 units
Planned machine hours (3 hours * 1,500 units)	4,500 hours
Actual machine hours	4,700 hours
Actual units produced	1,700 units
Standard machine hours allowed for actual production (3 hours * 1,700 units)	5,100 hours
Actual variable overhead cost	$1,269

Answer:

	Quantity	**x**	**Rate**	**=**	**Total**
+Standard	5,100	x	$0.25	=	$1,275.00
-Actual	4,700	x	$0.27*	=	$1,269.00
=Difference	400		($0.02)		$6.00

*Derived from given information: Actual Overhead / Actual Quantity

Efficiency Variance: (400) X $0.25 = $100.00 favorable

Spending Variance: ($0.02) X 4,700 = ($94.00) unfavorable

Total Variance = $100.00 + ($94.00) = $6.00 favorable

Exam Hint: Be sure to know of the variances for variable overhead and whether they are controllable by the production manager or uncontrollable:

Spending Variance - Measures variance due to changes in both rates and quantities of overhead items. It is a **controllable variance**.

Efficiency Variance - Measures the variance due to variations in the efficiency of the base used to allocate overhead (i.e., direct labor hours, machine hours, etc.). As long as the underlying allocation base is under the control of the production manager, it is a **controllable variance**.

II. Fixed Overhead

A. Fixed Overhead Volume Variance

1. Since fixed overhead does not change with changes in production volume, yet is applied to production based on a unit rate, anytime that actual production differs from planned production, a fixed overhead variance results. This variance is known as the **volume variance** and, since it is merely an artifact of the way that we assign fixed overhead to production, it is considered an **uncontrollable** variance.

2. The fixed overhead volume variance is calculated as:

> Budgeted Fixed Overhead - (Standard Fixed Overhead Rate * Std. Qty. Allowed for Actual Production)

Example:
McGorky Productions has budgeted fixed overhead of $40,000. The fixed overhead is applied to production based on direct labor hours: 0.5 direct labor hours (DLH) are required to produce each unit and the company has budgeted production of 100,000 units. Actual production is 120,000 units.

Fixed Overhead Application Rate = $40,000 / (100,000 units * .5 DLH per unit)
= $0.80 per DLH

Standard Quantity Allowed for Actual Production = 120,000 units * .5 DLH
= 60,000 DLH

Fixed Overhead Volume Variance = $40,000 - ($0.80 * 60,000)
= $40,000 - $48,000
= $8,000

B. Fixed Overhead Budget Variance

1. Even when actual production is exactly equal to planned production, it is still possible to have fixed overhead variances. The difference between the actual fixed overhead and the budgeted (or planned) fixed overhead is known as the budget variance.

2. The fixed overhead budget variance is calculated as:

> Actual Fixed Overhead - Budgeted Fixed Overhead

Example:
McGorky Productions' actual fixed overhead is $38,000. Its budgeted fixed overhead is $40,000.

Fixed Overhead Budget Variance = $38,000 - $40,000
= $2,000 favorable

C. A Graphic View of Fixed Overhead Variances

1. The four variances related to manufacturing overhead are illustrated by the graphics below:

   a. **Variable Overhead Variances**

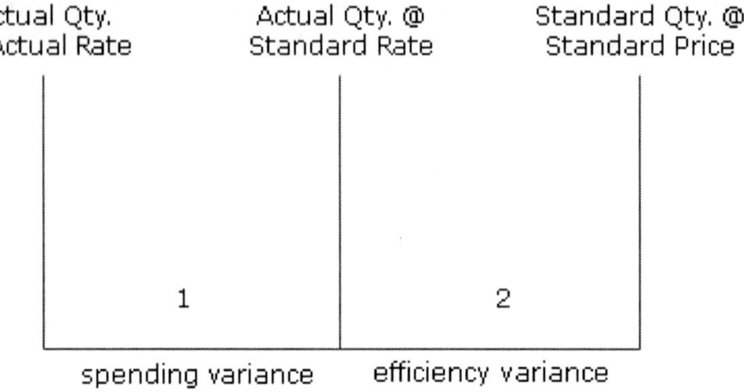

   b. **Fixed Overhead Variances**

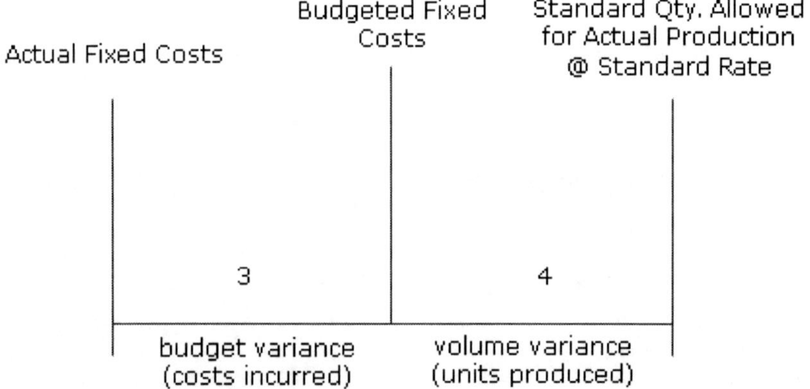

D. Because overhead variances can be difficult to interpret...

1. Some companies choose to combine the four basic overhead variances into subtotals that make the numbers easier to evaluate over time. Three combinations are generally found in practice and on the CPA exam:

   a. The two-way analysis;

   b. Three-way analysis;

   c. Four-way analysis.

2. **4-way analysis** -- Four-way analysis comprises the four variances shown above: the two variable overhead variances (spending variance and efficiency variance) and the two fixed overhead variances (budget variance and volume variance). Four-way analysis provides the most detailed variance information, but it is less commonly used than two-way and three-way analyses because of the difficulty of interpreting the information.

3. **3-way analysis** -- Three-way analysis combines the variable overhead spending variance and the fixed overhead budget (spending) variance into a single variance referred to as the total spending variance.

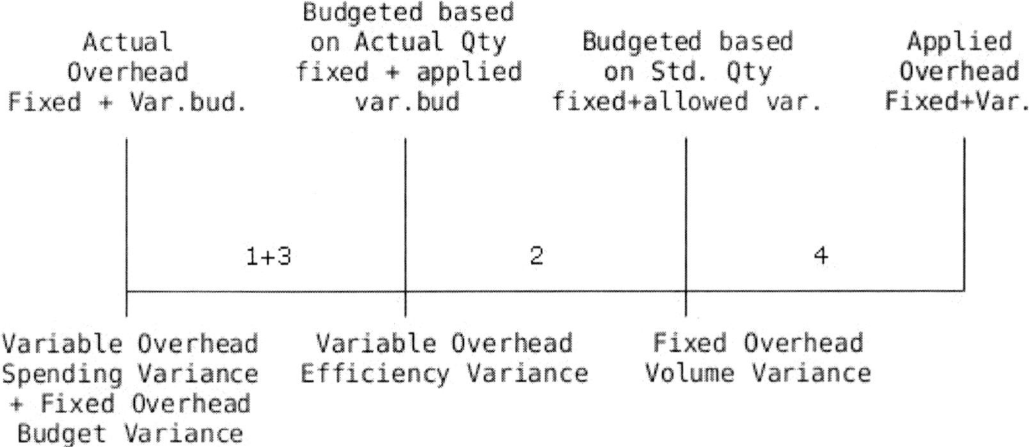

4. **2-way analysis --** Two-way analysis separates the overhead variances into a controllable and an uncontrollable variance. The two variable overhead variances are combined with the fixed overhead spending variance to create the controllable variance (often referred to as the flexible budget variance). The fixed overhead volume variance is isolated in the uncontrollable variance.

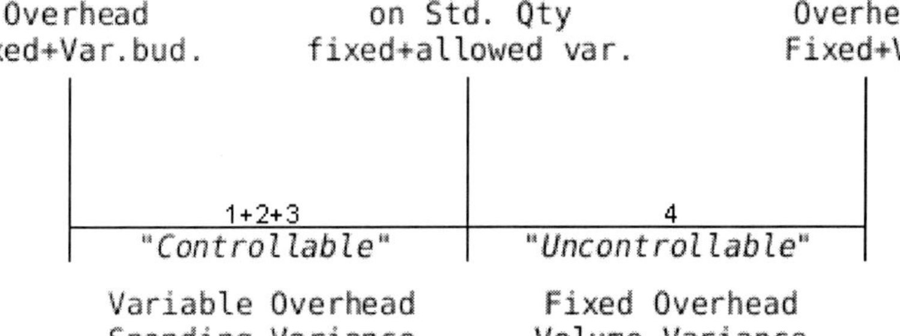

Variable Overhead
Spending Variance
+ Variable Overhead
Efficiency Variance
+ Fixed Overhead
Budget Variance

Fixed Overhead
Volume Variance

Study Tip:
Remember that although the efficiency variance is often controllable, it only reflects variation in units of the allocation base, not variance due to overhead itself.

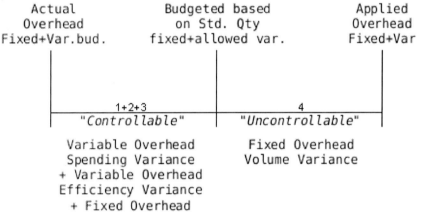

Decision Making

Relevant Costs, Part 1

The CPA exam typically tests four categories of decisions that focus on the identification of relevant costs: whether to process a product further or sell immediately, whether to keep or drop a product line, whether to accept or reject a special order, and whether to make or buy a product or component. This lesson covers the first two types of decisions; the next lesson covers the last two types of decisions. Decisions involving relevant costs are tested lightly on the exam - usually a single question about one of the four types of decisions per exam. This is, however, one of the few areas in Planning & Measurement for which questions tend to be computational rather than conceptual.

I. Introduction

A. The identification of relevant costs is a critical component in many production decisions: Should we buy a component or make it ourselves? Should we process a product further or sell it now? Should we keep producing a product or drop it?

B. Each possibility is characterized by its own set of costs and associated revenues. Which costs do we need to consider? Must we consider all of them? What about the revenues we lose when choosing one option means that we must forgo another option? The answer is that we must **consider all future factors that differ among alternatives** - these are the relevant factors: Relevant costs and benefits are the future costs and benefits that differ among alternatives.

1. **Avoidable costs** - costs that **can be eliminated by choosing one alternative over the other** - are relevant costs. **Opportunity costs** - the **benefits that are foregone** when the selection of one course of action precludes another course of action - are relevant costs.

2. **Unavoidable costs** - costs that will **remain the same** regardless of which alternative is chosen - are irrelevant to the decision process. Irrelevant costs fall into two general categories:

   a. **Sunk costs:** A sunk cost is a cost that **has already been incurred** and cannot be changed. For example, when deciding whether to buy a new car or keep your current car, the **price paid for the current car is irrelevant** as it occurred in the past and cannot be changed. On the other hand, the **market value of the current car** if you sold it **is relevant** to the decision as it differs between the two alternatives: if you buy the new car, you can sell the current car for its market value; if you keep the current car, you forgo receiving its market value.

   b. **Future costs and benefits that do not differ between alternatives:** Future costs that do not differ between alternatives tend to be fixed costs or allocated costs.

Example:
Remington Trucking is considering the purchase of a new delivery truck for $78,000. If they purchase the new truck, they will sell their current truck, which cost them $68,000 two years ago.

General maintenance and insurance on the current truck is approximately $2,800. However, this truck is also due for a major overhaul that will cost $1,500. Straight-line depreciation on the old truck is $8,000 per year.

General maintenance and insurance for the new truck will be approximately the same as for the old truck. If the new truck is purchased, depreciation on it will be $9,000 per year.

Irrelevant costs: When considering whether to purchase the new truck, the $68,000 purchase price is a sunk cost and is irrelevant. The general maintenance and insurance costs are also irrelevant because they are future costs, which do not differ between alternatives.

Relevant costs: The $1,500 cost of the major overhaul on the old truck is an avoidable cost and therefore is relevant (e.g., if the new truck is purchased, the cost of the overhaul can be avoided). The difference in depreciation is relevant but, since depreciation itself is a non-cash item, it is only relevant to the extent that it produces a cash difference due to its effect on income tax liability. The sales value of the current truck and the purchase price of the new truck are also relevant costs as they differ between the two alternatives.

II. Types of decisions using relevant costs

A. Several types of decisions involving the identification of relevant costs are frequently encountered. These decisions revolve around:

1. Whether to process a product further or sell it now;

2. Whether to keep or drop a product line or company segment;

3. Whether to make or buy a product or component;

4. Whether to accept or reject a special order.

III. Sell Now or Process Further Decisions

A. This type of decision usually involves processing decisions about joint products, although it can also be applied to processing decisions for a single product. In a joint product environment:

1. products are not separately identifiable until after the split-off point;

2. the costs incurred up to the split-off point cannot be separated or avoided.

B. When joint products are produced, separate products are identifiable after the split-off point. At that point producers frequently have the option of selling the products immediately or of performing additional processing on some or all of the products before selling them.

C. When making the decision to process a product further or not, **the only relevant facts are the differential future costs and benefits**: the **separable costs incurred beyond the split-off point and the difference between the revenue that can be earned** at split-off and the revenue that can be earned after further processing. Joint costs are not relevant.

D. Consider the following example:

1. Chemical Dynamics, Inc. produces three synthetic oils through a joint product production process. Chemical compounds are blended together, heated to 1200 degrees Farenheit, and left in vats to cool for two days. At the end of the two days, the three synthetic oils - Algon, Bessite, and Corex - can be separated from the material in the vats. Algon and Corex can be sold immediately after split-off but Bessite must be processed further before it can be sold. Additionally, Algon and Corex can each be processed further to create more concentrated products (Algon-Extra Duty and Corex-L). Based on the following sales volume, sales price and cost information, determine which products should be processed further and which should be sold at split-off (you may assume that none of the products can be disposed of as scrap):

		Algon	**Bessite**	**Corex**
Costs incurred up to split-off:				
Cost of raw materials	$40,000			
Cost of production processes	$20,000			
Volume at split-off:		25,000 gal.	20,000 gal.	5,000 gal.
Sales value per gallon at split-off:		$2.00/gal.	n/a	$4.00/gal.
Cost of additional processing:		$15,000	$20,000	$10,000
Volume after additional processing:		20,000 gal.	30,000 gal.	7,000 gal.
Sales value per unit after additional processing:		$3.00/gal.	$6.00/gal.	$4.50/gal.

2. When analyzing this decision, the first step is to eliminate the irrelevant information - the information that doesn't change. In this example, we can eliminate:

   a. The costs incurred up to split-off (raw materials of $40,000 and production process costs of $20,000) are sunk costs and are therefore not relevant: they have already been incurred and cannot be changed and so are irrelevant.

   b. The information about Bessite: production volumes, separable processing costs, and unit sales value. Since Bessite *must* be processed further and no other sales or disposal options can be considered, the treatment of Bessite cannot change and so the Bessite data is irrelevant.

3. The relevant costs and benefits, then, are related to Algon and Corex: the revenues realizable and costs incurred at split-off and the revenues realizable and costs incurred if the products are processed further. Each product needs to be considered separately because the highest return may be achieved when one product is sold immediately and the other receives further processing. The costs and benefits for each choice are summarized in the following table:

	Algon		Corex	
	Sell at Split-off	**Process Further**	**Sell at Split-off**	**Process Further**
Revenues:				
Price per gallon	$2.00/gal.	$3.00/gal.	$4.00/gal.	$4.50/gal
# of gallons	25,000 gal	20,000 gal	5,000 gal.	7,000 gal.
Total revenue	$50,000	$60,000	$20,000	$31,500
Additional costs:	- 0 -	$15,000	- 0 -	$10,000
Net realizable value:	$50,000	$45,000	$20,000	$21,500.00

4. Based on this analysis, it appears that the company should *not* process Algon further because its net realizable value is less when the goods are processed further. Corex, *should* be processed further because its net realizable value is greater when the goods are processed further.

IV. Keep or Drop a Product Line (or Business Segment) Decisions

A. When organizations track performance by product line or business segment, they often discover that some products and segments do not perform as well as others and that some may even be operating at a loss. The problem then becomes whether to continue producing the product or segment or whether to eliminate it.

B. The decision is not as straightforward as it might appear because:

1. some of the costs charged to the product or segment may not be eliminated if the product or segment is eliminated
2. changes in one part of the organization may impact other parts of the organization
3. there may or may not be alternative uses for the resources freed up by elimination of the product or segment.

Example:
Tres Piedres Auto Works is a automobile repair shop that provides brake and transmission service. About a year ago, the shop converted one of its repair bays to an oil change station so that it could offer quick oil change services. Tres Piedres now wants to review the results of this change to determine whether they should keep the oil change facility or convert it back to use for brake and transmission services. The following information is available:

	Brakes	**Transmissions**	**Oil Change**
Sales	$190,000	$230,000	$70,000
Costs:			
Variable costs	$114,000	$161,000	$56,000
Fixed costs	$28,000	$38,000	$22,000
Total costs	$142,000	$199,000	$78,000
Operating income (loss)	$ 48,000	$ 31,000	($ 8,000)

Additional information: If the Oil Change facility is dropped, the shop will be able to avoid $6,000 in fixed costs related to managing the facility. The shop will also be able to avoid $2,000 in advertising expenses designed to promote the oil change service.

The shop is not operating at capacity so recovery of the oil change bay if the oil change services were dropped would not increase sales of either brake or transmission services. Quite to the contrary, the manager estimates that brake and transmission service revenues will drop by $3,000 and $7,000, respectively, if the oil change services are dropped.

C. The preceding example contains several elements that are typical of keep or drop a product line decisions.

1. Notice that Oil Change Services **shows a net operating loss**. This is typical of CPA exam questions in this area. The unsophisticated candidate may quickly assume that dropping a product line that is operating at a loss must necessarily have a positive affect on the company's total net income. However, if the product line revenues are sufficient to cover its avoidable costs, this may not be the case. If the product line's net loss is due to unavoidable costs that have been allocated to it, total net income for the company may be reduced as a result of dropping the "unprofitable" product line.

2. Information is presented regarding variable costs and fixed costs:

   a. In general, **variable costs are avoidable costs**: if we don't provide oil change services, the variable costs related to the oil change services will not be incurred.

   b. **Fixed costs** are usually a **mix of avoidable costs and unavoidable costs**. In this instance, it appears that $6,000 of the $22,000 in fixed costs attributed to the Oil Change activity are avoidable, leaving $16,000 in unavoidable fixed costs.

3. Information is usually provided regarding **miscellaneous differential costs and revenues**. For example, if the oil change services are dropped, revenues for other services will actually decrease by $10,000 total as a result of lost synergies between the services provided. Additionally, $2,000 in advertising costs can also be avoided. Note that it is quite usual for the examiners to list these costs in addition to the other fixed and variable costs in hopes of causing the candidate to be confused as to whether the cost are included in the fixed and variable cost totals or not: **in the vast majority of cases these items are *in addition* to the other costs (or revenues)**.

D. To determine whether the oil change services should be kept or dropped, you will need to compare the total operating income with oil change services to the total operating income *without* oil change services. A typical analysis format for these types of decisions is shown below:

	Total with Oil Change	**Total without Oil Change**	**Difference Favorable (Unfavorable)**
Sales	$490,000	$410,000	($80,000)
Costs:			
Variable costs	$331,000	$268,300	$62,700
Fixed costs	$ 88,000	$ 82,000	$ 6,000
Total operating costs	$419,000	$350,300	$68,700
Other costs	$2,000	- 0 -	$ 2,000
Operating income (loss)	$ 69,000	$ 59,700	($ 9,300)

Study Tip:
This scenario described in the previous example (e.g., the line that may be dropped initially shows a net loss but further analysis reveals that the line contributes positively to the total organization's performance) is common to many CPA exam questions in this area.

E. Analysis of the changes in revenues and expenses reveals that, despite the net loss attributed to oil change services, the company will be **$9,300** *worse* **off** if it drops the oil change services. This is in part because the oil change revenues are greater than the avoidable costs associated with the revenues ($70,000 - ($56,000 + $6,000 + $2,000) =$6,000) and in part because the synergy between the oil change services and the other services offered was such that an additional $3,300 decrease in operating income ($10,000 decrease in brake and transmission service revenues less $6,700 in related cost savings) would occur if the oil change services were eliminated.

F. While some candidates prefer to perform the complete analysis as shown above, others prefer to look only at the **differential analysis**:

	Differences Favorable (Unfavorable)
Sales	($80,000)
Costs:	
Variable costs	$62,700
Fixed costs	$ 6,000
Total operating costs:	$68,700
Other costs	$ 2,000
Operating income (loss)	($9,300)

G. The results of the two analysis formats are the same, of course, but many candidates find it easier to look at only the differences.

Relevant Costs, Part 2

The CPA exam typically tests four categories of decisions that focus on the identification of relevant costs: whether to process a product further or sell immediately, whether to keep or drop a product line, whether to accept or reject a special order, and whether to make or buy a product or component. This lesson covers the first two types of decisions; the next lesson covers the last two types of decisions. Decisions involving relevant costs are tested lightly on the exam - usually a single question about one of the four types of decisions per exam. This is, however, one of the few areas in Planning & Measurement for which questions tend to be computational rather than conceptual.

I. Accept or Reject a Special Order

A. Special orders, whether for products or for services, require us to think differently about costs and prices specifically because they are "special" orders: **one-time opportunities that are not part of the organization's on-going business**. Normally, products are priced to cover "full" costs: not just variable production costs but fixed overhead and selling and administrative costs as well. All costs must be covered if the organization is to survive. Special orders, however, are not subject to this constraint. Since fixed overhead and selling and administrative costs have already been covered by regular product sales, they do not need to be considered when pricing special orders.

B. Special order decisions are usually short-term, profit-maximizing decisions. For these decisions, **the only relevant costs are the costs directly attributable to the special order** and, if the company is operating at capacity, the **opportunity costs** associated with production that must be canceled in order to complete the special order. Strategic considerations may also come into play if accepting the special order has the potential to compromise or, alternatively, promote management's objectives outside of profit maximization. For example, a company might be willing to accept a special order from a customer who represented a market segment that the company was trying to penetrate even if the company lost money on the special order.

C. **Considering a Special Order When there is Excess Capacity:** If the special order can be completed using existing capacity, only sales revenues and the variable costs of producing the order need be considered.

Example:

Marpro Industries produces an electronic flytrap that has proved to be very successful. Marpro plans to produce and sell 100,000 flytraps at $70 each during the upcoming year. The cost of producing and selling each flytrap is:

Direct materials	$25.00
Direct labor	$12.50
Variable manufacturing overhead	$7.00
Fixed manufacturing overhead	$4.00
Variable selling and administrative expense	$3.50
Fixed selling and administrative expenses	$4.50
Total cost per unit:	$56.50

A company that manages horseback riding stables for several ranch resorts has asked Marpro to build 1,000 custom flytraps for their use at a price of $55 apiece. Marpro estimates that the design and re-tooling costs associated with the customization would cost $3,000. In addition, direct materials cost would increase to $27.00 per unit, variable manufacturing overhead would decrease to $6.50 per unit and variable selling and administrative expenses would decrease to $1.00 per unit. The order would not affect sales of their standard flytrap and could be produced using existing excess capacity. Since the special order price is already less than the cost of a standard flytrap, Marpro initially rejected the order. However, they are now having second thoughts and want to re-evaluate the special order request. Should Marpro take the special order?

Answer: When considering whether to take a special order, the only relevant costs are the costs directly attributable to the order. In this case, the $3,000 design and re-tooling cost must be considered as well as the direct unit costs:

Direct materials	$27.00
Direct labor	$12.50
Variable manufacturing overhead	$6.50
Variable selling and administrative expense	$1.00
Cost per unit:	$47.00

Special order revenue (1,000 X $55)	$55,000
Less: special order unit costs (1,000 X $47)	($47,000)
Less: design and re-tooling costs for the order*	($3,000)
Net profit on the special order	$5,000

* The design and re-tooling costs could also have been expressed as $3.00 per unit ($3,000/1,000 units) and added to the other unit costs.

Note that the fixed manufacturing overhead and fixed selling and administrative costs have been eliminated from the special order analysis because they do not change as a result of accepting the special order. Based on this analysis, Marpro should accept the special order as it will increase profits by $5,000.

Study Tip:
CPA Exam questions sometimes take this approach to the treatment of opportunity costs. In these cases, it is important to remember that the opportunity cost of the foregone option is **added to the costs** of the option under consideration.

D. Considering a Special Order When there is *No* Excess Capacity

1. When no excess capacity exists, acceptance of a special order means that other units must be removed from the production schedule to make room for the special order. The **foregone profits** related the units that were removed from production represent an **opportunity cost** and must be included in the profitability analysis of the special order.
2. See Example on next page.

Example:
Consider the same facts as in the preceding example except assume that in order to produce the special order, Marpro will have to eliminate production of 1,500 of its standard flytraps. The relevant costs and benefits associated with the production and sale of the 1,500 standard flytraps are:

Direct materials	$25.00
Direct labor	$12.50
Variable manufacturing overhead	$7.00
Variable selling and administrative expense	$3.50
Total relevant cost per unit:	$48.00

Revenue for 1,500 standard units:	$105,000
Less: relevant costs for 1,500 standard units:	($72,000)
Net profit for the 1,500 standard units	$33,000

Note that the fixed costs allocated to the standard flytraps are unavoidable and, thus, irrelevant: they will remain the same regardless of whether the standard units or the special order units are produced.

Based on this analysis, the special order would not be accepted when there is no excess capacity. The special order would contribute a total of $5,000 profit to the firm but the regular sale of the 1,500 standard units would contribute a much larger amount: $33,000. The company would be $28,000 better off ($33,000 - $5,000) by rejecting the special order.

An alternative way of incorporating the opportunity cost associated with the 1,500 standard units into the analysis is to include the opportunity cost as one of the cost factors associated with the special order:

Direct materials	$27.00
Direct labor	$12.50
Variable manufacturing overhead	$6.50
Variable selling and administrative expense	$1.00
Cost per unit:	$47.00

Special order revenue (1,000 X $55)	$55,000
Less: special order unit costs (1,000 X $47)	($47,000)
Less: design and re-tooling costs for the order	($3,000)
Less: opportunity cost ($33,000)	($33,000)
Net loss on the special order	-$28,000.00

II. Make or Buy a Product or Component

A. Many organizations prefer to make their own product components rather than purchase them from external suppliers in order to maintain control of production quality and supply. In recent years, however, globalization and increasing price competition has caused many organizations to outsource component production: suppliers who specialize in large-scale production of a particular component can often provide the component at a lower cost than the organization can produce it.

B. The decision of whether to outsource production - to make or buy a component - is based on comparative analysis of the external purchase costs and the relevant costs of internal production.

Example:
Ozone Boards produces handcrafted surfboards. In order to maintain high quality, Ozone has traditionally built all of the board components themselves. Recently, costs associated with production of the board blanks that serve as the foundation of the board have increased substantially due to environmental concerns about some of the chemicals used in production of the blanks. Ozone reports the following costs associated with blank production:

Direct materials	$15.00
Direct labor	$20.00
Variable manufacturing overhead	$10.00
Fixed manufacturing overhead	$13.00
Total cost per unit:	$58.00

Ozone's production schedule requires production of 2,000 blanks per year. A company specializing in the production of board blanks has offered to sell Ozone 2,000 blanks per year at a cost of $48 per blank. Ozone has investigated the supplier and their product and is satisfied that they can produce and deliver a blank that meets Ozone's specifications. Ozone estimates that it will be able to avoid $4,000 in fixed manufacturing overhead costs if it purchases the board blanks instead of producing them. Should Ozone outsource production of the board blanks?

Answer: In order to compare the cost of internally produced board blanks with purchased blanks, all irrelevant costs (e.g., costs that continue regardless of whether the boards are produced internally or purchased from an external source) must be eliminated from the costs associated with the internally produced blanks. In this instance, total fixed manufacturing overhead costs are $26,000 ($13 per unit X 2,000 units) when the blanks are produced internally. However, if the production of the blanks is outsourced, $4,000 of those costs can be avoided: $22,000 ($22,000/2,000 units = $11.00 per unit) of the fixed manufacturing costs are irrelevant. When comparing the cost of internal production to the cost of purchasing the units from an external source, only the $4,000 of costs ($4,000/2,000 units = $2.00 per unit) that can be eliminated if production is outsourced are relevant production costs.

This leads to the following analysis:

	Make	**Buy**

Direct materials	$15.00	
Direct labor	$20.00	
Variable manufacturing overhead	$10.00	
Avoidable fixed manufacturing overhead ($4,000/2,000 units)	$2.00	
Cost per unit:	$47.00	$48.00
Total costs (unit cost X 2,000 units)	$94,000	$96,000
Difference in favor of producing blanks internally	$2,000	

When only the relevant costs of producing the blanks internally are considered, it becomes clear that Ozone is slightly better off financially when it produces the blanks internally instead of outsourcing them.

With that said, note that strategic considerations may enter into the analysis. For example, concerns over potential environmental liabilities if Ozone continues to produce the blanks internally might cause the company to decide that the $2,000 difference in costs was not sufficient to justify the risks associated with internal production of the blanks. Whenever possible, strategic concerns should be quantified and included in the analysis.

Transfer Pricing

Transfer prices, the prices charged when goods are transferred between organizational divisions, can be determined in several different ways. The method of choice depends on a variety of factors including the sales demand for the goods, the production capacity and costs of the selling unit, the strategic goals of the organization, and the regulatory environment in which the goods are produced. Transfer pricing is tested lightly on the CPA exam - perhaps one question per exam.

I. Introduction

A. When one division of a manufacturing organization supplies components or materials to another division, the **price charged by the selling division to the buying division** is known as the **transfer price**. Transfer prices are usually determined by one of the following methods:

> **Definitions:**
>
> *Market Price*: The price the purchasing unit would have to pay on the open market.
>
> *Cost-based Price*: One of several variations on the selling units' cost of production: variable cost, full cost, cost "plus" (a percentage or a fixed amount).
>
> *Negotiated Price*: A price that is mutually agreeable to both the selling and purchasing unit.

B. In decentralized organizations, the determination of the transfer price is problematic because the managers of the buying and selling departments each seek to maximize their own departmental revenues and minimize their own departmental costs. When both managers **act in their individual best interests, the organization as a whole may suffer** resulting in **suboptimization**. The existence of suboptimal decision-making usually indicates a problem with management's incentive and reward structure known as **goal incongruence**. Goal incongruence exists when **actions encouraged by the reward structure of a department conflict with goals for other departments or the organization as a whole**.

C. For this reason, senior management usually establishes the methodology for setting internal transfer prices in such a way as to promote **goal congruence**. Goal congruence occurs when the **department and division managers make decisions that are consistent with the goals and objectives of the organization as a whole**. Tax and production capacity issues can also complicate the transfer pricing decision.

> **Study Tip:**
> Candidates should be sure to know the definitions of goal congruence, goal incongruence, and suboptimization. These definitions are sometimes tested directly but are also used as distracters in other questions.

II. General transfer pricing rule

A. The following transfer pricing rule helps to ensure goal congruence among department and divisional managers:

> Transfer Price per unit = Additional outlay cost per unit + Opportunity cost per unit

B. The additional outlay cost -- Includes the variable production costs incurred by the selling unit (raw materials, direct labor, and variable factory overhead) plus any additional costs incurred by the selling unit such as storage costs, transportation costs, and administrative selling costs.

> **Study Tip:**
> Market price is the "theoretically correct" transfer price.

C. **Opportunity cost --** Is the **benefit that is forgone as a result of selling internally** rather than externally. Depending on the sales volume and production capacity of the selling unit, there may or may not be an opportunity cost associated with the internal transfer of the goods.

1. **Selling unit is operating at full capacity --** When the selling unit is both producing at full capacity and selling all that it produces, the opportunity cost per unit is equal to the revenue given up if the unit is sold internally less the additional outlay incurred in the production and sale of the unit:

> Opportunity cost per unit = Selling price per unit - Additional outlay cost per unit

Example:
Trotter Parts Supplier, Inc. has two production divisions. Division A produces a Component X, which is used by Division B. Division A pays $8.00 in direct materials, direct labor, and variable factory overhead to produce a unit of Component X and sells to external customers for $14.00 per unit. Based on this information, the opportunity cost associated a unit of Component X is:

Opportunity cost = $14.00 - $8.00 = $6.00

And the transfer price should be:

Transfer price = $8.00 + $6.00 = $14.00

In other words, when the selling unit is operating at full capacity and can sell all that it can produce, the **transfer price should be equal to the market price**. A transfer price that is less than market price is de-motivating for the selling division's manager because that division's return is decreased for every unit sold internally instead of externally.

D. **Selling unit is operating at less than full capacity --** The picture changes when Division A is producing at less than full capacity and has met all of its sales demand. If Division A produces additional units to sell to Division B, no opportunity cost is incurred because no external sales opportunities were forgone: opportunity cost equals zero. The transfer price under these conditions is:

> Transfer price = $8.00 + $0.00 = $8.00

E. That is, when the selling division has excess production capacity, the **transfer price should be equal to the additional costs incurred to produce each unit**. However, because this price provides no additional return to the selling division for units sold internally, most selling units find it unacceptable. In practice, this price usually serves as the lower threshold in a transfer price negotiation or as the basis for cost-based pricing.

III. Negotiated transfer prices

A. In keeping with the concept of decentralization, many organizations permit the buying and selling divisions to negotiate the transfer price directly. The buying division's maximum price will be equal to the minimum price for the item on the open market. The selling division's minimum price will be equal to: 1) its direct costs if it has excess capacity; or 2) its market price if it does not have excess capacity. When no external markets exist for the component being transferred, negotiations are typically based on standard costs and divisional profitability considerations.

B. Although negotiated transfer prices can work well when divisions are on equal footing and when managers are well informed and cooperative, oftentimes this is not the case. When division managers focus primarily on their own profits or are simply not effective negotiators, negotiated transfer prices can lead to divisional strife and run counter to the organization's efforts to create goal congruence among its divisions.

IV. Cost-based pricing

A. Under cost-based pricing, the transfer cost is determined by the selling division's production costs. Although cost-based pricing subject to significant inherent limitations, as long as the selling unit has excess capacity and standard costs are used to set the price, it is a simple, easy-to-understand method to set transfer prices and is used extensively in practice. Several variations on cost-based pricing are common.

1. **Variable cost pricing --** The transfer price is set at the variable costs incurred by the selling division to produce and sell the unit to the purchasing division. In general, these are direct materials costs, direct labor costs, variable factory overhead costs, and variable selling and administrative costs. Note that the **transfer price should always be based on standard costs** rather than actual costs: using actual costs to set the transfer price allows manufacturing inefficiencies to be passed on to the purchasing division and provides no incentive to the selling division to control costs.

   a. Although variable cost pricing is generally attractive to the purchasing division, it does not appropriately motivate the selling division since it only covers the cost of production and does not provide any profit to the selling division.

2. **Full-cost (absorption) pricing --** An allocated portion of the fixed costs of the selling division is added to the product's variable costs to determine the transfer price. Although this price usually has some appeal to both the selling division (it receives some "extra" money to cover fixed costs) and the purchasing division (full absorption cost is likely to be less than the market price), it is problematic for the organization as a whole. Why? Because **the fixed costs allocated to the product by the selling division become variable costs to the purchasing division** as well as to any other divisions who receive the product subsequent to the original purchasing division. When fixed costs are treated like variable costs, any analysis that uses these costs to value earning opportunities will tend to understate profitability.

Example:
Tree House Restaurant runs a catering business in addition to its dine-in restaurant. The two businesses are treated as separate divisions in which the catering business buys products from the restaurant business and then resells them.

The catering business recently had an opportunity to cater a 500-plate luncheon for $7.00 per plate, but rejected the offer because it was not high enough to cover the $5.00 transfer price of the food plus the catering business' additional out-of-pocket costs of $2.50 per plate. The catering manager later discovered that the $5.00 transfer cost included $1.50 of allocated fixed costs and that the actual out-of-pocket costs of producing each plate was only $3.50.

Had the catering job been accepted, the restaurant as a whole would have been $500 better off ($7.00 - ($3.50 + $2.50) = $1.00 contribution margin per plate X 500 plates).

3. **Cost-plus pricing --** The transfer price is based on the selling division's additional costs per unit plus either a fixed dollar amount or a fixed percentage of the cost. Cost-plus pricing has the same advantages and disadvantages as full-cost (absorption) pricing: although it is simple and easily understood, the inclusion of an arbitrary charge as part of the unit cost to the purchasing division may lead to suboptimal decisions later on.

V. Dual pricing

A. Dual pricing is an attempt to eliminate the internal conflicts associated with transfer prices by giving both the buying and selling divisions the price that "works best" for them:

1. **The selling division --** Uses the market price as its transfer (out) price: this eliminates the potential for the selling division to see a decrease in its returns just because it sells products internally instead of externally;

2. **The purchasing division --** Uses standard variable costs as its transfer (in) price: this enhances the usefulness of product costs for decision making purposes and eliminates the need for the purchasing division to "share profits" with the selling division by agreeing to a transfer price above cost.

B. Unfortunately, by giving both the buying and selling divisions prices that enhance their profitability, much of the value of pricing as an incentive for divisions to control costs is lost.

VI. Other considerations

A. Transfer pricing can be a useful tool in promoting goal congruence among organizational divisions, but when production takes place in an international environment, it can be an even more **important tool for reducing tax liability**. Because taxes and import duties vary substantially among countries, the transfer price used to value products as they flow across national boundaries can have a significant affect on the amount of taxes and duties paid. In some domestic instances, transfers of goods across state boundaries can create a similar effect. When these factors enter into play, transfer prices are usually determined by the tax accountant rather than the divisional or corporate managers.

Performance Measures & Management Techniques

Responsibility Accounting

Responsibility accounting - accounting and reporting designed to measure the manager's performance by reporting only those items that are under the manager's control - is fundamental to the management and control processes of all but the smallest organizations. Responsibility accounting is tested regularly, but lightly, on the CPA exam. Questions are almost always conceptual rather than computational.

I. Responsibility Accounting

A. In decentralized organizations, management control is usually established by dividing the organization into **segments - smaller organizational units for which responsibility can be assigned**. Segments can be of many types and sizes: divisions, regions, stores, departments, product lines, sales territories, etc.

B. Segments are also known as **responsibility centers**. Three types of responsibility centers are commonly found:

1. **Cost center** -- An organizational unit whose **manager is responsible only for costs**; cost centers are often service or staff **departments that do not generate revenue**, such as the personnel department, the custodial services department, and production department.
2. **Revenue center** -- An organizational unit whose **manager is responsible only for revenues**; revenue centers are usually sales and marketing departments who have no responsibility for managing costs.
3. **Profit center** -- An organizational unit whose **manager is responsible for both revenues and costs**; profit centers are usually organized around individual stores and/or product types.
4. **Investment center** -- An organizational unit whose **manager is responsible for the return on investment** earned by the center. That is, the manager is not only responsible for revenues and costs, but is also responsible for the **size of the profit earned in relation to the resources invested** in the unit.

Example:

Boggy Farms, Inc. is an integrated organic food company that operates plant research and seed production facilities, a number of small farms which are used both to grow crops and to produce organic fertilizers, and twenty-four retail outlets which sell its products as well as other organic products. Boggy Farms' responsibility and reporting structure is shown below:

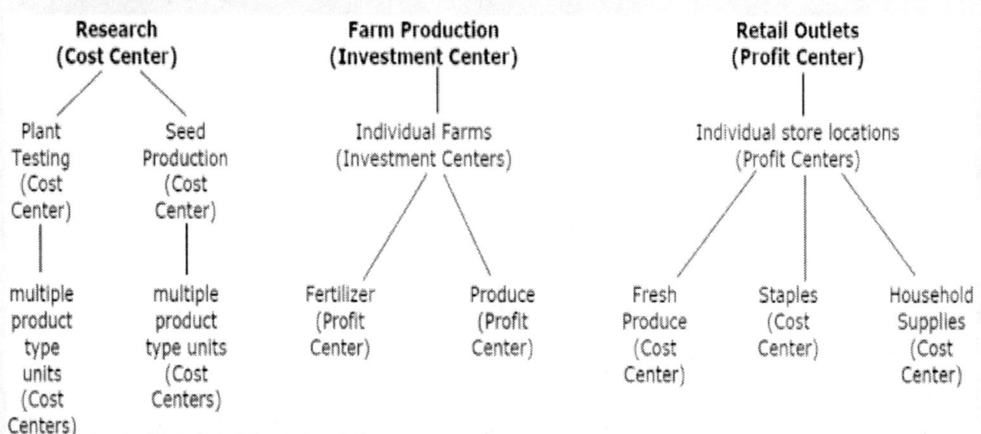

The company is divided into three primary segments (Research, Farm Production, and Retail Outlets), each of which is also a responsibility center. Each main segment is broken down into multiple sub-segments, which are broken down into still smaller sub-segments. Each of these is also an individual responsibility center with a director or manager who is responsible for managing costs, profits, or return on investment.

C. **Responsibility accounting --** Is the name given to the accounting procedures and reports used to measure the performance of the responsibility centers. Responsibility accounting is one of the tools used by management to support goal congruence: goal congruence occurs when all of the segments within an organization and the individuals within each subunit work towards the same goals - the organizational goals set by top management.

D. **Controllability --** A fundamental concept underlying responsibility accounting is controllability - Managers should **only be responsible for costs and/or revenues which they can control**. For example, if the manager of a retail sales outlet cannot choose or negotiate prices for the products sold in the store, the manager should not be held accountable for cost of goods sold as it is outside his/her realm of control. Although there is no universal rule that specifies absolutely which costs are controllable and which costs are uncontrollable, most managers should not be held responsible for depreciation expense or insurance expense because they likely did not make the decisions that generated these costs.

   1. **Allocated costs --** Costs incurred by another unit that are charged to units that benefit from the costs (e.g., custodial costs); **allocated costs are not controllable** by the unit receiving the charge.

E. Just because a cost is uncontrollable at one level does not necessarily mean that it is uncontrollable at other levels. Continuing the retail outlet example, suppose that the performance of all the retail outlets is the responsibility of the vice president of the retail sales division. Though depreciation and insurance costs were uncontrollable for the retail outlet manager, the vice president of the division has the authority to make these decisions and thus depreciation and insurance costs are controllable at the division level.

Study Tip:
Most CPA exam questions about responsibility accounting ask you to either: 1) identify an organizational unit as a cost center, profit center, or investment center; or 2) identify costs as controllable or uncontrollable by a specific manager.

II. Segment reporting

A. Segment reporting can be used both to evaluate manager performance in responsibility centers and to evaluate the overall performance of the organizational divisions themselves. Segment reporting **differs from financial reporting not only in scope** (e.g., specified organizational units rather than the organization as a whole) but in **format** as well. The following is an example of a segment report for the Retail Sales Division:

	Retail Sales	**West Store**	**East Store**	**South Store**
Sales	1,500,000	800,000	400,000	300,000
Variable Operating Expenses:				
Personnel	250,000	130,000	70,000	50,000
Cost of merchandise	450,000	235,000	130,000	85,000
Occupancy	100,000	45,000	30,000	25,000
Other	300,000	140,000	100,000	60,000
Total Variable Operating Exp.	1,100,000	550,000	330,000	220,000
Segment contribution margin	400,000	250,000	70,000	80,000
Less: Controllable fixed expenses	115,000	80,000	20,000	15,000
Profit controllable by manager:	285,000	170,000	50,000	65,000
Less: Traceable fixed expenses	130,000	80,000	25,000	25,000
Segment profit margin	155,000	90,000	25,000	40,000
Less: common fixed expenses	55,000			
Income before taxes	100,000			
Income taxes	39,000			
Net income	61,000			

B. Segment reporting uses a **contribution format**: variable expenses are deducted from revenues to determine the contribution margin. **Fixed costs** are separated into:

1. **Controllable fixed expenses --** Fixed costs that are both traceable to the segment and controllable by the manager:

   a. Deducted from the contribution margin to determine the **profit controllable by the manager**.

b. Used to evaluate the manager's performance.

2. **Traceable fixed expenses --** Fixed costs that can be traced to a particular segment but which are beyond the control of the manager.
   a. Deducted from the profit controllable by the manager to arrive at the segment profit margin.
   b. Used to evaluate overall segment performance.
3. **Common fixed expenses --** Fixed costs that are incurred to benefit more than one segment.

C. Segment performance is tracked through traceable fixed expenses: since common fixed expenses are not allocated to the operational units, only the overall income for the organization is affected by common fixed expenses.

Total Quality Management

The BEC part of the CPA exam has often included content on Total Quality Management (TQM). TQM considers both the quality of design and conformance quality in formulating a company's strategy on the quality dimension. TQM shares a common philosophy with Just-In-Time, and quality is an important dimension to both topics. Categorizing costs in one or more of the four categories of cost of quality (COQ) comprises frequent content tested in this area.

I. Introduction

A. In an increasingly competitive global market, organizations cannot rely solely on price competition as a means of gaining market share. Consumers are only too well aware of the trade-off between price and performance and will abandon low-priced products that fail to perform as expected. The continued improvement in quality across a broad range of products and services partly as a result of modern, automated manufacturing techniques and of the widespread adoption of international quality standards, has significantly increased the average consumer's expectation of quality. Recognizing this, most organizations find it important to make product quality a significant part of their strategic plan.

II. Measuring Quality

A. The basic concept behind quality management is customer satisfaction: customers are satisfied when the products they buy perform as expected. In general, the more a product meets or exceeds a customer's expectations, the higher the level of customer satisfaction. While most firms make periodic attempts to measure customer satisfaction directly through surveys, focus groups, etc., the most commonly used measures of satisfaction are:

1. Sales returns;
2. Warranty costs; and
3. Customer complaints.

> **Study Tip:**
> The examiners frequently ask the candidate to identify measures of customer satisfaction. The measures cited above are the commonly presented examples. The commonly presented distracters (e.g., items which are *not* **measures of customer satisfaction**) include: (1)time required to produce the product; (2)design costs; and (3)testing costs.

III. What is quality?

A. The concept of quality as used in Total Quality Management (TQM) often differs from the the traditional concepts of quality. "Quality" is most commonly used to refer to "grade." For example, a platinum bracelet is usually considered to be of higher quality than a silver bracelet and a Mercedes is usually considered to be a higher quality vehicle than a Ford.

B. However, in TQM, the concept of quality has to do with **how well the item meets its design specifications**. That is, does it perform as it is expected to perform? Using this concept of quality, a car that is designed to have high fuel economy but not a lot of power (as defined by its ability to go from zero to sixty miles per hour in a specified number of seconds) and meets those objectives without experiencing any other significant failures is a much higher quality vehicle than a high-end sports car that has a lot of power but is plagued by constant engine problems and so is often under repair. This concept of quality is known as **"quality of conformance."**

> "The quality of conformance refers to the degree to which a product meets its design specifications and/or customer expectations."

C. TQM relies on Quality of Conformance as evidenced by the fact that the TQM philosophy includes measuring results frequently. That is, if results are measured frequently, then they must have certain expectations in mind to evaluate the results. This is quality of conformance (AKA conformance to specifications). On the other hand, conformance to a product design that the customer does not want is destined to failure. Therefore, quality of design is also important. Thus, quality addresses two perspectives in TQM:

1. Failure to execute the product design as specified;
2. Failure to design the product appropriately; **quality of design** is defined as **meeting or exceeding the needs and wants of customers**.

D. The customer's perception of quality depends on both high quality of conformance and high quality of design. Thus, TQM attempts to satisfy both of these definitions of quality.

IV. Cost of Quality

A. The costs incurred by an organization to ensure that its products and/or services have a high "quality of conformance" are known as **costs of quality** and are divided into four categories:

1. **Prevention costs --** Costs incurred to **prevent the production of defective products**:
   a. Re-engineering to improve product design;
   b. Improved production processes;
   c. Better quality materials;
   d. Programs to train personnel.
2. **Appraisal costs --** Costs incurred to **identify defective products during the manufacturing process**:
   a. Inspection;
   b. Testing.
3. **Internal failure costs --** Costs of **defective components and final products identified prior to shipment**:
   a. Scrap;
   b. Rework;
   c. Costs of delays due to defective products.
4. **External failure costs --** Costs caused by **failure of products in the hands of the customer**:
   a. Field repairs;
   b. Returns;
   c. Warranty expenses;
   d. Litigation.

Study Tip:
There is almost always one question about TQM in Planning & Measurement and it usually asks the candidate to match a cost of quality (e.g., cost of using better quality materials, cost of scrap, cost of sales returns, etc.) with its appropriate category (i.e., prevention costs, appraisal costs, internal failure costs, or external failure costs).

V. Total Cost of Quality

A. An organization's total cost of quality is the sum of its prevention, appraisal, internal failure, and external failure costs. There is inverse tradeoff between the cost of failure (internal or external), and the cost of prevention and appraisal in determining the total quality of conformance:

1. When the **overall quality of conformance is low**, more of the total cost of quality is typically related to **cost of failure**. For example, a manufacturer substitutes a lower quality power cord connection on one of its products with the result that, after a short period of use, the power cords tended to break, rendering the product unusable. This problem causes the quality of conformance for the product to be lower and the cost of external failure to be higher.

2. **Increases in the costs of prevention** and the **cost of appraisal** are usually accompanied by **decreases in the cost of failure** and **increases in the quality of conformance**. Continuing with the power cord example, if the manufacturer increased the amount of testing completed before the product was shipped, more defective products would be discovered. This would **increase the cost of internal failure**, but **decrease the cost of external failure**. Since the cost of an external failure is normally greater per unit than the cost of an internal failure (that is, it is less expensive to identify a faulty product before it is has left the factory than to replace or refund a faulty product in the hands of a consumer or distributor), the **overall cost of failure decreases**.

    a. An even more effective method of reducing the overall cost of failure is to increase efforts to **prevent** failures. Although increasing product quality testing (costs of appraisal) saves the difference between the cost of an internal failure and an external failure, the testing itself incurs additional costs and does nothing to increase the product's overall quality of conformance. On the other hand, increased spending on prevention potentially both reduces the cost of failure and increases the quality of conformance. Returning to the power cord example, if the company increases the quality of the power cord connection (thus, making the product less likely to fail) and makes no changes to product testing, the costs of failure due to this problem can perhaps be eliminated completely and the quality of conformance is greatly improved. In general, **the cost of prevention is both less than the cost of appraisal** ***and*** **less than the cost of failure**.

VI. ISO 9000 Standards

A. In 1987, the International Standards Organization (ISO) issued **a set of quality control standards known as the ISO 9000 standard**. Though directed primarily towards companies selling products in the European market, the standard is largely accepted in the international community. The ISO 9000 standard is actually a "family" of standards (ISO 9001, ISO 9002, ISO 9003 and ISO 9004) and has been updated several times: once in 1994 and again in 2000. The ISO 9000 standard specifies requirements of an effective overall program of quality management, including:

    1. Documented procedures to manage quality across the organization;

    2. For each product, a set of quality objectives, tests, and procedures to document the test results for use in improving product quality;

    3. Facilitating continuous improvement by regularly reviewing the individual processes and the quality system.

B. ISO 9000 compliance is certified by a number of accreditation bodies. It is important to note that certification to an ISO 9000 standard **does not guarantee the quality of end products and services**; rather, it **certifies that consistent business processes are being applied**.

Inventory Management

The Economic Order Quantity (EOQ) model and the Just-in-time (JIT) inventory model are the push and pull models (respectively) illustrated and discussed in the inventory management area. Topics related to these models are also covered, including backflush costing. These models and related features are tested regularly, though not heavily on the CPA exam (usually one question per exam). Questions in this area are often conceptual tending to focus on the conditions necessary to successfully implement JIT processes and recall characteristics of the EOQ approach. Unless otherwise stated, models tend to focus on a cost minimization approach to inventory management, with the only tradeoff being the maintenance of adequate inventory to service operations.

I. Just-in-time Inventory Management

A. Just-in-time inventory management is a key component of the "pull" production processes that have transformed much of the manufacturing world over the past twenty years. The central idea of just-in-time inventory management is simple: **do not do any work until demanded by customer orders**. Thus, customer demand "pulls" material orders, labor, and all other manufacturing activity through the plant.

1. By ordering inventory items only as they are needed, **carrying costs related to the raw materials inventory can be dramatically reduced or even eliminated**.
2. When costs are reduced, resources - both financial and operational - are made available for other productive uses. For example, if a custom wooden shingle manufacturer changed to JIT inventory management, not only would the company avoid the cost of putting the raw lumber stock into storage and then moving it to the production line when it was needed, it could use the freed-up cash and warehouse space to expand its operations.

B. Though the JIT concept was initially directed at purchases of raw materials inventory, it was soon extended to work-in-process and finished goods inventories as well. The application of JIT concepts to finished goods inventories gave rise to "pull" production processes. Prior to JIT inventory management, most goods were produced using **"push" production practices**:

1. In contrast to JIT, "push" systems manufacture based on forecasted sales and budget projections. A **production schedule is created based on the budgeted sales** volume and units are "pushed" through the production process into finished goods inventory in accordance with the schedule.
2. When actual sales are less than budgeted sales, finished goods inventory accumulates in the warehouse.

C. In a **"pull" production process**, the **production schedule is determined by the actual sale of goods**:

1. As customer orders are received, goods are scheduled for production.
2. In a multi-step production process, the later steps "pull" production through the earlier steps. For example, consider the wooden shingle manufacturer's three-step production process:
    - **a.** Lengths of raw lumber are cut into shingle-sized pieces.
    - **b.** The raw shingles are soaked in a chemical bath to preserve their color and to increase their fire resistance and then removed and dried.
    - **c.** The dried shingles are packaged for delivery.

d. Under pull production processes, when customer orders are received, the packaging process requests dried shingles from the preserving process, the preserving process requests raw shingles from the cutting process and, finally, the cutting process requests only enough raw lumber to fill the current order.

D. In a well-managed JIT system, *all* **inventories will be eliminated**: there will be no raw materials inventory, no work-in-process inventories for any production period and no finished goods inventory.

E. Of course, in order for JIT inventory and production management to work properly, all supply and production processes must function flawlessly: a **problem in any production or supply process will be felt immediately** throughout the entire production line because there are no inventories (buffer stock) to cushion a break in the flow of production. In particular, the following characteristics must be present in order for JIT inventory management to function properly:

1. The company places **many small orders** that the suppliers must **deliver frequently in a timely manner**.
2. To motivate suppliers to provide a high level of performance and reliability, buyers usually negotiate **long-term contracts** with a much **smaller number of (certified) suppliers** than would be the case in a traditional processing environment. Certified suppliers guarantee the delivery time and quality of the units according to the terms of the long-term contract. Vendors often **use electronic funds transfer to pay invoices, and factories often have systems to provide real-time order information to suppliers**.
3. Raw materials must be of **consistently high quality**. Because, there is little or no excess inventory to fall back on, the entire production process may be delayed if any materials are faulty.
4. When the company is confident that the goods are of high quality and when there is a strong relationship with the supplier, **inspection of materials** can be reduced to a minimum. Most inspection is done by highly skilled direct laborers directly on the manufacturing line. These laborers work cooperatively in U-shaped "islands" or manufacturing "cells" and also maintain their own workspace, keeping the area clean and often doing their own machine maintenance.
5. **Order and payment processing costs must be reduced**, often by use of an electronic order and payment system known as integrated computer based manufacturing (ICBM). Because of the higher level of trust between the customer and the supplier, some of the controls and procedures usually present between trading partners are dropped. For example, suppliers may check the production schedule directly and make ordering decisions independently. Also, suppliers are often paid on a periodic basis (e.g., monthly) rather than for each delivery (based on the terms of the long-term contracts mentioned earlier).

F. Changes in the purchasing and delivery processes are only the first changes that must take place. Once the raw materials are received, the production process must also be modified in order to support production of small batches of products. Just-in-time production environments are characterized by:

1. A flexible manufacturing environment that can be **set up quickly** when a different product needs to be produced. Emphasis is on constantly reducing setup time, lead time, and cycle time, and simplifying production processes.
2. A **skilled, flexible, and empowered workforce** that can **perform multiple tasks**. In just-in-time production environments, workers are often organized in teams or manufacturing cells. In this environment, each worker is able to perform many or all of the tasks necessary to complete the product and can

Study Tip:
The characteristics necessary for JIT to function properly and the characteristics of a JIT production environment are the most frequently tested concepts in this section.

switch from one task to another as necessary to keep the production flow moving. This approach aids in production line smoothing. Employees are cross-trained to improve production flexibility and work cooperation. They are empowered to stop the production line to resolve problems.

3. A very **low rate of defects**. Because there are few or no "extra" units in the production process, virtually all units must be good or the production line will not be able to produce the required units of finished goods.

Study Tip:
JIT and TQM were both championed by the same person, Dr. W. Edwards Deming. Accordingly, both methods stress the importance of quality and share a common philosophy and body of knowledge.

G. As can be seen from the foregoing discussion, JIT inventory management processes are consistent with:

1. **Total Quality Management (TQM)**, which encourages elimination of product defects in order to minimize costs of quality.

H. Just as JIT management ultimately necessitates just-in-time production management, a JIT production environment is often accompanied by a specialized product costing technique called **backflush costing**. Backflush costing is a product costing approach in which **costing is delayed until goods are completed** or, in some cases, until the goods are sold.

I. Traditional costing begins by flowing costs into work-in-process inventory and through each processing procedure until they flow into finished goods when production is complete. As goods are purchased by customers, costs flow out of finished goods into cost of goods sold. This approach is known as "sequential tracking" cost accounting.

J. In contrast, backflush costing is premised on the idea that when JIT inventory and production management practices are in place, there will be little or no raw materials, work-in-process inventory, or finished goods inventory. Because virtually all costs pass immediately through the raw materials and work-in-process inventories into finished goods and on to the cost of goods sold, it makes little sense to spend time and money tracking costs through these inventories:

1. Rather than flowing costs into raw material and work-in-process, the **actual costs of production are accumulated in a control account**.
2. When goods are completed, **finished goods is debited for the standard cost** of the number of units produced and the control account is credited (alternatively, if there is little or no finished goods inventory, the standard cost of the units sold may be debited to cost of goods sold).
3. Any **balance remaining in the control account** (the difference between the actual costs of production and the standard cost of production) is normally **written off to cost of goods sold**.
4. To the extent that there is work-in-process inventory, costs are **moved out of finished goods** (e.g., credited to Finished Goods) and **debited to work-in-process** at the standard price.
5. In other words: "**...standard costs are flushed backward through the system to assign costs to products**. The result is that **detailed tracking of costs is eliminated**."

K. Although **backflush costing simplifies the costing process**, it fails to allocate significant variances back to the product inventories and thus inventories on the balance sheet may be undervalued. Because of this problem, **backflush costing is** *not* **consistent with GAAP**.

II. Economic Order Quantity Model (EOQ)

A. EOQ is an annual model used to determine the most economical amount to order by minimizing the total sum of ordering costs and carrying costs over the year.

B. Costs of ordering inventory decrease with the size of orders.

C. Costs of carrying inventory increase with the size of orders.

D. Ordering costs are usually stated explicitly in computations, but they normally include purchasing, shipping, setup, and lost quantity discounts.

E. Carrying costs include costs of storage, obsolescence and/or perishability, insurance, rent, property taxes, security, depreciation, handling, and the cost of capital of the inventory itself (opportunity cost). Understand that the opportunity cost of the inventory is not equal to the cost of the units of inventory themselves. The inventory cost itself is neither an ordering nor a carrying cost.

Note: Although tedious, the questions often have asked the candidate to identify which costs are in each category, so be prepared for this.

$$EOQ = \sqrt{\frac{2\ DO}{C}}$$

Where,

D = annual unit 'D'emand
O = 'O'rdering cost
C = 'C'arrying cost per unit

III. EOQ Model Features

A. The primary disadvantage of the EOQ model is that its assumption of constant demand may not be realistic.

B. Safety stock is the minimum amount of inventory that must be maintained to prevent stockouts (running out of inventory).

C. In the EOQ model, safety stock represents the planned inventory level at the reorder point less inventory used during lead time (allowed for shipping).

D. Safety stock is calculated as (max lead time - mean lead time in days) x (average usage per day).

E. Stockout costs are primarily lost sales and customer dissatisfaction.

F. Ideally (and similar to the tradeoff of order costs and carrying costs), the cost of safety stock and stockouts should be minimized.

Note:
The reorder point in the EOQ model is equal to the safety stock amount plus the amount of units in inventory that are expected to be used while waiting for inventory to be replenished (i.e., used during lead time).

Balanced Scorecard and Benchmarking

The balanced scorecard and benchmarking are tools for evaluating organizational performance within the context of its overall business strategy. The balanced scorecard identifies financial and non-financial critical success factors within a four-category classification system (Financial, Customer, Internal Procedures, & Learning and Growth) and defines performance measures to evaluate the organization's success in each category. Benchmarking identifies the "best practices" for the organization's critical success factors and continuously compares them to the organization's policies and procedures. The balanced scorecard and benchmarking are lightly tested on the CPA exam (one question every exam or two). Most balanced scorecard questions ask the candidate to identify performance measures in one of the four classifications.

I. Introduction

A. This topic demonstrates how value creation can be linked to strategy using the Balanced Scorecard and other initiatives.

II. Balanced Scorecard

A. The *balanced scorecard* translates an organization's mission and strategy into a comprehensive set of performance metrics.

B. The BSC does *not* focus solely on financial metrics.

C. It highlights both nonfinancial and financial metrics that an organization can use to measure strategic progress.

III. Balanced Scorecard Perspectives

A. The Balanced Scorecard is viewed from the following four perspectives:

1. **Financial** - specific measures of financial performance
2. **Customer** - performance related to targeted customer and market segments
3. **Internal Business Processes** - performance of the internal operations that create value (i.e., new product development, production, distribution, after-the-sale customer service)
4. **Learning, Innovation, and Growth** - performance characteristics of the company's personnel and abilities to adapt and respond to change (e.g., employee skills, employee training and certification, employee morale, and employee empowerment)

B. These classifications facilitate evaluation of the organization's fundamental resources - its people, its processes, and its customers - in relation to its financial performance.

C. Different strategies call for different scorecards. Within each of the four classifications, the organization identifies its

1. **strategic goals,**
2. **critical success factors,**
3. **tactics, and**
4. **performance measures.**

Example:
Marfu Manufacturing, a producer of kitchen and bathroom countertops, has decided to pursue a strategy of high quality and product innovation and has identified the following critical success factors, tactics, and performance measures related to this strategy:

	Critical Success Factor	Tactic	Performance Measure
Financial Perspective	Maintain high margins while gradually growing	Gradually phase out low margin jobs	Percentage of jobs with margins over 50%
Customer Perspective	Develop a high level of customer recognition as a cutting edge design firm	Maintain a high profile through participation in design competitions	Number of competitions entered; number of awards won.
Internal Business Processes Perspective	Execute designs with an extremely high level of craftsmanship	Develop quality specifications for each job and evaluate at project completion	Number of quality inspection problems noted per job
Learning, Innovation, and Growth Perspective	Attract and retain highly qualified, innovative designers	Promote employee development through continued education and support of professional certification activities	Percentage of design employees who have acquired professional certifications

D. Effective scorecards are designed so that the **tactics that promote achievement of strategic goals in one area support achievement of strategic goals in other areas**. For example:

1. aggressive hiring of employees with strong research and development skills (a tactic from the Learning, Innovation, and Growth perspective) should result in more new and improved products (a strategic goal from the Internal Business Processes perspective);
2. new and improved products should help the company penetrate new markets (a strategic goal from the Customer perspective);
3. penetration of new markets should lead to additional revenues, which should improve financial performance (a strategic goal from the Financial perspective).

IV. Creating the Balanced Scorecard

A. The first step in creating a balanced scorecard is identification of the organization's strategic objectives in each of the four areas. Once the objectives have been determined, **SWOT analysis** (see Strategic Management) is used to identify the critical success factors necessary for the organization to achieve its strategic objectives within each of the four perspectives.

B. The organization must then develop operational tactics - courses of action - designed to achieve the goals specified by the critical success factors. Finally, performance measures must be developed for each tactic to determine whether the tactics have been successfully implemented.

Study Tip:
Most balanced scorecard questions on the CPA exam ask the candidate to identify performance measures associated with one of the four classifications or, conversely, to identify the classification in which a particular performance measure would be found.

C. Common performance measures include:

1. **Financial:** Gross profit margin, sales growth, profitability per job or product, stock price, achievement of cash flow goals, any of the standard financial ratios (inventory turnover, return on investment, current ratio, etc.);
2. **Customer:** Market share, product returns as a percentage of sales, number of new customers, percentage of repeat customers, customer satisfaction as measured by customer surveys, customer complaints, sales trends, etc.;
3. **Internal Business Processes:** Percentage of production downtime, **delivery cycle time** (time between order and delivery), **manufacturing cycle time/throughput** (the time required to turn raw materials into completed products), **manufacturing cycle efficiency** (ratio of time required for nonvalue-adding activities to the total manufacturing cycle time), standard cost variances, product defect rate, amount of scrap and rework;
4. **Learning, Innovation, and Growth:** Percentage of employees with professional certifications, hours of training per employee, number of new products developed, employee turnover, number of customer requests for specific designers, percentage of project proposals accepted, and employee satisfaction levels.

Study Tip:
Definitions of the manufacturing performance measures listed in the Internal Business Processes section (**delivery cycle time, manufacturing cycle time, and manufacturing cycle efficiency**) occasionally appear in CPA exam questions.

V. Features of a good balanced scorecard

A. Articulates a company's strategy by trying to map a sequence of cause-and-effect relationships through metrics.

B. Assists in communicating the strategy to all members of the organization by translating the strategy into a coherent and linked set of measurable operational targets.

C. The scorecard limits the number of measures used by identifying only the most critical ones (Kaplan and Norton suggest a total of 15 to 20).

D. The scorecard highlights suboptimal tradeoffs that managers may make.

VI. Pitfalls that should be avoided when implementing a balanced scorecard.

A. Don't assume the cause-and-effect linkages to be precise.

B. Don't seek improvements across all measures all the time.

C. Don't use only objective measures on the scorecard.

D. Don't fail to consider both costs and benefits of initiatives such as spending on information technology and research and development.

E. Don't ignore nonfinancial metrics when evaluating managers and employees.

VII. Common problems with metric choices

A. Items chosen leave out important criteria (e.g., both speed and quality are important but can often be traded off, so measuring one without the other will encourage dysfunctional results).

B. The metric may be either too broad or too specific.

VIII. Benchmarking

A. **Benchmarking --** is a technique of organizational self-assessment via internal and external comparison to sources of excellence in performance. In other words, you try to find someone who is doing it better than you and attempt to emulate their performance!

B. **Benchmarking should be done systematically --** Identify companies that are best-in-class performers,

1. measure and compare your performance to others,
2. attempt to determine drivers of performance,
3. establish goals, and
4. formulate a plan to increase performance compatible with strategy.

C. **Important points and features of benchmarking**

1. A company can't be the best at everything. Benchmarking should be done in the key areas that create a unique competitive advantage as determined by the company's distinctive competencies.
2. Because best practices change over time, benchmarking should be an ongoing process within the organization. In this way, benchmarking supports continuous learning and improvement. Priorities for benchmarking can change over time - expect this.
3. Don't try to focus on improving in every benchmark all the time.

D. Benchmarking is one tool that can be used to help create an atmosphere that supports a **learning organization**. Learning organizations are able to remain competitive in volatile environments because of their **ability to evaluate and interpret information** and their **willingness to embrace change**. Learning organizations are characterized by flexibility - a willingness to adopt new ideas and new processes - and efficiency in the acquisition and distribution of information. Human capital is especially important in learning organizations, as it is the source of the organization's creativity and vitality.

Strategic Management

Strategic management is the process of formulating organizational goals and objectives, developing tactics to achieve these goals, and designing performance measures to evaluate whether the goals and objectives are being met. To date, strategic management has been very lightly tested on the CPA exam.

I. **Introduction --** Organizational strategy defines how the organization competes in the marketplace. It is the driving force behind operations and the foundation upon which both short-term and long-term decisions are made. Most organizations have a number of strategies in place at any given time: a personnel strategy, an operations strategy, a marketing strategy, etc. However, all of these strategies derive from the overall organizational strategy and mission statement.

II. **Evaluating competitive intensity**

A. Numerous models have been developed to help formulate organizational strategy. One widely used model developed by Michael Porter and generally known as "Porter's Five Forces" evaluates the competitive intensity of the organization's industry by analyzing the market on five dimensions

B. **Bargaining power of customers**

1. An analysis of customer characteristics and the product choice options available to them; characteristics of interest include:

   a. Size of the customer base;

   b. Buyer volume;

   c. Availability of substitute products;

   d. Cost of switching to alternate products.

2. In general, environments in which there are relatively few customers, where alternative products are available, where the cost of switching to alternative products is low, and/or where high volume purchases are common tend to favor the customer and create a more difficult competitive environment.

C. **Bargaining power of suppliers**

1. An analysis of the supplier characteristics that affect the ability of the organization to negotiate for favorable treatment when purchasing materials or services characteristics of interest include:

   a. Number of suppliers relative to the number of firms;

   b. Availability of alternative product inputs;

   c. Cost of switching to an alternate product input.

2. When there are relatively few suppliers, few alternative products, and/or when the cost of switching to an alternative product is high, the supplier has an advantage over the buyer; the buyer's inability to negotiate effectively limits the competitive options available to him/her.

D. **Threat of new entrants**

1. Factors that affect the ability of new companies to enter the market include:

a. The amount of capital required to enter the market;

b. The extent of government regulation of the industry;

c. The existence of brand identity and loyalty;

d. The existence of product patents;

e. The availability of distribution channels;

f. The existence of other barriers to entry.

2. The easier it is for companies to enter the market, the greater the potential for competition within the market.

E. Threat of substitute products

1. The availability of alternative products or technologies limits the competitive strategies available to the organization. The threat of substitutes is impacted by:

a. The perceived level of product differentiation;

b. The cost of switching from one product to another;

c. The relative performance of substitute products;

d. The cost of substitute products.

2. Low levels of perceived differentiation, low switching costs and substitute costs, and little difference in performance significantly increase the threat of substitute products to the organization.

F. Intensity of competition

1. The current level of competition in the market also limits the competitive strategies available to the organization. Intensity of competition can be assessed by evaluating:

a. The number and diversity of competitors in the market;

b. The existence of barriers to exit;

c. The growth rate of the market.

G. The existence of a large number of diverse competitors, high barriers to exit, and/or a low growth rate make it much more difficult for an organization to compete.

H. Analysis of the five forces provides an understanding of the competitive forces in the marketplace upon which the organization's competitive strategy can be built.

I. This analysis shows how a firm can use these forces to obtain a sustainable competitive advantage. Porter modifies Chandler's dictum about structure following strategy by introducing a second level of structure: Organizational structure follows strategy, which in turn follows industry structure. Porter's generic strategies detail the interaction between **cost minimization strategies, product differentiation strategies, and market focus strategies**.

III. Competitive strategies

A. An organization's competitive strategy defines the way in which it positions itself to compete in the marketplace. Porter's model identifies two generic strategies of competition in broad, typically national or international, markets:

1. **Product differentiation**

a. A differentiated product is perceived to offer unique features or benefits to the customer (e.g., gasoline that contains additives to improve engine longevity); in general, differentiated products inspire higher levels of brand loyalty in customers, making them less sensitive to price differences among products.

b. In order to support a strategy of product differentiation, the organization must:

i. Foster continued product innovation and improvement through investment in research and development;

ii. Effectively market the product to maintain the brand distinction.

2. **Cost leadership** -- Cost leadership focuses on the organization's ability to sell a high volume of low cost products. In order to be able to implement this strategy, the organization must have high levels of productivity and efficiency and access to extensive distribution resources. Additional factors affecting the successful implementation of a cost leadership strategy include:

a. Proprietary production technology;

b. Access to low-cost production inputs (raw materials, labor, etc.);

c. Access to low-cost capital.

B. It is also possible to segment the market, selecting a few target markets in which to compete rather than trying to compete across the entire market. Segmentation of the marketplace yields a third competitive strategy known as a **focus strategy** or, more generically, **"niche marketing."** Segments (or niches) may be based on geographic regions, population demographics, or a variety of special interests or needs. Competitive advantage is gained by customizing the product to meet the needs of the specialized market segment. Competition within market segments can be based either on low cost (**cost focus**) or on product differentiation (**focused differentiation**).

C. **"Quick response" strategies** -- Which focus on either being the first to bring a product to market or in providing quick delivery of the product to the customer, are variations of focus strategy.

IV. **Environmental Scanning**

A. In recent years, increased competition and rapid changes in the competitive environment have necessitated more frequent reviews of the organization's strategies to ensure that the strategies remain viable in the changing marketplace. **Environmental scanning** is a process in which the **organization continuously gathers and evaluates information that could impact its ability to compete** using its current organizational strategies. The information gathered in environmental scanning comes from many sources including (but not limited to):

1. **Economic sources** -- Productivity measures (GDP, GNP), economic growth rate, exchange rate, unemployment rate, rate of inflation;

2. **Regulatory sources** -- Tax regulations, industry requirements, political climate, monopoly laws, safety guidelines (OHSA), international tariffs and duties;

3. **Environmental sources** -- Climate change, environmental consciousness/awareness, access to natural resources, transportation and communication infrastructure.

Study Tip:
Questions about SWOT analysis appear occasionally on the CPA exam. Questions in this area usually require identification of the SWOT analysis categories (Strengths, Weaknesses, Opportunities, Threats) and/or examples of items that would appear in the categories.

B. Once the information is gathered, **SWOT analysis** (identification of **S**trengths, **W**eaknesses, **O**pportunities, and **T**hreats), is often used to develop the organization's competitive profile: the strategies the organization can employ to pursue opportunities and counter threats. SWOT analysis analyzes the organization's **internal factors (strengths and weaknesses)** in the context of the relevant **external factors (opportunities and threats)** to develop competitive strategies. The matrix format shown below is useful in identifying strategies within the context of a SWOT analysis (sample Strengths, Weaknesses, Opportunities, Threats are provided):

	Strengths (favorable location; access to inexpensive raw materials; loyal, experienced employees)	**W**eaknesses (limited access to capital, long manufacturing cycle time)
Opportunities (high growth rate, limited number of competitors)	Strategies that use organizational Strengths to take advantage of Opportunities	Strategies that minimize organizational Weaknesses to take advantage of Opportunities
Threats (potential for government regulation, dependence on foreign supply sources)	Strategies that use organizational Strengths to take counter Threats	Strategies that minimize organizational Weaknesses to avoid Threats

V. Theory of Constraints

A. The theory of constraints identifies strategies to maximize income when the organization is faced with **bottleneck operations**. A bottleneck operation occurs when the **work to be performed exceeds the capacity of the production facilities**. Over the short run, revenue is maximized by maximizing the contribution margin of the constrained resource.

B. Revenue can also be improved by finding ways to relax the constraint. The following are commonly used methods of relaxing the constraint (eliminating the bottleneck):

1. Re-engineer the production process to make it more efficient;
2. Re-engineer the product to make it simpler to produce;
3. Eliminate nonvalue-added activities at the bottleneck operation;
4. Work overtime at the bottleneck operation;
5. Outsource some or all production at the bottleneck operation.

VI. Product mix decisions under constrained resources

A. In instances when production capacity is insufficient to meet demand, producing the item that **maximizes the contribution margin per unit of the constrained resource** maximizes profitability for the organization:

> **Study Tip:**
> Production decisions under constrained resources are tested regularly, though not heavily, on the CPA exam. In these questions, it is each product's **contribution margin per unit of the constrained resource** that determines profitability, not the product's individual unit contribution margin.

Example:
Fusion Foods produces two organic cereals: Granola Gems and Mixed Grain Magic. Cost data for the two products is shown below:

	Granola Gems	**Mixed Grain Magic**
Sales Price (per 2 lb. bag)	$5.00	$7.00
Variable costs:		
Direct materials	$1.50	$1.85
Direct labor	$1.00	$1.25
Variable overhead	$1.50	$1.95
Variable selling & administrative	$0.50	$1.00
Total variable costs:	$4.50	$6.00
Total Contribution Margin:	$0.50	$1.00
Contribution Margin as a Percentage of Sales Price	10%	14.2%

Although Fusion can sell as much of either of the types of cereals as it can produce, its baking ovens can only be run 12 hours per day, constraining the quantity of product that Fusion can produce. The baking ovens can process 72 pounds of Granola Gems in one hour; however, they can only process 30 lbs of Mixed Grain Magic in one hour. What product (or products) should Fusion produce?

Although Mixed Grain Magic is the more profitable of the two products in terms unit contribution margin ($1.00) and contribution margin percentage (14.2%), using all of the production capacity to produce Mixed Grain Magic will not maximize revenue. Why not? Because the amount of cereal that can be processed in a day is constrained by the amount of oven time available and Mixed Grain Magic requires over twice as much oven time than Granola Gems.

To determine which product to produce, we must determine the **contribution margin per hour of oven time**:

	Granola Gems	**Mixed Grain Magic**
Contribution margin per unit:	$0.50	$1.00
Number of pounds per oven hour	X 72 lbs.	X 30 lbs.
Contribution margin per hour	$36/hour	$30.00

Despite its smaller unit contribution margin, Granola Gems provides a higher total contribution margin than Mixed Grain Magic because of its higher contribution margin per unit of the constrained resource.

Competitive Analysis

Competitive analysis includes value based management, profitability/return analysis, target pricing markups, price elasticity, and key performance metrics such as return on investment, residual income, and economic value added

I. **Conventional Financial Performance Metrics --** These metrics have been around for many years and often tend to focus on external capital market analysis elements such as income and the investment base.

A. Return on Investment (ROI) = Net Income / Total Assets

> DuPont Formula = Return on Sales (ROS) x Asset Turnover, where
>
> ROS = Net Income / Sales
>
> Asset Turnover = Sales / Total Assets

1. The DuPont approach to ROI separates ROI into two parts for analysis. The two pieces allow a separate evaluation of profitability as a percent of sales and the efficiency with which assets were utilized to generate those sales. Multiplying the two parts together results in ROI.

Example:
A company is concerned that although profitability is comparable with competitors, their return results have been poor. The company has a new building with a significant degree of excess/idle capacity. The industry average ROI is 20%, with average profit margins of 10%. The company posted the following results for the current year: net income of $80,000; sales of $700,000; and assets of $530,000. How can the company explain the difference between profitability versus return?

Profit Margin * Asset Turnover = Return on Investment

(Net Income / Sales) * (Sales / Total Assets) = ROI

($80,000 / $700,000) * ($700,000 / $530,000) = ROI

11.43% * 1.32 = 15.1%

The profit margin of 11.43% is actually better than the industry average of 10%. However, the efficiency with which assets were used (as shown by the asset turnover) at 1.32 turns is lagging the industry average of 2 turns. Note: the industry average turnover can be found by dividing the ROI of 20% by the profit margin of 10%.

2. The focus on ROI is consistent with the approach taken by external financial analysts making ROI a very important performance metric by which companies are evaluated. However, for internal purposes, ROI suffers from potential accrual distortions and its vulnerability to the diluted hurdle rate problem.

Example:
Diluted Hurdle Rate: A manager (with incentive compensation based on ROI) has four assets with an average return (ROI) of 28%. The manager has idle cash to invest in a project that is expected to achieve a return of 25%. The company has a hurdle rate (i.e., required minimum return target) of 20%. Conclusion: The manager will be unwilling to invest in a project earning any amount less than the current 28% because it would dilute (i.e., reduce) the average return on the total. This manager's preferred decision is bad for the company since, if the decision is up to the manager, the cash will remain unused, not generating a return. The diluted hurdle rate problem is associated with virtually all metrics expressed as rates.

Note:
There are multiple ways of calculating residual income in the sense that some sources suggest using net income or NOPAT instead of operating income as shown above. The required rate of return is also referred to as the minimum required rate of return but can be equal to whatever management decides. Invested capital is usually total assets, but again can be modified to suit the needs of the user. This is why RI is referred to as a "general" form of economic profit.

B. Residual Income (RI) = Operating Income - required rate of return (invested capital)

C. Residual income (RI) is a general form of economic profit. Economic profit differs from accounting income in that it recognizes the cost of capital. RI has often been used as an alternative to ROI to preclude the diluted hurdle rate problem by expressing the return on investment in terms of dollars rather than a rate.

Example:
A company has a hurdle rate for investments of 20% and is considering basing the manager's bonus on return on either investment (ROI) or residual income (RI). The manager has achieved an impressive level of performance with an average cumulative return so far of 32%. A prospective investment of $1,000,000 is being considered that is estimated to earn $300,000 in profits. Which metric should be used (i.e., ROI or RI) and why?

The ROI is 30% = $300,000 / $1,000,000. This amount clearly exceeds the hurdle rate established for the manager of 20%, but if the manager's bonus is based on ROI, the manager has no personal incentive to make the investment since it would bring down (i.e., dilute) the current average return achieved of 32%. Thus, what's good for the company is not good for the manager personally. Residual income would be calculated as $100,000 = $300,000 - .2 ($1,000,000). The RI result provides a positive outcome where the income earned exceeds the cost of capital. Thus, with RI the manager and the company both are incentivized to make the investment. This is an outcome that provides goal congruence for the manager and organization.

II. Value-based Management (VBM) -- refers to relatively new financial metrics and processes for using them. The most popular VBM metrics and their creators include Economic Value Added (EVA) - Stern Stewart & Company and Cash Flow Return on Investment (CFROI) - Boston Consulting Group

Study Tip:
Economic value added is perhaps especially important since it is mentioned more than once in the detailed content specification outline.

A. EVA = NOPAT - WACC (Total Assets - Current Liabilities)

1. NOPAT = net operating profit after tax; WACC = weighted average cost of capital

WACC summarizes the overall cost of capital based on the weighted proportion of debt versus equity after reducing the cost of debt by the marginal tax rate.

Example:
For a firm that has $40 million in debt costing 10%, $60 million in owners' equity costing 14%, and a marginal tax rate of 40%, the WACC would be 10.8% = 40/100(10%)(1-.4) + 60/100(14%).

2. EVA is an **economic profit** (EP) metric and a **specific form of residual income**. Like other forms of residual income EVA is **stated in dollars**.
3. EVA is **often used for incentive compensation and investor relations**. This is likely due to the emphasis on the use of income (first part of the equation) exceeding the cost of capital (second part of the equation) in measuring wealth creation.
4. EVA suffers from its origins in **accrual-based** NOPAT and the difficulty in defining the nature of economic profit (i.e., economic profit is not cash-based, but it is often adjusted such that it is not strictly accrual-based either).

B. **CFROI = (CFO - ED) / cash invested**

1. For CFROI, economic depreciation (ED) is defined as the annual cash investment required to replace fixed assets; CFO is cash flow from operations.
2. CFROI is a **cash-based** metric that is designed to compute the real internal rate of return on a company's assets and is stated as a **rate**.
3. CFO - ED is designed to approximate free cash flow (FCF), which is approximately equal to cash flow from operations (CFO) less net investment in fixed assets. This amount represents cash that is potentially distributable to shareholders.
4. CFROI is often used for **incentive compensation, valuation, and capital budgeting**. This is likely due to the emphasis on cash flow, and the wide acceptance of cash flow for these purposes.
5. CFROI suffers from the weaknesses inherent in **rate-based** metrics (i.e., diluted hurdle rate problem, and the potential difficulty in applying rates to analysis where negative cash flows are involved).

Note:
Candidates are NOT expected to be asked to calculate CFROI, but should be aware of the conceptual tradeoffs of cash-based metrics versus economic profit type metrics like EVA. Candidates should expect to be required to calculate EVA.

C. Prevalent VBM Themes and Concepts

1. **Accrual-based metrics are discredited** -- this is because accrual-based concepts are designed to fulfill external reporting goals (e.g., consistency, conservatism, and matching) rather than provide economic substance.
2. **Cost of capital is increasingly emphasized** -- this emphasizes the economic income view that cost of capital is important to evaluation of wealth creation.
3. **Shareholders and shareholder value as the primary element of interest is common** -- this is about the importance of enhancing and protecting shareholder wealth.

4. **Relating VBM to strategy and making linkages to drivers of success is important** -- this recognizes the importance of causality and value drivers as related to strategic planning and execution (i.e., understanding causal performance linkages).

III. Price Elasticity Analysis

A. By definition, the **price elasticity of demand** is the percentage change in quantity demanded divided by the percentage change in price.

A price is considered elastic if the price elasticity of demand is greater than

$$\text{Price Elasticity of Demand} = \frac{\%\Delta Q}{\%\Delta P}$$

1 and inelastic if the elasticity of demand is less than 1.

B. Price elasticity is often tested using the concept of substitute and complimentary products. Effects of substitute and complimentary products are generally as follows: If products A and B are **substitutes**, an increase in the price of A will cause an increase in the demand for B. If products A and B are **complements**, an increase in the price of A will cause a decrease in the demand for product B.

Example:
The cost of playing golf versus the cost of playing tennis behave as products that are substitutes. As the cost of playing golf increases, the demand for tennis (i.e., an alternative to golf) increases. Tennis balls and tennis rackets are products that behave as complements. As the price for tennis balls increases, the demand for tennis rackets decreases.

C. Revenue is the result of both price and volume. If prices are relatively elastic (i.e., price **elasticity** > 1), then an increase in price will tend to decrease volume making the resulting increase/decrease in revenue uncertain. If prices are relatively **inelastic** (i.e., price elasticity < 1), then an increase in price will tend to increase revenue as volume remains unaffected.

IV. Target Pricing and markups

Target Pricing and markups -- The key to properly analyzing markups is to understand what the markup is based on. Sometimes the markup is based on a percent of cost or a specific type of cost (e.g., direct cost). Other times the markup is based on revenue. Thus, the candidate must focus on specific language that communicates the basis for the markup.

Example:

Given a sales target of 1,000 units, direct costs of $50 per unit, and total costs of $80,000, what is the target price necessary to achieve a 25% profit margin on direct costs?

In this case, the markup is based on **direct costs**. Thus, the desired profit is determined based on 25% of $50,000 = $12,500. Given that total costs are $80,000 the necessary price to achieve a total profit of $12,500 would be based on the equation,

Price (1,000 units) - $80,000 = $12,500

Price (1,000 units) = $92,500

Price = $92.50

Given the same set of facts above, what is the target price necessary to achieve a 20% profit margin on sales?

Here the markup is based on **sales**. Unfortunately, the sales number is not disclosed in the problem. But we do know the following: Sales - $80,000 = .20 (sales). Thus, to find price we have:

Price (1,000 units) - $80,000 = .20 (Price) (1,000 units)

.80 (Price) (1,000 units) = $80,000

800 (Price) = $80,000

Price = $100.00

Ratio Analysis

I. **Profitability and Return Metrics** -- The focus here is on margins, return metrics, profitability, and residual income. These are generally conventional financial metrics typically related to external financial reporting.

A. **Gross Margin = revenue - cost of goods sold** -- This is a conventional metric that reflects profitability prior to the recognition of period expenses (i.e., selling and general/administrative expenses).

B. **Contribution Margin = revenue - variable expenses** -- This is a metric primarily related to internal decision making. Contribution margin (as opposed to gross margin) focuses on cost behavior so that management can evaluate the consequences on profitability and the break-even point of alternative decision scenarios.

Note:
Although the traditional format above is consistent with absorption costing and the contribution format is consistent with variable costing, the difference between gross margin and contribution margin presentation is merely a format issue.

Example:

Traditional Format Income Statement		**Contribution Format Income Statement**	
Sales	$20,000,000	Sales	$20,000,000
Cost of Goods Sold	12,000,000	Variable Costs	7,000,000
Gross Margin (GM)	8,000,000	Contribution Margin (CM)	13,000,000
S, G, & A Expenses	3,000,000	Fixed Expenses	8,000,000
Operating Income	$5,000,000	Operating Income	$5,000,000

The income statements above reflect the traditional, gross margin (GM) and contribution margin (CM) formats. The traditional (GM) format is typical with absorption costing which is required for external (SEC and IRS) financial and tax reporting. This reflects the classification of costs by manufacturing/non-manufacturing. The CM format reflects classification by operational cost behavior (i.e., variable/fixed). The CM format is desirable for planning purposes since cost behavior allows management to examine what revenue and cost items are expected to change given different cost-volume-profit results.

C. **Operating profit margin = Operating Income / Sales** -- This is a useful metric for determining comparable performance without considering potential confounding interest and tax affects that usually have little to do with operations.

Note:
Operating income and Earnings before Interest and Taxes (EBIT) are considered the same thing.

D. **Profit Margin or Return on Sales = Net Income / Net Sales** -- This metric expresses the ability of revenue to generate profits and is an important external financial evaluation metric. As presented by the DuPont formula, Profit Margin or Return on Sales multiplied by capital or asset turnover is equal to return on investment.

E. **Return Metrics (Return on investment) --** These metrics are traditionally some of the most widely reported metrics used for providing an overall summary of externally reported financial results. There are several common variations of return, but all present some type of income divided by some type of investment base. Return on investment, return on assets, return on equity, and return on common equity are names that are quite common.

> **Note:**
> Any one specific ratio often will vary slightly in format from one text to another. Thus, it is important to know the general structure of the ratio and be prepared to calculate each as required based on the information given.

Return on Investment or Return on Assets = Net Income / Total Assets

Return on Equity or Return on Common Equity = Net Income / Common Stockholders' Equity

F. **DuPont version of Return on Investment**

DuPont Formula = Return on Sales (ROS) x Asset Turnover, where

Profit Margin or ROS = Net Income / Sales

Capital or Asset Turnover = Sales / Total Assets

The DuPont approach to ROI separates ROI into two parts for analysis. The two pieces allow a separate evaluation of profitability as a percent of sales and the efficiency with which assets were utilized to generate those sales. Multiplying the two parts together results in ROI.

G. **Residual Income = Operating Income - required rate of return (invested capital)**

1. Residual income (RI) is a general form of economic profit. Economic profit differs from accounting income in that it recognizes the cost of capital. RI has often been used as an alternative to ROI to preclude the diluted hurdle rate problem by expressing the return on investment in terms of dollars rather than a rate.

> **Note:**
> The DuPont formula analysis and Residual Income are covered in detail in the Competitive Analysis lesson.

II. **Asset Utilization --** These metrics are referred to alternatively as asset activity or asset management ratios and examine the efficiency with which assets are used to maintain and generate wealth.

A. **Receivables Turnover = Sales on Account / Average Accounts Receivable --** This metric provides data on the frequency with which (on average) receivables are collected.

B. **Days' Sales in Receivables or Average Collection Period = Average Accounts Receivable / Average Sales per Day --** Similar to receivable turnover, this provides an indication of the average length of the receivables collection period.

C. **Inventory Turnover = Cost of Goods Sold / Average Inventory --** This metric provides an indication of how quickly investment in inventory is being recovered.

D. **Fixed Asset Turnover = Sales / Average Net Fixed Asset --** This metric provides an indication of how efficiently productive assets are generating sales. This metric multiplied by the profit margin (AKA return on sales ratio) equals return on investment as used in DuPont analysis (covered in the Competitive Analysis lesson).

E. **Note --** Where turnover ratios are required, they are always structured such that the name of the ratio comprises the denominator in some form (i.e., it's "turned over" so that it's on the bottom). For example, "asset" turnover is Sales / assets, "inventory" turnover is CGS / inventory, and "receivables" turnover is sales / receivables.

1. Also, turnover ratios are related to their companion income statement accounts. For example, receivables turnover is related to sales and inventory is related to cost of goods sold, so these are the numerator accounts used, respectively.

III. **Liquidity** -- Often referred to as measures of short-term **solvency**, these ratios are used to evaluate an enterprise's ability to meet its short-term obligations.

A. **Current Ratio = Current Assets / Current Liabilities** -- This ratio measures the same concept that **working capital** does. The current ratio provides a comparison that is useful for standardizing working capital data when comparing organizations of differing sizes.

B. **Quick Ratio or Acid Test Ratio = (Current Assets - Inventory) / Current Liabilities** -- This metric removes inventory since inventory is often less liquid than other current assets such as short-term investments and receivables. Also, inventory may only be valued at liquidation value when a company is in distress making it less appropriate for meeting current obligations.

IV. **Debt Utilization (risk)** -- These metrics provide measures of balance sheet risk (i.e., in terms of financial leverage). An enterprise is considered more leveraged, and thus more risky, if it has a comparatively high amount of debt versus owners' equity. Risk from debt is due to the required obligation to pay interest regularly on long-term debt. Owners' equity financing is less risky than financing with debt since the periodic payment of dividends is not required.

A. **Debt to Total Assets** = Total Debt / Total Assets

B. **Debt to Equity** = Total Debt / Total Owners' Equity

C. **Times Interest Earned** -- Operating Income / Interest Expense. This approach measures the enterprise's ability to service its debt obligations by measuring the ability to make regular interest payments based on earnings. This reflects risk as reflected by the income statement.

Note:
Debt to Assets and Debt to Equity are generally balance sheet-based measures of leverage (i.e., the degree to which assets are being financed by debt) as a measure of risk. Analysts generally prefer one metric or the other, but both are designed to measure the same concept.

V. **Market Ratios** -- Market ratios are used to evaluate the value of the enterprise as based on capital market reflections of stock price as related to earnings and book value.

A. **Price earnings (PE) Ratio** -- Market Price per Share / Earnings per Share.

B. **Market-to-Book Ratio** -- Market Value per Share / Book Value per Share

Note:
Book Value per share = Common Stock Owners' Equity / # of Common Shares Outstanding

LaVergne, TN USA
15 February 2010
173212LV00001B/5/P

9 780974 654102